The Dakota Peoples

The Dakota Peoples

A History of the Dakota, Lakota and Nakota through 1863

Jessica Dawn Palmer

McFarland & Company, Inc., Publishers
Jefferson, North Carolina, and London

The present work is a reprint of the illustrated case bound edition of The Dakota Peoples: A History of the Dakota, Lakota and Nakota through 1863, *first published in 2008 by McFarland.*

LIBRARY OF CONGRESS CATALOGUING-IN-PUBLICATION DATA

Palmer, Jessica Dawn.
The Dakota peoples : a history of the Dakota, Lakota and Nakota through 1863 / Jessica Dawn Palmer.
    p.   cm.
Includes bibliographical references and index.

ISBN 978-0-7864-6621-4
softcover : 50# alkaline paper ♾

1. Dakota Indians—History.
2. Dakota Indians—Social life and customs.   I. Title.

E99.D1P185   2012   978.004'975243—dc22   2007042925

BRITISH LIBRARY CATALOGUING DATA ARE AVAILABLE

© 2008 Jessica Palmer. All rights reserved

No part of this book may be reproduced or transmitted in any form or by any means, electronic or mechanical, including photocopying or recording, or by any information storage and retrieval system, without permission in writing from the publisher.

Front cover: foreground image © 2012 Shutterstock; background portrait of Jack Red Cloud is a photograph by Herman Heyn, ca. 1899

Manufactured in the United States of America

*McFarland & Company, Inc., Publishers
Box 611, Jefferson, North Carolina 28640
www.mcfarlandpub.com*

In the name of the grandfathers

Contents

Introduction   1

1	The Origins of Man	3
2	Emergence	16
3	What's in a Word?	28
4	Who Were the Oceti Sawakin?	39
5	Democracy in Motion	53
6	Of Everyday Things: Robes and Moccasins, Home and Furnishings	65
7	Hunt and Harvest	81
8	Animals of Power	100
9	Politics and Trade	113
10	War and Peace	129
11	The Way of the Warrior	148
12	Social Graces	162
13	Within the Tipi	174
14	The Power of Women	185
15	Matters of Faith	193
16	Medicine and Power	207
17	Send a Voice	220
18	The Pursuit of Happiness	234
19	Wasicu	243

Chapter Notes   257
Bibliography   263
Index   265

Introduction

Many fine books exist about the Dakota people, such as Roy Meyers's *The History of the Santee Sioux: United States Indian Policy on Trial.* However, most tend to view the tribe only within the context of their involvement with the white man. The efforts of chroniclers like Joseph Epes Brown are invaluable in broadening the base of knowledge, but the methodology of research was to isolate and study a part of the culture to the exclusion of all others, which has contributed to the fragmentation of Dakota history. Some periods, such as the Indian or Plains Wars, have been quite literally done to death, and others have gone unchronicled by the early recorder simply because he was not there to observe them. So no epidemics were reported among the woodland Santee during the period of the smallpox pandemic of the 1700s, although it is unlikely they would have been exempt from its ravages.

To date, no comprehensive history of the Lakota/Nakota/Dakota peoples exists that views them as a nation-state, with politics and policy, whose history extends back to a time before the arrival of the European. In writing this book, my job has been that of a researcher, recorder and organizer, with the aim of providing a foundation upon which others can build. Every attempt has been made to provide early eyewitness accounts, especially those of internal eyewitnesses, the Dakota themselves. The text relies heavily on Dakota legends, traditions, and winter counts to reconstruct their history. Accordingly each chapter begins with a pertinent Dakota legend, allowing the people a chance to speak to the reader in their own voices.

The history of the Dakota has been maintained for centuries in their folklore and their traditions. Many of the stories told by the Dakota today portray actual events, and the characters named therein are historic personages. Other tales, the more metaphorical, give valuable insights into the Dakota perspective on life, their morals and their worldview. Their legends of love provide clues about lifestyle and marriage not found elsewhere, while their tales of war graphically reveal the politics of the tribe within the context of the international community, particularly as it existed before the appearance of Europeans.

The legends are meant to provide the reader with a framework upon which recorded facts can be hung, and a context in which the topic should be viewed. Lakota winter counts have been used not only for dating purposes, but as a record of events and trends. The pictographs portrayed the most momentous occasion that year, but the winter count also acted as a visual reminder of a whole series of events, such as numerous encounters with a particular foe or a disease running rampant through the tribe.

Final Note: About Words, Places and Names

The name used to represent the Dakota people as a whole presented something of a dilemma. The most familiar collective noun, Sioux, many find offensive. The names Lakota,

Nakota and Dakota reflect different dialects. The most logical option was to use the name they selected for themselves, *Oceti Sakawin*, or the People of the Seven Council Fires. However, the name only applied to the tribe after it had formed the seven hearths and did not pertain to the people when the tribes were still in process of formation, and that process is an important part of their history.

Since the Dakota are the acknowledged parent of the seven tribes, that name, their word for "allies" or "friends," was chosen. Thus, the word Dakota alone, or the phrase the Dakota peoples, means the nation as a whole. To avoid confusion the word Santee is applied to the woodland tribes, or the word Dakota is modified by the words woodland or Minnesota to differentiate them from their western (and eastern) relations. The Santee of the southeast coastal region are further qualified by their location in Carolina to distinguish them from the Minnesota Santee. The terms Lakota or Nakota are used when speaking of these tribes as a group. When applicable the pertinent tribe or band — such as Mdewakaton, Yankton, or Oglala — will be named specifically.

Another confusion for the English speaker is the spelling of Dakota/Lakota terms. Historically most words in the written language have been spelled phonetically, which tends to be entirely dependent on the "ear" of the listener. As a result, the reader of historical texts finds that the Two-faced Woman, *Anog Ite* (the g is pronounced as a soft "k") of Walker's books is spelled *Anukite* elsewhere, and neither spelling can be considered incorrect. In developing dictionaries, certain symbols have also been devised to portray sounds for which there are no English equivalents. However, no one system has taken precedence over another, and there can be any number of written transcriptions of a single sound. The soft "sh" of sound of "nikunsi" may be represented as an "s" with a dot over it; an "s" with an accent grave as in Beuchel's *Dictionary*; an unaccented "s"; or as "sh."

For purposes of this text, the most common spelling has been selected and the accent marks omitted. Whether a word given is Dakota or Lakota depends on the source or sources. For example: *Hanblecheya*, the Lakota word for vision quest, is found in numerous texts, while only one source gives the Dakota spelling. Since *Hanblecheya* is the word most likely to be recognized by the reader it is used rather than the Dakota word *Hambade*. Every endeavor has been made to be consistent, to pick a spelling and stick with it. The exceptions to these rules are quotes. If the original reporter or historian used the word Sioux, then its use is retained. Similarly, if the author quoted used a phonetic spelling that differed from the "accepted" spelling, then that spelling is preserved. If it is too different from the original, then the "correct" spelling or the English translation is embedded parenthetically in the text.

1. The Origins of Man

> *... before there was time, Han (night) existed, but Han was not as we know it now, with the stars and the moon drifting in an indigo sky. It was empty; it was void. Inyan lived alone in the vastness of space; but like Han, Inyan was not as it is now — not made of stone — instead Inyan contained within itself all things, all life, and his spirit was Wakan Tanka[1], the greatest of all mysteries, that which was both unknowable and unknown.*
>
> *Above all Inyan was power, and as time did not yet exist except in the sacred heart, Inyan decided that it would be good to have another being like himself. Yet there was naught but Inyan from which to create this other being, so Inyan took of himself, opening a vein and letting out his blood, the essence of life. It poured into the darkness, creating Skan[2] who contains the seed of change and transformation.*
>
> *Then Inyan spread a great disk before him and poured more blood upon it, making Maka, mother earth. Inyan looked at what he had done and saw that the world was without life. So Inyan bled the waters onto the earth, creating the oceans, rivers, lakes and streams, but in this act of creation, his life force was spent and Inyan turned to the stone that formed the backbone of mother earth (Maka). Hence the universe was born of blood and sacrifice. The newly-created earth remained shrouded in darkness. Maka complained to Skan. To silence her protests, Skan placed Anp, a ruddy red glow, in the sky to banish the eternal night; but still Maka shivered in cold and she complained again.*
>
> *Yet everything had been made already from the blood of Inyan, and, as Inyan had shown, something had to be sacrificed for something new to begin. To create warmth, Skan extracted parts from Inyan and from himself. He took pieces of Maka and the essence of water. From this, he fashioned the disk of the sun (Wi) and imbued it with spirit, giving it life of its own so that it might burn bright. The sun shone unceasingly and scorched mother earth, and Maka begged Skan to bring back the night. Skan ordered Anp to follow Han, so it came to pass that day followed night.*
>
> *In the beginning the great Mysteries of creation were isolated. Skan (sky) spanned the heavens. Night followed the sun across the sky. Only Maka, mother earth, with Inyan riding like a carbuncle upon her back, had companionship, company which she came to resent. Eventually the Mysteries came to desire someone of like spirit and mind. Skan made Tate from a portion of himself, and the wind was born. Wi, the sun, produced the moon Hanwi or night sun. Maka created Unk while Inyan grew tired of being rooted to the earth, unable to move and fashioned Wakinyan, thunder and storms, to walk abroad upon the planet to act as Inyan's hands and mouthpiece to the world. The Wakinyan were many in one and terrible to behold.*
>
> *Inyan sired two other offspring. The first he produced as an egg which Wakinyan hatched. This unnatural child was called Ksa, God of Wisdom; for he emerged from the egg as a man full grown and contained all the wisdom of the ages. Inyan's second son was born to Unk. Maka's daughter. His name was Iya and he became the chief of all evil beings.*
>
> *Unk was a contentious creature and soon she angered Skan. For her crimes Unk was cast into the water and became its ruler. It is Unk who creates the floods and causes people*

to drown. She slept with her own son, Iya. Thus, Unk became the mother of all demons. From this union, Gnaski was born. Gnaski was a being of great but deadly beauty, who had a deceitful nature.

The Mysteries feasted with their companions in a cavern in the belly of the earth, and Skan created the first man and first woman, Wa and Ka, to wait upon their table. Their human daughter, Ite, was renowned for her great beauty, and Tate fell in love with her. She became his wife, but Ite was a vain and proud woman. She considered herself the equal to the great mysteries and she set her sights upon the place of honor on Hanwi's seat next to Wi.

The demon Gnaski and Ksa the Wise decided that Ite must be humbled, and they devised a plan for her undoing. They enlisted the aid of Ite's parents, Wa and Ka, for in their foolishness and their pride, mother and father wished to see their daughter sit at the great Wi's side. Ka was the first mortal seer, and it had been told to her in a vision that if Ite sat with Wi, then Wa and Ka would live forever. One night at her parents' urging Ite took Hanwi's place at Wi's side. Wi gazed upon Ite's beauty with great longing. Shamed, Hanwi hid her face while Ite's husband, Tate, grieved.

For challenging the natural order of things, Skan condemned Ite to live upon the earth with her unborn child, Yum, and for her duplicity he twisted Ite's image, so that one face bore the countenance of her birth and was beautiful to behold while the other revealed the devious soul that lay within, and she became known as Anog Ite, the two-faced woman.

Like their daughter, Wa and Ka were banished to earth to live alone. Ka was transformed into a witch, whom Skan called Kanka (Wakanka) and Wa became a wizard, named Wazi (Waziya). So they became immortal as the vision foretold, doomed to remain forever alive and forever apart, and their dream was made reality to their eternal sorrow.

Because Ksa had used his wisdom to create discord, Skan sent him from the divine table and changed him into Inktomi, shape-shifter and trickster. Wi, who had allowed himself to be misled by a woman, lost his wife Hanwi who was given a time of her own, and now he travels the heavens alone, for Wi ruled the day while his wife reigned at night. Hanwi was compensated for the wrong done her when Skan gave her moontime, although she still hides her face in shame at the memory of Wi's betrayal.

After her banishment from the great banquet halls beneath the earth, Anog Ite grew lonely and Inktomi bored. The two got together and plotted to bring mankind up to the surface. Anog Ite made food and fine goods to tempt them. Inktomi transformed himself into the shape of a wolf and made his way to the caverns. When he arrived, the wolf spoke with an elder. Inktomi promised them beauty and plenty if they would travel with him to a place where the sun shone bright in the sky. Inktomi showed them the gifts that Anog Ite had wrought and promised them more if they would but follow.

A woman elder protested, refusing to leave the caves the Mysteries had given them as home, but a man known by the name as Tokahe, or first, with three others chose to go with the wolf to see what could be seen and decide if the region was safe for his family. The men were dazzled by the light after the darkness of the caves. Tokahe viewed a land of green and growing things. For the first time, he heard the song of the trees, felt the wind upon his cheek and the warmth of the sun upon his face.

The four friends returned to tell of all the wonders they had seen. Tokahe announced that he would take his family with him up to the surface, and he persuaded others to join them, and these seven families formed the core of the Dakota people, the Oceti Sakawin or the People of the Seven Council Fires.

The group made their way back to the land of the sun, but life was more harsh than they had imagined. The wide-open sky brought not only light, but rain and storm. The gentle breeze could also lash and whip while the winter wind could cut like a knife.

Heretofore, in the great banquet hall of Wakan Tanka, they had never wanted. They had never known hunger or cold, never been exposed to the elements. Food had always been a gift of the divine and shelter provided for them. They had been born to wait upon others, *and they knew nothing of life, so it was that Inktomi came among them as wolf to teach them the elements of society and culture while Wazi and Kanka took pity upon them. The old wizard instructed the people in the ways of the hunt, while the old woman sorceress clothed them. She showed them how to gather food and how to make the tools that they would need to survive.*

And from that time the red man spread far and wide across the face of the earth.

Curiously, the creation myth of the Lakota with *Inyan* or stone as creator reveals a more accurate portrayal of the origin of the universe than the Biblical one. The Lakota world view has been born out by science. From primal matter (Inyan or stone) all things are born and the first thing Inyan made was Skan, motion. Thus, creation takes place through motion, rapid expansion, which sounds suspiciously like the Big Bang theory. The legend implies that the Native American deduced from simple observation something which eluded "civilized" Europeans for centuries. While Christians were debating the number of angels that could dance the head of a pin, the aboriginal Americans had already evolved working theories about the cosmos that have withstood the test of time and scientific study.

Science further confirms stone (Inyan) as progenitor of earthly life, through lava flows (the blood of stone) which formed the landmasses and generated the gases from which the atmosphere (sky/Skan) was made. This, in turn, provided the basic ingredients from which the process of condensation could occur, with the end result of water. The combination of hot, mineral-rich earth, moistened by water, created pools in which the first single-celled organism was spawned and from which, eventually, all life emerged.

The Lakota creation myth also echoes Newtonian third law where "every action has an equal and opposite reaction." Acts do not take place in isolation. Inyan does not model with clay, which did not exist yet, pluck items out of the air or create by divine decree. When it was time to make warmth, the story states that "everything had already been made from the blood of Inyan" so Skan had to extract parts from himself and other beings. Therefore, the tale graphically illustrates the ideas set forth in the principles of conservation of energy and Einstein's Theory of Relativity. The former postulates that energy is a constant. Energy can be converted from one form to another, but it cannot be created or destroyed. As Einstein said in a lecture on atomic physics: "It followed from the special theory of relativity that mass and energy are both but different manifestations of the same thing."[3]

Likewise, in this tale the Lakota recognized their cave-dwelling antecedents, a fact largely ignored by the Bible. The concept of wolf (Inktomi transformed) as the teacher of culture may also contain more than a kernel of truth. Some sociologists contend that it was wolf who domesticated man rather than man who tamed wolf. Accordingly, pack members would attach themselves to human camps to obtain scraps. Man watched his lupine visitor and realized the advantage of the group in the hunt, so man expanded his villages to create packs of his own. Meanwhile the wolf warned the tribe of intruders, giving them protection. Those who formed attachments with wolves flourished. Similarly those wolves who cleaved to man thrived as dogs, while those who did not have been driven nearly to extinction. Thus, it has been argued that humanity then learned the social graces by observing the wolf pack and imitating its behavior.

Still, one question has puzzled the European psyche since their arrival on this continent. Where did the original inhabitants of America come from? Not content to steal the continent from the Indian, the white man had to justify his behavior. The question itself tends to negates the Indians' prior claim to the land, relegating them to the status of immigrants rather than original inhabitants, relative latecomers to be displaced by the second wave of immigrants, the Europeans.

Largely due to the repression of the native culture and their verbal tradition, the study of the origins has become something of a jigsaw puzzle with several pieces missing. It has required a multi-disciplinary approach to recreate a partial picture which has called upon the sciences of archeology, linguistics, climatology, geology, stratigraphy, dendrochronology, anthropology and most recently genetics. Viewed chronologically, the history of white man's study of the native population can be seen as a comedy of errors that reflected the biases of the time.

The idea that the first inhabitants migrated to North America from Asia is an old one and was recorded in the *History of the Triumphs of Our Holy Faith amongst the Most Barbarous and Fierce Peoples of the New World* (1645), by Jesuit missionary Andrés Pérez de Ribas. He described it as hearsay, which suggests that it was a widely held belief. He wrote: "...the most likely opinion ... is that these people arrived from Asia overland to the north or crossed some narrow stretch of sea...."[4]

The concept was not only popular among European conquistadors, it was of long standing. The Bering Strait as the place for this migration was posited by the Jesuit, José de Acosta in *Historia Natural y Moral de las Indias*, published in 1589.[5] He theorized that the ancestors of the then present-day inhabitants had followed a land route from Asia, at a place with only short stretches of open water to navigate. Acosta believed that these people had prospered and their descendants were the civilizations of Mexico with which he was acquainted. The hypothesis was remarkable considering the fact that the Bering Strait had yet to be discovered, an event that would not occur for nearly sixty years in 1648, when it was found by Russian navigator Semyan Ivanov Dezhnyov. The Danish navigator Vitus Bering further explored the strait in 1728.

One of the first systematic archeological excavations in North America was conducted by Thomas Jefferson in the 1780s. His primary attentions were directed at the burial mounds of his Virginia home, and he correctly surmised that they had been constructed by the forebears of the current tribes, a view that lost popularity later.

Still, the mounds and the origin of the mound builders continued to dominate archeological interest throughout the 1800s. Their construction was credited to everyone but the original inhabitants of this continent until 1839, when Samuel George Morton took measurements of eight skulls unearthed from various mounds and compared them with skulls of modern natives. He concluded they were of a single race, a fact which the study of genetics has confirmed.

The same year that Morton connected the mound builders with the native peoples, Albert Koch, the owner of a small museum in St. Louis, discovered mastodon bones and a stone point. Despite his having found the two together, Koch did not believe they were contemporary since it would have suggested a date of human arrival far earlier than what was then accepted. He sold the bones to the British Museum and the artifact to a private collector in Germany. As the Europeans moved west they continued to loot the mounds. One can only guess what knowledge and what treasures were lost through plunder.

A year later, perhaps a year too late (1840), Charles Lyell published the latest edition of his *Principles of Geology*, which included the subject of stratigraphy. Stratigraphy studied the layers or strata of rocks and developed a dating mechanism based on them. Therefore, the archeologist could date an item by the type of soils or rock in which it was found.

In 1869, the study of language began to contribute to the overall picture. Lewis Morgan studied common phrases and identified a linguistic connection between the Catawba people of the Carolinas and the western Dakota. Later, Horatio Hale suggested further east-west links between the Tutelo and the other Siouan languages. In 1881 Dr. A.S. Gatschet visited the Catawba and noted many of the terms were the same as those spoken by the Osage and Arkansas peoples of the Plains,[6] which suggested a common language base between the plains Osage and the Dakota. Gatschet took his list of vocabulary to James Owens Dorsey, an expert on the western "Sioux" and its dialects, who concluded that Catawba was a dialect of the Siouan tongue.[6] Further linguistic relationships were found during a study completed in 1891 by J.W. Powell, who isolated some fifty different language families spoken by the many diverse tribes.

Elsewhere, in 1876, C.C. Abbott began a study of the New Jersey Trenton Gravels based on stone tools that had been discovered there. He hoped to prove the antiquity of people in the New World and was among the first who believed their presence dated back to the Paleolithic times, prior to 35,000 BCE, but he was unable to provide sufficient evidence to support his premise. His standard was taken up by William Henry Holmes, who had both a strong background in geology and had worked with the United States Geological Survey in the western United States. In 1882, Holmes was commissioned to study native pottery, and in 1887, Holmes began to look for proof of Paleolithic man in North America.

At the beginning of the twentieth century, Ales Hrdlicka, a Czech-born physical anthropologist, set the hypothesis of early arrival back twenty years. Appointed to the head of the United States National Museum, Hrdlicka placed such stringent guidelines for accepting any artifact dated before 4000 BCE, the then-accepted timeline, that none could meet the criteria.

During Hrdlicka's administration, in 1906, the Antiquities Act was passed that belatedly protected native artifacts from unauthorized excavation, hoarding in private collection, and destruction. Meanwhile, Alfred L. Kroeber from the University of California introduced the concept of seriation and applied it to ceramic styles to construct an archeological timeline. First invented by William Flinders-Petrie, seriation is a technique which uses percentages of types of artifacts within a particular collection relative to artifacts in another collection in order to date them.

In 1892, anthropologist Adolf Bandelier developed a chronology of the Rio Grande region in New Mexico using seriation. His work, along with research done by Edgar L. Hewett and Walter Hough, lay the groundwork for later studies such as those by Nels C. Nelson, who in 1916 refined the science of chronology that would later be used in modern stratigraphic measurements.

Further north, George McJunkin discovered animal remains in an arroyo after the Folsom, New Mexico, flood of 1908. He knew the bones were too large to belong to either modern cattle or modern buffalo, and he told his tale to any who would listen, but it took fourteen years before Dr. J.D. Figgins of the Denver Museum of Natural History investigated the site. The following year, excavations revealed human artifacts, the now familiar Folsom point,[7] near a cache of bones of the *Bison taylori*,[8] a species that had been extinct for some ten thousand years.[9] Although conventional scholars have accepted this date for the advent of man on this continent — it's difficult to dispute — they seem to forget that, in order to spear the animal, man must have been here before the bison's extinction, in other words, before 10,000 years ago, which is now currently accepted as the date of human habitation. This is not to mention the years spent traveling from the Bering Strait to what is now the southwest United States, a fact omitted in many conjectures about human arrival.

In 1929, Dr. A.E. Douglass tested a piece of wood found in New Mexico's Pecos Pueblo excavations. The study of the tree rings and their growing seasons dated the structures to 11 CE (AD),[10] creating the science of dendrochronology, but contributing little to the question of origins since its use was limited to those places where wood was present. However, it has become invaluable to precise dating of later excavations.

Meanwhile, the list of related languages developed by Powell was refined by Edward J. Sapir from fifty to six parent groups, including Algonkin-Wakashan, Hokan-Siouan, Penutian, Nadene, Aztec-Tanoan, and Eskimo-Aleut, a variety which indicated a date of early arrival. It takes centuries for linguistic differences to appear, particularly to the point that the offshoot peoples can no longer understand the parent group. Therefore, each consolidation of language families into single parent group increases the length of time for differences to have evolved, indirectly pushing back the date of arrival.

In 1932, road construction crews near Clovis, New Mexico, uncovered more stone tools. The subsequent digs unearthed projectile points along with mammoth bones. The points differed from the Folsom points since they were fluted. Similar Clovis points have been found at excavation sites throughout North America. Bones adjacent to Clovis points dated as with radiocarbon years of 11,500, the Clovis points provided evidence of human occupation of the New World some one thousand five hundred years before Folsom, establishing a new accepted timeline.[11]

The following year (1933), Morris Swadish revealed further relationships between the six parent language families devised by Sapir, indicating fewer parent groups.[12] Discoveries made at Sandia cave near Albuquerque, New Mexico, in 1939 revealed two levels or layers of occupation. The familiar Folsom points were located in the first or upper layer. On the lower level, archeologists unearthed a different kind of lance point, much more crude than the Folsom finds. Using geological evidence and stratigraphy, Harvard Professor Brian Kirk estimated that the creators of these spearheads lived some 25,000 years ago.[13]

Elsewhere evidence of pre–Clovis man continues to accrue. In 1976, archeologists found the wooden foundations of pole-frame houses, along with a child's footprint, in Monte Verde, Chile. Here dendrochronology came into its own, and the structures have been dated to fifteen thousand years ago, some three thousand years before Clovis, and if one accepts that it would take centuries to travel on foot from the Bering Strait, and a period of time before the group became settled enough to build permanent or semi-permanent structures, this discovery seems to confirm the Sandia findings. However, as often happens with finds that place the Indian here before Clovis, some scientists claimed that the results of radiocarbon tests were contaminated, which sets the date to 12,500 years ago.

Around that same time, findings in Pennsylvania near the Ohio River provided additional proof of the existence of Paleoindians in the eastern United States that predate Clovis. Dr. James Adovasio excavated the large shelter between 1973 and 1977. The archeological remains were located 11.5 feet below the ground, with a total of 11 strata. The lowest contained traces of human occupation. The uppermost sublevel dates to between 10,950 and 7,950 years ago. It is separated from the middle sublevel by a layer of rock that was the roof and walls of the shelter. This middle layer dated to between 12,950 and 10,950 years ago, while the lowest sublevel — also sealed by rock from the roof and walls of the shelter — revealed radiocarbon dates from 19,600 to 13,230 years ago.

In Peru, human remains found near Ayacucho have been dated to 23,000 BCE. The founder of the Bolivian Archaeological Society, Arthur Posnansky, contended that the great temple complex of the Tiahuanaco (located in the basin of the Peruvian-Bolivian altiplano) was built around 15,000 BCE. Although his findings are controversial, if correct, they indicate not only had man arrived on the continent and made it down to Chile to create settlements, but had managed to develop great civilizations by this time.

In 1987, linguist Joseph Greenburg suggested the three-migration theory based on what he believed to be the major North American language groups found in the native population. His study included comparing languages based on phonetics, semantics and grammar. He used a list of 300 words that constituted a core language, such as pronouns, nouns for body parts and the names for family members. Greenberg took this information about language families and reconstructed them to create three "superfamily" groupings— Amerind, Na-Dene, and Eskaleut.

Advances in climatology began to make their contribution around this time.Scientists now propose that successive ice ages formed land bridges which allowed pedestrian traffic as the sea rose and fell. In the last million and a half years, North America has been covered in ice at least four times. The most recent period of glaciation, the Wisconsin, occurred between 122,000 and 10,000 years ago, lasting well over 110,000 years. Thus, during the Pleistocene epoch much of the New World was covered in ice. Glaciers inched their way down to present-day St. Louis. They topped the Rocky Mountains of Utah at times, and sculpted the Yosemite Valley. Ancient Lake Bonneville, a great inland sea and fresh-water habitat, spanned western Utah into parts of Idaho and Nevada. Evergreen forests covered a vast area between the Rockies and the Mississippi.

The land that first man confronted was the home of mega fauna. Bears, the short-faced bear, stood five feet at the shoulder (twelve feet fully upright) and weighed 1800 pounds, larger than the modern grizzly. Giant ground sloths sported twelve-inch claws and roamed the land. Those people who traveled down to South America would have found a predatory form of ground sloth. North America and South America would have been populated with the Columbian and wooly mammoths, the latter of which weighted in excess of 18,000 pounds, nearly twice the size of the average elephant, which weights in at 10,000. The ancient camels of North America were the originators of all camel lines in South America, Asia and Africa, a factor which will be important when one considers a possible cross pattern of human migration in between America and Asia. The Paleoindian also would have found a saber-toothed cat that stalked its way across the continent, preying upon all that crossed its path. The first inhabitants would have viewed the mega beaver with wonder, and the giant bison which became a part of Native American mythology, perhaps as a part of the collective memory from previous encounters.

When the ice retreated, a corridor was opened between the Laurentide ice sheet in the east and Cordilleran in the west, and it was through this passage east of the Rockies that scientists believe the red man advanced across the continent. The date given for the opening of this passage is about 12,000 years ago. However, excavations in Chile and elsewhere place man in the south and the east long before this event and challenge the accepted date of migration south.

A November 17, 2004, news release from the University of South Carolina announced the results of digs along the Savannah River in Allendale County, South Carolina. The excavations, conducted by archeologist Albert C. Goodyear, have yielded human artifacts in early Pleistocene soils. Samples of charcoal from a campfire located some 4 meters below the surface were sent to the laboratory at the University of California. Test results on the charred plant remains

The land the Paleo-Indian found was populated by huge creatures, including the saber-toothed tiger, short-faced bear, the Columbian mammoth and the mastodon. This stereo card (c. 1909) shows a mastodon skull with teeth revealed at an archeological dig somewhere in the United States. It was published in Los Angeles by J.Z. Gilbert & F.C. Winter on November 26, 1909.

yielded two dates: 50,300 and 51,700. This definitely places people in the eastern United States before the opening of the passage around 10,000 BCE, and if, as some authorities contend, it took 15,000 years to traverse the continent from the Bering Sea to the southeast, then the Native American may have arrived on this continent some 68,000 years ago.

It is only recently that genetics has come forward with new information. Global human-origins studies conducted by Mark Seielstad, of the Harvard School of Public Health, have now produced evidence that all humans, New World and Old World, are descended from the same human ancestors in Africa. From these and other genetic data, scientists are now able to reconstruct human migration events, trace genetic trails out of Africa and map genetic pathways of humankind the world over. It provides evidence for human migration and gene flow out of Africa beginning 137,000 years ago, plus or minus 15,000 years.

DNA research confirms a link between the original peoples of America and those of Asia. Early mitochondrial studies have allowed scientists to trace the four genetic lineages found in the Native American population (labeled A through D) to populations around Lake Baikal in Mongolia, West Siberia, "Beringia," Japan, and Korea. Genetic diversity studies support the presence of the Native American on this continent long before Clovis, indicating that the two populations separated approximately 40,000 years ago.

Genetics seems to corroborate this multiple-migration premise. Four genetic lineages suggest different migrations at different times, reinforcing Greenburg's theory. However, additional studies have muddied the waters as they often do. Working with a much larger data set, Andrew Merriweather of University of Pittsburgh discovered that the four lineages were further subdivided into nine distinct genetic subtypes. Additionally, all four lineages showed up in all three language groups. Merriweather concluded that it was unlikely that the same lineages could be found in all the resident population if they arrived by separate migrations. He posed the single-migration theory, whereby groups dispersed and evolved locally wherever they settled. Still, the proponents of the three-wave theory argue that multiple migrations could have brought the four haplogroups[14] to the New World singly, and intercontinental travel and intermarriage between the various groups mixed them.

The discovery of the haplogroup, X, found in twenty-five percent of the Ojibwa population and twelve percent of the Dakota, adds to the confusion. The X haplogroup has been traced to northern Europe. Some attribute its presence in DNA samples to sample contamination. The recent discovery of a European-style spear point in Virginia, which has been dated to 15,000 BCE, has led to conjecture that the Europeans were the "first Americans." Proponents of this theory point to presence of the X haplogroup in Native populations.

However, this assumption, which would deny the natives their status as the original inhabitants, completely ignores evidence of human occupation dating back thirty-eight thousand years and conveniently overlooks the possibility of Paleoindians developing similar styles of spearhead manufacture. No attempt has been made to explain how the gene appeared among the tribes of middle America without being found among the tribes of the east. If true, it suggests a far more easterly position for the Dakota people than previously supposed. The idea of the European as first man in America, and the progenitor of the X gene, also ignores the thorny question of how the two groups managed to intermarry if one of them had not made its way onto the continent at the time. The other possible source of the X-factor could be the Viking colony of Lief Ericson (1000 CE), and this too places the Dakota along the northeast coast, indicating they once claimed more land than formerly believed.

The X haplogroup seems to indicate that there were four rather than three sets of migrants who made their way onto this continent, and some propose a further seven migrations as a result of this X-factor. Merriweather contends that the presence of the X haplogroup in Central American populations confirms his premise of a single migration rather than negating it. His opponents suggest that this only indicates the possible of arrival Polynesian people along the southern coastal regions, ignoring the presence of the X-haplography in the North American interior.

DNA maps do reveal a preponderance of genetic types in certain areas, such as the B-group along the west coast down to the tip of South America, which helps to define the migrational routes for specific genetic families. To understand the inland movement of the Dakota, though, one must return to the study of linguistics before the "super families." The presence of the Siouan language in the east — noted by Lewis Morgan, Horatio Hale and A.S. Gatschet in the 1800s — allows us to trace, to a certain extent, the history of the Dakota people before the arrival of the white man.

If one considers the Hokan-Siouan stock, it includes:

- The Iroquois Family: Erie, Huron (Wyandot), Tuscarora, Mohawk, Cayuga, Onondaga, Cherokee, Oneida, Susquehana (Conestoga) and Seneca.
- The Caddoan Family: Wichita, Pawnee, Arikara (Ree) and Caddo.
- The Muskhogean Family: Choctaw, Chickasaw, Creek, Seminole, Alibamu, Natchez and Tuma.
- The Hokan Family: Yuma languages, from Delta California to the Mohave; Karok-Shasta of northern California; Pomo; Salinan-Seri languages, which included Chumash; and the Tequistlatecan languages, Oxaca of Sierra and Lowland Chontal; the Washo; and the Pacific coast inland region inland to the Sierras.
- The Siouan Family

The Siouan language family was not only one of the largest of the Hokan-Siouan stock, but also one of the widest spread. The many Siouan languages extended from Virginia and the Carolinas in the east to Florida and Biloxi, Mississippi, in the south. Anthropologist Clark Wissler contended that, at one time, Siouan-speakers dominated the entire southern half of the present-day United States.[15] At the time of European arrival, a form of it was spoken throughout the Midwest, across the Plains west to the Tetons and beyond our borders into Canada. All told, some form of the Siouan language is spoken by forty-five different tribes.

The following chart gives a breakdown of the two basic geographical divisions, east and west.

This map shows the migrations of DNA groups based on the three-migration theory. It also shows the prevalence of DNA haplogroups in certain locations. For example: the B-haplogroup along the Pacific coast. The controversial X group with its European origins is marked directly on the map since it is found only in isolated pockets in the northern plains and in central America.

EASTERN DIVISION						
Catawba Group				Tutelo Group		
Catawba (Iswa) Cheraw Congeree	**Eno Branch** Eno Keyauwee Shakori Sissipashaw Sugaree	**Peedee Branch** Cape Fear Peedee Waccamaw Winyaw	Santee Sewee Wateree Waxhaw Woccon Yadkin	Manahoac Manocan Moneton Nahyssan Occaneechi Saponi Tutelo	Biloxi Quapaw Ofo	
WESTERN DIVISION						
Dakota (Santee) Mdewankaton Sisseton Wahpkeute Wahpeton	Nakota Yankton Yanktonai Assiniboin	Lakota (Titawan) Oglala Sicangu Hunkpapa Mnikowoju Sihasapa Oohenunpa Itazico	**Gros Ventre** Hidasta Mandan Gros Ventre	Stone Absaroka (Crow) Black Foot	Winnebago Iowa Omaha Oto Kaw Ponca Missouri Osage	

Viewed as a family tree, the linguistic divisions are more complex than simply east and west, with three early branches: Catawba, Crow-Hidatsa, and Ohio Valley. Central Siouan, or the trunk, is then further subdivided into Mandan and Mississippi Valley branches. The latter is the largest, encompassing all the Dakotan languages (including Lakota and Nakota), Winnebago (Ho Chunk), Iowa, Missouri, Ponca, Oto, Omaha and Kaw (Kansa).

Just how similar or dissimilar were the languages? In the late 1700s, a German-born explorer Johann (or John) Lawson traveled throughout the Carolina territories. He wrote extensively in his journals, and his account remains one of the most accurate reports of the eastern tribes. He noted with a great deal of astonishment that the people of one village often could not understand the spoken language of their nearest neighbors, and Lawson was dealing with the Sugaree, the Congeree, the Sewee and the Santee, all Siouan languages. Thus, it would appear that there were vast differences in pronunciation.

Yet similarities exist. The Quapaw called the divine force that permeated all things *Wakontah*. Compare this against the Dakota term for the Great Mystery or Spirit: *Wakan tanka*. The following chart lists a few commonly used words, along with the numbers one through five, illustrating how closely allied the languages were and how divergent they could be. The bolded numbers "two" and "three" show similarities between the tribes of the west and east while numbers "one" and "five" reveal the contrast between the tongues. The Dakota/Lakota speaker could easily understand each other while the Biloxi of the south may have been able to guess with difficulty, but the Woccan of the east would have been mystified.

Term	*Lakota*	*Dakota*	*Biloxi*	*Woccan*
One	Wanzi	Wanji	Sonsa	Tonne
Two	**Nonpa**	**Nunpa**	**Nonpa**	**Numpere**
Three	**Yamni**	**Yamni**	**Dani**	**Nam-mee**
Four	Topa	Topa	Topa	Punnun-punne
Five	Zaptan	Zaptan	Ksa	Webtau
Sun	Wi	Wi	Ina	Wittapare
Moon	Hanwi	Hanwi	Ina	Wittapare
Man	Wicca	Wica	Anya	Unknown
Woman	Winyan	Winyan	Anxti	Yicau*

*Old woman

Altogether the Hokan-Siouan stock populated most of the continental United States into Canada. The language ranged from the far southeast, including Florida, north to Canada. The speakers claimed a territory from the northeast coast to the Midwest into the Great Plains, south through Wichita into Texas, north to the Canadian border and beyond. Some Hokan-Siouan speakers inhabited portions of the Rockies and the southwest while the Hokan language family had settled the deserts and the coastal and river regions of California up to Washington.

Meanwhile, in total land mass, the Siouan language family alone encompassed over two million square miles, more than fifty percent of the continental United States, or twenty-four of the forty-eight states, including Missouri, Arkansas, Iowa, Illinois, Minnesota, Wisconsin, Nebraska, Kansas, North Dakota, South Dakota, Wyoming, Montana, Idaho, and Colorado, continuing up into the Canadian provinces of Saskatchewan, Alberta, Manitoba, and into Ontario. According to contemporary accounts, the Siouan tongue in the southeast included Georgia, Virginia, South Carolina, North Carolina, Mississippi, Florida, and Louisiana.

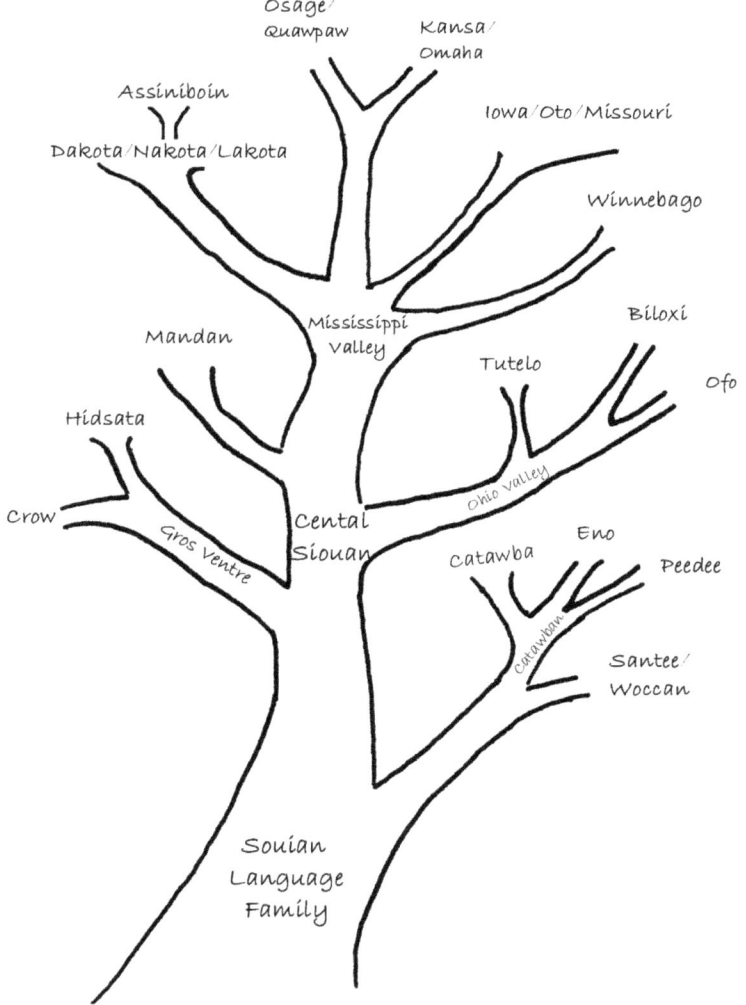

The family tree of Siouan language not only reveals distribution, but also provides a clue to the possible route of migration for the various groups. The first branch of the tree on the right includes the Carolinian tribes. Those on the left include the tribes that moved onto the Great Plains early, while the Lakota (top left) did not arrive on the prairie until around 1700.

The very diversity of native dialects suggests long occupation of this continent. Scholars estimate that it would have taken thirty-five thousand years for the Na-Dene language group to develop from a single mother tongue to 143 distinct languages, approximately 245 years per language. The Hokan-Siouan Stock consisted of 104 different languages. Assuming 245 years per language, it would have taken 25,480 years for these languages to evolve from the parent tongue. The forty-five Siouan languages would have developed in a period of 11,025 years and must have existed as a single tongue for a time before population pressures caused the splintering of the initial group.

All findings indicate that the first inhabitants of this continent were neither latecomers nor immigrants any more than the first settlers of Scandinavia or the British Isles were. Rather it sug-

The Dakota Peoples

(Left) At the time of Lawson (1700), the Carolinas were populated by numerous Siouan bands including an eastern branch of the Santee. The Siouan peoples were the original inhabitants of the area, predating either the Cherokee or the Powhatan, and it is believed at one time they occupied areas of Georgia and Florida.

(Right) This map reveals the widespread distribution of Siouan languages across the U.S. and Canada. In the north the Siouan Crow ranged into Alberta while the Dakota inhabited areas of Manitoba south along the eastern plains. Their land included the region around Lake Superior down to Iowa. Pond contended that the Dakota originated around Hudson Bay. Eventually their territory reached into Kansas. The Kansa, the Omaha and the Ponca inhabited the Ohio Valley until they moved west to Kansas, Missouri, Nebraska and Arkansas. The Mandan, Hidatsa, and the Gros Ventre ruled the western plains all the way to the Rockies. Siouan speakers were believed to be the first inhabitants of the southeast; their territory included the land from Florida up to Virginia. Wissler said the Siouan language dominated the southern half of the United States an assertion supported by the presence of Tutelo and the Biloxi in the present-day state of Mississippi, with the Biloxi along the gulf coast and the Tutelo further north.

gests that they were part of the first human dispersal from Africa that began 140,000 years ago and which saw the lands of Europe and Asia populated. Thus, the first Americans were a part of that epic journey, arriving here about the same time humans occupied Germany and Great Britain.

Some of their forebears stopped in Western Siberia, Mongolia, Japan and Korea, while the original Americans continued their travels across the Bering Strait until their influence stretched across the two continents. Sea travel would not have been impossible even with the technology that existed at the time. In fact, travel need not have been one way. Seaworthy ships in the Pacific Northwest and in the Aleutian Islands were in use by native tribes when the European first arrived to "discover" them. Likewise the Maya and the Aztecs had vessels capable of traveling in the Gulf of Mexico and were known to follow trade routes up the Mississippi River, while the Polynesian peoples managed to cross incredible distances with their outrigger canoes, which enabled them to populate the islands all across the Pacific. Indeed, the fall of the Soviet Union reunited cousins from eastern Siberia and western Alaska, indicating long established interaction between the peoples of the two continents.

At this time any answer to the date of their arrival must still be considered conjectural, a "best guess" based on the information currently available, although dates of at least 50,000 years ago are now generally accepted. Still, new hypotheses are proposed as new evidence appears to refute old theorems. New excavations push back the date of arrival while climatological data become more precise and modify accepted timelines. Dates and the theories themselves are constantly being updated, revised and refined.

The Lakota scholar Vine Deloria, Jr., dismissed the Beringiean theory that portrays natives as "latecomers who had barely unpacked before Columbus came knocking on the door" as a "white lie,"[16] and science supported him. All things considered, the Dakota and other great nations of North America have more claim to this continent than the Celts and their descendants have to the British isles, for archeology has proven that the Celts were not the builders of the Stonehenge and did not arrive on British shores until much later. They supplanted the previous inhabitants and the builders of that great monument. Thus, the question of where the original people came from becomes moot. They can only be viewed as the first citizens of this land and, more importantly, its discoverers.

2. Emergence

The rays of Wi (the sun) caressed mother earth (Maka) and from this warm touch came all the plants and the animals, the four-legged and the winged ones. Then one day, a two-legged one appeared. Called "First Born," he was a man and more than a man. He wandered the earth and spoke the language of the animals — for then all languages were one — and he understood animal ways. First Born moved freely among the four-legged; he conversed with the birds, and he listened to the song of the trees.

First Born set up his lodge in the center of the world. From there he could view all things, and nothing escaped his notice, but First Born was alone. He craved the companionship of one of his own kind, but there was no one, so like Inyan before him, First Born took something from himself, a splinter from his toe, and fashioned a child. Like all children, the boy was trusting, innocent and helpless. First Born was pleased and named him "Little Boy Man." First Born taught his brother all that he knew. From this wisdom came the sacred beliefs and customs of the Dakota people. He gave Little Boy Man the knowledge of animal speech. He explained their ways and their means.

From afar, the trickster Inktomi watched the boy mature, and the spider grew jealous. He could look into the boy's heart and he could see the future, for had he not once been Ksa, the god of wisdom who had been given the gift of sight? And Inktomi did not wish to be supplanted by this upstart.

Sitting in his web, he sent his messengers among the animals and Inktomi advised them to be rid of the Little Boy Man before he became a man fully grown. "He will subjugate you all. He will be master of all the people — the four-legged and the winged ones, those that swim, creep, slither or crawl."

But the animal nations did not heed Inktomi's warning. The child walked among them, and they saw no harm in him. Rather they saw the joy and playfulness of youth. Only Unk, ruler under the water and mother of all demons, listened to Inktomi. At her bidding her children rose up and killed Little Boy Man, and then, fearing the response of First Born, they hid the body at the bottom of the sea.

From his home at the center of the world, First Born searched for his brother and found his reflection in the deep. First Born brought Little Boy Man's bones up to the surface. Then First Born built the first ini ti (sweat lodge). He made a fire and gathered cedar and sage. He pulled sacred stones from the water of the stream. He placed the youth's bones inside the lodge. He made the sacred vapor and sang the sacred songs, which are sung by the Dakota to this day.

Sweet Grandfather's breath restored Little Boy Man's life to him once more, and they returned to the lodge at the center of the earth. For a while they roamed in peace among the whispering pines, fearing no one. But Inktomi was never far away. He grew ever more restive and envious of this comely youth whose back was straight and heart was true, unlike Inktomi's own twisted visage.

He sowed discontent across the land. "Look," he said, "how big he has grown and how strong he has become." Inktomi again sent his messengers far and wide, asking the animals to make war against Little Boy Man. They debated the issue. Soon this talk reached the youth's ears and he grieved.

His elder brother saw Little Boy Man's troubled expression and he asked: "What worries you so?"

Little Boy Man told First Born all he had heard. His older brother frowned. Then he made the youth a bow and some arrows, a war-club and a spear, and he demonstrated their use as he instructed his brother in the arts of war.

"It is time," said First Born, "for you to fight."

Little Boy Man opened his mouth to protest, but First Born silenced him. "It is they who have brought this upon themselves, not you upon them. If they attack you, you must defend yourself."

As the young man practiced with club and bow, First Born cast a stone into the air. Where it fell a wall of rock rose beside the lodge. He tossed another pebble into the air, and another wall appeared, another and another, until the barricade surrounded their lodge on all four sides.

Little Boy Man stood at the top of the walls and watched for his enemies day and night. Then one day as the sun rose, the four-legged appeared on the horizon, and the rolling hills of the prairies turned black as if they were covered in a great blanket. The buffalo charged and the ground thundered under their hoofs. The elk galloped forward with the deer at their heels to batter at the walls. Bears and wolves advanced, growling. The smaller animals, the badgers, gophers and prairie dogs, burrowed beneath the walls, attempting to undermine them.

Sadly Little Boy Man strung his bow and then loosed his arrow into the buffalos' breasts, and the animals dropped before him. Little Boy Man swung his great club and row upon row of his enemies fell. Then the insects attacked, with their whining and their stinging. Little Boy Man struck his club against the rocks. Sparks flew and the grass caught fire. The smoke drove the insects away, and the rest of the animals scattered before the flames.

The youth watched them go with a heavy heart.

The four-legged ones licked their wounds, and then they gathered to sue for peace with First Born and his younger brother. First Born agreed, but to compensate Little Boy Man for the insult done him, the animal people had to furnish him with flesh for his food and skins for his clothes. Harmony reigned once more among the great nations.

Not many moons had passed before First Born sent for his brother. "You are grown," he said, "and you can no longer be called little. You are a man, but you will remain always a boy to me. It is time, though, for you to go out into the world to find a wife."

"But how am I to do this?" the young man objected. "We are alone."

First Born repeated: "You must find a wife. You must make children, so your kind will continue."

Confused, Little Boy Man left his father's lodge. Then one night as he made camp, he met another like himself, yet different. Softer, smaller, pretty, she spoke with a musical voice that sounded for all the world like the morning chorus of birds in the trees. The girl was dressed in gray, and she carried a basket of chokecherries under her arm. She offered him some and he was smitten by her beauty and generosity.

That night he, who knew nothing of the ways of love, made love to her. The next morning when he awoke, he looked around, but she was gone. He scanned the clearing; he saw nothing save a tiny robin. It sang a beautiful song of greeting to the dawn, nodded at him and flew away. The youth searched for the woman, day and night, but he found naught but the haunting melody of bird song. He mourned her loss.

The next day another woman, plump and industrious, entered the clearing next to the lake. She bustled around the camp, chopping wood, and busied herself building them a fine lodge of wood. For a while they lived together as man and wife. When their child was born, the young man wanted to take them — his wife and his child — to visit his brother, but the *beaver woman refused. He left her in their camp alone, and when he returned, his lodge was gone; his wife and child had vanished.*

He sat grieving beside a stream when a third woman approached. She had beautiful thick black hair. She reached out to him and brought him to her with a great bear hug, and he was comforted. Of this union, Boy Man had many children, and he hoped that from his home at the center of the earth, First Born watched them and knew that his little brother was happy, but Boy Man would not leave his wife, for he remembered what had happened before.

Life, though, never runs smooth or to our liking, and somehow they became separated in the woods. Other women followed, caring for Boy Man and loving him each in their turn, and each gave him many fine children who became the ancestors of the human race.

The Dakota creation tale told by Charles Eastman in *The Soul of an Indian*[1] differs from the Oglala version relayed in the previous chapter, although it contains many of the same elements. Unk, the ruler of the deep and mother of all demons, appears as the enemy of fledgling man. The trickster Inktomi (spelled Unk-to-mee by Eastman, according to the Dakota pronunciation) figures large in this version and the Lakota story. In both the trickster, as wolf or as spider, acts as "teacher of man." In the Dakota version Inktomi teaches through adversity, as he often does, hence providing the motivation for first man to learn the arts of war. Inktomi's role as instructor is more direct in the Lakota.

Like the Oglala version, the Dakota tradition reflects scientific fact when it places a great sea where none should be and may refer to the period when Lake Bonneville covered nearly twenty thousand square miles in the Great Basin region of the United States.

The Dakota creation story accurately depicts the use of walls as defensive structures. Their description resembles the type of earthworks built in the upper Mississippi region in the prehistoric period. Accounts from the historic period tell of Dakota towns surrounded by earthworks into which sharpened wooden stakes had been driven. Meanwhile the beaver's lodge hints at the type of wooden structure, the *tipi tonka,* used as a summer home by the Minnesota Santee.

The reach of the Dakota, rather than the Siouan, peoples is best illustrated by the presence of the Santee, in both the east and the west (see chart, page). The Dakota Santee (*Isanti*) of the north derived their name from Ble (Lakota) or Mde (Dakota) Isanti, Knife Lake, a name bestowed upon them by the Dakota people themselves. Scholars recognized a direct relationship between the Santee of Piedmont Carolina and the Minnesota-based Santee. The two tribes shared many customs and religious beliefs. For example, the snake was held in awe by the Santee of east and west and the Dakota. As a sign of this respect, neither the Dakota-Santee nor the western Lakota would step over a snake. Instead, they go around it. Further east, in 1700, the explorer John Lawson described the same custom when he wrote in his journal about the curious habits of the Indians of Carolina. "...Snakes, they avoid it, if they lie in their way...."[2]

Both branches of the Santee played a form of ball game. Lawson described the game of the eastern tribes: "These Indians are much addicted to a Sport they call *Chenco,* [a ball] which is carried on a staff with a Bowl made of Stone, which they trundled upon a smooth Place."[3] Later he mentioned a game played with "Batoon and a Ball." Each description displays striking similarities to the northern Santees' lacrosse, where a net or a small bag replaces the stone bowl of the eastern Santee. In *Indian Boyhood,* Ohiyesa referred to the game as a part of the midsummer festivals of his youth.[4] The tribes competed to ascertain who was the fastest and the fleetest of all warriors. Dakota women also played a version of it during the maiden feast.

The two Santee tribes also shared the game of pips or stones. Lawson described the Carolina Indians playing it in 1700. Seth Eastman documented the women of the Minnesota Santee playing the same game in an illustration he made some 150 years later, and a form of this game made its way onto the plains with the Lakota.

Both Dakota and Carolinian Santee used counting sticks in their record keeping, in their communications and as a diversion. The Santee of the east used what Lawson called a parcel of marked reeds. The Dakota woodland Santee and the Lakota also had counting sticks. Santee Ohiyesa (Charles Eastman) described them in his book *Indian Boyhood* as "variously colored sticks about five inches long" which they kept to record the years.[5] The stick as a form of record keeping changed with the plains tribes. When the Lakota warrior Crazy Horse surrendered in 1877, an eighty-four-year-old man in his band carried a "stick about six feet long, covered in notches, thousands of them." An American officer asked him what it was; "he said it was the history of the world from the beginning handed down by his fathers."[6]

Where sticks were a limited resource, the *Titowan* (Lakota) switched to hides to keep winter counts with pictographs that commemorated the most important event of a given year. The Siouan tribes of the eastern seaboard, woodland Minnesota and the Great Plains all used pictographs as a form of written language which, in the case of the Carolinian Santee, Lawson described as "Heiroglyphicks."[7] The Dakota of both woods and plains sent wands to other tribes, which were specially painted and marked in order to convey a message to the recipient.

Tribes all cross the United States had some form of ritual sweat for purification, but the structure of the southeastern Santee sweat lodge most closely resembled the *ini ti*[8] of their northern relations. "[T]hey take Reeds, or small Wands, and bend them Umbrella-fashion, covering them with Skins or Matchcoats. They have a large Fire not far off; wherein they heat Stones.... There is a Pot of Water in the *Bagnio*."[9]

Both were river Indians. The Carolina Santee and the northern Dakota built houses of bark and canoes of hollow logs. The lodges differed slightly in structure. The Carolinian "wigwam" was round and where the weather was warmer, the residents lived in them year-round. The Dakota's bark houses were oblong or rectangular, although curved at the corners, and they used as them residences only during the summer months.

The Santee of east and west followed similar mourning rituals, including faces blackened with "Smoake of Pitch and Ash." The four-day funeral feast of the east coast Santee also finds its reflection in the final phase of the "Keeping of the Soul" ceremony of the western group.

John Lawson described the Carolina Santee as "a well humour'd and affable people."[10] Furthermore he discussed how other tribes deferred to the Santee at gatherings. "The Indian King of the Santee ... was the most absolute Ruler in these parts, although he rules over a small People...." His predecessor was "a Man of Great Power, not only among his own Subjects, but dreaded by other neighbouring Nations for his great Valour and Conduct."[11]

The Carolina Santee were treated with reverence by adjacent tribes, signifying an elevated status, because the Santee or Dakota were considered the progenitors of their people. The Mdewakanton Santee in particular were held in esteem since they were considered the descendants of the fabled *Tokahe,* or "first" to emerge from the caves.

A physical resemblance was also noted. In 1946 State Representative W.R. Bradford (NY) expressed that there was a similarity in face and feature between the Siouan-speaking Catawba of the east and the western Dakota. So how did the people, the language and their influence spread so far? And what route did they take? Their common heritage suggests a possible route that the two tribes traveled during their migration across the continent, with the Dakota Santee staying behind while the Carolingian Santee drifted further east.

The accepted school of thought is that the Siouan tribes of the southeast once inhabited the Ohio Valley or headwaters of the Ohio river. Historian Philip Edward Pearson, born in 1786 around Monticello, later moved to Fairfield, North Carolina, where he learned the local legends that indicated northwestern antecedents to the Catawba and suggested Canadian origins. According to Pearson, the bands divided. One remained on the Kentucky River, the other moved into Virginia.[12] Although his memoirs, written in 1842 at the request of the Governor James Henry Hammond of South Carolina, have caused much controversy due to some erroneous dates, they cannot be entirely discounted.

Dr. James Mooney, of the Smithsonian Bureau of Ethnology, in his first major work, *A Handbook of Indians North of Mexico* (1885), attempted to chronicle all the tribes in the United States and Canada. Mooney outlined a route of Siouan migration whereby "one branch crossed the mountains to the waters of Virginia and Carolina while the other followed along the Ohio and the lakes toward the west. Linguistic evidence indicates that the eastern tribes ... were established upon the Atlantic slope long before the western tribes ... had reached the plains."[13]

Writing in *The Southern Indian* (1935), R.S. Cotterill agreed with Mooney, describing the western migration of the Eastern group "...down the Ohio to divide at its mouth sending one group up the Mississippi to rejoin the parent stock, and a second one down the river to become the Quapaw and the Osage," with Siouan fragments left in the present-day state of Mississippi, in the form of the Ofo of the north and the Biloxi in the south.[14]

The phrase "parent stock" is a telling one. From it, one can infer a previous split took place further north in Canada around the Great Lakes along the north shore of Lake Superior. Thus, the Siouan peoples of the east, and later of the south and southwest, would be offshoots. It also suggests that a "parent population" remained in the region for a period of time only to move into Minnesota.

However, another view exists based on the verbal tradition of the Winnebago (Hochunk or Hochungra). Their name translated into English means "people of the big speech" or "parent speech" and implies the Hochunk were the originators of all the Siouan-speaking tribes. Dakota verbal traditions, and what is known of their history, seems to contradict this. Both describe the Dakota sweeping south and assimilating much of the area occupied by the Winnebago, Iowa and other tribes, which — if the Siouan language originated in the north — indicates that the Dakota would have been the parent tribe.

In an article for *American Archeologist* (April–June 1935), Frank G. Speck postulated that the Siouan people of Carolina were, in fact, the earliest inhabitants of the region, older than the Powhatan and much older than the Cherokee.[15] A century earlier, Cotterill had also placed the Siouan speakers among the first inhabitants of the southeast, predating the tribes current during the Revolutionary War period.

Mooney concurred: "The Indians who at the close of the American Revolution occupied those regions of the South then claimed and partially possessed by the United States were comparative latecomers. Preceding them had been a branch of those who were called Sioux by unadmiring neighbors and who in some remote pre–Columbian period had broken from their northern brethren in the neighborhood of the Great Lakes to become the oldest inhabitants of the South."[16]

This places the Siouan tribes in Carolina long before the 1500s when the Powatan also peopled the eastern shore. The Siouan tribes remained and were among the people to meet Hernando de Soto during his expedition from Florida to Arkansas from 1538 through 1542. Scholars now believe that the Siouan speakers were firmly established in the southeast by the 1400s and were possibly present as early as 1100. This implies that the split between the Dakota and the Siouan tribes of the east must have occurred around 1000 CE, an estimate that appears to be confirmed by their own traditions. For example, the Battiste Good winter count carries Dakota/Lakota history back to their origins as a separate entity to a period some 900 years ago.

As the most ancient of all the southeastern tribes, some authorities believe they also claimed territory in Florida and Alabama. The estimated date suggests that the Siouan tribes were living in the south during the zenith of the mound-building period. Authorities agree that the heyday of the eastern mound construction predates the tribes of the Revolutionary War Period, all the way back to the original inhabitants—the Siouan speakers.

Mound builders were still at work when the first Spanish explorers landed on the coast and continued to be active until the 1700s, and the Santee of the Carolinas were among them. The contemporary eyewitness account of John Lawson described the Carolina Santee burial rites, including their mounds. "The manner of their Interment, is thus: A Mole or Pyramid of Earth is raised, the Mould thereof worked smooth, sometimes higher or lower depending on the Dignity of the Person whose Monument it is."[17]

A map of mound distribution according to Henry Clyde Shetrone. Notice the large number of mounds located in areas once occupied by Siouan-speakers, along the Ohio Valley, in the Virginias, the Carolinas, along the Mississippi River valley, and in the states of Mississippi, Wisconsin, Iowa, and Minnesota.

It is interesting to note, also, that the major distribution of mounds follows the routes of Siouan migration acknowledged by the experts. The heaviest distribution of the mounds included many of the places inhabited at one time or another by one of the many Siouan tribes, including Ontario, Ohio, Michigan, Indiana, Illinois, Wisconsin, Minnesota, Iowa, Kansas, Pennsylvania, Kentucky, Tennessee, Alabama, Arkansas, Missouri, Mississippi, and the Piedmont region of Carolina. Compare this list against those states whose inhabitants spoke the tongue noted on page 13.

One of the first reputable American archeologists, Thomas Jefferson, excavated the burial mounds of his native Virginia. He found numerous bodies, a discovery similar to the charnel houses and tombs of the Santee recorded by Lawson 100 years earlier. Jefferson attributed the mounds to the native tribes in his *Notes on Virginia* (1781)[18] where he described his findings. "I first dug superficially in several parts of it and came to collections of human bones, at different depths, from six inches to three feet below the surface."[19] His reported finds are reflected in a drawing of the warriors' tomb completed by John White and published in the 1590s.

Ignoring the evidence, Victorian writers discounted the idea that the aboriginal people of their time could have built such great structures. A premise put forward by Caleb Atwater in the early 1800s credited the mounds to the Mesopotamians and Egyptians, even the lost tribes of Israel. The myth was perpetuated by Ephraim Squire and Edwin Hamilton Davis in 1845, who believed the current natives did not have the sophistication to build the mounds. It took many authorities, including James McColloh, George Samuel Morton, and Henry Rowe Schoolcraft, and absolute proof provided by Cyrus Thomas, to dispel this misapprehension. In 1891 anthropologist J.W. Powell described the mentality of the time: "For more than a century the ghosts of a vanished nation continent, and the forest covered mounds [were] usually regarded as the mysterious sepulchers of its kings and nobles. It was an alluring conjecture that the powerful people, superior to the Indians, once occupied the valley of the Ohio and the Appalachia ranges ... all swept away by the invasion of the copper-hued Hun..."[20]

Climate was the more likely cause for the destruction of the mound-building cultures. The Little Ice Age began around 1300 CE and lasted until the mid–nineteenth century. While it signified a decrease of global temperatures of only a few degrees, the results devastated Europe. The Little Ice Age was either indirectly or directly the responsible for some of the biggest disasters of the time, including the Black Death and the Irish potato famine. As a worldwide phenomenon, the climatic shift also existed in America, with similar consequences: crop failures, famine and pestilence. The construction of temple mounds required thousands of man-hours, which indicates a large settled population. Starvation and death as horticulture failed would have cut into this population base and caused the survivors to disperse.

One of the reasons why the Indians were dismissed as the mound builders was the presence of copper jewelry, weapons and breastplates in the mounds, since the local natives seemed to have lost the skill of metallurgy. Yet copper in an almost pure state came from an area around Isle Royal in Michigan, an area of migration for the Siouan tribes, and was traded across the country. The fact that metal ornamentation was still worn by the native population is documented in some of the earliest accounts of Europeans' interaction with the indigenous population. The hapless native would be questioned about other, more valuable metals, such as silver or gold.

If the inquirer did not like the answer he received, as happened with the explorer Hernando de Soto, the city was sacked in search of the more precious metals and everything of value taken, including the copper breastplates. Most of the time, early Europeans left pestilence in their wake. By the time the British arrived some 100 years later, following a century of illness and devastation, not only would the copper items have been lost, but the knowledge of how to make such items also would have been forgotten. The further decrease in population occasioned by disease

This picture was taken at Indian Mound State Park, in St. Paul, Minnesota, which was well within the Dakota range; however, they denied building these mounds. The Dakota credit their creation to the Siouan Iowa and the Winnebago. The view, looking down from above, reveals a series of several mounds with the Mississippi River in the background. The photographer is unknown. It was published in 1898 by the Detroit Publishing Company.

destroyed what was left of the manpower required to build great monuments, and with no stable land base the desire to create such tributes to honor the dead would have been lost also.

Mound design varied from region to region as did the tribal traditions. Mississippian people built towns of earthen mounds that could reach heights of a hundred feet, and they had sufficient grasp of astronomy and math to align each of their mounds according to the exact position of the sun when it rose and set on the equinox and solstice. In the east, mounds were built primarily for burial, although other types of earthworks were also found. Lawson described towns and villages, some abandoned, that were built on mounds and surrounded by earthen palisades similar to those found in the Mississippi region.

This much is known: both the east-coast Santee and the Siouan Catawba were mound builders. Possibly the northern Santee could be included among their number, although it is unlikely that they were the builders of the major Mississippi mounds, attributed to the Cahokia. In the 1800s, the Wahpeton medicine man Weyuha described the mound "Minnewakan Chantay, where a great leader Chotanka lies buried,"[21] which suggest a burial mound near Devil's Lake (*Minnewakan Chantay*) which had been preserved by the people who created it.[22] Additionally, archeologist Lloyd A. Wilford, who studied the mounds around Mille Lacs in 1946, credited the one-time resident Santee tribe, the Mdewakanton, with their creation.[23] Meanwhile the Dakota themselves give credit to the Iowa, another of the many Siouan speakers.

The best source of information about their travels across the continent must, of course, come from the Indians' own tradition. In his journal *A New Voyage to Carolina*, John Lawson

There were mounds all along the Gulf Coast, the most impressive in Alabama. Some were located where the Siouan Biloxi lived. As a matter of fact, mounds existed in every area inhabited for any length of time by the Siouan-speaking tribes. The Carolina Santee were known mound builders. The mound pictured is located off Georgia Highway 17 and Georgia Highway 75, Nacoochee, White County, GA and was part of the Historic American Buildings Survey, 1933.

recorded that, when he questioned the residents about the land of their forefathers, they would point west, "where the sun sleeps."[24] Meanwhile the Catawba pointed northwest toward the Ohio Valley and Canada, seeming to confirm the theories of Mooney and Cotterill. The western Siouan speakers claimed eastern origins. An Osage chieftain told John Sibley in 1834 that they had come from the east in great numbers. Mandan farmers of the Missouri River region repeated a similar story while the Kansa (Kaw) and Omaha say the shells they prized were brought with them when they came from the great waters of the sunrise.[25] The plains Lakota, the Titonwan, also point to the east, toward the Minnesota home of the Dakota.

The Minnesota Santee point neither east nor south as the one-time Ohio valley tribes do, but north, indicating the route suggested by Pearson in his memoirs,[26] reaffirming their "parent" status. The upheavals occasioned by the abandonment of the major Cahokia settlements created a vacuum which may have drawn the Dakotas south in the 1400s to the place they occupied at the time of contact.

Samuel Pond, who lived among the Dakota Santee in Minnesota for twenty years in the 1800s, confirmed their northern origins. In his book, *The Dakota or Sioux in Minnesota as They Were in 1834,* he said: "The Indians have lived here for generations, supported by their own exertions, and they have also lived in colder latitudes than this, around the frozen shores of the Hudson Bay and far up toward the Arctic Circle."[27] Later he elaborated: "It is believed by them that they came here from the north, and they may have formerly lived very far north, as they were familiar with some of the habits of the Esquimaux, for whom they have a name, calling them 'Eaters of raw food.'"[28]

Sources indicate that when the Dakota were first "discovered" by the French, they were living northwest of Lake Superior, and some of the Assiniboines, a tribe who were descendents of the Nakota, were living still father north.

Thus, native verbal traditions seem to confirm the theories espoused by the authorities. Combining the available facts with the Dakota legends, one can attempt to trace their inland path. The Siouan people originated in the far north. They knew the Inuit and may have lived alongside them and traded with them for a time. Changing climate, lack of resources or population pressures caused the northern Dakota to move south from the Hudson Bay region during what is called the Medieval Warm Period between 900 and 1300 CE to an area north of the Great Lakes.

At that time the tribe seems to have divided. Whether they did this far north of the Great Lakes or along Lake Superior is unknown. At least one authority places the collective Siouan tribes east of Lake Michigan for a period of time. Certainly as canoe Indians, the Santee and the Catawba could have crossed the Lake Superior near Sault St. Marie, and they could then have followed the shoreline south. The Catawba continued to travel further south, perhaps with the southern contingent of Santee and the many other Siouan tribes, who eventually turned

The natives of this country often created artwork with their mounds, such as the giant snake found in present-day Ohio. Pictured here is the Rock Eagle Mound, located in Rock Eagle State Park, U.S. Route 441, Eatonton vicinity, Putnam County, GA. Part of the Historic American Buildings Survey, 1933 Library of Congress, photographer unknown.

Burial mounds were found all across the United States and not just in the eastern half, although it is estimated that there were at least 10,000 mounds along the Mississippi River and further east. Despite much proof to the contrary, Victorian America credited their creation to European or Middle Eastern groups, including the Lost Tribes of Israel. The photograph was taken by Prokudin-Gorskii, Sergei Mikhailovica sometime between 1905 and 1915 (Library of Congress).

east. The later cooling of the Little Ice Age may have drawn the northern Santee further south, while Cotterill's "parent stock" remained around the Great Lakes and still lived there when they met early explorers in 1650.

The migrations east and south would have been accomplished in stages. Evidence suggests that many of the tribes remained in the Ohio Valley, east of the Mississippi and west of the Appalachian Mountains, for a while, a theory supported by their own legends. This would make them neighbors of the Iroquois, and their relationship terms are surprisingly similar, denoting a fairly long association and interaction between the two nations.

Several hundred years ago, though, the Dhegiha Sioux (Osage, Quapaw, Kansa, Omaha, and Ponca) were forced to leave their homes along the lower Ohio and Wabash Rivers for locations west of the Mississippi. The Omaha group have been credited with the effigy earthworks of southern Ohio. The first to leave was the Quapaw around 1400–1500. They crossed the Mississippi and headed south into Arkansas. The Omaha, Ponca, and Kansa continued up the Missouri River, skirting Illini territory, and continued west to the Kansas City region where the Kansa stayed while the other two tribes moved on. The Ponca and Omaha tribes remained united as a single tribe the longest, moving together as far as Iowa and Minnesota before separating in the 1700s. The Osage settled along the lower river in central Missouri.

The Missouri Indians belong to the Chiwere Siouan language group. They called themselves the "Niutachi." The name "Missouri" was given to them by the Illini, and meant "the people with dugout canoes." This group included three other tribes: the Iowa, the Oto, and the Winnebago. Originally one tribe, their early prehistoric home was northern Ohio, along the Great Lakes. The Winnebago were the first to separate from the rest. The other three divisions occurred after they crossed the Mississippi River in late prehistoric times.

Another part of the Ohio Valley branch on the language tree, the Biloxi also traveled west along the Ohio River. Unlike their sister tribes, who turned north when they arrived along the shores of the Mississippi River, the Biloxi went south until they reached the Gulf of Mexico.

What became the Carolina Santee, the Sewee and the Wateree, the Catawba and the Woccon, formed a separate group who continued south and east to settle South Carolina and possibly as far south as Florida. The Tutelo seemed to have moved due east and then south, until they too reached the northern areas of the Carolinas.

The Dakota, after their arrival from the north, stayed in the region around the Great Lakes, where they grew and prospered, expanding west until they took over the northern plains to the Great Basin region, from Kansas north into Canada. All told, Cotterill's parent stock, the Dakota, have endured as a people with a recorded history for at least 900 years, as noted in the Battiste Good winter count. Thus as a nation the Dakotas have existed nearly as long as England, if one dates British origin, as they do, to the time of the Norman invasion in 1066. At it is the history of the "parent stock" specifically which will be addressed in the following chapters.

3. What's in a Word?

The surface of the earth lay empty except for those beings who, by flouting the rules of correct and moral conduct, had been exiled from the sacred lodge. Inktomi, who was the cleverest of all, quickly grew bored early on, for he would have others with whom he could play, others with whom he could converse. Creatures he could trick.

Inktomi stood proud—for he was fair then and had yet to assume his arachnid shape—and whenever he spoke a single word, the animal so named appeared before him. He spoke the eagle and the owl, the buffalo and the bear, and with this act, Inktomi imparted not only character, but form to his creations, for words were important things to be used sparingly.

He made the beasts who walked through the woods and the fields and the birds who ride the winds of heaven. He made those who swim in dark waters, those that slither and those that creep. He named the trees and each blade of grass, and Maka sported a fine new robe of infinite color. But Inktomi was not as clever as he thought, for he had forgotten to name himself. So Inktomi was left a mere miscellany of shifting parts—eight legs, two bodies—hence a spider.

Forever restless, Inktomi soon grew bored again, and at the instigation of Anog Ite, he brought man to the populate the planet. All the tribes—the four-legged, the two-legged and the winged ones—lived in peace. Men conversed with animals, and animals with man.

The tribes of animals were many, but the buffalo, deer and antelope were most numerous and considered themselves better than the rest. They grew bloated with hubris and pride. They called a council where they decided to prey upon the others, and the buffalo, elk, deer and antelope made war upon the rest of creation.

This angered the Great Spirit, who came to the place known as Minnewakan Chatay[1] and put up His tipi. He called all the animals to attend His council. When each emerged from the lodge, they were greatly changed. The buffalo who had led the rebellion was made the most ugly and ungainly of all creatures, while the antelope, elk and deer were weighted down with horns.

The bear and the wolf tribe had always been the most learned and much favored by the Great Mystery. It was decreed that the bear and wolf would prey upon the buffalo, deer and elk, who had grown too numerous and too arrogant.

And the power of speech was taken from them. The one voice splintered into a thousand different tongues, each with their grunts and growls, their shrieks and snarls. The scream of the hawk. The warble of the lark. The wolf and the coyote each had their song. Not one of the animal tribes could understand the other. Only man, created by Wakan Tanka and not born by the word of Inktomi, was left in his own shape, and only those specially gifted by the Great Spirit retained the knowledge of animal speech and can talk with them. These holy men and women were bound by oaths and vows not to reveal this sacred tongue to anyone else, for its knowledge is the gift of the divine and the power of the word is not to be taken lightly.[2]

3. What's in a Word?

Before leaving the subject of language, one must consider the language itself, for language tells a great deal about a people. The story is a cautionary tale about the power of the word and the waste that occurs when words are expended foolishly. It warns against sin, in this case conceit or pride, which inevitably leads to downfall and could be compared to the Biblical account of Babel. The people — the four-legged, two-legged and winged ones — are struck dumb, unable either to communicate with or understand each other. The tale also reflects the attitude of the people who tell it.

Nothing demonstrates history better than language. English is a good example, with its overlay of words from the Celts, the Romans, the Saxons, the Viking Norse and the Norman French. Each word or phrase reveals another wave of invasion. The conquerors may have been overthrown, left voluntarily or been assimilated into the people; but they left their mark upon the people in their tongue. The American government understood how essential language was to the identity of a people. The suppression of the native tongue became an integral part of the government's plan to assimilate the indigenous people into "civilized" U.S. society.

The Dakota placed great importance on language. Its mastery turned a prisoner into a member of the band. A captive was accepted on equal footing as any other tribe member as soon as he learned to speak Dakota. Understanding the language, both spoken and unspoken turned an enemy into a partner and friend. The Dakota valued their orators and their storytellers who kept their history and traditions alive. Their leaders were often good speakers, able to sway great numbers of people with their words.

Dakota was not to be spoken quickly or thoughtlessly. Like Chinese, changing the accent in a word or phrase can radically alter its meaning. The Lakota word *má ga* with the accent on the first syllable means "field," while *ma gá with its accented second syllable means "goose."* Syllables often are repeated, the number of times repeated indicated quantity, frequency or intensity, which would require due consideration to ensure the speaker conveyed the correct emphasis.

Eugene Buechel, who devised the first Lakota dictionary, found them precise and exact in their speech, and he said: "Detesting hurried, indistinct speaking, the Lakota speak slowly. Every syllable has its pound or ounce of weight and sound."[3] Likewise, Lawson described the Siouan tribes of the east as being measured and unhurried speech, speaking at length without fear of interruption.

The words now used as a name — Lakota and Dakota, and the lesser known Nakota — mean friend or ally. Individually they represent linguistic subgroups or dialects. Simplistically speaking, if the Dakota used a "d" in a word then the Nakota used "n" and the Lakota "l." Hence the three distinct forms of the word "friend."

In truth, the variations were more complex. Neither Dakota or Nakota contained the letter "l" in their spoken language. "L" is unique to Lakota. Thus, *Ble Wakan*, the Lakota name for Spirit Lake, becomes immediately recognizable as Lakota, while the Dakota would say: *Mde Wakan*. The Dakota word *nina*, or "very," becomes *lila* in Lakota, but remains *nina* in Nakota. The "hd" of Nakota is pronounced "kd" in Dakota and "gl" in Lakota. The Yankton's *hda*, meaning "go home," becomes the Santee's *kda* and the Titowan *gla*.

There are other differences in pronunciation. The biggest disparity seems to be between Lakota and its two sister tongues. Spoken Dakota and Nakota sound similar. Whatever the dialectic variations, they were not so severe that the three groups could not communicate with one another.

Early European settlers found the languages of the Dakota, Nakota and Lakota peoples less offensive to the ear than the those of the eastern Iroquois and Algonquin. Dakota was less harsh, less guttural, with fewer glottal stops. Still, Samuel Pond described it as difficult for an adult to master, with many unfamiliar sounds to imitate. "The language is easy in acquisition to those who learn it from childhood, for it has few irregularities and its system of vowel sound is very simple indeed."[4]

Syntax is tricky, particularly for the English-speaker. Like French and Spanish, one has the "ball red" rather than the "red ball." Additionally *kin*, described by Buechel as the article "the," often follows the modifier, so the phrase becomes "ball red the," Sometimes *kin* not only follows the noun but precedes it — turning "the red ball" into "the ball red the."

As in English the predicate (verb) usually followed the subject (noun), but sentence structure seems inverted to the English speaker. For a better understanding of the differences in sentence structure, consider the following phrase from Buechel.[5]

> The English: All kind of trees grew.
> The Lakota: *Can owe kin oyasin icage.*
> Translated literally back into English: "Trees kind the all grew."

An object added to the sentence increases the English-speaker's confusion. "None of you will go home" in Titowan Lakota becomes *Waniji yaglapi kte sni* which, when translated word for word back into English, becomes "none you will not go home."[6]

However, what appears muddled at first glance becomes clear when viewed within the context of Native American sign. Sign language, ingenious in its simplicity, allowed the Algonquin trader to speak to the Dakota and vice versa. Many of the signs would easily be comprehended by the people of today who were not acquainted with it. As in mime, old age is depicted as a man standing back hunched over or leaning on a stick. Infirmity is shown as shaking, palsied hands.

Sign, as a language of warfare and trade, meant the object — the thing being traded or the recipient of the attack — was more important than the subject, which usually consisted of the participants of the conversion. They would be omitted, implied, or indicated simply enough by pointing. Often the speaker was the actor, hence the subject of the sentence, and could also be omitted, much as the word "you" is omitted in the imperative sentence. One does not say: "You stop"; rather one says: "Stop"— the "you" is implied. Transitive verbs, such as "are" or "is," become unnecessary, losing their meaning, and did not exist in sign language.

Other things had to be depicted symbolically, affecting order and presentation, and there were limits to the number and kinds of signs the human hand could form, which also influenced order. Case in point, the thumb of one hand pressed against the thumb of the other, with forefingers either touching or nearly touching to form a circle — symbolizes something circular, something contained. Modifiers indicate the type of container.

For example: "Lake" combined the sign for "water," the hand cupped in front of the mouth; an open circle, indicating something large; and the sign for "rain." A well was differentiated from a lake by the size of the circle. Here the fingers and thumb touched, indicating something small, but the sequence remained essentially the same, with the final modifier "drink" the definitive one — meaning that this water was good to drink. The concept of "island"— land surrounded by "water"— shifts the emphasis. The circle precedes water (hand cupped in front of the mouth), which is secondary, defined by a circular sweep of the palm held flat for "surround." In other usages, the same circle followed by interlocked fingers meant a corral or pen. The preceding signs followed by a steepling of index fingers indicated a cabin.

Comprehension then becomes a process where the initial item requires delineators in order to clarify. It must have had an influence on the spoken word, used as they were in conjunction with one another. Certainly, the two mirrored each other in other ways. In both the spoken language and in sign, emphasis was revealed by repetition of a word or an act. The sign for strike, of course, meant strike. Used repeatedly it indicated some kind of attack.

Another reflection of the people, the Dakota language has no passive voice. Rather than saying "the boy was killed by a wolf," one must say: "a wolf killed the boy."[7] This says a great deal about the psychology of the culture as a whole, that it was active in its stance rather than passive. Like sign language, Dakota dialects have no "is." If one wants to make a simple declarative statement that "John is tall" it is sufficient to say "John tall." No verb is required.

Tense, such as past or present tense, did not exist in the spoken language, a reflection of the Dakota view about time, which was of little or lesser import in their culture. It was understood in the context of the sentence. If time was essential to the meaning of the sentence, then the common delineators (the sun/day, the winter/year, the moon/month) would be incorporated and specific number given. In the spoken language, the words *kte* or *kta* in the sentence indicated that this was a future occurrence, two days hence rather than two days ago.[8]

Often the spoken word was used with sign for clarification. Daytime designations in sign consisted of the thumb and forefinger in a half circle for sun. The position in which it was held and the distance from the shoulder indicated the time of day; shown at its zenith (above the head) meant noon. The addition of the sign for night following the sun symbolized the "night sun," that is, the moon, or month. The number of days or months were counted out upon one's fingers.

While Pond grumbled that Dakota was restricted when it came to adding the new concepts and devices brought by the white man and white commerce, it proved itself to be quite adaptable. Guns were called thunder sticks or fire sticks, either or both, a perfectly apt description of the object in question. In this, the language could be compared to present-day German where old words are added together to illustrate new concepts. Alcohol was either fire water or *wakan* water, in this usage meaning crazy, another accurate description. The definition of *wakan* is mysterious, which entailed a number of nuances including madness.

Dakota and most of the Native American tongues are descriptive, as illustrated by the names of the month. The chart below gives two versions. The first column reveals the months as recorded by the Count Giovanni Beltrami in 1828.[9] The second is attributed to Stephen Riggs in 1852.[10] The differences in spelling are vast, dependent not only on the original language of the hearer (French as opposed to English or Spanish), but his knowledge and educational background. Thus, translations vary, and Beltrami, unfamiliar with the local grains, called wild rice "oats." Other changes in month names can be explained by the period and by placement. In the later version, the Dakota had acquired a greater reliance on buffalo than agriculture, so August became the buffalo moon, replacing the old harvest moon.

Month	Santee	Translation	Dakota	Translation
January	Onkiwari-ouì	The moon of valous	Wi-tehi	The hard moon
February	Owiciatà-ouì	The moon of wild cats	Wicata-wi	Raccoon moon
March	Wisthaocia-ouì	The moon of bad eyes	Istwicayazan-wi	Sore-eye moon
April	Mograhoandì-ouì	The moon of game	Magahokada-wi	Moon when geese lay eggs
May	Mogahacandà-ouì	The moon of nests	Wojupi-wi	The planting moon
June	Wojusticiascià-ouì	Strawberry moon	Wajustecasa-wi	Strawberry moon
July	Campaseià-ouì	Cherry moon	Canpasapa-wi	Chokecherry moon
August	Yanklankakiocù-ouì	Buffalo moon	Wasuton-wi	The harvest moon
September	Wasipì-ouì	Moon of oats	Psinhnkaetu-wi	Wild rice moon
October	Sciowastiapì-ouì	Second moon of oats	Wi-wajup	Drying rice moon
November	Takiouka-ouì	The moon of roebuck	Takiyuha-with	Rutting moon
December	Abesciatakiouskà-ouì	Budding horns moon	Tahecapsun-wi	Moon when deer shed their horns

Not only were there the three dialects, but within the dialects, there were two, possibly three distinct "languages" which revealed aspects of Dakota culture.

Women did not use the imperative voice. Certain words such as *wo*, *yo*, or *po* at the end of a sentence indicated a command. These words were the provenance of men. Women used the softer and more moderate *we, ye, pi* which suggest entreaty as opposed to an order or demand. A man also used *ye* in a plea or petition.[11] However, if a command must be given by a woman to her husband or her son, it was phrased in the form of petition as a sign of respect.

An analogy could be drawn between Dakota and French, with its two forms of the word "you": *tu,* the informal singular, or *vous* which was either plural or formal singular and the only correct form of address if speaking to one's superior. Such nuances showed deference and so the language reveals much about relationships. Other terms whose use was restricted to men included the participle *lo, hau* used as a greeting or approval, or *haun* an expression of extreme grief.

Respect as a reflection of the spoken word was shown in other ways. After a boy reached a certain age the young man's sisters were not supposed to speak to him directly. Their question had to be addressed to a younger sibling who could then relay the question to its recipient and the answer back to the questioner. How often this was actually practiced within the confines of the lodge where it would become cumbersome is impossible to say. This concept of who could speak to whom directly and how was called *wistelkiciyapi* (to make ashamed),[12] and it was not limited to the Dakota, numerous other tribes of other language groups had similar injunctions.

No one, either male or female, could talk to or even look at one's in-laws. It required a third party — presumably one's spouse or another interpreter, often in the form of the "sacred transvestite" — to communicate with the parents. If a young man or a young woman alone in a tipi was visited by his or her spouse's parents, the latter would not enter the lodge until another could be found to act as intermediary.

Buechel claimed the Lakota did not have words *per se* but 500 syllables which could be strung together to create words.[13] Such a description makes the language sound casual and imprecise. Nothing could be further from the truth, and this was best illustrated by relationship names. There were no less than sixty-two names to denote one's relationship to another individual, which told not only how they were related but indicated the gender of the speaker and the gender of the person addressed, so a woman's nephew was *Toska* while a man's nephew was called *Tonska.* To a certain extent the terms revealed the degree of consanguinity and connection, for example, to one's parents. A man could be an "uncle" or "father" depending up whether he was brother to one's mother or one's father. All elders were called grandfathers, or some variant of the word, or grandmothers.

The relationship names also gave their standing within the family unit with separate words for first-born son, then second son down to the last-born, and the same was true for daughters. These words acted as names until another had been earned. Meanwhile when speaking of a son, but not a specific son, a different word was used. Variations existed between tribes or dialects. Thus, the Dakota called the first-born daughter *Winona* and the Lakota would call her *Witokape.* (A complete list of the Lakota relationship names can be found at the end of the chapter.)

The fact that so much attention is paid to relationship stresses the importance of the extended family among the Dakota people, and it served a further purpose by delineating whom one could marry. It defined one's position among the people and ensured that people did not marry anyone too close in the consanguinity.

A third form of Dakota was "sacred language." This language, used in prayer, rite and song, was the exclusive provenance of medicine men and women and holy men and women. The Dakotas' concept of sacred language reflects their respect for the divine. It might be compared to Latin in the old Catholic Church, although in this instance the words are obviously Dakota in origin. For example: the abbreviated name for the Mystery of sky, *Skan,* originated in the sacred language of old and the word was not used by common man. He would have spoken of *Takuskanskan.* It is only recently that *Skan* has becames adopted into common usage.

In his long career painting the natives of forest and plains, Frederic Remington recorded what appears to be the creation of a winter count. The winter count covered the period from one winter to the next or a year. Warriors also used pictographs to relay their achievements on either tipi or robe. This illustration was painted in 1889 and published in 1890 by Houghton, Mifflin & Co.; Copley print copyright 1903 by Curtis & Cameron.

    Sometimes the words of sacred language were incomprehensible even to the holy man. For instance, the sacred songs, which are "songs without words." The first song sung as the people enter the circle during the sun dance is an example of a song without words. This apparent incongruity of prayers that no one understands does not trouble Dakota as long as it is pleasing to the divine. The songs — revealed in a vision — were sacred, and became further consecrated by time, tradition and repetition.

    Contrary to popular belief, the Dakota people had a form of writing, although the early settlers did not dignify it as written language since it came in the form of pictographs. Referring to the Carolina Santee, Lawson described it variously as hieroglyphics or more disparagingly as "doodling and scribblings." Unlike Egyptian hieroglyphs, where images often depicted sounds, Dakota pictographs were purely representational. A horse meant a horse and man on horseback meant a man on horseback.

    Lodges were decorated with the exploits of the warrior who dwelled therein. Each scene told a story that could immediately be understood by the members of the tribe. Robes would be similarly adorned. The figures always told a story and, like the paints worn by the brave, the symbols were anything but

The picture writing of the Dakota was representational. A tree stood for a tree. If the picture was surrounded by a series of dots or dashes, it indicated many. So, a tree encircled by dots meant forest. A single campfire suggested a camp or a band. Surrounded by lines it meant "many" or a council fire and a meeting of the tribes.

Entries from the 1888 Red Cloud census collected at the Pine Ridge reservation in 1888. Each pictograph gave the name of the head of a household which then became the family name. On the top is the pictograph for Red Cloud. Bottom, Slow Bear, with its backwards slant, gives the impression of reluctance, or slow. The illustration demonstrates just how versatile this form of writing could be.

Cross roads
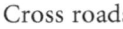
Trade

River

Notification of events also required the ability to communicate the place and the type of event, as shown here.

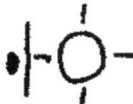  

Communications of events, such as tribal council, needed to convey the concept of time. The method used is both as simple and understandable, even to the uninitiated, as it is ingenious. The symbol for the sun is immediately recognizable while a series of slashes or lines next to it indicate the number of days, or suns (*center*). A circle, or oval, of black meant night. The placement of the two symbols — night and day — along a thin line of "number" indicated past or future events. Hence the sun next to the night symbol followed by the line meant tomorrow. If the line separated the sun from circle of night, it meant yesterday (*left*). The number of days could also be conveyed by alternating sun and nights strung together (*right*).

arbitrary. Even the Europeans had to acknowledge that their writing worked well as form of communication.

As a written language, it was practical enough that it allowed the Lakota to keep a record of years in their winter counts which can still be understood today, and it was in such common usage that pictographs were recognized and accepted by census officials in 1880, who would receive boards or hides adorned with the head of the household's name depicted graphically.[14]

The Dakota also used wands to communicate. They were sent as invitations. The sticks would be marked or painted in such a way to convey a message, not only of the type of event, war, feast or ceremony, but to whom it was addressed. For instance, if a man had been injured in battle and was subsequently invited to join a warrior society, the wand sent to him was painted red, symbolic of the blood spilled when he was wounded.

The Dakota utilized many other forms of communication. Sign language was not only used to speak with an outsider; it was used within the tribe, during the hunt or a raid to ensure their presence would not be betrayed by talking. Animal sounds kept them in contact with other members of the war party without revealing their position to the enemy. Among themselves, they had a system of shouts. The "soldiers' shout" told the tribe of a decree about to be enforced and a call of alarm. Altogether, this allowed them to communicate information quickly without the use of words.

Blanket signals transmitted information soundlessly from a distance. This was important when noise might alarm local game or alert a rival tribe. A blanket swung unfolded overhead signaled some sort of discovery. If the blanket was rolled up and held at both ends, it meant buffalo. If the blanket was then spread out across the ground, it depicted a large herd. To throw a blanket overhead several times indicated danger.[15]

Smoke signals could broadcast information from much father away. The messenger did not have to be within sight of the camp. Smoke signals could transmit information during the daytime. Their use was not restricted to night as the Roman and British system of signal fires had been. A single puff of smoke warned of danger. Two signaled "all's well" while three was a plea for assistance.

Trail markers conveyed valuable information between bands, even between tribes of different languages. The markers could be tufts of grass knotted, single branches broken, or grass or sticks hanging on a forked stick. Where trees were available, the message could be notched into the trunk. Elsewhere stones could be stacked or arranged in certain way. Therefore using simple means the prairie people could express a large variety of information. A single small stone stacked upon a larger rock meant "this way"—as did a handful of grass knotted but standing upright. When the grass was bent, it pointed in the correct direction, left or right. If the knotted grass was torn up and lying on the ground, it meant danger. A stack of stones with a long flat stone pointing in a particular direction indicated the place where water could be found. A series of sticks planted in the ground then conveyed the number of days hence. Four sticks meant four days. Five sticks, five days.[16]

Viewed as a whole, Dakota communication was not restrictive, as Pond complained. Viewed as a reflection of a culture, it reveals a people who were precise and patient, deliberate in their speech

Once the message was created on a wand, hide or bark, it had to be relayed to its recipient. Before the arrival of the horse this meant human couriers. Later, of course, the horse replaced travel on foot or canoe. Within the village or environment, a herald announced news or events to the community. Another of Frederic Remington's paintings, this one, called *The Indian Runner*, was published in, 1890 by Houghton, Mifflin & Co. and again in 1903 by Curtis & Cameron.

and manner. Their form of nonverbal communication was highly creative, allowing commerce between people who had no common language, and something for which the European culture of the time had no equivalent. The Dakota language reveals an adaptable people who could adjust their means of communication to necessity and circumstance, a people who valued clarity in communication and who respected correct use of the language itself.

Blanket signals. This painting by Frederic Remington, published in 1909, shows two riders on horseback signaling with a blanket. The blanket signals allowed people approaching a village or a camp to warn them of their arrival or to send news from a distance. If, for example, the blanket were rolled up and held by both ends, showing a half-circle to the far observer, it indicated horns or buffalo. The signal thus conveyed the presence of a herd without disturbing it.

Left: Stacks of stones were another means of long-distance and long-term communication between tribes. The one on the right indicates that the observer should go "this way." The other stack not only indicates the presence of water, the top stone also points the way. A series of sticks placed next to this stack would indicate the number of days to the water source. Woodland tribes could use a series of notches on the bark of a tree to convey similar information.

RELATIONSHIP NAMES (LAKOTA) from Walker and Powers.[17]

1. *Hunkake* ancestors
2. *Mihigna* my husband, *mitawicu* my wife
3. *Tunkan* grandfather; may be used by anyone
4. *Tunkansi/Tunkasi* a child's maternal grandfather, or father-in-law when used by anyone other than a child
5. *Tunkansila* paternal grandfather and a term of respect addressed to any elder
6. *Kun, Kunsi* paternal grandmother. The first could be used by anyone, while the second was specifically used when children addressing their grandmother
7. *Unci/Onci, Uncisi/Onicisi* maternal grandmother. The former was used as a sign of respect. The latter was addressed by one's grandchildren, and mother-in-law

8. *Atku, Ate* father. The first a formal form of address; the second informal (Papa), used by children
9. *Hun, Ina* mother formal and informal
10. *Leski* uncle mother's brother
11. *Tonwin* aunt father's sister
12. *Sic'e* a woman's brother-in-law
13. *Tanhan* a man's brother-in-law
14. *Sicepan/Scepan* woman's sister-in-law
15. *Hanka* a man's sister-in-law
16. *Takos* son-in-law or daughter-in-law
17. *Ciye* a boy's eldest brother
18. *Sunka* a youngest brother, used by either a male or a female
19. *Tiblo* a sister's eldest brother
20. *Cunwe* a boy's eldest sister
21. *Tanke* a girl's eldest sister
22. *Tanka* a girl's younger sister
23. *Tankasi* a boy's younger sister
24. *Hankasi* a male's male cousin
25. *Sicesi* a male's female cousin
26. *Sicepansi* a female's female cousin
27. *Ohmawaheton* a form of address between a woman's parents and her husband's parents
28. *Tawin* wife
29. *Hingna* husband of sole wife
30. *Bluze* husband of more than one wife
31. *Teyak* second wife who is not a sister of the first wife
32. *Miteyak* second wife who is a sister of the first
33. *Wincu* captured wife
34. *Tawicu* consummated wife

Younger generation

1. *Cin* son when used as an indefinite descriptor
2. *Cun* daughter when used as an indefinite descriptor
3. *Cinhan* son when speaking of a specific person
4. *Cunwin* daughter when speaking of a specific person
5. *Cinksi* when a parent is speaking of one's son
6. *Cunksi* when a parent is speaking of one's daughter

Children's placement names (Sisseton)

1. *Caske* first son
2. *Hepan* second son
3. *Hepi* third son
4. *Hake* fourth son
5. *Wake-Wa-Gu-Gu-Na* fifth son
6. *Winona* first daughter
7. *Hapan* second daughter
8. *Hapsti* third daughter
9. *Wanske* fourth daughter
10. *Wihake* fifth daughter

Children placement names (Oglala)

1. *Caske* first son
2. *Hepan* second son
3. *Hepi* third son
4. *Catan* fourth son
5. *Hake* fifth son
6. *Witokape* first daughter
7. *Hapan* second daughter
8. *Hepistanna* third daughter
9. *Wanska* fourth daughter
10. *Wihake* fifth daughter
11. *Hakata* last-born either male or female
12. *Cekpa* one of twins of either gender

Additionally there were:

1. *Tawagan* stepchild
2. *Takos* child-in-law
3. *Tonska* a man's nephew
4. *Tonzan* a man's niece
5. *Toska* a woman's nephew
6. *Tozan* a woman's niece
7. *Takoza* grandchild
8. *Wicatakoza* grandson
9. *Winotakoza* granddaughter
10. *Hunka* relative adopted by ceremony
11. *Winohtin* sister of a fraternal manner
12. *Hunkawanzi* brother of a fraternal manner

4. Who Were the Oceti Sawakin?

Many winters ago, when humankind was young and new to this earth, they angered Unktehi, spirit of water and mother of all evil beings, or perhaps they had offended the Great Spirit himself, for Unktehi declared war on the people, and Wakan Tanka did not stop her. Unktehi caused the rivers to swell until they burst their banks. The water rose and rose and spread across the face of the earth until there was none left, except a small promontory of rock near the place where the sacred pipestone was quarried.

Many drowned as they fled before the flood, moving to higher ground until they reached the hill, and it seemed that Wakan Tanka had turned his face from this world. The people clambered up its sides until the hill was covered and they were packed tight, backs against the giant boulders.

Still the flood waters came, for Unktehi was not done with man yet. Waves crashed against the rocks, crumbling the walls and pinnacles which fell and crushed the people clinging to the hill below. The waters turned red, staining the rock with their blood, and that is why pipestone is sacred, for it is made with the flesh and blood of our ancient ancestors.

Soaring in the heavens, Wambli gleska, the great spotted eagle, saw all that happened beneath him; but there was little he could do to help. There were so many, and he was just one. This most powerful and magical of all eagles viewed the plight of the people and grieved their loss as the boulders came tumbling down. Suddenly he spotted a lone woman struggling in the surf. This one, at least, he could save. Wambli gleska swerved, and catching the currents of the winds he ascended high into the heavens. Then he swooped. The mighty bird clasped her arm gently in his huge talons. His wings beat, creating eddies and currents in the water's face, he lifted her and carried her away. Wambli gleska took her to his lodge far above the flood.

The young woman mourned the people, and the eagle kept his distance, waiting patiently for her to turn her face to him, for Wambli gleska found her a good woman and he grew to love her, and she, after her grief had passed, grew to love him too. They married and she had many fine babies.

Wakan Tanka watched the children grow into adulthood, brave and strong, and was satisfied that not all men had perished, and he punished Unktehi for her harshness, turning her as hard as her judgment by turning her to stone. Her bones now form the Badlands. Her back is the high ridges, and her vertebrae are found in the red and yellow stone.[1]

Meanwhile the descendants of the eagle and the last woman, her children and her children's children, became the Cangleska Oyate, the Dakota people or Hoop Nation.

As the name suggests, the *Cangleska Oyate* describes unity, and all who are contained within the *Cangleska Wakan*, or sacred hoop, are both protected and blessed. It might also be considered among their first names, for at one time, the Dakota formed a single tribe which, according to this legend, were the descendants of eagles.

Part of the rare book collection, this sketch was drawn by John White. The engraving is by Theodor de Bry and was published in *Americae pars decima* in 1619. While it depicts an Algonquin village of Secotan, the houses and the agricultural plots were similar to those found in woodland Dakota summer camps. The standard *tipi tonka* was rectangular in form and made of woven bark. It was large enough to house up to four families.

The process that began when the Siouan-language speakers spread across the continent continued with the parent band that remained in the Great Lakes region. As the Dakota population expanded, the single band formed divisions, creating separate bands which further subdivided as necessity dictated. The process took generations.

While the formation of distinct dialects may not take the full 245 years required to form separate languages, it helps to provide a baseline. Not only were the dialects firmly established by the time white men arrived on the scene in the 1500s, but cultural differences had accrued between the groups.

Their linguistic cousins Crow and Hidatsa had already branched into new tribes, developing new languages. These tribes never performed the eastward trek that took so many of the other Siouan bands in a wide circle through the Ohio Valley. The Hidatsa and Crow were direct offshoots of the Dakota, and the first of the Siouan tribes to move out onto the American plains. The Assiniboin who splintered from Nakota later also developed a distinct language. This suggests a timeline of 980 years to form four distinct languages, and more time would have been required to evolve three dialects, which confirms the existence of the Dakota as a tribe since around or even before the ninth century.

The northern Dakotas were long established at the time of the first recorded mention of them by Father Paul LeJeune in 1640, when he referred to them as the Nadowesioux, the Chippewa word for "snake." However, there are other interpretations for the origin of the name Sioux. Indeed, one theory dismisses any derogatory intent, suggesting that the term dated back to the time when the tribes, living further south, worshipped the snake. Clifford Cancu, Head of Dakota Studies at the Sisseton Wahpeton Community College, proposed another hypothesis, believing the name resulted from a Native American sign for river. The Santee were river Indians, and the sign for river consists of the index finger, pointed forward, drawing an undulating course in the air which was misinterpreted by the white traders to mean snake rather than river.

The other names that the Dakota gave themselves actually reflect their division. For example: the word *da* (*la* or *na*), "considered," plus *koda*, "friends," shows that the single tribe had by this time disbanded into separate but allied units.[2] Meanwhile *Oceti Sakawin*, translated as the People of the Seven Council Fires, describes the Dakota after the process of division was complete and the seven hearths, or tribes, had formed.

The council fire itself represented the autonomy of the tribe. Each hearth, or tribe, preserved its sacred fire by carrying coals from the previous council fire to the new campsite, which would then be used to light the new council fire. It symbolized *Wi* or the sun, and its coals were used to light the *canupe* or sacred pipe also kept by each band. Each band formed a *tiospaye*, and each *tiospaye* had its own leader or *Itancan*. The chiefs came together during the summer months for intertribal councils. The chief of the most powerful band within a tribe was recognized as the spokesman for the group during these intertribal council fires. Collectively the tribal chiefs were known as *Naca Ominicia*, who could alternatively choose one among their number to represent or lead them.[3]

Divisions required the consent of the parent tribe. Said Robert M. Utley in *The Lance and the Shield, The Life and Times of Sitting Bull*: "Sioux camps had been governed by strict compact: No family belonged without the consent of the council; no family withdrew without the consent of council."[4]

Divisions could also arise as a result of a dispute. A person could be cast out or he could be shunned and choose to leave his band voluntarily, and with its tacit permission. If a man was exiled and others chose to join him, they became a separate band within the tribe. If a large number of people followed that particular leader, or if they grew to a band of significance, they became a tribe or separate council fire. An example of this former is the Inkpaduta band which

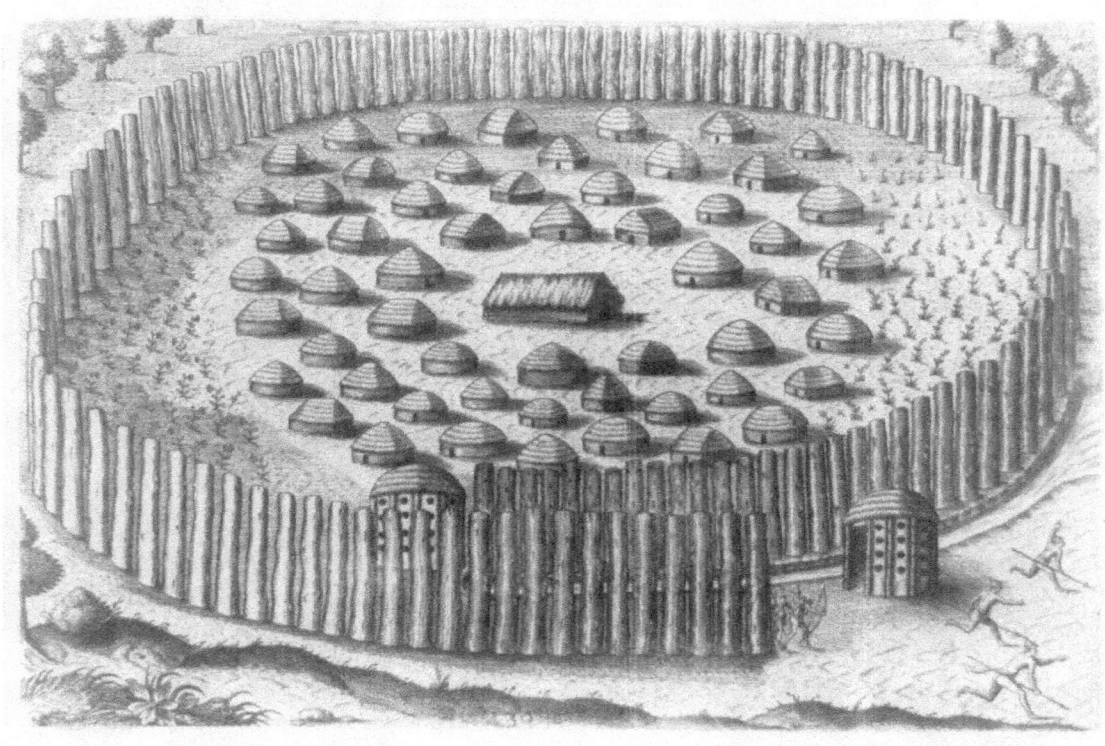

Some of the tribes, particularly the Siouan tribes of Carolina including the eastern Santee, used circular construction for home and village structures, as did the Dakota Wahpeton. Later in the 1815 No Ears winter count, it was noted that Itazipcho (Sans Arc) experimented with circular homes. This illustration drawn in the 1500s by John White shows a fortified village with an enclosing stockade. Part of the Library of Congress Rare Book Collection, the engraving was done by Theodor de Bry after a watercolor by John White and published in *Wunderbarliche, doch warhafftige Erklärung, von der Gelegenheit vnd Sitten der Wilden in Virginia ... / Erstlich in engelländischer Sprach beschrieben durch Thomam Hariot, vnd newlich durch Christ. P. in Teutsch gebracht.* Franckfort am Mayn: Gedruckt bey J. Wechel, in Verlegung D. Bry, 1590, plate 19.

was formed when a man named Wamdesapa killed his old rival Chief Tasagi and was banished. Others followed and a new band was born, which became known to the other Dakota people as the Wahpekute renegades.

John Blount Horn explained the process and its progression for James Walker in the early 1900s. Divisions usually occurred when the lack of game in a region caused a group to move farther away from the parent branch in the search for food. "Then some wandered so far in the summertime that they did not return to the winter camp...." According to Horn a portion of these people made their home on Knife Lake (*Ble* or *Mde Isanti*) and became known as the Isanti, or in modern parlance, the Santee. Later the people of Knife Lake (Santee) moved to the place "where leaves fall," making two council fires, the Wahpukte and Wahpeton, while one of the bands moved onto the *tinte* or plains. A separate group remained at the lake year round and, said Horn, "they stank like fish so they were called *sin sin* (Sisseton). So there were four council fires."[5] Then one of the plains group who had made their home upon the plains moved further west. They no longer participated in council fires. They sent messengers with rough voices to speak to the parent tribe and became known as the Assiniboin ("those who spoke with rough voices"). Those who stayed became the Upper and Lower Yankton ("End Dwellers") and the Yanktonai ("Little End Dwellers").[6]

At the time of their introduction to the French, Dakota territory stretched from Manitoba north of Lake Superior south through Minnesota to Wisconsin, taking in the northwestern corner of Iowa and portions of Missouri. Some of their stories name locations around the southern tip of Lake Michigan, such as stinking or "skunk" marsh (Chicago), which suggests they considered Illinois part of their hunting grounds. The fact that the resident Illini viewed them as serious competitors for territory and furs indicate that this is correct. Later what is now the state of Missouri was held by a portion of the tribe that would eventually become the Titowan ("dwellers on the plain") while the Yanktonai moved out to Nebraska. Increased population pressures caused by the juxtaposition of eastern tribes forced some of the bands to move farther west and south again until the lower Nakota bands inhabited parts of Kansas. Meanwhile, the Assiniboin headed further north. The Crow continued west into the Rockies, and the Titowan took their place upon the prairies.

Each tribe developed an individual identity. Therefore, the Dakota, Lakota and Nakota peoples were distinguished from each other by more than language. In matters of dress, the outside observer could usually differentiate between the woodland Dakota and the plains Lakota. While both wore braids, the Santee would burn off their hair in the front, forming bangs. Even within a tribe, there could be variations. Thus, the Sisseton, considered a Santee tribe, dressed more like the plains Lakota than the woodland Dakota.

The names of the subdivision say something about the group, how it was formed or how the people within the group were viewed by the rest of the tribe. Consider the Itazipcho (Sans Arc) bands: Mazpegnaka ("Wear metal in the hair"); Tatankachesli ("Dung of the buffalo"). Each label contains a seed that may refer to the tribe's or band's origin, or describes a distinguishing characteristic, such as metal ornamentation. The names are of great antiquity, and many of the meanings have become lost in the mists of time. Similarly, the names can often be subject to differing interpretations.

The number of bands and sub-bands attributed to a tribe varied, depending upon the year and the success of the particular tribe during that time period. In their heyday the Titowan band of the Oglala consisted of some twenty divisions (or sub-bands). They now consist of a single unit. It is also important to grasp the breadth of the *Oyate* and to remember that each sub-band represented between 100 and 400 souls. A sobering thought, for those bands who no longer exist and the people who once populated them — along with their progeny — have been eliminated. In the case of the Oglala, this means the loss of some 1800 to 7600 individuals.

The first to meet the Europeans were the Isanti, or the Santee. The woodland branch consisted of four of the seven hearths or tribes. The Dakota had semi-permanent summer camps and, with some exceptions, they lived in bark houses similar to the Algonquin long house for a portion of the year, a lifestyle which they shared with the Nakota.

Ranked as first among the Santee were the Mdewakantonwan, or Mdewakanton ("The People of Spirit Lake"), believed, according to one tradition, to be descendants of Tokahe, the first man to emerge from the caves. All agreed they were the original council fire from which all other tribes sprung. As first, they were considered the leaders of their people by uneducated outsiders, like white traders who did not understand the autonomy of each group. Therefore, during the early reservation period, the Mdewakanton were forced — by the simple expedient of withholding their annual payment — to bring rebel bands, such as the one led by Inkpaduta, under their control after the Spirit Lake Massacre of 1857.

Mdewakanton Bands
- Kiuska
- Kaposia
- Pinisha
- Reyata Otonwa

Because they were considered the oldest tribe and the progenitors of the all the Dakota peoples, the Mdewakanton had pride of place in inter-tribal councils, with their tents set up opposite the entrance to the camp. One band was called the "Kiuksa," violators of custom or rule breakers, for in their attempt to keep the bloodline pure, they married within the band, thereby breaking the accepted rules of consanguinity that required tribe members to marry outside their own band.

In 1805, Zebulon Pike described them, whom he called "Mino Kantongs," as the only Dakota who built log huts, made canoes and cultivated corn. In dress, Mdewakanton more closely resembled the Algonquin than their Lakota cousins. They wore cloth turbans rather than the leather headband.

They were traders. One authority credited the spread of the other bands into the plains not to lack of food or as a result of population pressure, but as something that was economically motivated in order to maintain the woodland Dakota with pelts for trade, which suggests that the *Oceti Sawakan* could and did act according to a unified policy.

The Mdewakanton, indeed many of the Santee, were virtually wiped out during the 1862 uprising. After that time, they lost much of their prestige within the Dakota nation and ceased to be a driving political force. As with most tribes, the number of the bands varied. For instance, in an 1820 census report, the Mdewakanton bands were given as Keoxa (Kiuksa), 400; Eanbosandata (Khemnichan), 100; Kapozha, 300; Oanoska (Ohanhanska), 200; Tetankatane (Tintaotonwe), 150; Taoapa, 300; Weakaote (Khenlnichan), 50. Thus the five noted by Buechel, found in the box, represent only those groups that survived into the twentieth century.

Depending on the source, the Wahpekute ("Shooters among the Leaves") were the second or possibly the third hearth to form. Their history is one of the most convoluted and, as a group, they appear to be the most controversial. According to one author, Roy Meyers, they separated from the Mdewakanton after they lost their homeland at Mde Wakan in 1753;[7] however, this would make them one of the last bands to separate rather than one of the first. Pike called them "the most stupid and inactive" of all tribes, whose members consisted of those people who had been expelled from other bands.[8]

> **Wahpekute Bands**
> - Inyan ceyaka atonwan — Village at the Rapid
> - Takapsicaotonwan — Those who swell at the Shinny-ground
> - Wiyaka otina — Dwellers on the Sand
> - Otehi otonwe — Village on the Thicket
> - Wita Otina — Dwellers in the Island
> - Wakpa otonwe — Village on the River
> - Can kaga otina — Dwellers in Log

Even the woodland Santee viewed the Wahpekute as a lawless band and the least successful of all tribes. According to one tradition, the band betrayed the Iowa, who had been given permission to travel across their land, by rising up and slaughtering invited guests, including their chieftain, after the feast. As result they were cursed by Wakan Tanka and never prospered.

Historically ill-luck seems to have followed them into modern times. During the War of 1812, one of their bands, the Fire Leaf, became renegade among the Wahpekute when they chose to side with the Americans over the British. Later, in the 1840s, the renegade Inkpaduta saw their beginning. These renegades continued to make trouble for all the Dakota people when they declared war on the white settlers in southern Minnesota and northern Iowa that resulted in the Spirit Lake Massacre.

The Wahpekutes' main settlement was located on Cannon Lake. The Me-da-te-peton-ka ("Lake of the Big Village") and their territory included Inyan Bosndata or Standing Rock River. In dress and tradition, the Wahpekute so closely resembled their Spirit Lake relations that they were often lumped with the Mdewakanton by early explorers. This changed as time progressed. By 1823, Chronicler William Keating described the Wahpekute as a lawless band[9] who had adopted a nomadic style of life and plains dress.

4. Who Were the Oceti Sawakin?   45

Most Dakota tribes favored the tipi. The plains tribes used it almost exclusively. The woodland Santee had their summer homes, but they switched to the tipi during the cold winter months, allowing them to follow game wherever it went. The photograph, taken by Edward S. Curtis, for his book *North American Indian*, shows a Dakota winter camp. Library of Congress, The Curtis Collection. *North American Indian*, suppl. vol. 3, plate 106.

The next division of the Dakota tribes were the Wahpetonwan (Wahpeton) or "Dwellers among the Leaves." At the time of initial contact in the mid–1600s with European traders and missionaries such as Father Louis Hennepin, both the Sisseton and Wahpeton bands resided in settlements that extended from Manitoba, Canada, to their present homelands on Lake Traverse, and further south into Minnesota and northern Iowa. In 1766, Jonathon Carver listed them as one of the plains tribes. While white settlers looked to the Mdewakanton for help, in fact, the honor of bringing the peace between whites and the Dakota after the Spirit Lake Massacre belonged to the Wahpeton when they retrieved the white women captured by the Inkpaduta band and returned them to their families in 1857.

Around 1834, the Wahpeton included some seven bands which inhabited the area around Carver, St. Lawrence, Traverse des Sioux, Swan Lake, Lac Qui Parle. Additionally there were bands that lived with the Sisseton and the Yankton around Big Stone and Traverse Lakes. Because of the close association between the Sisseton and the Wahpeton, the latter were often mistaken for the Sisseton by their American or European neighbors rather than being afforded individual status as a separate tribe.

Whatever their placement, the Wahpetons remained woodland in their culture while the Sisseton adapted prairie lifestyle and dress. The Wahpeton maintained separate summer and winter lodges. Their summer homes were located at permanent bases or campsites. Much like the Carolina Santee, Wahpeton houses were dome-shaped rather than the oblong structures build by the Mdewakantan. Their lodges were constructed of wood covered in mud. However, by 1834, this kind of dwelling had been replaced by the more standard hide tipi.

The fourth group were the Sisitonwan (Sisseton) the "People of the Fish Ground (or Marsh)," those whom Blount Horn called *sin sin*, who stank of fish. They were among the first tribes to migrate to the Minnesota River valley. In dress, they resembled the plains Lakota, although they lived in settlements along the banks of lakes. Their territory at the time of the War of 1812 included Big Stone Lake on the upper Minnesota River up to an area northwest of Lake Superior in Manitoba. Like many of the other hearths, the Sisseton tribe was divided into numerous bands.

Sissseton Bands

- Wita waziyata otina — Dwellers at the Northern Island Ohdihe
- Basdece sni — Those who do not split (the backbone of the buffalo)
- Itokah tina
- Okahmi Otonwe — Village at the Bend (with further division in to Canska Otina)
- Manin tina — Those who pitched their tents away from the main camp
- Keze — Barbed, as a fishhook (a name of ridicule)
- Kapoza — Those who travel with light burdens
- Abdowapuskiyapi — Dry on their shoulders

According to census figures of the early 1800s, the four hearths of the Santee numbered 7000,[10] representing 20 percent of the total population of the Dakota nation. During the summer months, they usually formed permanent settlements. Women and children remained in villages to tend fields or went to separate sites to collect food, such as the annual maple sugar harvest, while the men hunted. However, in winter, they switched to the familiar tipi and followed the migratory lifestyles associated with the Lakota further west. They were among the first tribes to be "tamed" by the Americans, in 1824, Keating reported that the Santee had settled into permanent villages.[11]

Yankton Bands

- Chankute
- Chagu
- Wakmuhaoin
- Ihaisdaye
- Wacheunpa
- Ikmun
- Oyateshicha
- Washichunchincha

The next two hearths, or tribes, represented different linguistic groups from the Dakota. The Nakota encompassed the Yankton and Yanktonai tribes. The Nakota lived in the fringes of western Minnesota in the plains. Indeed the name Ihanktonwan (Yankton) means the "people of the end" while the Ihanktonwanna (Yanktonai) were the "little dwellers of the end." In the 1700s, they were involved in quarrying pipestone and trading it, and they were an integral part of the Dakota trade network. Early sources describe them as one of the more agrarian tribes, while in 1805, Pike said they were never stationary, which suggests that

On February 23, 1867, a Santee Sioux delegation attended a reception in the East Room of the White House. Members included representatives of the Yankton and Upper Missouri tribes and the illustration shows them with President Andrew Johnson and others government officials. It also reveals the differences in dress between the woodland Dakota and the plains Lakota. Note the cloth and fur turbans of the Santee, along with the distinctive cut of the leggings without fringe. The print came from a photograph by Alexander Gardner (1821–1881) which was published in *Harper's Weekly* on March 16, 1867.

they had adopted the nomadic lifestyle of the plains. The combined Nakota tribes numbered about 2500, a little less than one third their Dakota counterparts.

In 1850 Culbertson mentioned two Yankton bands, including one, "who do not cook," and another, "who eat no geese," that can not be identified with any of these divisions found in other sources. Either these tribes vanished from history or the listing is in error. Such mistakes happened from time to time; for example, when writing *History of the Indian Tribes of the United States* (published in Philadelphia by Lippincott, Grambo and Company, 1851), Henry Rowe Schoolcraft incorrectly included the "Wahnaataa" as one of the Yankton bands.

Despite the name "Little Dwellers of the End," which suggests a diminutive, it is believed that the Yanktonai were the elder of the two Nakota tribes. They were closely associated with the Lakota Hunkpapa throughout the nineteenth century. Their bands were listed as the Kiyuksa, Wazikute, Hunkpatina, and the unidentified Hahatonwanna, Honetaparteenwaz, and Zaartar, or as Hunkpatina, Pabaksa, and Wazikute. In the *Handbook of American Indians North of Mexico,* published by the Smithsonian Institution Bureau of American Ethnology (1905), James Owen Dorsey gives the Upper Yanktonai subdivisions as Wazikute, Takini, Shikshichena, Bakihon, Kiyuksa, and Pabaksa, and the subdivisions of the Lower Yanktonai as Hunkpatina (also called Putetemini), Shungikcheka, Takhuhayuta, Sanona, Ihasha, Iteghu, and Pteyuteshni. There were further English translations for Yanktonai bands about which little else is known beyond the name, including "the band that wishes life" and "the few that lived," which may refer to

> **Lakota Bands**
>
> - Oglala (Scatter their own)
> - Sicangu (Burned thighs)
> - Hunkpapa (End of Circle)
> - Mnikowoju (Planters beside the tream)
> - Sihasapa (Black Foot)
> - Oohenunpa (Two Kettle)
> - Itazipco (Without bows)

bands that had been destroyed by the ravages of war or disease.

The final hearth in the list of seven are the Titonwan, whom we now think of as the Lakota. Their formal name *Titowan* means "prairie village," and they gave their name to the Teton Mountains which became the western limits of their range. When they met Lewis and Clark in 1804, the Titonwan consisted of four council fires: the Sicangu, the Oglala, the Minicounjou (Mnikowoju), and the Saone. Around 1830, the Soane broke up to form three additional bands, completing the seven Lakota bands known today.[12]

Despite the fact that the Lakota represented only a single hearth of the seven, it claimed the largest population base, with over 25,000 members, which means the one tribe contained approximately seventy-four percent of the total Dakota population. The Lakota were so numerous that their seven bands each attained the status of tribes which further divided into bands and sub-bands.

The Oglala ranked first among the Teton bands and after the fall of the Mdewakanton, they took the place of precedence in intertribal councils. They maintained a chiefs' council of seven. They were mentioned by Lewis and Clark in 1806. Later Pierre De Smet, who spent a great deal of time among the Crow, called them: "The worst among the hostile bands..." along with the Blackfeet, the Hunkpapas and the Santees.

There has been much conjecture about the origin of the name Oglala, which means to "scatter their own." Some ascribe it to a specific incident, while others suggest that it originated from the fact they were the first of the Titowan who fathered the rest and then spread or "scattered" across the prairie. The latter definition appears to be confirmed by a quote from Pierre-Charles Le Seuer in 1701 where he refers to them as "villages dispersed in several small bands."[13] However, it takes a great stretch of the imagination to equate "oujatespouitan" with Oglala, and one wonders if he was speaking of the Dakota people as a whole. Still by the middle of the nineteen century, the Oglala claimed a territory that stretched from the Smoky Hill River in Kansas to the Black Hills.

In 1841, the Oglala fought among themselves and the Kiyuska band (meaning "the cut-offs") separated from the rest. The Oglala experimented for a time with agriculture when they settled with the Arikara and adopted their horticultural economy, but this was cut short when smallpox arrived on the scene.

In 1913, James Walker listed seven Oglala bands. Twenty-nine years earlier, the Rev. W.J. Cleveland (1884) enumerated a full 20 bands.

> **Oglala Bands (circa 1884)**
>
> | | | |
> |---|---|---|
> | (1) Iteshicha | (8) Peshlaptechela | (14) Kiyuksa |
> | (2) Payahya | (9) Tashnahecha | (15) Wacheonpa |
> | (3) Oyukhpe | (10) Iwayusota | (16) Wachape |
> | (4) Tapishlecha | (11) Wakan | (17) Tiyochesli |
> | (5) Peshla | (12) (a) Iglakatekhila | (18) Waglukhe |
> | (6) Chekhuhaton | (b) Iteshicha | (19) Oglala |
> | (7) Wablenicha | (13) Iteshichaetanhan | (20) Ieskachincha |

Sicangu has been translated both as Burnt Thigh, or the "people of burnt woods." According to verbal tradition, the name originated when a prairie fire destroyed a village. Men, women and children, who traveled by foot some distance from the village, were burned to death. Those who could get to a nearby lake saved themselves. Many were badly burned from running through tall, burning grasses. The English adapted the French word for burned, "Brule," to describe the tribe.

The Sicangu maintained a chiefs' council of ten, and like the Oglala, they once consisted of 20 bands along with the parent group. In 1806 they lived east of the Missouri River, along the Niobrara River. Their proximity to the trails of European trade meant that Sicangu suffered more loss due to disease than any other Lakota tribe. Even before they met Lewis and Clark, the Sicangu had experienced five separate outbreaks of smallpox.

Sicangu Bands		
(1) Kakeglia	(8) Tiglabu	(15) Oglalaichichagha
(2) Hinhanshunwapa	(9) Wacheunpa	(16) Tiyochesli
(3) Shunkahanapin	(10) Waglukhe	(17) Wazhazha
(4) Hihakanhanhanwin	(11) Isanyati	(18) Ieskachincha
(5) Hunkuwanicha	(12) Wagmezayuha	(19) Ohenonpa
(6) Miniskuyakichun	(13) Waleghaonwohan	(20) Okaghawichasha
(7) Kiyuksa	(14) Wakhna	

The Sihasapa, or Blackfoot/Blackfeet, got their name when "their feet had been blackened by walking through an area that had a prairie fire." They were an offshoot of the Soane, and should not be confused with the Algonquin Blackfoot/Blackfeet (Siksika) whose name came from the black moccasins they wore. The Lakota Sihaspa divided into seven bands, including the Sihasapakhcha, Kanghishunpegnaka, Glaglahecha. Wazhazhe, Hohe and Wamnughaoin. They often lived near the Hunkpapas and the Itazipcho (Sans Arc).

The Mnikowoju (Miniconjou) were "planters next to the stream." While many believe the Oglala were the only Titowan tribe to attempt agriculture on the plain, the name suggests this band too was agrarian and for them it was not an experiment, but a trait for which they became renowned. In 1837, George Caitlin immortalized the Miniconjou warrior known as "Corn," a name that also suggests an agricultural connection. It was a Miniconjou band, under Big Foot, who were almost completely eradicated at Wounded Knee.

The Itazipcho (San Arc or "those who hunt without bows") were closely related to the Miniconjou, possibly even an offshoot of the other band. They most likely followed the same settled lifestyle, for in 1815, the No Ears winter count marked their living in a "big house" or *titanka*, a term used to describe log homes of the Europeans and the circular dwellings used by the Ree (Arikara). Lakota scholar Vine Deloria believes the *ti tanka* refers to the latter rather than the former, and Lone Dog's winter count seems to support this belief. Speaking of the same event, the winter count reads: "The Sans Arc made their first attempt a dirt lodge."[14] The Itazipcho seem to have separated themselves both physically and in lifestyle from the other tribes for a such long time that their return to the fold was a newsworthy event that deserved mention in the 1846 Big Missouri winter count when the Itazipcho camped with the other tribes.[15]

The Itazipcho consisted of six different divisions: the Shinalutaoin ("Scarlet cloth earring"); Wolutayuta ("Eat dried venison from the hindquarter"); Mazpegnaka ("Wear metal in the hair"); Tatankachesli ("Dung of a buffalo bull"); Shikshichela ("Bad ones of different kinds"); Tiyopaoshanunpa ("Smokes at the entrance to the lodge").

Little has been documented about the next band, the Oohenunpa. The name, meaning "two kettles," seems to have originated "one year they were starving and only had two kettles

Above: Wahpeton houses were described as dome-shaped wooden structures that were covered with mud, similar to the Mandan earthen lodge pictured here. Later, the Sans Arc adapted the round house of the Arikara. This photograph was taken in North Dakota by Edward S. Curtis (c. 1908) and is part of the Edward S. Curtis Collection. It was published in *The North American Indian* (Seattle, Wash.): Edward S. Curtis, 1907–30, v. 5, p. 4.

Below: While winter's hardships necessitated smaller camps, in the summer months the council fires came together, and their camps could be huge. During the time of the annual sun dance when several tribes came together, the population could number in the thousands. The photographic print by F.B. Fiske shows a large camp, with one of the many summer storms that hit the plains in the background. It was taken in Fort Yates, North Dakota (c. 1902).

THE HEARTHS OF THE SEVEN COUNCIL FIRES AND THEIR BANDS

Mdewakanton	Wahpekute	Wahpetonwan	Sisseton	Yankton	Yanktonai	Titonwan
Kiuska	Me-da-te-peton-ka (Lake of the big village)	Inyan Ceyaka Atonwan (Village at the Rapids)	Wita Waziyata Otina (Dwellers at the Northern Island)	Chankute	Wazikute	Oglala (Scatter their own)
Kaposia	Inkpaduta	Takapsicato Onwan (Those who dwell at the Shinny-ground)	Ohdihe	Chagu	Kiyuksa	Sicangu (Burned thighs)
Pinisha		Wiyaka Otina (Dwellers on the Sand)	Basdece sni (Those who do not split the backbone of the buffalo)	Wakmuhaoin	Hunkpatina	Hunkpapa (End of Circle)
Reyata Otonwa		Otehi Otonwe (Village on the Thicket)	Itokah Tina (Dwellers at the South)	Ihaisdaye	Hahatonwanna	Mnikowoju (Planters beside the Stream)
Titonwan		Wita Otina (Dwellers in the Island)	Okahmi Otonwe (Village at the Bend)	Wacheunpa	Honetaparteen waz	Sihasapa (Blackfoot)
Ohanhanska		Wakpa Otonwe (Village on the River)	Manin Tina Those who pitched their tents away from the main camp	Ikmun	Zaartar	Oohenunpa (Two Kettle)
Tacanhpisapa		Can Kaga Otina (Dwellers in Log)	Keze (Barbed)	Oyateshicha	Pabaksa	Itazipco (without bows)
Anoginajin			Caknute (Shooters at trees)	Washichunchincha	Takini	
Oyateshicha					Shikshichena	
Khemnichan					Bakihon	

of corn left." If one can surmise something from the name, it also indicates another plains tribe who depended at least in part on agriculture for food. Elsewhere, however, the name is translated as "two boilings," which contradicts a horticultural connection. This particular division of the plains Lakota continue to exist as a separate entity and now reside on the Cheyenne River reservation.

The Hunkpapas, who often allied themselves with the Yankton, remained unnoticed by Europeans and later by the Americans, with no mention of them in the records until 1825, when the name appeared in a treaty which the Hunkpapa refused to sign. Hunkpapa means "end of the horn" and described their position in the camp structure, at the end of the circle near the entrance. The placement indicates they were one of the last bands formed. The Hunkpapas consisted of eight to ten bands, such as Chankaokhan ("Sore backs"), Cheokhba ("Sleepy kettle"), Tinazipeshicha ("Bad bows"), Talonapin ("Fresh meat necklace people"), Kiglashka, Chegnakeokisela ("Half breechclout people"), Shikshichela, Wakan ("Medicine-man band") and Hunskachantozhuha. Culbertson, writing to the Smithsonian in 1850, omitted the Shikshichela and the Hunskachantozhuha, but added "Those that carry Fire-Hearts," or Chantaapeta, as part of the Hunkpapa.

It is the Lakota tribes with which history is most familiar, and when one talks about the Sioux, it is the image of the plains peoples that springs to mind. It is the Oglala chief and medicine man, Red Cloud and Crazy Horse, and the Hunkpapa Sitting Bull who are remembered. Yet in discussing the *Oceti Sawakin* before the arrival of the white man, the historian must reach back to their Dakota roots to view what life must have been like in the past.

5. Democracy in Motion

　　Many winters ago one of the great nations of the winged ones, the crows, declared war upon a village, or so it seemed, for they descended upon the people, eating everything in sight. Children strove valiantly to chase the birds away, throwing rocks at them until the rocks were gone, when the little boys would run at the crows, waving their arms and shouting. Still the crows came. The women tried hard to keep them from their tipis. Both women and children raced back and forth, back and forth, but it was impossible to drive the birds away from the lines where they hung the jerked meat.

　　The headmen met to discuss this plague upon their village. Women already had spoken their minds within their tipis and their voices were heard in the soldiers' lodge. The council members smoked many pipes over the issue and talked. When all agreed, they declared war upon the birds.

　　The chief told the camp crier to ride from tipi to tipi, giving his orders: The crows' nests were to be destroyed wherever they were found, their eggs broken. Grown birds would be shot on sight until not a one was left in the land. Everyone would participate. Men and boys would kill the adults with their deadly arrows while women and their daughters swept across the land, smashing eggs and nests alike.

　　The war lasted for seven days, and the surviving crows fled, flying away never to return, and the skies were empty of their raucous cries. Slowly, one by one, the other birds — the meadowlark and the hawk — made their way back to the village, and the women were happy again, for these birds hunted insects and vermin who often besieged their tipis.

　　The chief held a great feast to celebrate their victory over the crows. As they ate, one of the warriors approached the chief. In his hands he held a single bird, gawky and spindly, little more than a nestling, and he gave the last of the crow race to the chief so he could pass judgment. Wise, generous, and ever looking toward the future, the chief spared the bird. The crow lived in the chief's tipi, and the chief taught the bird to speak. When it finally mastered Dakota, the far-sighted chief taught the crow to speak other tongues, of both enemy and ally, and then he set it free.

　　The bird rejoiced in its newfound freedom. It flew and it flew, and when it spied an enemy camp, the bird alighted and listened to all that was said and done. Then it returned to the chief and reported all that it had seen and had heard, for the crow was grateful for the generosity of the chief. Thus, the chief knew the movements of the other tribes, friend and foe alike. When battle threatened, the wise chief sent men to intercept the enemy war party long before it arrived at the village. So it was said that the chief could predict the future, for it seemed he knew when the next raid would occur, and more importantly he knew where the attacking party could best be waylaid. Soon the other tribes learned not to make war upon this particular band. They feared this chief who could foresee their movements.

　　Under his guidance, the band prospered, for the bird brought back news of big herds, and their kettles and their bellies were always full. Then one day the bird returned to the

This picture shows Chief Little Wound in council. They sit in a semi-circle around the speaker. Council members would discuss all matters of import from camp moves to the hunt or war. The council nominated the men who policed the tribe in each one of these situations, the *akitcita*. Photo by Herman Heyn of Heyn & Matzen, possibly for the Trans-Mississippi and International Exposition in Omaha in 1898.

chief's tipi. The avian head hung low, and it refused to speak. The chief pressed it to tell him what ailed it, but the crow would not. Neither would it would eat.

The chief threatened to gather his warriors and search for the source of the bird's sorrow, and finally the crow spoke: "Don't go, for I overheard three medicine men talking as I flew in the mountains, and what I heard grieves me. They envy your power and they have cursed you and your brother who enforces your decisions. You are going to be struck by lightning in three days time. It does not matter where you go; this fate will find you."

The two men looked at each other, for they knew they had to leave the village so no others would suffer the same fate. The people were saddened over the loss of two great leaders, but they busied themselves building the men a fine tipi far from camp.

On the third day, the village held a feast, and after feasting, six maids brought the war ponies forward. The horses were painted for battle. One maiden walked ahead of the chiefs' horses, with two women on either side of them. In the hands of the first were the chief's bow and arrows. The last woman followed behind, bearing his brother's bow and arrows. Thus they were escorted to the lodge in honor and ceremony.

Then the sad cavalcade turned aside and rode away. As soon the brothers had entered the door, thunder boomed just on the other side of the horizon. They lifted the flap to watch as dark clouds of storm streaked across a once-clear sky. Further away the procession halted and turned to stare as lightning danced around the tipi.

The next day the people dressed in their finest regalia and gathered in the center of the village. The warriors rode out to see what had become of their chiefs. When the escort arrived they found the two brothers lying cold as stone in death, their weapons still in their hands, warriors to the end. Their brave ponies lay beside them. The men left everything as they found it as a token of respect. Here the lodge would remain, a reminder to the people of the sacrifice they had made, and they were remembered long in story and song.

When the warriors started back to the village they heard a forlorn caw. They swung around to see the crow perched upon a tent. It rose on the winds and flew away — its debt paid — and to this day, no crows will go near this particular tribe.[1]

The myth contains many of the elements of government among the Dakota. For example: Two chiefs who were brothers, reflecting the structure of the village with more than one leader and the emphasis on clan. It shows the decision-making process through council and near-universal suffrage. It reveals the primary attributes required of a leader: generosity, wisdom and a willingness to sacrifice himself for his people. It also illustrates the system of dissemination of information through town criers (*akitcita*) who announce the decisions of the council.

Another of Herman Heyn's photographs from the same period. This shows Red Cloud, along with other unnamed chiefs. The chief's council, or **Wakiconza,** consisted of the most prestigious men of the tribe. Each man was a member of the Chiefs' Society, and among the most experienced and accomplished warriors. The first man (left) in bottom row is wearing the scalp shirt which reveals he was leading member, able to bear the regalia of the Chiefs' Society.

Early settlers were impressed by the democracy of Indian government. Our constitution owes much to the Native American, borrowing heavily from the Iroquois League.[2] Benjamin Franklin was the first to recognize the Indian system as a potential model for the fledgling colony. In 1754, Franklin advocated incorporating its elements into colonial government structure, in which each tribe (town) had its council house where local issues were discussed and decisions made, with elected delegates to attend the national assemblies and represent the community views.[3] Thomas Jefferson, creator of the Declaration of Independence, also wrote extensively about Iroquois political traditions. In the end, not only Benjamin Franklin and Thomas Jefferson, but Thomas Paine, George Washington and Thomas Charles adapted elements of the Iroquois form of government to fit American needs.[4]

The members of the Six Nations of the Iroquois were not the only "democrats." One warrior explained the Huron philosophy. "We are born free and united brothers, each as much a great lord as the other, while you are all slaves of one sole man. I am the master of my body, I dispose of myself, I do what I wish, I am the first and last of my nation ... subject only to the Great Spirit."[5] The Algonquin also prided themselves on individual freedom and looked down on the European class system.

Elsewhere, the Siouan Waxshaw of Carolina used open council for its most important decisions. One such public discussion was witnessed by John Lawson and his impressions recorded. "These meet in all general Councils and Debates, concerning War, Peace, Trade, Hunting and the Adventures and Accidents of Human Affairs.... Affairs are discoursed of and argued *pro* and *con*, very deliberately (without making any manner of Parties or Divisions) for the Good of the Publick; for as they meet there to treat, they discharge their Duty with all Integrity imaginable, never looking toward their Own Interest, before the Publick Good. After every Man has given his Opinion, that which has the most voices, or in the Summing up is found the most reasonable, that they make use of without any Jars and Wrangling, and put into Execution, the first Opportunity that offers."[6]

The Dakota shared this form of government by general council as Samuel Pond learned after observing the Minnesota Santee. "The government of the Dakotas was purely democratic, the people holding all the powers of government in their hands.... They claimed and exercised the right of deciding all questions which concerned the public interest."[7]

Comparing Pond's reports to Lawson's, there were other similarities between the eastern Siouan tribes and the Dakota of the west. Each maintained a council house in the center of the village where all negotiations and business were transacted. Pond's description of tribal organization reflects that of their eastern cousins. It included a chief, which Lawson called "King," a war-captain or war chief, and councilors "who are picked from among the ancientest of Men"[8] and who determined "their Business of Moment, with a great deal of Deliberation and wariness."[9]

Like the Iroquois, the Dakota elected men who would then represent them in intertribal councils. Unlike the Iroquois, Dakota women did not have a "vote." However, they had ways of making their opinions known and their voices given due consideration in a council.[10] For instance, moves would be delayed to let the women finish drying meat. Women elders could speak in council, and some even held office within the village structure.

The Lakota system described by Walker incorporated a series of checks and balances. For example: each band had several leaders, or chiefs. The chief was known as *itancan*. Historically chiefs numbered two, four or six, although some had more. The practice of a single chief seems to be a modern manifestation, a concept thrust upon them by white men who expected each tribe to have a single man, like a European king, to rule them and, therefore, represent them.

The chiefs each had at least two assistants (war-chief/chief soldiers); and a separate council of advisors, or headmen; along with the enforcers of local custom, the *akitcita*, often referred to by white writers as police or marshals. The chiefs or headmen either directly or indirectly selected the *akitcita* to police the tribe, but once the *akitcita* were elected, the same men who appointed them had to submit to the *akitcita*'s authority, subject to the same laws and suffered the same reprisals for breaking them as any other tribal member.

                    Wakiconza   ⇔   *Naca Ominicia*
    ⇗   Tribal Council   who elected   Chief(s)
selected   selected
Naca Ominicia   *Akitcita*
Chiefs' Society   ⇔   to police the tribe

Within these basics, there were any number of variations. For example, the different ways that a man may be named as chief. The simplest was by common consent of the general populace. In the forming of the new band, the first man to separate from the parent band usually became chief among those who followed him. In already established tribes the chiefs were nominated by the Chiefs' Society (also known as the *Naca Ominicia*) from one of their number. In some bands, the chief/chiefs were elected by the headmen (council) from among themselves, who were also members of the Chiefs' Society. Once named, he would be given a place of honor with his lodge adjoining the council tent.

According to the Oglala Red Feather, the post of chief was a limited one, lasting about a

The tribes relied on hunting for their livelihood. Camps had to be mobile to ensure no region was overhunted. The sketch shows a camp move, with women and horses dragging lodge poles and many of the travelers on foot. With as many as four hundred people in a band — hence, living in a village — moves required a great deal of organization with specific people called *akitcita* nominated to oversee them. The wood engraving, from a picture drawn by Theo. R. Davis, was published in ***Harper's Weekly***, May 21, 1870, p. 324.

year.[11] Those who remained in the office for a longer period of time did so because they were reelected. If that happened, then the wife of the sitting chief would be notified when the *akitcita* placed a counting stick inside her tipi. She would prepare a banquet, and then take stick and food so the newly reinstated chief, the headmen and the *akitcita* would feast together. If a new chief was chosen to replace the incumbent, he would carry his tobacco pouch and pipe and take his place inside the *iyokihe* (the tipi adjacent to the council house).

Another mistaken belief was that the office of chief was hereditary, although it often passed to a son. While clans and family ties were important, the son had to prove himself as a warrior-hunter and become a member of the Chiefs' Society to qualify, and the heir could easily be passed over if others felt he was unequal to the task.

If the people lost confidence in their leaders, they could replace them, and if they did not agree with their decisions they could simply refuse to comply. Likewise an acting chief could be ousted from the office if he regularly broke the rules of the tribe. Neither was the tribe subject to any of the chief's decrees if they proved unpopular. Hence, tribal members felt no great compunction to acknowledge the articles of any treaty their chief had signed with the U.S. when he acted without their consent.

There were limitations to the post beyond that of time. The chief could direct the men to war, but he did not participate. He was forsworn to protect the women and children; thus he stayed behind to defend them.[12] Much of his authority was delegated. This had practical applications, ensuring the best warriors, the members of the Chiefs' Society, guarded the camp. As a Silent Eater and Shirt Wearer, Sitting Bull was obliged to sit out the battle of Greasy Grass (Little Bighorn). The Chief was also sworn to ensure no one went hungry. So he was honor bound to give away both his food and his possessions. Often the chief was the poorest member of the band, a fact reflected by the fact that Sitting Bull's tent was the shabbiest in the camp.[13]

Even in the time of a single chief, he did not operate alone, but in concert with the council, or headmen. These head chiefs were called *wakiconza*. The number of the latter varied from tribe to tribe. The Oglala had seven and the Sicangu ten.[14] The headmen constituted the ultimate authority within the tribe.

The *wakiconza,* or headmen, counseled the chief in all matters. The council consisted of the older, more experienced members of the tribe. Also included among their numbers were shamans, braves, hunters, and medicine men/women. Councils, though, were not limited to the these advisors. Often others would be asked into the council lodge to consult with the headmen or chiefs if they had a particular area of expertise. The invitation took the form of a beaded wand or one that was decorated with porcupine quills which was then sent to the individual's tipi to request the person's presence in council. If the matter was important enough, a general council was called where all men, and some women, had a voice.

Women often found a whole new world open up for them when they left childbearing years. Old women spoke at councils, and some became elders, particularly those who were members of the Chiefs' Society from which leaders were selected. According to legend, one woman ruled as chief or headman within her tribe for as long as she lived,[15] and 18th century census rolls indicate a woman could head a family,[16] and this gave her a say and a vote in the general council, like her male counterparts.

In the Siouan east, Lawson was amazed by the courtesy found in these meetings. "Whenever an aged man is speaking, no one ever interrupts.... Indeed, the Indians are a people who never interrupt one another during Discourse; no man so much as offering to open his Mouth, till the speaker has uttered his Intent."[17] Like the Waxshaw, the Dakota treated their elders with respect, and no one dared to interrupt them. Dakota elders taught the children and kept their history. Their wisdom and their counsel were often sought.

The *wakiconza* (council of headmen) was the arbiter when the ruling of the *akitcita* was disputed. *Itancan* (chiefs) may change, but the council stayed the same, so they provided continuity within a camp. Once accepted, the man or woman remained a member of the council until he died or was deposed. The council maintained peace within the community through conciliation and compromise. They sat in judgment in difficult cases where laws were violated. They set policy in trade and war and decided whether it was time to move camp or time to hunt.

The next category, the *akitcita*, was the most difficult for the outside observer to understand since they fulfilled many functions, such as town crier. According to Thomas Tryon, writing in 1897, once selected the *akitcita* was one the highest officers in the camp. His word superseded even that of chief, in that if a chief disobeyed the rules, then he must submit to the *akitcita*'s punishment. The term *akitcita* meant "to find the right way to do a thing,"[18] and this was the function the *akitcita* performed by enforcing the rules of the tribe.

The way and means of their selection also varied between the major tribes and bands. In some, the headmen as a group chose the individual *akitcita* while in others it was the chief who did so. Elsewhere the Chiefs' Society appointed the *akitcita*. Or, according to Iron Tail, the *akitcita* society itself was nominated, with the selection of the candidates taking place among society members.[19]

The candidates had to belong to certain societies in order to be eligible, just as the chief belonged to the Chiefs' Society. *Akitcita* societies could also be warrior societies; some were not. *Cante Tinza* ("Braves hearts"), the *Tokala* ("Fox"), *Wikin ska* ("White marked"), *Sotka yaha* ("Wand carriers"), *Kangi yuha* ("Crow owners"), *Ihoka* ("Badgers").

Once chosen by the chief, the *wakiconza* or their respective societies, the original four became *akitcita itancan*, who in turn picked four assistants.[20] Women could also be also called upon to act as *akitcita,* although it was rare.[21] Like the chief, the *akitcita* normally served a term of one year. If the situation warranted it, they could serve longer until the chief or headmen called upon another society to replace the first or until the task was complete.[22] However, Thomas Tyon and John Blunt Horn claimed that they stayed in their office as long as they were physically capable.

All the *akitcita* together were the *tiyotipi* or "soldiers' lodge." Once installed in their office, the *akitcita* painted a black stripe from eye to the lower jaw as a badge of office. The chief *akitcita* acted as town crier or herald *(Yamaha)*. He wore three stripes to distinguish himself from the rest of the *akitcita*. In other bands, the black stripe was drawn from the forehead near outer ridge of the eyebrow down to the chin. Red Feather described two black stripes worn by all *akitcita* rather than one.[23]

Just as the *akitcita* were selected from specific groups, their authority was often restricted to specific situations. There were *akitcita* for the hunt, *akitcita* for the camp, *akitcita* for a move and *akitcita* for war.[24] The rules enforced by the *akitcita* varied according to the situation as did the people who enforced them.

The *akitcita* of the hunt directed the hunt as if it were a war. All men were required to stay together. No one could preempt the hunt, taking advantage of game before the other members of the band. Silence was mandatory to prevent stampeding the herd. If anyone in the hunting party or in the camp broke this rule, he was punished. This included dogs. Those that barked could be killed. Once the hunt was completed the meat was distributed fairly among all members of the tribe so that no one went hungry.

Once they were installed in their office, the power of the *akitcita* was absolute. They had control over band members and visitors alike, as trader Henry Hasting Sibley discovered in 1847 when he broke camp rules and was subjected to chastisement as if he were a member of the tribe. While the chiefs could give orders to the *akitcita* and, in delicate situations, they were consulted to pass judgment on the lawbreaker, still the chiefs were subject to the ruling of the *akitcita*.

Edward S. Curtis (1868–1952) photographed the Lakota tribes extensively. Here he shows a village herald going about on horseback. The herald was the chief *akitcita,* or *yamaha.* It was his job to announce major events, such as dances, celebrations and feasts, along with any council decisions, such as major moves and hunting or war parties. In some bands, he would nominate further assistants while in others, the council named the *akitcita* society, who would then select the four *akitcita* and elect their leader.

Penalties for wrongdoers included, but were not limited to beating the offender, confiscation or destruction of property, banishment, and in extreme cases, such as murder or resisting the *akitcita*, execution. During the 1870s, the *akitcita* placed a death sentence on any Lakota who defected to an agency.[25] While in Canada, Sitting Bull sentenced three young men who had stolen horses, thereby breaking an oath Sitting Bull had made to the "Redcoats." The perpetrators were stripped and staked to the ground for a week, exposed to sun and elements, insects and wildlife, not to mention the ridicule of the tribe.[26]

In a large camp situations, several of these groups could be functioning simultaneously as new bands joined the encampment and hunting parties left to feed the expanding population. In such a situation where two or more bands formed a single camp then the rules and governing body of the parent band took precedence, and the other bands obeyed the chief, the headmen, the *akitcita,* and the customs of the first. If unrelated tribes joined then the older governed the camp. Thus, the Mdewakanton would take precedence over the Hunkpapa.

The concept of *Cangleska Oyate*, the Sacred Hoop, found its reflection in the structure of their camps. The *tiyopa*, door or accepted entrance, always faced east and any who came in peace entered the village this way. At best, entrance by any other direction indicated ignorance of custom, if not downright enmity or insult, and, therefore, the individual would immediately be considered suspect.[27]

The position of honor in camp or lodge was opposite the entrance, or in the west. In early times when the bands met, this place was reserved for the Mdwakanton, the parent tribe of the Dakota people. The second oldest tribe, the Wahpekute, took their position to the left (southwest) of the Mdwakanton. The third, the Wahpeton, were stationed to their right in the northwest. The fourth band to evolve, the Sisseton, set up to the left of the Wahpekute, and the Yankton camped at the northeast side of the circle. The Yanktonai were positioned south of the entrance, and the Titowan, as the youngest, maintained their place in the east, north of the entrance. The Hunkpapa, as the last Titowan tribe formed, camped closest to the entrance in the east. This structure carried in all formal camps, and one could determine the esteem with which a tribe or band was held, or its age, by its position within the circle.[28] The politics of the period also found its reflection in the camp circle, so that in later years, the Titowan Oglala replaced the Mdewakanton after the 1862 uprising as the tribe in the position of honor opposite the "door" or in the west.

Societies were an integral part of the running of the camp. Chief Society members were among the most powerful and most skilled men in the tribe. Each man invited to join the Chiefs' Society was asked if he was ready to give up the warpath and become a gentleman. The duties

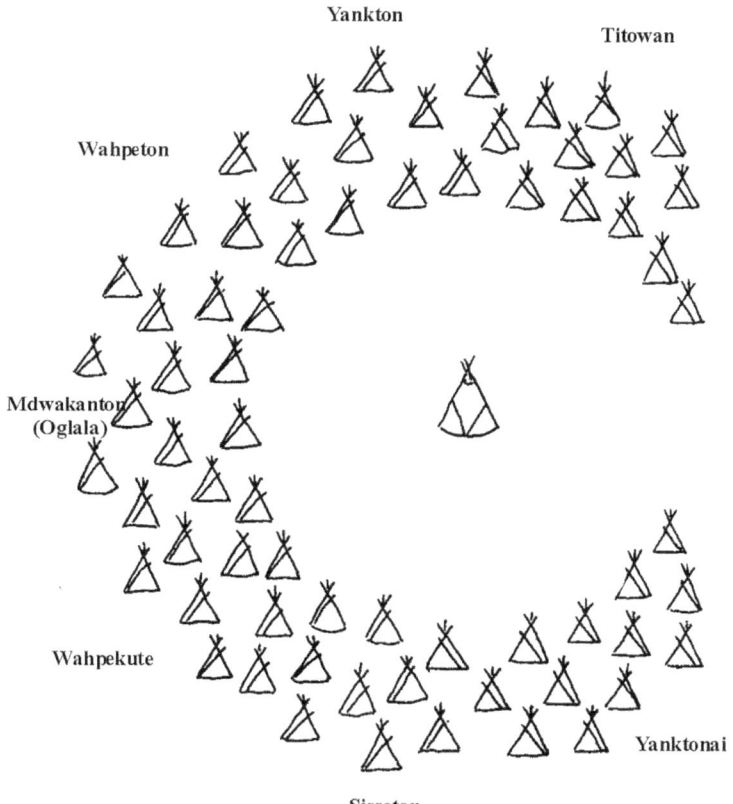

During an intertribal council, a band's position within the camp circle was established according to the age and status of the tribe. It also found its reflection in the positions normally assigned within the home setting, with the man given the honored place opposite the door, which always faced east. The tipi in the center of the circle was the council chamber. The chief of the chosen or dominant tribe put up his tipi next to this lodge. Interestingly enough, inside the home, the woman's place was at the center next to the fire, indicating her preeminence within the family. The positions shown here were subject to change, depending on the number of tribes in the camp and the status they held at the time. Before the 1862 conflict, the Mdewakanton were located in the position of honor, opposite the entrance. Later, the Mdewakanton were replaced by the Oglala, who took this place of distinction as progenitors of all the Lakota tribes.

of its members included protecting the camp in time of war. They swore to provide a horse to any old woman who fell behind when they moved camp and ensure that no orphan went unnoticed.

Members also became known as the Big Bellies or Silent Eaters, since they had given up the active life as a warrior to become an advisor. Later the society was given the additional name *Pahin ptechala*, or short hair, referring to the short hair of the buffalo headdress.[29] The Silent Eaters (*Naca Ominicia/Takanka Waipahu*) had four pipe bearers and four shirt wearers. The former carried the sacred pipe upon which all oaths, negotiations or truces were based. As a result, they carried the more authority not only within the society, but also within their tribe. The shirt wearers were a later manifestation. The office originated in 1851. The shirt wearers acted as intermediaries between headmen, council and *akitcita*.[30]

Akitcita societies provided the men who enforced the laws. Some societies were testing grounds for the later investiture in the major governing bodies. For instance, members of the *Ska yula* (white horse owners, created by Sitting Bull) became the candidates for election to the Chiefs' Society. The *Ska yula* were warriors, and if, through his service to this society, a man was found worthy, then he would be invited to put his weapons aside and join the Chiefs' Society. At a time when war was constant, defense of the community was paramount; therefore, one-time members of warrior societies would be a logical choice of candidates to be left behind to defend the women and the children..

Likewise societies acted as a filter. Men of ill repute or bad character would not be accepted as members, and those members who had not proven their prowess would not be promoted to a ruling body, thereby eliminating the unworthy from positions of responsibilities.

Societies could be complex with a number of "societies" within societies. The *Miwatani* (Mandan or no-flight society) consisted of members of the Braves' Society who vowed to hold their position in battle.

The Chiefs' Society had their Shirt Wearers (*Onglage Un*), and at least one source stated that it was the shirt wearers, and not the pipe bearers, who became headmen of a camp.[31] The scalp shirt, which was the badge of office, was worn only at important functions, such as the sun dance, when all the tribe had gathered. The shirt wearers often would join the *akitcita* in patrolling the camp.

Of course, nothing said that an individual could not be invested with more than one office or belong to more than one society. Sitting Bull belonged to the *akitcita* societies, the Kit Fox[32] and the Strong Hearts, and to the dream societies of buffalo and *heyoka*. Later he joined the Silent Eaters (Chiefs' Society) and in that context, he became both a pipe bearer and a shirt wearer, and *Wicasa Itancan*. He founded of the White Horse Society in 1875 or 1876.[33] So societies allowed a man to prove his worth, and he who had earned more than one honor would become a leader among his people.

The government of the *Titowan* was well documented by Walker. Meanwhile, information available about the organization of the woodland Dakota is sparse. The best description comes from Samuel Ponds, who wrote about the Dakota before 1834.[34] According to Pond, the Dakota maintained only two "permanent" officials—one chief and one chief warrior. The chief did not interfere much with the life of the tribe. Neither was he consulted often.

The structure he describes appears less stratified, with most of the work done by general council where the majority of the tribe members would have to agree on important matters such as moving camp or initiating a hunt. The decision was reached by majority will. Voting was an informal affair. Once discussed, the measure would be proposed at which time the people could give their assent. If the response of "yes" was loud, then the measure would be enacted. If, however, the response was weak or the people remained silent then the matter would be dropped.

Pond believed that disputes within the tribe were settled by retaliation, with the wrongdoer punished by the wronged, or chastised by public opinion with the community acting against the rule breaker in a form of shunning. Meanwhile the people to enforce the laws did not appear to have permanent posts, but would be nominated on an as-needed basis, which suggests *akitcita*.

Whether these apparent differences between Lakota and Dakota government occurred because the system had already been irrevocably altered by their interaction with white men, or because Pond was not aware of the nuances within the tribal environment, is unclear. It is unlikely he would have been privy to closed council, and by this time, the idea of one ruler — thrust upon them by the U.S. government that would only treat with one chief whom, they presumed, could act as spokesman for and representative of his people — had become ingrained.

In a history commission by the Sisseton-Wahpeton Tribe, Ehanna Woyakapi said the way a chief was chosen changed around the late 1700s. Individual wisdom and powers were replaced by a hereditary system of chieftainship. These chiefs had limited powers except in council where they reigned supreme. They had a choice of picking the headman, who stayed in the office for life. Much relied on kinship. Relationship by clans held great weight. The band council, headed by the chief, was the main governmental body. Each clan had a *wakincun* or counselor representing them and no councilman had more power than another. Each camp had a messenger to announce decisions after the vote.[35] Charles Eastman (Ohiyesa), who grew up among the Wahpeton, describes a more formal camp structure than that portrayed by Pond. Young braves had to consult with and obtain permission from the medicine men before they formed a war party,[36] and medicine men were by default members of the governing council. Likewise, he made reference to "police" who enforced camp rules during the hunt.[37] In other words, *akitcita*. The *akitcita* would assign a territory to be hunted by a specific group of men, thereby ensuring the areas did not overlap or become overhunted, and disputes were avoided.

Also note that having a chief and a warrior chief means the Dakota had two chiefs like the Lakota. For both the woodland and plains tribes, important decisions required a general council where all men/clans were consulted, and neither Lakota nor Dakota could claim personal vendetta against a wrongdoer as their exclusive domain. However, if an act of revenge threatened to disrupt the peace of the tribe, the *akitcita* would intervene and the perpetrator punished. Thus, what appear at first glance to be differences between the woodland Dakota and the plains Lakota dissolve under closer examination. The Dakota maintained all the same elements: two chiefs, a council of elders, and people to police the tribe.

To review, the organization was efficient in its simplicity. A body of elders, men who have proven their ability and their worth, would choose leaders from among their numbers. This ruling body would make decisions which were then implemented by the *akitcita*. If the decision was to move, special *akitcita* would be selected for their knowledge of the terrain. They would scout ahead, pick the next site and make sure that the main body stayed together, that no one straggled and no one was left behind. At night when they formed the camp, the camp *akitcita* would take their place, although the other group would not relinquish their offices until the camp had reached its final destination. If disputes occurred which the camp *akitcita* could not resolve, the problem would be taken to the chief counselors, who then acted as a judiciary body.

If the camp came upon a herd during a move and a hunt was called, then further hunt *akitcita* would be appointed for the task. They would lead the hunt while camp *akitcita* would stay behind with the women and children to defend them and enforce the hunt laws, such as the rules of silence. Once the hunt was completed, the camp would then continue its migration and the *akitcita* specifically nominated for that task would take over again. It was an ingenious organization that by separating responsibilities ensured no one society or group would gain too much power.

At certain times of year, the many bands would meet, at which time the headmen would discuss national issues, matters of mutual importance. The structure remained the same with the chief and headmen of each band representing his people. The council would set national policy as happened before the Battle of Greasy Grass, when Oglala Crazy Horse and Hunkpapa agreed to maintain a defensive posture against the whites,[38] a policy they would later be forced to abandon.

Many deny the Dakota the status of a nation, saying they lacked a central government. Yet they did have national councils. Some prefer the term confederacy, but a confederacy consists of linked groups which were culturally and linguistically different, which means the Dakota did not meet the criteria. However, it was as a nation-state that the Dakota were recognized in the Fort Laramie Treaty.

The Dakota government was fluid, as illustrated by the formation of new bands, or *tiospaye*. It can be viewed as a loose affiliation of tribes with each unit acting independently throughout much of the year, but coming together for shared events, such as religious festivals or the autumnal hunt, and working in unison with important matters, such as trade and national defense.

The Dakota tribes often worked as a whole, revealing a unified purpose and a single policy. National councils of elected representatives were held annually where the Dakotas would devise an integrated policy that governed trade and territory. If the results of the council led to a conflict with another tribe, the council selected an individual to lead in this effort. Thus in times of crisis, they had both representative and executive offices.

Each tribe remained autonomous outside this national network, similar to the divisions found in state and federal governments. Meanwhile the separate bands could be compared to the local county and town, and each town had the right to choose its own selection process for its officials.

The fact that the faces of the national council and its leaders changed as needs changed or as local selection replaced their representative in this office, picking the best man for the job, does not discount the idea of a centralized government; rather it reinforces it, just as the American electorate often replaces their elected officials.

The picture that emerges is sophisticated. These were not a primitive people governed by a hereditary chief (king) who led by arbitrary rules, such as those found in Europe at the time of contact. Rather the system is similar to that of Rome before the Caesars, where consuls would be elected from the numbers of the senate, the voting and advising body of the time, to serve for a period of twelve months, and if an issue were important enough it would be placed to a vote among all qualified individuals. The Dakota government was a democracy like that of Greece, where all free-born males had a voice in the affairs of the community, and Dakota freedom far outstripped that which was current in Europe when the first white settlers arrived on these shores.

6. Of Everyday Things: Robes and Moccasins, Home and Furnishings

The old woman bent over her work. The wind howled outside her door, and she lifted her head to listen. Her skin was dark and her face was seamed from years of exposure to the sun and wind. Her eyes were almost colorless, the irises bleached blue, and they had the blank, unblinking gaze of the blind.

Her foot rested against the warm back of her dog. The fire guttered, and she hissed at him. The dog blinked and yawned. His head dipped as if he acknowledged an unspoken command. Then he turned, grabbed a stick from the pile next to the door and put it on the fire.

"Good dog," she said; she patted his head. "I don't know what I'd do without you."

The woman spoke true, for the dog was her eyes and her ears, and often her hands. He was a comfort to her, and his broad back against her feet kept her warm at night. The old woman lived on the meat that he lay on her doorstep each morning; a rabbit or a squirrel, sometimes a raccoon. He was as old and scarred as she was, and she didn't care to think what was going to happen to her when he died.

But this wasn't just any dog; he had been sent to her by spirit. Wise beyond his years, wise even beyond her years, he knew the secrets of the universe. You could see it in his eyes, and he had been sent to guard the woman as she labored, here at the edge of the universe.

She sighed, turned back to her work and squinted, trying to focus on the pattern. All she could see were colors — light, dark and shadow — the vaguest sense of shape. The figures formed by the beads were blurred, but she could remember what they were supposed to look like: The sharp peak of mountaintop, triangles, which were then inverted below to create a diamond design, followed by the winged shape of moth for protection. By her side stood a row of clay pots, each containing brightly colored beads. Her hand brushed a bowl, nearly knocking it over onto its side. Even the colors were starting to get dim.

The old woman stood, fragile old bones crackling with the effort. Her faithful hound raised his head. His eyes followed each movement as the old woman hobbled toward the kettle, led to it by the flickering light of the fire. Her back was curved under the weight of years. The dog stood and moved silently over to her seat.

The old woman gave the contents of the kettle a quick stir and stepped outside the door, for blind as she was she could still feel the sun upon her face and the wind in her hair, and she could still remember a time when she had had a family, with many fine children and many fat grandchildren playing around the fire. A time when she was not alone here where the earth ended. A time when her son returned from the hunt every day, a huge buck slung over his back.

Inside, the dog tore into the design she had been weaving. He plucked a single thread in his teeth and gave it a gentle tug. The strand broke and the beads scattered on the floor of the tipi. Patiently, working one by one, the dog started to unravel everything that she had done.

Blessedly the old woman could no longer recall how much time had passed since she had seen her son. The tribe had waited many moons for his return. Eventually, they had to move on to follow the herds. But the old woman was stubborn and she had stayed behind, and she waited still. She no longer counted the days, the moons or even the seasons. She had long since abandoned any effort at keeping track of time. Her counting sticks lay forgotten in some perfleche somewhere.

With the delicacy born of practice, the dog pulled another thread from the hide. The beads tumbled onto the floor, mixing with the colors that had gone before, and if you looked close by you could see the ground was covered with a brightly colored mosaic of beads packed in the dirt.

Outside, the woman glowered at the horizon that she sensed rather than saw, as if she could make his figure suddenly appear. Nothing moved. The wind picked a up steel-gray braid and slapped her in the face. She shivered and she swung back to the tipi. Time was wasting, and she had much to do. She must finish the robe before he returned.

The dog sat as the woman ducked inside the door. His wagging tail sent loose beads skittering across the floor, clearing a path for her. To the hound Wakan Tanka had given a sacred trust, to prevent the coming of the blue and red days that heralded the end of time, and to do that, the old woman's work must never be completed, for should women's hands ever grow idle, the world would end.

Still, the dog loved the old woman and would not have her fall.

The grandmother tottered back to her seat and lowered herself in a cacophony of ancient bones. Her fingers felt for the design, and there was none. She frowned. She would've sworn that she had gotten farther than that.

"Oh well," she said to no one in particular and began counting the beads again.

Dress among the Native American tribes showed an evolution throughout the centuries, never more so than with the Dakota woodland Santee. Before their contact with white men, their clothes were made of soft and pliable deerskin. Later after prolonged interaction, they switched to broadcloth. Before the Lakotas' immigration west, dress between the two branches of the tribe would have been similar if not the same. However, even before the move differences started to appear.

The basics of men's dress included a breechclout of hide brought through a belt from front to back, with the ends hanging down to mid-thigh. Thigh-length leggings were tied in place by thongs to this same belt or girdle. A poncho, a deerskin with a hole cut in the center, was added during inclement weather. In winter, sleeves were provided by tying or sewing the slit shut under the arms.

In 1700, Lawson described virtually the same dress for the Santee of the eastern seaboard; however, by this time, the Carolina Santee had already begun the shift to cloth which would take place among the western Santee in the 1800s. "Betwixt their Legs comes a Piece of Cloth, that is tucked in by a Belt before and behind.... They wear Shooes, of Bucks and sometimes Bears Skin, which they tan.... These have no Heels and are made as fit for the Feet, as the Glove is for the Hand.... Their Thread being the Sinews of a Deer divided vary small."[1]

Women, like men, wore a form of breechcloth, or modesty panel, and leggings from ankle to knee. Throughout their history, though, women's dress style changed more than men's. According to Josephine Paterek in *Encyclopedia of American Indian Costume*, originally Dakota women wore a wraparound skirt with a poncho added for inclement weather.[2] If true, this sug-

Early Eastern tribes' dress A native woman of Pomeick (an Algonquin tribe) carrying a clay vessel, and her daughter holding a doll and a rattle. The watercolor by John White was first published in 1590. The fact that it was later used to illustrate John Lawson's *Voyages*, where he describes the Siouan tribes of Carolina, suggests that the pictures reflected the mode of dress of such tribes as the Santee. Library of Congress Rare Book Collection: from an engraving by Theodor de Bry after a watercolor by John White in *Admiranda narratio, fida tamen, de commodis et incolarvm ritibvs Virginiæ [...]*. Wecheli : svmtibvs T. de Bry, 1590, plate 8.

gests they wore a waist-high skirt, rather than a dress, with a poncho that could be shed, and indicates less emphasis on modesty. This mode of dress would have been identical to that worn by the women of the Siouan tribes of the Carolinas during the time of Lawson.

As a style, it was practical, for it also would be suitable to a warmer climate, provided the poncho could be shed. Therefore, it might date back to the last Halocene period. Certainly it

This John White illustration reveals the similarities in dress between the tribes, and is titled "How the chief ladies of the town of Dasamonquepeio dress and carry their children." The skirt is similar to that in use by the Dakota in the early period. Due to Dakota modesty laws, it is likely that Dakota women wore the poncho full time. From the Library of Congress Rare Book Collection: Engraving by Theodor de Bry after a watercolor by John White in *Admiranda narratio, fida tamen, de commodis et incolarvm ritibvs Virginiæ [...]*. Wecheli : svmtibvs T. de Bry, 1590, plate 10.

confirms a common heritage for the Siouan tribes of east and west. Later though, the skirt-poncho of the north was most likely worn, with the poncho a permanent part of the attire.

The skirt and poncho later developed into a strap-and-sleeve type dress. Made from a single skin sewn at the side, it was suspended from the shoulders by thongs or straps of hide where the sleeves could be tied for additional warmth in cold weather. The style originated further east,[3] and was worn by women of the Algonquin tribes, indicating commerce and long interaction between the two groups.

While women's fashions went through more shifts than men's, styles were not then as they are now, with one becoming passé and being summarily dropped within a season. Style and design were dictated more by the quantity and kind of available material and by the garment's adaptability. A perfectly serviceable design was often in use for centuries. Thus, the strap-and-sleeve dress developed in the 1600s was still worn by Lakota women of the plains as late as 1833[4] and by the Yankton in 1834. The style was still in use by other tribes in 1851, as illustrated in a sketch of a Cree woman drawn by Rudolph Kurz in that same year.[5]

However, women's clothes continued to evolve from the simple wraparound dress to the more elaborate two-skin, side-fold dresses. Great care was taken to preserve the shape and features of the animal in the skin, which revealed the skill of the maker. To tan a hide and maintain the neck, tail, head and legs still attached was much more difficult than a simple straight cut would have been. Meanwhile the still-intact skin endowed the wearer with the animal's power and protection.

Once the hides were tanned, the two skins were sewn together horizontally. The top quarter of the dress, or a full half of one of the hides, was folded over, hiding the horizontal seam. Then it was laced or sewn up the side. The left side was longer and a strap went over the right shoulder. A beaded flounce was often stitched onto the bottom of the skirt for decoration.

The over-the-shoulder or single-skin deer dress was simple in design, with a fold at the top to create a yoke and a single seam. A strap or straps secured it. Sleeves could be added by lacing them onto the straps. A poncho or robe added further warmth. This design was as easy to make as it was utilitarian. Great care was taken to maintain the shape of the hide, which revealed the skill of the maker.

Moccasins for both men and women were one-piece and soft-soled with the seam along the outer edge and up the heel. A tongue could be attached. Another style used by the Dakota included a central seam sewn up the front. Cuffs could be added. In the winter, they would fill their moccasins with fur or dried grass to provide additional protection and warmth. Until replaced by the blanket, buffalo robes provided winter warmth for men. Deer or beaver skin were used for elders, women and children.

The Santee in full dress cut an impressive figure as indicated by French explorer Pierre Esprit Radisson, who described their arrival at the Feast of the Dead in 1660 as the most spectacular of all the eighteen nations represented. Young warriors wore feathers as prominent as royal jewels. Their faces were painted several colors; their hair burned off except for a tuft ornamented with pearls or "turkey" stones. The tuft was treated with bear grease mixed with red earth and made to stand upright. They dressed in deerskin robes, beaded and quill-worked leggings. Moccasins were adorned with buffalo hide which dragged more than a foot and a half behind them. Beaver-skin robes were painted white. They carried weapons and shields. The elders wore no paints; their hair was treated the same as that of the young men. The elders wore buffalo robes that swept along the ground.[6]

A decade later Father Louis Hennepin found styles little changed. "Some had their short hair full of bear grease and decorated with red and white feathers. Others sprinkled their heads with the down of birds which clung to the grease."[7] Two centuries later Mary Henderson-Eastman described many of the same styles and adornments, meaning they were still in use.

However, as time went on, the woodland Dakota adopted the long hair more familiar to us now. Ohiyesa described the warriors as they prepared for a lacrosse match. "Some banged and singed their hair; others did little more by adding powder. The Grecian knot was located on the wrong side of the head, being tied tightly over the forehead. A great many simply brushed back their long locks and tied them with a strip of otter skin."[8] He added, "It was an impressive spectacle — a fine collection of agile forms, almost stripped of garments and painted in wild imitation of the rainbow and sunset sky on a human canvas. Some had undertaken to depict the Milky Way across their tawny bodies, and one or two made bold attempts to reproduce lightning. Others contented themselves with painting the figure of a fleet animal or swift bird on their muscular chests...."[9]

Regional and tribal variations existed. As the Sisseton, one of the Dakota Santee, moved out onto the prairie, they adopted the plains style of dress. Men and women alike parted their hair in the center, and formed two braids or hair ties on each side. These were further wrapped with otter fur, a practical solution to the prairie winds. Meanwhile the Wahpeton, another Dakota Santee tribe, maintained the woodland style of dress longer and continued to keep their hair banged in front and back. They wore four braids, two braids in front and two in back.

Costume also differed between the two. The shirts of the Sisseton males were loose. They had long fringe and were trimmed with weasel or otter skin. The leggings were tight, also with long fringe and similarly trimmed with small animal skin and/or hair, while Wahpeton shirts were tight fitting with short fringe. Wahpeton leggings had large ankle flaps. Two pairs of strings fastened them onto the belt and beaded garters were worn below the knee. The Wahpeton also maintained the woodland tradition of wearing their triangular knife sheath on the chest. The Sisseton did not.

Quite often dress styles moved across tribal boundaries, coming with trade. For example, the Sisseton and Wahpeton women adopted the two-piece dress with cape, similar to the costume worn by the central Algonquin. This variation of the two-hide dress no longer maintained the shape of the animal. Instead two skins cut square were sewn together at the sides. The top was folded down and supported by two straps rather than a single strap. Additionally, it had a cape-like or turtle top. Sleeves were sewn from elbows to wrist, laced at the back and attached to the dress by thongs.

The next adaptation came from the west, originating with the tribes of the plateau. By this time the migration of the Titowan Lakota west would have been in full swing and was eventually picked up by the woodland Santee. The design placed two intact skins, back to back. In forming the upper dress, the tail part of the hide was folded over on the outside and sewn straight across. The folded skin was sewn down to give the appearance of a yoke. The triangular tail with its fur still on formed an ornament on the chest. The sides were then sewn or laced closed.

The three-skin dress was the last revision until the late 1800s. The third skin lengthened the yoke and stiffened it for more elaborate beadwork. A dip left in the center of the yoke indicated where the deer tail had once been. Both styles had fringe work attached under their arms and along the side seam.

6. Of Everyday Things 71

Eines alten Manns von Pomeiooc IX.
Winterkleydung.

Ie alten Männer zu Pomeiooc werden bedeckt mit einer grossen Haut/ so vber den Schultern zusammen gebunden / von der einen seiten her biß vnter die Knie hervnter hanget/ auff der andern seiten steckt herauß der ander Arm/daß der desto freyer sey. Es sind aber die Häute zugleich mit ihren Haaren zubereitet/ oder mit andern haarechten Häuten gefüttert. Die jungen Gesellen können nicht ein einigs Härlein vmb den Mund vnnd am Kien vertragen/ sondern so viel derselbigen sich herfür thun/die reissen sie alsbald herauß. Wann sie aber alt worden sind/ alsdann lassen sie die wachsen/ wi ewol sie deren gar wenig zu haben pflegen. Die Haar binden sie auch hindern Kopff zusammen/ vnd tragen auff dem Scheitel deß Haupts einen Kamm/ gleich wie auch die andern. Die beyliegende Landschafft ist also fruchtbar vnd bequeme/daß auch Engelland selbst mit ihr nicht möge verglichen werden.

John White also captured an old man in his winter clothes. The tunic is similar to the one-skin dress worn by Dakota women. As a mode of dress, it had staying power and was worn into the mid–1800s. Library of Congress Rare Book Collection: Engraving by Theodor de Bry after a watercolor by John White in *Wunderbarliche, doch warhafftige Erklärung, von der Gelegenheit vnd Sitten der Wilden in Virginia … / Erstlich in engelländischer Sprach beschrieben durch Thomam Hariot, vnd newlich durch Christ.* P. in Teutsch gebracht. Franckfort am Mayn: Gedruckt bey J. Wechel, in Verlegung D. Bry, 1590, plate 9.

By the 1700s, the Lakota had moved out onto the prairies, and differences in dress between the plains of the west and the woodlands of the east became more pronounced, although some basics remained the same, especially among the warriors. Men wore breechclouts of leather that covered from mid-thigh in the front and longer in the back. During the early period, they also had a kilt-type skirt. Thigh-length leggings had side seams and fringe. Large flaps often hung over the moccasins. The leggings could be painted with appropriate markings for counting coup, battle wounds or kills in battle.

Early shirts were made of a single hide tied or sewn under the arms to create loose sleeves. Fringe under the arms, thongs, horsetail or human hair were wrapped along the bottom. Quill and beadwork fringe were also added along the shoulders. Triangular patches at the neck, both front and back, were reminiscent of the sheaths once worn there. Painted shirts were worn by the medicine men and holy men during special occasions.

Early moccasins for the plains Lakota followed the one-piece soft-soled woodland type of their Dakota cousins. Then they adopted the hard-soled moccasin. During this transitional period, the soft-soled moccasins were beaded and hard-soled were not. Eventually, the Lakota adopted the hard-soled two-piece moccasins common on the prairie. Tongues and cuffs were added. Sometime the footwear was left plain; other times it was decorated with beadwork. Foxtails and sometimes the full pelt of a skunk were attached to the heels, endowing the wearer with the courage of the animals involved.

Winter wear included footwear made of dressed buffalo skin with the hair left on and turned inside out to provide insulation; the soles were made of stiff elk hide. Buffalo robes were prized possessions. It was only later in the 19th century that the blanket came into common use as part of the plains apparel. The Dakota of both woods and plains used snowshoes of wood or rawhide, frozen to make them more pliable, or of the bent-frame and cross-hatch thong variety.

The most common hairstyle among the western Lakota was the familiar two braids with a center part. Men added a third braid, or scalplock, that hung from the crown of the head. Braids

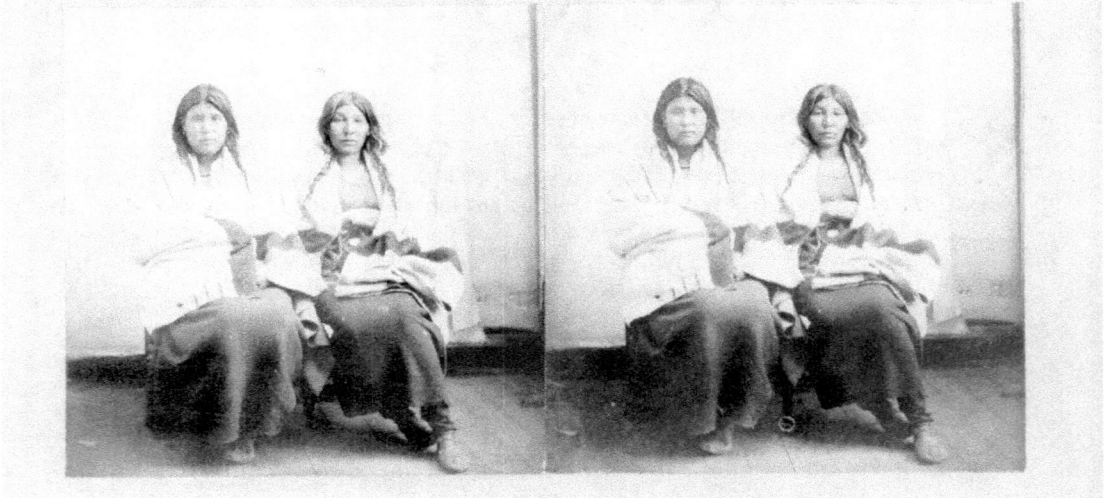

The Santee were the first to adapt cloth into their attire. By the reservation era when this picture was taken, cloth had completely replaced hides. However, certain elements of design remained with the skirt drawn through a belt which could be raised or lowered for ease of walking. Leggings are still present and the blanket remained a more effective means for warmth than the coat. Library of Congress: Entitled *Santee Women*, the print was reproduced on a stereo card, photographed by C.L. Hamilton, Sioux City, Iowa, between 1868 and 1880.

were wrapped in otter or trade cloth or quilled bands. During mourning, men would shave their heads, leaving only the scalplock. Some men gathered their hair into a club at the back. Others might leave a single forelock hanging over the nose. Besides the typical braids, Lakota women wore their hair free-flowing or gathered into bag at the back. Some women wore the hair clubbed into large locks and piled over the temples.

By 1834, in fact by as early as 1775,[10] the attire, dress and personal appearance of the woodland Santee had changed through prolonged exposure to the white trader. Pond, describing their dress, indicated that cloth had replaced most leather items, particularly in women's apparel. Skirts and leggings were made of broadcloth. Coats were made of blankets, even gloves were cotton. However, the Santee maintained certain basics. Skirts consisted of a single length of cloth that was wrapped around and brought up through a girdle. The exterior piece overlapped the interior, but did not entirely cover it. This allowed skirts to be lengthened and shortened as needed. When walking through long grasses or in snow, the women would pull the cloth up, for ease of movement or to keep it dry. The skirts were flat in front and gathered at the sides. Overcoats had tight sleeves and were sewn shut over the breast, but left open at top and bottom. Leggings stretched from the knee to the top of the moccasin.

Men wore blankets sewn to fit, of white, green, red or blue. In the summer months, men wore cotton shirts and the breechcloth was made of blue broadcloth. It was looped through a belt or a girdle, from the inside out. The men still wore leggings of leather or cloth, depending on the weather, the season or the availability of material.

Dress moccasins were beaded. Those used for everyday wear were unembellished. Socks were oblong strips of blankets wrapped around the feet and ankles. During the winter months or on long marches, dried grasses or the down from cattails were stuffed inside the moccasin for protection and insulation.

Ornaments included silver disks which were worn across the chest. Beads, embroidery and quillwork adorned skirts and overcoats on women, breechcloth and shirts on men. Men wore bear-claw necklaces. Some tribes had prohibitions against women handling a bear's remains. As jewelry, women favored pipe beads. Women often wore many strings of beads and several pairs of earrings, and it was estimated by Pond that one woman wore some seven pounds of jewelry.[11] Such finery was not used for everyday wear, but would be brought out for special occasions.

Women kept their hair smooth and braided, while Santee men continued to cut theirs in bangs and often had several small braids plaited around their face, along with the standard scalp lock. The braids were often beaded while the scalp lock was reserved for badges of office. Women rarely painted their faces, except for red on the parting of their hair and along their forehead to display their status as buffalo women. Young women might also place red dots on their cheeks.

Men, like women, wore paint appropriate to their memberships in certain societies, such as the *Hunka* society, or as required by the situation. The wearing of paint was generally reserved for war parties, festivals, dances or other ceremonial occasions. Young men often adorned themselves with the skins of skunks attached to their ankles as a symbol of bravery, for the skunk never ran from an enemy.

In the late period, winter coats of the Lakota consisted of a blanket wrapped around their waist and then bound in a girdle. The blanket was doubled across the front and reached down to the knees while the back portion could be brought up to cover shoulders and head. Buffalo robes were still used and worn in much the same fashion. Older men and women had robes made of deerskin, which was warmer than cloth but lighter than buffalo.

Tribes of east and west, both men and women, used pouches which they would hang from their belts to keep personal possessions. Pouches were made from the skin of a small animal, such as mink, weasel or skunk, that was removed whole, with the meat being drawn up through the throat. In these bags, pipes, smoke, flint and tinder, along with other tools, were kept. They were attached by drawing the head through the belt or girdle. Knives at one time were kept in a sheath that was hung by a thong around the neck. Later they were suspended from the belt. Pouches were also used to carry "medicine" or articles that were sacred to the bearer — such as navel amulets which were quilled or beaded in the turtle design and contained the umbilical cord of the wearer.

Trade cloth existed amongst the Lakota even before they met the white man, due to trade with the eastern Dakota. However, cloth was considered too valuable to use to make complete garments and was generally reserved for accent pieces attached to leggings, the yokes of dresses

Men's casual dress included breechcloth and moccasins, pictured here. It allowed freedom of movement and was used as everyday wear in the summer months. Leggings and shirt could be added for protection or warmth. The photograph, taken by Herman Heyn on June 20, 1900, pictures Mato Wammyomni holding a peace pipe in a full-length portrait.

or men's shirts. In the late 19th century, women's dress in the plains went through one final shift. The three-skin dresses had a yoke as a separate piece, which was further decorated. The dresses had notched sleeves and the hem was cut straight across the bottom.

Ornamentation, beadwork and the use of quills, jewelry and headgear, what we might call accessories, did not go through the same evolution that attire did, partly because it was such an individual thing, entirely dependent upon the tastes of the wearer. While tribes often acquired finely worked pieces through trade, more often than not beaded items were made by the women of the household, thus dependent upon the skill of the creator. Although there are tribal variations in design, because of trade the delineation is not as marked as one might think.

Likewise, ornament and design were often influenced, even dictated, by membership in specific societies, so certain styles might change with the group as a whole, but remain current for a select few within a chosen tradition. A *Sicangu* (Brule) buffalo robe, acquired in 1855, had been used in the initiation ceremony of a young buffalo woman. The design consisted of twenty-eight parallel lines, one for each day of the month or "moon," and twelve tufts of red wool across each line, possibly indicating the twelve months of the year. Lines, in particular, were highly symbolic and said to represent the trail on which women travel.[12]

Members of the Santee Badger Society wore war shirts with otter-skin collars. Buffalo Dancers wore buffalo headdresses with horns and carried shields with buffalo symbols. The Bear Medicine men wore the skins of the bear as hood and robe and painted their bodies red. Lakota warriors also carried shields, adorned with skins and feathers and painted with individual symbols. Members of the Tall Ones Society wore headdresses of owl feathers. Kit Fox members wore the headdress of a wolf, with a fox skin around the neck, head in front and tail in back, and a coyote jawbone. Crow Owners wore the stuffed skin of a crow around the neck. Omaha dance members wore an otter-skin collar, crow bustle and roach headdress.

The symbols used in design often served a dual purpose besides the purely aesthetic. It was believed that the spider web had magical properties, for it had been observed that arrows and even bullets passed through it, leaving it torn but relatively intact. As a result, the web design often appeared on children's robes as a form of protection. Lakota women used geometric patterns in their own robes while pictorial art appeared on men's robes depicting certain victories.

Changes were also be seen due to other environmental influences, for instance with beadwork. After the Lakota left for the plains, the Santee adopted the floral designs of the Algonquin while the Lakota adapted geometric patterns. Similarly it has been said that Santee women lost their skills at beadwork since they could obtain finely crafted items from their one-time enemies, the Ojibwa.[13] However, in 1834, Pond was still impressed with Dakota artistry.

The earliest examples of quillwork come from the woodlands of the east. Sophisticated techniques of application had already been developed by the sixteenth century. The plains people brought the skills of their forebears with them as they migrated west. However, archeological evidence from caves in Nevada and Utah indicates that quills were used as a bonding element as early as 530 BCE, and the use of quills in the decoration of moccasins dated back nearly fourteen centuries.[14]

Quills were used to decorate pipe bags and cradles. Wrapping techniques were used on pipe bags and in hair ornaments. Quills were worked into hides like embroidery and geometric patterns were often explained in mythological terms, as the spider web symbolism noted above.

The use of porcupine quills was limited by availability. Thus, the people of the southern plains used porcupine quills less than those of the north who had greater accessibility to the animal or to the product which could be obtained through trade. Santee were the main producers of bird-quillwork, although the Ojibwa, the Yankton and the sedentary tribes of the upper Missouri — the Mandan, Hidatsa and Arikara — also used bird quills in their decorations.

Trade also influenced the media used. Elk's teeth were found in Lakota women's dresses long before the tribe had migrated far enough west to be within the range of the elk herds. Dentalium and cowrie shells were also obtained through trade. Later, things like ribbons and metal were brought in by white traders, and eventually the use of beads had almost completely replaced quills.

Lakota women showed particular pride in their beadwork. They favored monochromatic backgrounds with right-angled and isosceles triangles alone or combined with diamonds or hourglass shapes and used the lazy stitch almost exclusively.[15] This consisted of several beads strung together before anchoring. Oglala warrior Thomas Tyon spoke of the particular skill of women who had dreamed of the double or two-faced woman, *Anog Ite*. They were believed to be the best artisans, inspired in their designs, although they were driven mad by their experience.[16]

Beads and quills adorned the shoulders and bands down the sleeves of ceremonial shirts. The number of bands and their width varied. In the northwest plateau region and the central plains these decorative bands were often large, but moving further east they dwindled in proportion until with the eastern Santee such beaded bands on shirts were small or nonexistent. Quilled or beaded disks were also found on ceremonial shirts. It is believed they originated in circular pieces of shell or metal disks of the early period in the woodland east. The iridescent disks were symbols of the sun for the tribes of the Great Lakes region and when combined with the shell, the ornament also represented water spirits.

Ceremonial objects were frequently covered with red paint. The color itself was *wakan*, symbolizing life, blood and the sacrifice of *Inyan*. In order to handle ceremonial objects, the person had to paint his hands red. Lakota leaders wore hair shirts. Originally made of scalps, later people would use hair donated by other tribe members or the hair from a horse's tail.

Headgear ranged from the purely practical to highly significant. In the early era, the Dakota tribes wore hoods in the winter for warmth and in the summer to protect them from mosquitoes. This form of headgear seems to have been dropped by the Sisseton as they moved west, but maintained by the Wahpeton. In the winter, the Titowan Lakota wrapped skins around their heads like a turban while the leather thong tied around the brow was practical in keeping the hair out of the eyes.

Once the tribes began to drift apart, styles changed and the Mdewakanton and the Wahpeton switched to a cloth sash wrapped around the head similar to those worn by the Algonquin of the east. Often the cloth was beaded with the Algonquin-style floral design. The Santee were first to adopt the roach as this style was known; however, this too eventually made its way west and became part of the regalia of the Lakota Omaha society in the late period.

Simplified versions of the feathered headdress developed in the eastern woodlands. These

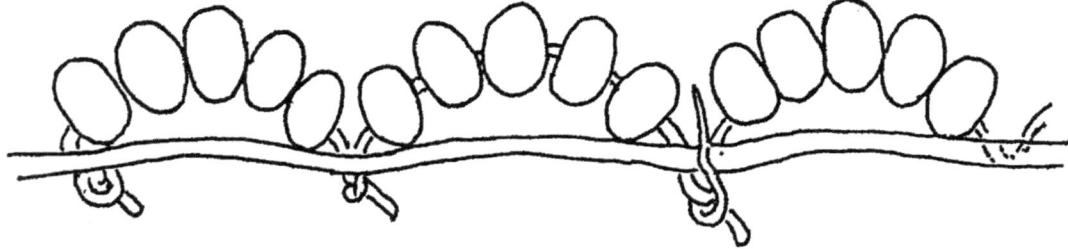

The lazy stitch was accomplished by stringing four or five beads together before anchoring it to the hide or cloth. Not only was it easier than anchoring one bead at a time, the lazy stitch created an artistic affect not achieved by the former, with raised rows that worked well with geometric patterns. Lakota women prided themselves on their beadwork, and the items thus beaded were considered works of art.

became more elaborate with the flared style adopted by the Lakota of the west. The latter were constructed with loops at the bottom of the feathers for lacing to a buckskin skullcap. This resulted in freedom of movement. The feathers were flared by running a second lace through the quill halfway up the feather. The headdress became the embodiment of the eagle as messenger of the sun while the soft down represented the mystery of motion or *Skan*. The horned bonnet was another style of headdress which invoked the protective power of the buffalo.

Housing varied from tribe to tribe, with more than the basic divisions found between woodlands and plains. Case in point, the woodland Dakota Wahpetons maintained a permanent summer house. The *tipi tonka* was made of bark and had a gabled roof. The woodland Mdewakanton shared this type of summer dwelling. However, in the winter months, the Wahpeton created an earth-covered, dome-shaped lodge while the Mdewakanton used the typical tipi.

The Siouan tribes of the east, including the Santee of the Carolinas, shared the bark lodges of the Dakota Santee, but unlike their western cousins, they lived in them year round and the buildings differed slightly in structure. According to Lawson, their homes were "*wigwams* or Cabins built of Bark, which are made round as an oven, to prevent Damage by hard Gale of Wind."[17]

Both men and women participated in the building of the summer house. Posts were set about a foot or two apart. The posts along the side of the house were five to six feet tall, and taller in the center of the end, forming a gable. Forked posts were used to support the ridge pole. Struts rested on the ridge pole in the center and rested on the upright posts along the end. Smaller posts were placed across the upright posts and the rafters and were anchored with basswork bark. According to Pond, it resembled a "wickerwork."[18]

The bark most often used for the external walls was elm, with a single piece cut from each tree. These were five or six feet long and of varying widths, depending on the size of the tree. These were also fastened to the crosspieces with basswood bark. The roof was constructed by Wahpeton men since it was considered work unbefitting a woman. It too was made of bark with the pieces set to overlap, like shingles. Doors were placed on the ends, two doors if a large house and one if a smaller dwelling.

The semi-permanent *tipi tonka* had a platform for sitting and sleeping which measured five to six feet wide and two to two-and-a-half feet above ground level. This wrapped around the inside of the house, except the wall, or walls, with the door. The platforms were covered with buffalo skins and mats of woven cattail leaves.

Each house had a separate shed which consisted of a roof supported by posts that extended about 8 to 10 feet out from the dwelling. It served the same function as a porch and was used for outside seating and for sleeping on hot summer nights. Corn and other vegetables were hung there to dry. Some homes had a medicine pole set in front to protect the residents, although not all authorities, such as Pond, mentioned its presence.

Housing also changed, depending upon the historical periods. So the Wahpeton of Ohiyesa's time, who once maintained the wooden summer lodges of the Santee, used the hide tipi entirely after they were ousted from their Minnesota homeland. In the late period, after the Sisseton migrated to the plains, they built permanent homes similar in structure to those of the Mandan. These were dug into the ground, with an earthen bench left around the walls to take the place of the woven platform. All had a round or sometimes octagonal stockade, built about two feet high. Four upright, forked posts placed in the center formed a square and supported ridge poles bound by basswood bark or leather thongs. Additional poles were laid from the stockade to the central support and woven together with bark, ash or basswood. This was then covered with more bark followed by a mixture of clay and hay, similar to wattle and daub used in Europe. As noted in the 1815 No Ears winter count, the Sans Arc experimented with Arikara-style log

Before the skin could be fashioned into clothing it had to be fleshed and then dried. If the hair was left in place, it was used as a blanket or a robe. With the hair removed, it was sewn into clothes. While the picture here shows the drying of walrus hide in Diomede, Alaska, the procedure used by the Dakota would have been the same. Part of the Edward S. Curtis Collection, Library of Congress, the photograph was published in *The North American Indian* by Edward S. Curtis (Seattle, Wash), v. 20, p. 124.

dwellings. Deloria described them as circular while Lone Dog described them as a "dirt lodge."[19] This suggests similarities to the Sisseton-Mandan style *ti-tanka*.

The standard hide tipi was made of approximately eight skins sewn together by sinew. The Mdewakanton, who often obtained hides through trade, used deer sinew. On the plains they used buffalo. The Dakota tipi was about twelve feet tall and twelve feet in diameter. Three poles were tied together to form a tripod. Nine more poles rested against this support. The tipi cover was laid on the ground, folded in half, raised by a pole attached to the top and wrapped easily around the structure. Straw or dried grass was patted against the inside walls during the winter months as a form of insulation. In the summer, the hide walls could be folded back or raised to provide ventilation. Robes were placed on the ground away from the door to create their beds.

In each one of the structures, the permanent summer home or the more mobile tipi, the hearth was the center of activity, and it was placed in the center of the domicile. Smoke escaped through a hole in the middle of the roof. Sticks demarcated the hearth place. Beds were made of buffalo robes, woven mats and pillows stuffed with down.

When living in their tipis the Dakota carried cooking vessels. Originally they used the paunch or stomach of the buffalo, which they could suspend next to an outdoor fire. Food was cooked by adding heated stones to the water. The woodland Dakota also made pots of black clay. Early authorities did not ascribe these clay vessels to the Dakota; however, said Pond: "I have seen specimens of it, and certainly it is no better than was to be expected at their hands. They who have seen the ornamental work of Dakota women will admit that much of it was tastefully designed and skillfully executed."[20] From this statement, one might infer that he recognized the designs. After the arrival of the European, clay pots were replaced by the metal kettle, a process which had reached its completion by 1775 when Peter Pond visited Santee and Yankton camps.[21]

Bowls and spoons were usually made of wood, although sometimes spoons were fashioned from antlers or buffalo horns. In 1766, Jonathan Carver mentioned bowls of clay or stone and plates made of the knotty excrescences of maple.[22] Peter Pond meanwhile was given a bark dish and a buffalo horn spoon with which to partake in the feast the Yankton had prepared for him.[23] Fifty-nine years later, Samuel Pond added to these descriptions. "Their wooden dishes were well formed and valuable. They were made of the hard knots cut from the sides of trees, hewn into shape with a hatchet and finished with a knife bent on one end. Their spoons and ladles were made the same way, but provided with a handle."[24]

The latter Pond applauded their workmanship. "There can be no better canoes than those made by the Dakotas, from the trunks of trees, with no tools but an axe and a clumsy adze."[25] Elsewhere it has been said that they used the birch bark canoe, which indicates either a regional variation or a change necessitated by material.

The woodland Dakota made storage containers of bark. The bark was wrapped around hoops and a seam sewn at the side. The bottom was formed by another piece of bark cut round and sewn into place. These containers held from two to five bushels. The women would fill them with corn or wild rice and bury them for long-term storage.[26] In the past, women also would have made bark wallets or parfleches from a single piece of bark folded in thirds. Two-thirds were folded in half and sewn together along the side, the remaining third acted as a flap which could be tied shut to prevent spillage.

Although the Dakota are not associated with weaving, they made cloth from yarn spun from the bark of nettles or from basswood bark which was softened by boiling. This could be dyed and then used to create the sashes and broad garters worn by men. Broader pieces of cloth had regular patterns or figures woven into them. These were then sewn into bags where the women stored their best clothes and ornaments. With the arrival of manufactured goods, they replaced the woven-bark bags with those made of yarn.

Inside the home, the furnishings of the Lakota would have been similar to those found in the winter tipis of the Mdewakanton. However, for a completely nomadic tribe, clay pots would have been impractical. The cooking vessel of buffalo paunch was used almost exclusively until iron kettles became common. Lakota storage containers, or parfleches, were made of stiff rawhide, folded and sewn together at the side, with a flap to hold goods in place. Women also made a kind of backrest or half-seat from stiff rawhide. These were often beaded works of art.

The Dakota cradle was a simple affair, according to Pond, little more than a single piece of wood where a baby could be secured, while the cradles of the Lakota plains were described as elaborate, with much time and attention spent on the beading. Both men and women would work on their creation. The same down from cattails that insulated their shoes provided absorbency and was used to pad children's clothes in place of a diaper

Standard tools for the Dakota women of both woods and plains included an awl, a needle, a knife and an axe. The more agrarian tribes also had a hoe for planting. Some consisted of little more than heavy wooden sticks, usually hickory, sharpened into a point. Often a piece of antler would be attached to the end for digging. In the prairies, the scapula of a buffalo was preferred and used to level the ground inside a tipi and to dig up roots.

Horses' halters were made of buffalo hide with the hair scraped off. A band was passed over the head and behind the ears. Another band was attached to this which slipped over the horse's snout and around the jaws. Saddles for men differed from those used by women. Indeed, men rarely used saddles. When they did, men's saddles consisted of two pieces of wood about twenty inches long and one-half inch thick which fit on the horse just behind the withers. These were held in place by two pieces of elk horn that formed an arch. The whole was scraped smooth and fitted with green buffalo hide, sewn in place and dried. According Walker, the Lakota saddle served as the basis for the McClellan saddle adopted by U.S. cavalry.[27] The saddle, if well made, often lasted for generations.

Women's saddles were different in structure. They were adapted for the woman's specific needs and were more utilitarian. From them, women needed to be able to suspend travois poles or lodge poles and be able to hang the papoose and other valuables.

Here as elsewhere, the Dakota peoples revealed ingenuity in adapting the native resources. They were a practical people, using the material at hand. When traveling and on the plains, their hide tipis were warm, comfortable and dry in the winter and open and airy in the summer. The summer lodge of the woodland Santee, meanwhile, was well suited to the environment—capitalizing on a resource (wood) that was unavailable to the people of the plains. They could with the simplest supplies make beds, cushions and hard seats as back supports. They created their own tools, fulfilling all their own needs, until the white man came along and created new ones—the fire-stick and the iron kettle.

While practical, the Dakota also revealed themselves as artists and artisans. The Lakota were renowned for their skill in beadwork, and Pond confessed his admiration of the beading done by the woodland Dakotas. Through their efforts women added value to each item. The untanned hide was turned into a prized robe, colorful moccasins, or a treasured cradle. Their goods were durable, their clothing practical. Most early explorers learned to imitate the dress of the Indian. Leather wore better than cloth in harsh, uncertain terrain, and was easier to replace. Thus, the Dakota truly conquered their environment, and they did it by living with it and within it, adapting to it and what it could provide to fulfill their needs.

7. Hunt and Harvest

Once there were ten brothers who lived in the woods with their sister. They were kind to her and were good providers, and she was happy. She gathered the mdo and the psincha to fill their pots and took care of their lodge. Every day the brothers would go out and bring home plenty of meat. Then one day the eldest did not return from the hunt.

The sister worried, but her brothers assured her that he must have chased the game a bit too far. Surely he would arrive home on the morrow with a deer slung over his back and a story to tell. However to calm her fears, the second promised he would find their brother if he did not appear in the morning.

With the next day's dawning, the eldest still had not arrived. True to his word, the second brother went in search of his brother. That night the second was nowhere to be found. The following day, the third brother went to look for the other two, and so it went until all the brothers were gone.

She wept and wandered the woods, calling their names, but she was alone. As she walked near a river, she glanced down at a stone of sparkling beauty. She plucked it from its bed and put it in the bodice of her gown. Exhausted from her efforts to find her brothers, she lay down next to the water to sleep. When she awoke the next morning, she felt a weight against her breast. She looked down and discovered a small child clinging to her bodice. His skin was cold to the touch, and she realized that he was made of the river rock she had picked up the previous day. She called him Stone Boy.

The child was clever and precocious, able to walk on the first day, and they returned to the lodge. She rejoiced; she was alone no more. The boy saw the ten quivers hanging on their hooks and he reached up to grab one, but she stopped him.

"Leave them," she said. "Those belong to your uncles. Someday they might return." Then she made him a fine bow and arrows, along with a beaded quiver that was just the right size for a child. He hunted small game, enough to provide for the two of them, and they were content. During the day, she tended the corn and at night, she taught him the history of the tribe, telling him all their sacred tales.

Moons passed; seasons passed and then years, until the Stone Boy was a young man. Each night he contemplated the quivers until one day he announced that he was going to find his uncles and bring them home. She argued; she wept and pleaded with him, but he was as unmovable as the stone of which he was made. He placed a pillow in the corner and said: "Do not fear for me. As long as this pillow stays in its place, I will be safe."

He traveled until he came upon a grizzly. The bear, angry at being disturbed, challenged him to a fight. The Stone Boy accepted, and the bear attacked, but he hurt his claws and shattered his teeth on the rock-hard body. The grizzly broke off the combat and withdrew, snarling, but the Stone Boy just laughed, pulled an arrow from his quiver, and shot the bear in the heart. He cut trophies from the body and traveled on until he found a tree that had been struck by lightning. Stone Boy studied the ground and realized that a great battle had been waged here on this spot. Then he came across some arrows and recognized them from the quivers that hung around the lodge. His uncles had been here, and they had fought a great battle.

The maple sugar harvest was one of the most important events in the Dakota year, taking place during February and March, before the thaw. Santee men went to hunt deer while the women and children would set up camp and prepare, felling trees, chopping wood for the fires where the raw sap would be boiled, and creating the troughs which would be used for boiling by hollowing out logs. This photograph shows a woman tapping maple sap after it has begun to flow. Photographic print by Roland Reed, c. 1908.

Just then, a black speck appeared on the horizon flying low and fast toward him. It expanded as it approached, and as he squinted at it, there was a blinding flash. A man stood before him and, like the bear before him, the man challenged Stone Boy. Flush from his victory with the bear, Stone Boy agreed.

The man grew as large as a giant. Lightning crackled around them as they wrestled, but the Stone Boy had skin that could not be broken or pierced. The warrior began to sweat and it began to rain. Finally, the Stone Boy threw his attacker to the ground. Around him the sky murmured and the storm flowed away.

Stone Boy bent and cut away the scalplock. He examined it, for it was made of the soft red down of a woodpecker. He blew on it, and it drifted up into the heavens. Stone Boy followed

7. Hunt and Harvest

The woodland Dakota and the Nakota maintained plots of corn. Early in their history, the Lakota did also. It was the woman's responsibility to tend crops. Even after their move to the plains, some of the tribes maintained this tradition. The name Miniconjou means "planters next to the stream." The Sans Arc (Itazipcho) were believed to be an offshoot of the former tribe. They adopted permanent homes in 1815, which suggests they became farmers. The Oglala also experimented with agriculture. The Dakota grew two varieties. The dried corn would be ground and used to thicken stews or soups. Corn was a universal among the tribes. The pictures shows an Apache woman hoeing rows of corn with an infant in a cradleboard on her back. Photographic print, Edward S. Curtis, c. 1906, December 19. Edward S. Curtis Collection (Library of Congress).

the floating feathers until he arrived at a nest filled with blood-red eggs. He clambered up into the tree. The people of a nearby village emerged from their lodges and ran to him pleading.

"Give me my heart," each shouted in turn.

He looked from them to the eggs and then he took one in each hand and smashed them. Two warriors fell to the ground, stone dead. Stone Boy seized more of the eggs and held them high over their heads. "One of your kind has hurt my uncles. Tell me where they are or I will break all the eggs."

The people turned their backs on him. So Stone Boy broke the eggs, one by one, until only four remained. Ignoring the dead bodies, he climbed down from his perch with the eggs tucked in his shirt. Then he searched the village until he came upon the four survivors.

"Where are my uncles?" he demanded.

The youths looked at their fallen comrades and took him to a place of bones. Stone Boy instructed the young men to bring him sticks, wood, water and stones, for he had learned his lessons well. Then as First Born had done, Stone Boy built an ini ti (sweat lodge) over the pile of bones. He heated the rocks and covered them with water. Sacred steam rose, and he withdrew to wait. From inside the sweat lodge, he heard the murmur of voices raised in medicine songs. Stone Boy opened the door and there stood his uncles.

When they emerged, he discovered one was missing a finger so he broke the rest of the eggs and cut a finger from one of the youths. The men returned to their lodge, and there was much joy and celebration. Eventually life settled down to the easy rhythm of days. The uncles hunted; the mother tended the corn and gathered herbs while her son wandered the wood, hunting like his uncles, but he did not bring his meat home to feed the family. Instead he cut off ears, teeth and claws and carried them around as trophies and left the meat to be eaten by carrion. His mother and her brothers warned him that he must not be wasteful, for he would anger the Great Spirit who had decreed that animals must sacrifice their lives so that the children of Little Boy Man, the two-legged ones, might live; but the youth was stubborn and did not listen.

Then one day he came home, his expression uneasy. His mother pressed him to discover what bothered him so, and he said: "I heard the animals plotting to wage war against us. They have sworn to kill us all, but," he drew himself upright, "I will protect you."

He turned again to the teachings, the tales told to him by his mother of First Born, and Stone Boy threw a pebble into the air and a circle of stone surrounded their tipi. He threw another and another and another, creating concentric rings around the first. Then he tossed two more stones into the air. Each became stone lodges, one on top of the other.

The army of the angry beasts advanced upon their defenses and the brothers loosed arrows one after another into the mass of fur and snarls, but still the animals came. The bodies fell in heaps which others used as bridges until they had breached first one ring and then another. The family retreated into the lodges, but the badgers and the gophers had been busy, undermining the stone foundations of their home. Elsewhere the beavers reversed the course of the river, and waters from the nearby stream poured into the lodge. The water rose, and the woman and her brothers drowned.

But made of stone as he was, the Stone Boy could not be killed. Rather he was buried when his stone pillow that he had placed so casually in the corner one day fell on top of him. There he stays to this day, watching over the rubble, punished for spurning sacred law and the agreement made by the Great Mystery between animals and man. He had abused his strength and his power, preying upon the weak for his amusement, and not honoring those creatures who sacrificed their lives so that others might live.[1]

This legend tells of waste and lack of gratitude to the divine and lack of respect for the animals who died so that man might live. It speaks of the connection between the hunter and the hunted. Stone Boy calls upon the wisdom of First Born, but for Stone Boy, the magic doesn't work as planned for he has misused his power in the past. The animals win because their cause is just.

Yet the story only addresses one aspect of prehistoric food production, for the natives of the continent utilized any number of resources. The cultivation of corn began on this continent long ago. Agriculture made the great civilizations feasible, and recent finds indicate that Caral in Peru and the Mayan culture in Mexico date back to 2600 BCE, which means farming would have had to have been not only established but the skills honed and refined by this time in order to support the large populations found in these centers.

Climate had a direct effect on prehistoric food production. The natives of each period became hunter-gatherers or farmers, depending on the available resources. The Middle Archaic Period (5000–3000 BCE) was marked by a major climatic drying period throughout most of the central United States. This resulted in an increase in sedentary lifestyle across the continent with multi-seasonal base camps and some permanent habitation sites. Activities centered on

The picture of the *Mound Builders Gathering Their Crops* gives a more accurate portrayal of the Dakota management of their crops. Harvest was a community affair that included both women and children. For the Siouan tribes of the east who relied more on agriculture, farming, along with hunting, was the man's activity as family provider. The Dakota, however, deemed it woman's work. Photogravure by Gebbie & Husson Co., Ltd. of a painting by H.N. Cady published March 30, 1892.

agriculture. Fabrics, basketry, and cordage along with new tool types, such as grooved axes, appeared during this time.

The drying period ended during the Late Archaic Period (3000–1000 BCE). Still farming continued. Artifacts from this time included digging tools, numerous plant processing tools, and the first pottery in the Midwest. Gourd and squash remains from the period are the earliest physical evidence of agriculture. Late Archaic burial mounds are also found.

Remains from the Early Woodland Period (1000–500 BCE) are rare, although it appears that the Late Archaic cultural patterns persisted into this time. Where represented, Early Woodland culture showed an increased use of ceramic pots to prepare food. As with the Early Woodland Period, the Middle Woodland Period (500 BCE–CE 400) reflects a further increase in the use of pots, with ceramic styles becoming more numerous. Again, the reliance on pottery suggests a settled and agrarian lifestyle, for clay pots are heavy to transport and do not travel well.

The Late Woodland Period (CE 400–900) was split, climatologically speaking. Around 500 CE there was a shift to cooler temperatures on the plains that made it ideally suited for the buffalo. Herds then grew to the sizes found later in the 1800s, up to sixty to seventy million. This had a detrimental effect on cultivation. Large herds trampled crops, making the agricultural lifestyle precarious and precipitating a switch among the prairie people to a more pedestrian lifestyle where the tribes followed the herds.

But the bulk of the Late Woodland Period took place during what is known climatically as the Holocene period, a time when the global temperatures were warmer and the American plains was peopled entirely by agrarian communities. The Late Woodland culture saw the introduction of the bow and arrow and widespread cultivation of a number of plants, including maize.

Meat had to be dried or jerked to preserve it. The picture, called *In camp*, shows two Lakota women cutting meat and drying buffalo meat on poles. The meat could then be ground and soaked to feed the very young or it could be mixed with fruit to make *wasna* or pemmican. Further east, fish was dried on specially constructed racks. The woodland Dakota also dried corn and wild rice which was then stored in bark or hide containers and buried in the ground for later consumption. Photo taken by Edward Curtis, c. 1908. Edward S. Curtis Collection. Published in *The North American Indian*, Edward S. Curtis. (Seattle, Wash.): Edward S. Curtis, 1907–30, v. 3, p. 6. 1908.

Typical sites include villages or hamlets along stream valleys and small earthen and stone cairns or mounds located on hills and ridges overlooking the villages, such as the one near Devil's Lake described by storyteller Smoky Day in Eastman's *Indian Boyhood*.

The Mississippian Period (CE 900–1700) included the Cahokia, near the confluences of the Mississippi, Missouri, and Illinois Rivers. These sedentary cultures were based on maize. Small notched, triangular arrow points were found.

While it is impossible to pinpoint where the Dakota peoples were during the Late Woodland period, they would have had to have arrived in the Minnesota region by the Mississippi period in order to be "discovered" by European explorers in 1649. It's interesting to note that the stone arrowheads, which mark Late Woodland sites, were never used by Dakota. According to the records of Samuel Pond and Ohiyesa, antler was the preferred medium. Eastman said that others had tried shooting with arrowheads found in the area and found them useless.

Having existed as a people, the Dakota would have lived through the many transitions described above. Their style of life during the Halocene period depended not only upon the when, but the where, of their migration. If they arrived from due north, they would have been more reliant on hunting. If they moved through the prairies of the west, as claimed by Iowa oral tradition, it is likely they placed a greater emphasis on agriculture, with the nomadic lifestyle coming with the mini-ice age that gripped the planet from 1100 to 1865 CE.

Starting in the 1700s, winter counts recorded times of want and plenty, as they documented the weather. For example, twenty different winter counts listed 1826, 1827 and 1828 as years of scarcity when the weather was cold and the snows so deep that they hunted on snowshoes and ate boiled rushes. At least three winter counts recorded an incident of cannibalism in 1826 as a result of starvation. Meanwhile 1830 was called the year of big famine. The Big Missouri winter count for 1853 said: "the winter was so cold and feed so scarce that horses died."[2] Four years later was a time of plenty.[3]

The importance of the hunt was revealed in the winter counts. The first four years of the No Ears winter counts (1759, 1760, 1761, 1762) mention the hunt or hunters, with 1759, 1760, and 1761 marking the deaths of fishermen, hunters, and trappers; the last entry, 1762, told of men swimming after buffalo, which suggests floods.[4] The No Ears winter count commemorates the privations of 1827 with "They used snowshoes," presumably to hunt, while Iron Crow notes "the winter of deep snows."[5]

The cooling temperatures reduced reliance on agriculture, particularly in the north, until the Dakota lived as the hunter-gatherers the Europeans first encountered, who planted little more than tobacco and corn in their garden plots. Indeed the Wahpeton writer Charles Eastman seemed to believe that the switch from an agrarian-type culture to a more nomadic one was a conscious choice. "It was not, then, wholly from ignorance or improvidence that he [the Indian] failed to establish permanent towns and to develop a material civilization. To the untutored sage, the concentration of population was the prolific mother of all evils, moral no less than physical."[6]

Writing in the 1680s, Hennepin said that the Dakota did little farming, although he admits they kept small plots. In 1775, Peter Pond stated that the bands living at the mouth of the Minnesota River, the Sisseton: "Rase plenty of Corn for thare one [own] Concumtion."[7] The Santee of the Carolina coast relied on corn and tobacco, and in the crop-dependent south, it was man's job, as provider, to plant the seed and tend the fields.

If one accepts their traditions of northern antecedents, it is unlikely that the early Dakota Santee were ever completely dependent on agriculture, and if they lived parallel to the Inuit peoples, then they may have developed a similar lifestyle. Likewise, if status is a measure of importance and the status of the Dakota male was determined by his ability to hunt, one must assume that the Dakota relied upon hunting and supplemented it with crops for much of their history.

Both woodland Santee and prairie Lakota/Nakota relied on the buffalo for at least part of the year and supplemented their diet with other game, such as deer. After white traders made it financially lucrative, the plains tribes came to rely on the bison almost exclusively. While the hunt was organized for the group, once begun it became a distinctly individual affair. The picture, entitled *Doomed*, by Charles Schreyvogel, artist, was painted in oils sometime around 1901.

Evidence, however, seems to suggest that at one time there was much heavier reliance on crops before white men came to trade. With the woodland Dakota acting as intermediaries between the tribes of the west and the European of the east, commerce replaced farming which supplemented the hunt and trade in furs. Meanwhile the Wahpeton-Sisseton of Lake Traverse, though, continued to concentrate on agriculture, growing a surplus of corn to trade as late as 1835.[8] According to both winter counts and tribal names, four of the seven Lakota bands raised crops for at least part of their tenure on the prairies.

In Samuel Pond's time, most Dakota villages maintained small plots of corn. They cleared their fields as they had for centuries, through the process of girdling or barking, which cut off a crucial part of the tree. The bark could then be used to build or repair the *tipi tonka*. Within a few months, the trees would die, leaving an abundance of wood and ample sun for their crops.[9] Unlike the east-coast Santee, tilling the soil was woman's work for the Minnesota-based Dakota.

Planting took place when the first wild strawberries ripened in June, for they knew then that the crops were safe from late frost. The women usually chose soil where the wild artichoke grew, where the earth was rich and much easier to dig. Like most native peoples, the Dakota planted in mounds rather than in rows. They hand-picked each seed and then soaked it in preparation for planting. When the first four leaves appeared, they would loosen the soil around the seedling. Later, the mound was shored up to support the plant. Cross-pollination was done by hand, putting corn pollen of one type on the silk of another variety.[10] According to Samuel

Pond, the Dakota concentrated on two different kinds of corn. One type was short and had a fast growing season of approximately sixty days. It was the preferred crop, although they grew another, taller kind that required a longer growing season.[11] The crops were guarded from blackbirds by women and children.

Corn would be eaten still green, or it could be dried by removing the husks and hanging the ears. Once dry, it was pounded into meal. For longer preservation, corn would be boiled, after which the kernels would be scraped from the cob with mussel shells and then spread out to dry. This too would be pounded into meal which was stored in bark barrels and buried in the ground.

Corn was supplemented by gathering food from the environment. In March, the woodland bands would divide, with the women and children going off to collect the sap of the maple trees while men hunted elsewhere. Maple was not the only tree exploited for its sugar. Sap from birch and ash made a dark and bitter sugar which was used for medicinal purposes. Box elder yielded a sweet white sugar.[12]

One of the best descriptions of maple season comes from Eastman's *Indian Boyhood*. The women felled trees and hollowed logs to contain the sap. They continued to cut wood for fires until April when the sap would start to flow. Once this occurred the women had little time for any other activity besides its collection and production. V-shaped slashes were cut in the bark with axes, and the sap collected in buckets or troughs made of birch bark. Often women and children had to compete with rabbits and squirrels who were happy to devour the sap the Dakota gathered for their cooking pots.

The Dakota maintained a hut for boiling. The long fires were tended by the boys, who also had to ensure that the sap did not boil over, while the girls worked with the women. After the arrival of the European goods, metal kettles were used to hold the sap. Prior to this period they may also have used clay pots. The completed product was patted into cakes and wrapped in birch, or stored in hollow canes. Some of it would be crushed and stored in rawhide bags. The entire process took nearly six weeks.

Additionally, Dakota women would gather *psincha, psinchincha,* and *mdo*, the wild turnip and the water lily. Both *psincha* and *psinchincha* were underwater roots. The latter was the same shape and about half the size of a chicken egg, while the former was round and an inch in diameter. They were dug up by foot, the *psinchincha*, once uprooted, would rise to the surface of the pond, where it could be reached. The *psincha* did not float; however, it grew in marshy margins where the water was not deep. The *mdo* was a form of sweet potato. The wild, or prairie, turnip was found across the plains and was a staple of all three groups, the Dakota, the Nakota and the Lakota.

In the summer months, they would pick blueberries and wild spikenard, *Aralia racemosa* or American spikenard, which grows two to four feet tall. A close relative of sarsaparilla, it had medicinal purposes, as a remedy for respiratory ailments in both man and domesticated animals. The roots are aromatic and spicy; spikenard once was a basic ingredient in root beer.

In the prairies the people gathered sand plums as they ripened in July.

Wild rice of the Minnesota lakes was harvested by the woodland Dakota in August. As often happened the band would split in two, with half going to hunt and half to harvest the grain. Fifteen or twenty families would descend on a lake where they maintained family plots of wild rice. Said Eastman: "On the appointed day all canoes were carried to the shore and placed on the water with prayers and proper offerings. Each family took possession of an allotted field, and all the grain therein was tied in bundles of convenient size, allowing it to stand for a few days."[13]

Then they would enter the lake again with two people per canoe. One would paddle while the second drew the ends of each bundle into the canoe, shaking the grains into the bottom of

While the Lakota are most often associated with buffalo, the woodland Dakota relied on deer. Only when they began their westward migration did they expand their diets to include the American bison. This photograph (photographer unknown), called *A noble buck in peril from a Sioux hunter*, was published as a stereo card, December 4, 1908, by International Stereograph Co., copyrighted by C.L. Wasson.

the boat. The rice would be taken to the land and spread to dry on grass mats or buffalo robes. If the season was drawing to an early close, the women built scaffolds upon which green grass was placed, followed by the newly harvested rice. A fire expedited the drying process. To hull the grain, the dried rice would be heated over a pit approximately two foot by two foot. Men would then put on new moccasins and tread upon the rice, separating the grain from the chaff. The women would pour it onto a robe which was shaken to separate the inedible hull from the edible grain. Caches were dug, lined with bark and dried grass, or with a deerskin, where the rice would be stored until it was needed.

Acorns were also collected in autumn. Only the best were chosen, those with their caps intact, for a nut without its protective cap indicated it was infested with worms. The acorns were dried, shelled and ground into a meal. The tannin was removed by leaching or rinsing it with water over a mound of fine sand near a spring or a river to make it palatable. According to Lawson, the Siouan tribes of the east roasted acorns and beat them into meal which they would use to thicken their soups. "They use them instead of Bread, boiling them until the Oil swims on top of the Water, which they preserve for use, eating the Acorns with the Flesh-meat."[14]

Infants were nursed for a period up to two years. In addition to mother's milk, Dakota babies were fed soft food which consisted of cooked wild rice and venison broth. Another dish included dried venison pounded into a powder and soaked in water to capture all of the nourishing juices. This was then mixed with ground corn that had been browned over a fire. The porridge of rice, softened venison, and crushed corn was a staple for many Dakota infants, particularly the orphaned. As children developed teeth, more foods were added to their diets, including meat (elk, bison, deer, rabbit, ducks) and fish.

They also ate a variety of berries, plums, and nuts wherever they could be found growing wild. Another staple of young and old alike was *wasna*, more commonly known by the Algonquin name, pemmican. It was made of dried buffalo or deer meat ground into a meal mixed with some kind of fruit, usually chokecherry, along with enough fat or grease to bind the mixture.

The buffalo hunt must have fascinated the Americans who all but destroyed the tradition as it destroyed the species. In the period from 1880 through 1890, two and one half million were killed in the state of Kansas alone, as part of a government campaign to deny the plains tribes their way of life. This fact is well documented by the bounties paid for every skin brought in. This half-tone reproduction of a painting by Charles M. Russell was copyrighted by Charles Schatzlein. The illustration was used in *Field and Stream*, May 1898, p. 65.

To the outside observer, the division of labor appeared uneven. While women gathered food, orchestrated the moves and prepared hides, men appeared inactive or were completely absent from the camp, but the women preferred to have their men off in pursuit of game, for meat still provided the bulk of their diet. Samuel Pond, for one, felt the division was equitable. Hunting was a dangerous activity and no sport for a people who depended upon game to survive. The huntsman never lost his a sense of danger. Lurking behind any tree could be a predator, or worse, a human enemy. Prey was never cooperative, so the hunter could be charged and gored by a buck, and many Lakota warriors met their end under the hooves of a buffalo. Neither was success guaranteed. The hunter could leave early in the morning and return at night empty-handed. Often if he had chased the deer too far he would not be able to get home. If he returned without success, he would fast all day.

Training for the hunt began early. Ohiyesa stated that he was three when he stood with his first bow and arrows in his hands.[15] Boys concentrated on small game which their weapons could fell, such as rabbits, chipmunks, squirrels, small birds and grouse. They would be sent out singly to search for signs of a deer's day bed or scratches on bark which indicated the presence of a bear. A broken branch, crushed grass, a single print or a tuft of fur left in a tree,[16] or a deer trail could reveal the quarry for the following day. The information they took back to camp was used by the adults to assist them in the next day's hunt.

Ohiyesa's uncle taught him to observe nature. "In hunting, you will be guided by the habits of the animal you seek. Remember that a moose stays in swampy or low land or between high mountains near a spring or a lake...."[17] Thereby his uncle shared his experience but only through silent observation would Ohiyesa be able to expand upon this knowledge.

Childhood games also developed hunting skills. Boys would run foot races, as they might have to race after prey. They practiced archery, both standing and running, and, after 1700, they practiced horsemanship in their races as they practiced archery on horseback.

Since the hunt provided the primary food source, it governed the life of the tribe. In *One Vast Winter Count*, Colin Calloway said: "Hunting people lived with as well as on animals."[18] Moves were orchestrated because of the presence or lack of game in a region, and their ceremonial religion and dances were based on the hunt. New bands were formed because of it. For the woodland Dakota and in the earlier period the Nakota and the Lakota, hunting, like gathering, was seasonal. In the spring, nests were plundered for eggs, a job shared by women and children. As the year progressed, young geese and ducklings provided further nourishment. Immediately after the spring thaw, around March, the boys of the village hunted chipmunks when they first emerged from their dens and gathered in large groups, at which time they could be easily picked off.

Winter was the best time for fur trapping, when the animals' coats were thickest, although the season provided new challenges with both hunter and hunted encumbered by the snow. The Dakota developed snowshoes and created sleds to carry traps and meat. In the mid–seventeenth century, the Dakota trappers concentrated on muskrat while their plains relations focused on the beaver that had been depleted further east. The spring hunt that began before the first thaw was one of the most important, for the furs collected then were considered the most valuable.

The hunter carried a few provisions on his back. He took traps for otters and separate heavier traps for muskrat. The brave would approach the den and shove a spear into the soft earth. If occupied, the den was cut open and the animals removed. As spring thaw progressed, traps were laid. These could then be visited by canoe at night. Muskrats were also shot as they swam around in their lakes at dusk. As spring turned to summer, the coats grew shabby and even the flesh of the muskrat was deemed inedible.[19]

Come summer, the Santee returned to their permanent summer camp where they could

The Lakota of the late plains period were primarily known as buffalo hunters. However, they took advantage of the many diverse food sources available to them at the time. The Shoshone got their name as the "eaters of sheep," but the Dakota hunted sheep too. Pictured here is a Brule man who stands on vantage point looking for the mountain sheep. Called *The Sentinel*, this photographic print was another taken by Edward S. Curtis, c. 1905.

tend their fields of corn. Although the Dakota hunted deer at any time of year, the primary deer hunt began in October and lasted through December. The Santee bands broke up into smaller units and scattered throughout their territory. They carried little with them, and they left behind only those who were too old, or in some way invalided, therefore unable to walk. A few warriors or *akitcita* remained in the summer camp to guard them. Any of the elders who could keep up would come along to care for and to teach the children the tales of their ancestors.

Each group kept to a particular area for this period and would return to the unified camp in January. After a region had been thoroughly hunted for a radius of six miles, the band would move on. The area was left to recover until the following year to allow the herds the chance to renew; thus, no region was overhunted and the game was conserved. The number of deer must have been considerable even in the later period, for trader Oliver Faribault told Samuel Pond that he purchased fifteen hundred skins from two bands in a single year. Pond estimated that, assuming the Dakota killed an additional five hundred deer for personal use, it would leave only two or three deer per person per full year.[20]

The woodland bands would follow the food source as did the Lakota. According to the Wahpeton, Ohiyesa, differences existed between the hunter of the plains and the hunter of the woods. They were dependent on the buffalo as a food source, and sometimes the Dakota looked down on their western brethren. The Dakota also hunted buffalo, but they had other sources of meat. Thus, Eastman boasted that they were the better hunters since they had to learn diverse skills in order to track the many different animals that formed their diet. "The hunting of the prairie boys was limited and their knowledge of natural history imperfect. They were, as a rule, good riders, but in all-round physical development much inferior to the red man of the forest."[21]

His perspective is simplistic, not taking into account that the original prairie huntsmen were primarily trappers who pursued the same game that had been extirpated in the Minnesota Dakota's woodland environment. In the beginning, the Lakota were not a mounted tribe, with the first trade for a horse recorded in the winter count of 1707.[22] Until that point, the Lakota did not rely upon buffalo for sustenance; instead it represented a supplement to their food supply. Prior to the introduction of the horse, the buffalo hunt popularized in our imagination did not exist. The tribe migrated with the herds. The weak and the aged buffalo would be picked off or culled.

With bison able to run at speeds up to thirty-five miles per hour and the hunter on foot, a stampede profited no one and quickly resulted in their food source disappearing over the horizon. The Carolina Santee donned the skins of deer to cover the human scent. This required an intimate knowledge of one's quarry in order to mimic its behaviors accurately; thus the religious initiations and dances had a practical aspect. Like the Siouan hunters of the east, the plainsmen would disguise themselves.

The unmounted Yankton, Sisseton and Lakota of the early plains period dressed themselves in buffalo hides which they found bulky and cumbersome, so they took an unusual tactic, disguising themselves in wolf skins, for the bison did not fear the wolf it could see, particularly the lone wolf.[23] In the earliest period when Dakota tribes still inhabited the region around the Hudson Bay they may have worn seal skins and hunted seal as did the Inuit people, with whom the Dakota were acquainted. When skins were not available, they would camouflage themselves with plants tied to their bodies. They also armed themselves with an assortment of whistles and decoys to lure their prey to them.

In the autumn when stores must be built up, several tribes would gather for the great hunt, where the herd was driven into a natural pen, into a pit, or over the edge of cliffs, a technique that had been used for thousands of years on the Great Plains. Only during this annual event would hunters be permitted to stampede the herds, run them to exhaustion and send them over an embankment. They could then harvest the carcasses.

The mass hunt became more refined after the Paleo-period. In central Canada, the Dakota's one-time neighbors and long-term enemies, the Ojibwa, perfected a system where they erected bush and pole "scarecrows" across vast regions of tundra in an ever-narrowing path. Then they would drive the caribou between these figures, funneling the frightened animals into a wooden stockade. The Yankton offshoot, the Assiniboin, made pounds of logs and dirt. The tribes of New England, who like the forest-based Dakota relied on deer, planted and maintained hedges through with their prey could be safely channeled. Perhaps in the early period, the Santee used a similar technique.[24]

Even after the Lakota became reliant on the buffalo as a food source, they often had to supplement their food supply with other meat when the herd absented themselves from the region. Then they would hunt and trap whatever small animals were available: squirrels, prairie dogs and rattlesnakes, to name only a few.

In both woodland and plains, traps supplemented meat obtained through hunting. Some traps were elementary but highly efficient, developed after close observation of the animal. Rabbits, for example, were disabled by littering their paths with burrs and sharp thorns, effectively crippling them so they could not run.[25] Snares and deadfalls were common. A piece of meat placed on a pile of loose logs would attract mink, ermine, otter, wolves and marten. When an animal tugged on the bait, it would unseat a peg and trigger a fall which would crush the animal.[26] The first snares were made with rawhide looped across the path which caught and strangled the quarry. This changed in the later period when horsehair knotted into a noose replaced rawhide, and later still when wire replaced horse hair. The noose would be anchored to the branch of the tree. When a small animal ran into the snare, the knot would tighten and

Although the John White watercolor depicts the tribes of the east coast in 1560, it still captures the many means used by the Dakota to catch fish as described by Charles A. Eastman, including spearing, netting and fishing with line. The illustration pictures native men and women in a dugout canoe fishing while others in the background stand in the river and spear fish. The illustration comes from the Library of Congress Rare Book Collection: Engraving by Theodor de Bry after a watercolor by John White in *Wunderbarliche, doch warhafftige Erklärung, von der Gelegenheit vnd Sitten der Wilden in Virginia ... / Erstlich in engelländischer Sprach beschrieben durch Thomam Hariot, vnd newlich durch Christ. P. in Teutsch gebracht.* Franckfort am Mayn: Gedruckt bey J. Wechel, in Verlegung D. Bry, 1590, plate 13.

the branch would snap back, hanging the animal out of harm's way from most predators until it could be collected by the huntsman.

In *Native Roots,* Jack Weatherford described another kind of snare specifically devised to capture the most sacred of all creatures. "On the plain, where the eagle feather had such high value, hunters devised a way to trap the animal without harming or marring the quality of feathers. They dug a pit covered with branches and secured a small animal or bird on top of the branches as bait." The hunter waited inside the pit. When the eagle landed, but was unable to take off with the secured prey, the hunter would reach up from the pit, grab the bird and strangle it,[27] after which the animal was honored by ceremonies.

Meat was augmented by fish which could also be snared on line, speared or shot with bow and arrow. The fishing line was made of sinew of either deer or buffalo. Later when white trade provided horses and other goods, fishing line was made of horsehair and hemp. In the autumn when fish were sluggish, they could be caught by hand and thrown out onto the shore. As a cooperative effort, streams would be dammed and large fish driven into baskets. During the winter months, they cut holes in the ice and fished with line or bow and arrow.

Despite the fact that the choice of game had changed, the governance of the camp hunt remained the same between the woodland Dakota and plains Lakota and Nakota. The decision to hunt was discussed amongst the headmen of the tribe. If the council called for a hunt, special *akitcita* were assigned to manage it. If the hunt required a move, further *akitcita* would be selected to oversee it. If lack of game required the band split into smaller groups, then an area would be assigned by the *akitcita* to each group to ensure that they did not trespass on another's hunting grounds. If smaller bands separated from the first, they became self-governing, with new *akitcita* chosen to lead the hunt and another set of *akitcita* to direct the move.

After the morning meal was eaten, the *akitcita* of the march would assemble on the hill nearby and women would break down the camp. The location of the next camp, near water and a supply of wood, had already been selected by the scouts the previous night. During the march, men could hunt for game alongside the column if they obtained permission.[28]

The rules of the hunt and the move surrounding it were stringent. Silence was essential to ensure the camp did not scare game away. People who disobeyed were severely punished, their home and goods destroyed. Barking dogs were put to death. Likewise, any hunter or group of hunters who infringed on another's assigned territory was forced to turn over his kill and could have his camp destroyed, as happened to Ohiyesa's grandmother when her son broke established hunt laws.[29] Any hunter who took off on his own to hunt without permission was subject to severe penalties, including having his horse killed.[30] Women also hunted. Many stories and cautionary tales describe women taking over the hunt when men were absent.

Before the hunt, the *wasicun wakan* would make medicines and charms and perform ceremonies to ensure good luck in the chase. Besides preparing their weapons, the hunters would participate in the *inipi* to purify their bodies and spirits.[31] If another band was asked to join the hunt, a holy man would gather tobacco and send invitational wands.

In the woodlands where deer were the object of the hunt, smaller groups would go out during the day, not returning until long after dark. Once the supply of game was depleted, the headmen debated a further move. Similarly in the west, they would discuss whether they should follow the herd or remain until hides had been treated and the meat made into jerky.

On the day of a buffalo hunt, scouts would meet the hunters as soon as it was light enough and report the location of the herd. The huntsmen would mount as silently as possible and advance as close to the herd as they could without being seen. The *akitcita* of the hunt would decide the best access point and dispose of their huntsmen to ensure each had equal advantage. After the initial rush, each man acted singly.[32]

Even after the arrival of the horse, the favored weapon of the Lakota remained the bow

7. Hunt and Harvest

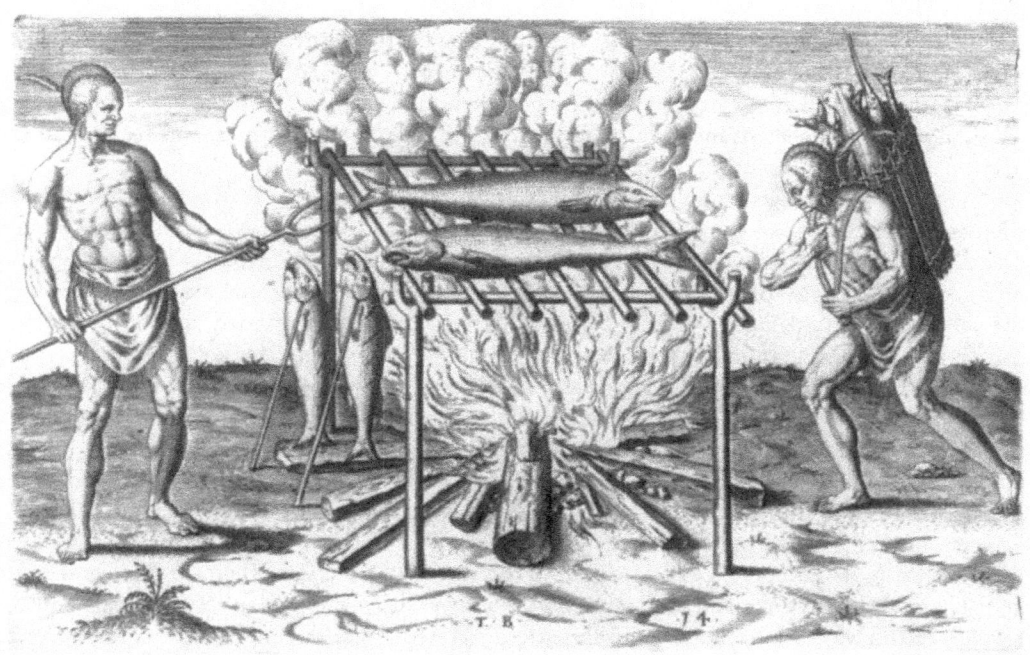

Ein höltzern Roost, darauff sie die Fische besengen. XIIII.

Wann sie eine grosse menge Fische haben gefangen, begeben sie sich auff einen darzu verordneten Platz, welcher die Speiß zu bereiten bequeme ist, daselbst stecken sie vier Gabeln auff einem viereckten Platz in die Erden hinein, auff diese legen sie vier Höltzer, vnd auff dieselbigen andere zwerchsweise, also, daß es einem Roost, der da hoch gnugsam sey, gleichförmig werde. Wann sie die Fische auff den Roost gelegt, machen sie ein Fewer darvnter, doch nicht nach der weise der Völcker von Florida, welche die Fisch allein besengen, vnnd im Rauch außtrücknen, die sie den gantzen Winter vber behalten. Diese Völcker aber braten alles verzehrens, vñ behalten nichts in vorraht, darnach, wann sie dessen dörfftig sind, braten oder sieden sie frische, wie wir hernach sehen werden. Wann aber der Roost so groß nicht ist, daß die Fisch alle möchten darauff gelegt werden, stecken sie kleine stecklein am Fewer in die Erden, vnnd hencken die vbrigen Fische durch die Ohren auff, vnd braten sie vollendt so lang es gnug sey. Sie sehen aber mit fleiß zu, daß sie nicht verbrennt werden. Wann die ersten gebraten sind, legen sie andere, so sie frisch herzu gebracht, auff den Roost. Vnd also widerholen sie diß braten so lange, biß sie der Speise gnugsam zu haben vermeynen.

This illustration showed how the tribes of the east cooked fish. A similar means would have been used with drying although coals would have been damped. Library of Congress Rare Books Collection: Engraving by Theodor de Bry after a watercolor by John White in *Wunderbarliche, doch warhafftige Erklärung, von der Gelegenheit vnd Sitten der Wilden in Virginia ... / Erstlich in engelländischer Sprach beschrieben durch Thomam Hariot, vnd newlich durch Christ. P.* in Teutsch gebracht. Franckfort am Mayn: Gedruckt bey J. Wechel, in Verlegung D. Bry, 1590, plate 14.

and arrow over the gun or lance. The most desirable approach was from behind so the arrow entered the body of the bison above the flank, passing through the viscera and lodging inside the body. If this was not possible, then the hunter would shoot from the side. With this method, though, the arrow could possibly pass completely through the buffalo which, while it left the beast fatally wounded, allowed it to run unimpeded for a long time. The lance or spear was then used to finish the kill.[33]

When a man acquired a new horse, the animal had to be trained for the rigors of the hunt. Training began with the horse ridden alongside or directly into herds of other horses. Buffalo hides would be rubbed against their skin to get the horses familiar with the scent, so they that would not balk when surrounded by bison instead of horses. Once the pony was trained for the hunt, it was used for no other purpose.

The division of food among the hunters was not as cut and dried as one might think, with the person who shot the game becoming its sole possessor. Instead the Dakota hunter would give notice to the others by giving a particular shout that was recognized among the tribes. If no one came, then he could cut the carcass up and carry it home. If someone showed up, then the venison was divided equally. If one hunter arrived, then it was divided in half, if two, then thirds; and if three, then in quarters,[34] while the man who shot the deer kept the skin.

The Lakota also divided the goods among other members of the band, while the hunter who shot the animal was allowed to keep the liver, entrails, brains and hide. To shoot a white buffalo was considered sacred and was mentioned in three separate entries of the Big Missouri winter count for 1830,[35] 1831[36] and 1848.[37] The hunter who made the kill was obliged to hold a ghost lodge. If a dispute about possession arose, the hunt *akitcita* would view the body and the arrow found embedded in the flesh. The hunter who made the killing shot got the hide. The liver was eaten raw, dipped in gall which, it was believed, would endow them strength and courage. The entrails were cooked and eaten by the party, with the tripe laid on the coals and the inside peeled away. The Dakota Mdewakanton disdained to eat raw meat, although the Santee tribe, the Wahpeton of Ohiyesa's day, would eat the liver of the buffalo raw, as did their prairie brethren.[38]

When the Dakota hunter returned with his deerskin to the camp, his success was announced to the village, and feasts were held. On the plains, the women, children and elders of the Yankton and the Lakota came to the scene of the chase with horses and travois in order to haul meat way. As soon as the chase ended, the holy man chose a carcass to give as an offering to *Taku wakan*. The skin was removed and the meat left where the spirit of the buffalo would take up permanent abode.[39]

Like all aboriginal men, the Dakota peoples honored their prey. They proved themselves skilled trappers and hunters, adapting to new needs and new environments and adopting new technologies, when useful, and mastering them. They were also practical enough to stick to tried-and-true methods when they proved more efficient. Their hunts were carefully coordinated and orchestrated and not the helter-skelter image conveyed by the media. Similarly they were skilled in adapting to both circumstance and season. They were adept at exploiting their environment without harming it. They gathered food from many different sources, and even in the later period when they relied heavily upon the buffalo, they supplemented their diet with native plants, such as the prairie turnip.

Meanwhile from the time of their arrival on this continent, the Europeans learned how to live in the harsher milieu of the Americas from the resident tribes. The natives taught the white men what was good to eat and what was not, and how to grow food here where European methods proved inadequate. Settling the plains was no exception. Like the agrarian tribes of the prairies, the first Europeans to inhabit the plains built their homes of sod. Whether from observation or active instruction on the part of the tribes, the white settlers discovered which plants

Starting prairie fire—This Remington print shows the use of fire as a fire break, a strategy still used by firefighters today. Fires were also started deliberately to burn off old grass as a means of drawing buffalo into an area. The dead grass would be replaced by new shoots which would attract the herd to fresh pastures. The picture, *Burning a refuge to escape from the oncoming prairie fire*, was painted by Frederic Remington in 1907.

were edible. They used the same herbs for their medicinal effect and to provide comfort in their homes. They stuffed their mattresses with daisy fleabane. In a place with no wood, the early pioneers burned buffalo dung in their fires, as did their native neighbors, and it was one of the child's duties to collect it. Thus, when pressed with the same challenges, the white farmer applied the solutions learned from the resident tribes.

8. Animals of Power

The land where Wakan Tanka, the spirit of Inyan, made his great banqueting hall was sacred. Here he feasted with all his relations. He paid little heed to that which happened upon the earth, leaving the inhabitants to their own devices unless need presented itself.

Yet not all was as it should be above ground, for there was much consternation among the winged ones and their four-legged cousins. Each vied for a position of supremacy amongst the many animal tribes. No one knew where he or she belonged in the structure of things. The elk and the buffalo as biggest thought they should take precedence over the rest.

So a race was proposed to clarify the order and rank of each species. Each tribe was supposed to pick one from among their number, their fastest and the best of their species to represent them in the race.

Excitement ran through the animal community as they debated the assets of their members. The buffalo picked their swiftest runner, a sleek, light cow. The wolves chose one who was fast and fleet of foot, as did the badger, the beaver and the bear. The winged ones, likewise, selected their best to fly in the race. As the choices were made, criers went around the many animal camps announcing the representatives of each species until the skies echoed with their voices.

The day of the race was fast approaching. In preparation, the animals painted themselves in many fine colors, so they could be distinguished from the rest. The skunk drew a white stripe down his back that he may not be missed. The coyote dipped his tail in paint, and these colors they wear to this day.

When the sun rose on the morning of the race, the animal tribes gathered around the track. The chosen among four-legged and the winged ones lined up, straining to be off. The signal was given, and the animals leapt forward. The smallest chosen to represent their people, the rabbit and the squirrel, were nearly trampled in the rush. The ground thundered beneath their feet as the other animals raced alongside the runners, roaring their encouragement.

The track ran above the great hall, disturbing the feast, and Wakan Tanka took notice. Inyan flexed his mighty back of stone, and the ground began to swell and roll. The land rattled. It shook. The animals swerved to avoid the place were the earth bulged along Inyan's spine, and the world exploded around them. The air was filled with flying rocks and leaping flames.

The animals scattered, the race forgotten.

When the sky cleared, mountains stood where the track once had been, and so the Black Hills were born as a result of this great race.

Called Paha Sapa in the language of the People, they were the home of Wakan Tanka, and they became sacred to those who served him. For Wakan Tanka was the giver of life, and Bear Butte became his most sacred altar. Paha Sapa was also the home of Inyan's companion, Wakinyan. It is said that the Thunderbird who sends storms out upon the plains dwells where the stone needles touch the sky. The rocks were wakan, and at night their spirits come to life to sing sacred songs to the people.

The buffalo became so important to the Lakota people that it was the only animal species that warranted a spirit guardian — the white buffalo. The bison provided not only food and hides for clothing and tipis, but its sinew was used as thread, the paunch as a cooking vessel. The bladder made the ball for the sacred ball game. The horns were sculpted into utensils. The skull and horns were an integral part of the rituals. The scapula formed the Lakota hoe, and the ribs were used in sleds. The Lakota made glue from the hooves, and shields were cut from rawhide. Although government figures say that the herds originally numbered thirty million, other authorities contend that there were as many as sixty million. At one time, there were two subspecies, the plains and the woodland bison. Only the plains buffalo exists in the continental United States today. Panoramic photograph by Christian T. Pelck; Pelck's Scenic & Art Studio; May 1, 1906.

> So Paha Sapa also became known as Wamaka Og'naka Icante, the heart of everything that is, or the navel of the universe. It is the place where the sky, clouds, earth, and the underworld meet, and spiritual home of the Dakota peoples.

The legend recounts the birth of the Black Hills. It credits their creation to the animals, as it elaborates upon the differences between the species. It gives an explanation of their unique appearance, along with at least some of their identifying characteristics. In a world where all are related, animals were important in the scheme of things, and the Dakota claimed a special relationship with them. One legend traced the tribe's origin to the mighty eagle, and the eagle feather became a symbol of constancy and virtue. Another ascribes their beginnings to the matrilineal clans through marriages between animals and man, specifically Little Boy Man.

The Dakota attributed not only wisdom to animals, but spirit and soul. Said Ohiyesa in *The Soul of an Indian*: "We believed that the spirit pervades all creation and that every creature possess a soul in some degree, though not necessarily a soul conscious of itself. The tree, the waterfall, the grizzly bear, each is an embodied Force, and as such an object of reverence."[1]

In this, the Dakota were not unique. Hunter-gatherers have shared veneration of animals throughout the ages. Colin Calloway explained the connection in *One Vast Winter Count* where hunters "touched the spirits as well as the bodies of the animals that gave them life.... Hunters danced to prepare themselves and the animals for hunting, and they prayed to the spirits of the prey. They butchered the kill in ritual manner lest the animal spirit take offense. Ritual hunting and adherence to the obligations established with animal kin guaranteed success in the short term and ensured the renewal of the animals for the future."[2]

Hunting was both a religious activity and an economic one. It represented a way of living in relation to natural forces. All hunting cultures have maintained a way of life based on a ritual of thanks for the sacrifice and acknowledged a reciprocal relation with animals. The Dakota virtue of *wacantognaka* (generosity) was based on a belief that animals who sacrificed their lives fell to generous hunters who performed the correct rituals and displayed the proper respect.

Calloway contends: "Hunting people ... existed in such close relationship that the lines between animal and human often became blurred.... People inscribed animal figures on drums, shields and tipi covers, wore animal masks and parts in ceremony, mimicked animal movements in dance, sang songs that connected them to the animals and to their ancestors and sought contact with animals in dreams and visions."[3]

Their totems included the sacred beast represented by its skin or by a painting. These symbols were treated with reverence and carried into battle to ensure the guardianship of the animal spirits. The attributes of an animal, such as wisdom, cunning, and courage, were conferred upon the wearer of the badge. Likewise, the animal's medicine was granted to members of the animal's lodge to which the practitioner belonged. However, some men claimed a special relationship with an animal, conveyed by revelation.

Traditional narratives taught lessons about personal conduct, using animal characters and animal characteristics, so tales about rabbits cautioned against cowardice and stories about deer warned against seduction. Many stories existed where animals and man married, imparting their attributes to their offspring.

Creation myths often credit earth's creation, and the creation of man, to animals. While the Dakota attributed human origins directly to *Wakan Tanka,* it was divine Inktomi, in the form of a wolf, who brought man up to the earth and taught him the rudiments of culture. In their close relationship to animals, the Dakota had many stories about the interdependence of people, animals and their environment. Tied to place by matrilineal animal clan and family memories, their legends connected the people not only to the land, but also to a tribal history whose lessons they must not forget. Similarly, their tales described the natural world in which the Dakota managed to survive only by maintaining proper relations with other creatures, as noted in the expression *Mitakuye Oyasin* (all are related).

The term totem refers to a familial animal, or more appropriately an animal representative whose characteristics are attributed to a clan, a family and tribal grouping. Ohiyesa explained the Dakota perspective. "Ever seeking to establish spiritual comradeship with the animal creation, the Indian adopted this or that animal as his 'totem,' the emblematic device of his society, family or clan. It is probable that the creature chosen was the traditional ancestress."[4] So it was that "...animal totems so general among the tribes were said to have descended to them from their great-grandmother's clan, and the legend was often quoted in support of our close friendship with the animal people."[5]

Both Christian Genesis and Dakota tradition agree that man was created last; however, the significance of this placement in birth order and its subsequent interpretation shows a perspective that is diametrically opposed and reveals a basic difference in thinking. For the Christian, man was last, therefore more advanced — presuming, one supposes, that God had become more practiced in his craft. As last and best, man was placed to rule over the animals of forest and field and the birds of the air. For the Dakota, though, man as last was youngest and as a child of the universe, he must learn from his elders and his betters, the animals.

The fact that animals take precedence over man reveals a great deal about Native American culture and Native American thinking, for this concept seems to be universal. Animals, as first-born and first to roam the earth, become the mentors, the teachers of man. It is from animals that humanity must learn how to live upon the surface when they eventually emerge as latecomers from the confinement of the caves. Animals came first before man and they became the elder brothers and sisters to man and, as such, humanity's teachers. According to Dakota tradition, it was from bear that the people learned which herbs, roots and berries were safe to eat. Other myths credit this to Inktomi.

8. Animals of Power

As one of the primary prey species for the woodland Dakota, the deer was surrounded by many myths and legends. It was believed to have magic to confound the hunter, and according to the Lakota, it had the power to seduce young men and cause madness in any young warrior who had allowed himself to be seduced. The illustration is called *The home of the deer*, from a lithograph published by Currier & Ives, c. 1870, New York (Library of Congress).

Bear held other wisdom. The Santee performed a bear ceremony before each war party, in which a chosen man acted as bear. He would wear the bearskin, and they would reenact the hunt. The first brave to lay his hand on the bear was said to have bear power. Bear also imparted healing powers. In *Indian Boyhood*, Ohiyesa described a Wahpeton Bear Dance where he asked to act as proxy for a youth who was too sick to participate in his initiation as a bear medicine man. A den was dug two hundred yards from camp. A bear man sang, and men and boys gathered around the den. The potential initiate would emerge and chase the men who, in turn, attacked the symbolic bear by striking him with switches and shots of powder. Any man who touched the bear without being touched would overcome an enemy. If one fell down during the contest, a death or some other sort of reverse would be visited upon the family.[6] Thus, animals presaged events.

In a later book, *Soul of an Indian*, Eastman described the relationship between man and animals. "The Indian loved to come into sympathy and spiritual communion with his brothers of the animal kingdom, whose inarticulate souls had for him something of the sinless purity. He had faith in their instincts as in the mysterious wisdom given from above; and while he humbly accepted the supposedly voluntary sacrifice of their bodies to preserve his own, he paid homage to their spirits in prescribed prayers and offerings."[7]

More importantly, the Dakota belief does not divorce man from his environment where humankind are only one small, and the least significant, part of the whole. So when the Native speaks of "all my relations," or *Mitakuye Oyasin*, he includes the family of animals and man. It could even be said that the aboriginal Americans were the first ecologists, for as early as the

1700s the eastern tribes were pleading with the European migrants not to destroy the environment. They knew that each species no matter how insignificant had its niche to fill, that the loss of one meant the impoverishment of the whole. The Dakota, too, understood the concept of conservation as evidenced by their hunting practices.

They honored animals who sacrificed so much in order for man to live. Eastman elaborated: "His respect for the immortal part of the animal, his brother, often leads him so far as to lay out the body of his game and decorate the head with symbolic paint or feathers. Then he stands before it in the prayer attitude, holding up the filled pipe, in token that he has freed with honor the spirit of his brother, whose body his need compelled him to take to sustain his own life."[8]

For the Dakota, Lakota and the Nakota people, animal kinships could also be individual. The person did not choose the animal; the animal chose the woman or the man, and once chosen, the power could not be "given away." If someone showed an affinity for an animal, which would indicate that he had been adopted by a species, then he could be educated by the appropriate shaman in its ways or initiated into a special society. In the later period, though, Pond revealed that this concept had been greatly diluted when he said that animal powers could be purchased from someone who had seen that animal during a vision quest.

An individual could have a multiplicity of animal mentors—one for his little (physical) self, another for his big or greater (spiritual) self. In addition, he or she may have an animal as a special protector, messenger, or guide. He or she may have a particular medicine, which would also be represented by an animal. Thus, a person had "buffalo" or "bear" medicine, "badger" or "otter." Medicine men were restricted in the type of treatment they could give by the kind of animal involved. So Mato (bear) healers treated broken bones, wolf medicine men removed arrows, while buffalo practitioners understood women's complaints.

An animal might also appear to a person with a particular lesson that was relevant to circumstances at that time or to impart a power that the individual may need during a personal crisis. These animals might be called temporary mentors or messengers. They did not become guardian spirits; they were simply teachers along the way.

If a person dreamed of an animal three times, he became a member of their society. A performer, or dancer, was one who had dreamt of an animal twice and a man twice. An individual could belong to more than one organization, many represented by an animal. Thus, a young man may become a member of the Kit Fox society and an Elk dreamer. A woman could become a Buffalo woman and also join the Kit Fox society as a singer. For example: Sitting Bull was a *Heyoka* warrior, therefore was associated with coyote. He also claimed eagle power and a special affinity to many birds, including meadowlark and bob o link, and was a practitioner of wolf medicine.

On a physical level, the spirit pole (a stick about 4 to 6 foot in length, adorned with the appropriate talismans—fur and feathers) replaced the totem pole of the northwest, although the woodland Santee put up medicine poles in front of their homes which could be compared to the northwestern totem. However, according to Joseph Epes Brown, Lakota animal associations can be broken down into three basic categories[9] which do not include totem:

1) Master Guardians, or master spirit—a spirit animal that guards an entire species.
2) Power animals—the spiritual essence of an animal or a species.
3) Guardian Spirits—the animals that appear during a dream or vision. Personal protectors, teachers or guides.

The White Buffalo is an example of a Master Guardian, for both the buffalo and the buffalo people (*pte*), the Lakota. After the beaver populations had dwindled, the plains tribes owed

Elk was the "male" equivalent to the deer. Elk dreamers had power over "love magic" and the elk dance included the use of mirrors contained within a hoop. Elk was a symbol of stamina and endurance. The picture above comes from the New York Zoological Society and was photographed by Gottscho-Schleisner, October 13, 1941. Gottscho-Schleisner Collection (Library of Congress).

their survival to the bison. The animal provided not only sustenance, but clothing, thread, homes and cooking pots to the Lakota and the plains Nakota, and it became the most important of all creatures. Nothing was wasted. The hooves were boiled for glue; the bones provided tools; even the bladder was cleansed, inflated and used in the sacred ball game. Accordingly only the buffalo rated a master guardian.

Elsewhere, other species had master guardians; for example, the quintessential creator raven of the Pacific northwest, whose earthly descendants are but a pale reflection of the original, and the trickster coyote of the Great Basin region. Similarly the woodland Dakota, who had a much wider range of prey, gave equal precedence to other animals.

The term "power animal" used by English speakers is something of a misnomer, resulting from mistranslation, or an inaccurate translation that does not take into account the juxtaposition of words in the Dakota language. In other words, it is a too-literal translation. The noun in this instance is "power" and the descriptor is "animal." Thus, it describes the power of an animal — its attributes, its associations and its strengths — and what Europeans think of as "power animal" is, in fact, the Guardian Spirit. Both individuals and societies could have guardian spirits. For example: the coyote was the guardian spirit of the *Heyoka* warrior.

The meanings or spiritual attributes of a species varied between tribes, sometimes within tribes. All the Dakota, Nakota and Lakota tribes agreed that the deer is *wakan*. However, the kind of power invested in the animal was dependent not only on the kind of deer, but on the tribe. Some holy men said the white-tailed deer was a seducer of men; others attributed this power to black-tail or mule deer. Both were considered capable of casting spells to confound the hunter.

Certain animals were considered more powerful — two examples being the buffalo and the wolf — but no animal was considered insignificant or without magic. For example: the skin of the drake's head carried within it the power of Okaga (the south wind) and symbolized comfort and well-being.[10] Some animals were more often associated with women — such as the buffalo or "pte" and deer — while men were equated with wolf and elk.

Wolf was a teacher. It was so important to the Native American that in sign language, the gesture for wolf, two fingers extended, also was the base of the sign for other important words or concepts, such as spirit, hunt, scout, strategy and warfare. When Ohiyesa's uncle was teaching him to hunt, he advised the youth to be like the wolf and "take a second look at everything you see."[11] So wolf imparted sight, such as scouting skill, and it imparted wisdom.

Horse was another "male animal" and it was believed if a woman rode a fast horse she would ruin it and the family would never proper.[12] There is more practicality to this injunction than superstition. Women used their horses differently. They needed them for hauling heavy loads. They needed stability. A slow, sure, even-footed gait was more important than speed, and they would have trained their horses that way.

Similar prohibitions surrounded bear. Women were not supposed to handle bear hide. If they did, the skin suffered no ill effects; the women did, becoming grumpy and irascible like a bear. However, there are documented instances when women did handle bearskin; for instance, when four Dakota women presented bear hides to Pierre Radisson and his fellow traders in 1660. Similarly, Ohiyesa described a woman who claimed to have bear medicine and she owned a bear-tooth necklace. Both suggest that such prohibitions were not hard and fast, but varied between bands and between lodges or societies.

The animals the *Oceti Sakawin* chose to emulate tells a great deal about their society. It is women, like buffalo, banding together that form the backbone of the herd. In the plains, it was buffalo who fed the people, provided their wealth. Dakota women were the property owners. Through their labors, they brought prosperity, turning a simple piece of leather into a beaded work of art. Through their toil, their families were fed, and through their bodies, they brought new life into the community, giving them their greatest wealth, their people.

Meanwhile the hunts and the warriors (men) were represented by wolves. Wolf endowed its bearer with the power of speed and endurance. Sitting Bull was among the warriors who claimed special protection from the wolf, with whom he could converse. He composed a song for it after he had pulled two arrows from a wounded animal.[13]

Wolf gave strength through the solidarity of the pack. It was associated with war; hence the use of the spirit/wolf hand signal in American sign language as basis as the sign for war. According to tradition, wolf created the wind when it howled. When it howled a second time, its voice brought forth fog. So wolf could lend invisibility to a war party, and its power was invoked by member of the *Hanskaska* society. Since wolf presided over the affairs of war,[14] a man with wolf medicine was called upon to invoke its power as a party set out on the warpath. Many warriors painted their faces with a smear of red across eyes and mouth to emulate a wolf after a successful hunt, with blood across muzzle and snout, and so invoke its power.

The Dakota perception of an animal's power came from keen observation of species habits, which led to some interesting connections and not immediately fathomable associations. The Lakota perceived a link between the swallow, the woodpecker, cocoon and moth, butterfly, dragonfly and spider's web. These animals were, in turn, allied with the *Heyoka* coyote. Because the swallow "flew before storm" and the woodpecker beat a tattoo before it arrived and gave a particular cry that warned people of its coming, both birds became associated with thunder and vicariously with lightning, or *Heyoka*. The cocoon resembled the whirlwind, the tornado, hence storm, which also made it *Heyoka*. The emergent moth became associated with whirlwind by extension. Its beating wings and bouncing progress evoked air currents. Similarly dragonfly and butterfly became associated with wind, whirlwind and storm. The whirlwind muddied the mind and was invoked to confuse the enemy. Once linked to storm, they became indirectly associated with the *Heyoka* spirit, coyote, who had provided one of the songs for the Sun Dance ceremony. *Heyoka* warrior Sitting Bull wrote songs for both the thunderbirds and the woodpecker who, he believed, had saved him from a bear in a dream.[15]

Meanwhile the spider's web and cobweb withstood the onslaught of wind and rain. Arrows, even bullets, passed through it and left the web relatively intact, so it came to represent strength and protection. These symbols were used on children's robes to protect them, and when placed on the warrior's shield or incorporated into the design of his shirt, it made the person impervious to all missiles that might be thrown his way.

Inktomi, as spider, had his lessons to convey to man. Of the divines, *Ksa cum Inktomi* is often dismissed as trickster. This is an over simplification of the tradition, which saw clever Inktomi as one of the most complex of all sacred creatures. Meanwhile observation revealed spiders in many forms, unlike wolf or even buffalo who had one basic shape. There were tiny spiders, scarcely bigger

One legend of the Dakota claims the tribe descended from the eagle. The story is one of the many universal flood myths, where the last woman married the eagle who had rescued her from the turbulent waters. It is the juvenile form of the bald eagle, *wambli gleska* or spotted eagle, that supplied the feathers for Dakota headdresses. Photographic print published between 1900 and 1930 and taken by S. Sexton, photographer, that forms part of the Frank and Frances Carpenter collection (Library of Congress).

than the head of a pin, and large spiders; those which were delicate with frail, spindly legs and those whose with thick legs and bodies that were covered in fur.

Similarly spiders had successfully occupied every environment. They built their homes everywhere. They built webs in trees and in rocks. Some species made their nests in water, surrounded by protective pockets of air. Others, like the wolf spider, hid in dens underneath the earth. Some could fly, weaving parachutes of silk which they could shoot into the air and float upon the breeze. Indeed, wily spider had conquered each element and been able to make it home. Who better, then, to lead man onto the planet? Who better to teach them its ways than the one who could reach into every corner of the environment? Even though a mischievous being at the best of times, Inktomi actually does more good than harm. Despite obvious differences, the two animals, spider and coyote, became linked, both known as tricksters.

Those people who dreamt of coyote, Wakinayan or lightning, were deemed *Heyoka*. Simply stated, *Heyoka* refers to backwards thinking and backwards doing. Those with coyote medicine were the tribal clowns, and it was their solemn duty to teach by example, albeit the wrong one. By doing things opposite from the way it would be expected, they made people laugh while leaving their audience to ponder the consequences of flouting tribal traditions.

This group also included the mad who were considered sacred by virtue of special medicine and protected by the tribe, although some believed they were infected by bad spirits. However, the insane were fed, clothed, even revered, for it was believed that they heard the voices of the gods. Their opinion was sought, even if it was taken by doing the reverse of that which was advised. Thus, the native exhibited a humanity not found in white culture even today. The insane were accepted as part of the tribe rather than isolated, exiled or hidden away in shame. Contrast the images of Bedlam and the British madwoman in the attic with a picture of an individual warm, fed and honored in such a way that they become integral to their community.

All animals had their tale to tell, their moral to be learned. The meadowlark was the herald of the south, the bringer of good things; it imparted clarity. Sitting Bull believed the meadowlark had a special relationship with the Lakota and often lectured his men to be kind to them. Sitting Bull also had a special affinity for other birds and composed a song for bob o links.[16] In *Lakota Belief and Ritual,* Red Rabbit stated that meadowlarks were *Okaga's* (south) *akitcita* and the crane his messenger who held many of the same attributes of the meadowlark.[17]

Even the prairie chicken with its fanciful mating dance had a power that was associated with love, as was the song of the whippoorwill. The singing of frog brought rain. Lowly gopher darting from cover to cover represented indecision and distraction, while skunk was noted for its bravery. According to Joseph Epes Brown, skunks possessed the same no-flight quality as the badger, and its skin attached to the heel was a warrior's promise to the people not to flee battle.[18]

While eagle feathers symbolized constancy and virtue, only those who had special power to do mysterious things were allowed to wear hawk feathers. Thus, it imparted a connection to the divine.[19]

In one tale recorded by Marie L. McLaughlin, the rabbit nation was overrun by other animals, so it symbolized cowardice and fear and, because of some obvious attributes, it also evoked images of love. The rabbit dance was one of the few dances where men and women danced together. Rabbits also had their positive aspect and were admired for their agility and for perceived humility.

Even goats who lived in the mountainous regions outside the range of the Lakota for much of their history were prized and represented by a society. Men who dreamt of goats were sure-footed and agile, and had special abilities to scale heights.

Fox, like wolf, was associated with war. It represented persistence. It was believed to have a gentler spirit than wolf, which suggested protection of the tribe. Thus, the Kit Fox or *Tokala* society was an *akitcita* society rather than a warrior society. Because it had its dens underground, fox had knowledge of things hidden from view and had an affinity for roots and herbs that could cure.

Many medicines contained both dark and light elements, such as owl medicine. Owl had the ability to see in the dark. Its appearance near a village was believed to be a precursor of death. Its hooting near a camp meant a ghost was near. This association with death was based on fact. The hoot of an owl, as one of the easiest for man to emulate, was used to signal a night attack. An owl's presence at night would not have been considered foreign or strange. However, one ignored it to one's peril, and Ohiyesa described the entire tribe going on alert when an owl was heard near the camp. Owl, with its night vision and its connection to death, gave its bearer a certain kind of sight that allowed him to see what was normally hidden from view. Its link with darkness suggested the dark arts. An owl appeared in a dream to the founder of one of the most important warrior societies, the *Miwatani* society. Thus, its medicine could be good, and the talent to see beyond the immediately apparent was an important skill for a warrior and a hunter to have.

To obtain the feathers required for their regalia, the plains tribes hunted the eagle by going to a height and digging a hole large enough to house a man, over which a mat would be laid and prey staked. The eagle would land to collect the prey and the hunter would leap from cover and strangle it. Although eagle attacks on man would have been rare, the parent with eggs or young to protect would have vigorously defended the nest. The above picture, titled **Dazed by an eagle's unexpected attack**, shows a golden eagle swooping down on an Indian hunter. From a stereograph copyrighted by C.L. Wasson (International Stereograph Co.), December 4, 1908.

Prohibitions often surrounded different animals. Weasel endowed its bearer with cunning, but contact with weasel skin was supposed to make a man, or a menstruating woman, ill. To hurt or kill a mountain lion carried a curse which doomed the perpetrator to suffer a crippling injury. Snake too brought bad luck, yet the Sacred Bow Society was based on snake.[20] Raven was watchful and crow observant, desirable qualities in a warrior, represented by the *akitcita* society, the Crow Owners. The regalia of the Omaha society included crow skins.[21] When an arrow was loosed, crow was invoked, and camp sentinels wore raven skins as insignia, although many associated the birds with black magic.

Badger imparted strength and tenacity, and was represented by the *Ihoka akitcita* society. It also gave the ability to cure, using roots and herbs. Bear was endowed with these same powers; but because badger was small, its ability to heal was associated with children. The chart below gives some of the major mentors and their associated powers.[22]

While a family as a whole could claim heritage through the maternal grandmother, most animal associations were not bequeathed to the next generation. Neither was a name, although it could be adopted after a death. If a person's father was known as Lone Wolf, this did not automatically mean that the sons would take the name or that the family grouping had the wolf as a power animal. It is only since the beginning of the U.S. census of Native Americans, in the mid–1800s, that the name of the head of the household — usually, but not always, an animal name — became the family name or last name that was passed on the next generation. In essence, this made the Lakota way of naming through vision quest illegal.

Name	*Animal*	*Attributes & Powers*
Tatanka	great buffalo	Strength, plenty
Mato	bear	Healing, medicinal herbs
Wambli	spotted eagle	Messenger to the divine
Sungmanitu	wolf	Warrior, teacher, pathfinder
Mica	coyote	Joker, *Heyoka*, "backwards thinking"
Sunka	dog	Protection, friendship, cunning
Hehakamale	elk	Sexuality, endurance
Capo	beaver	Industry and fidelity
Cetan	hawk	Speed, endurance
Zuzeca	snake	Lying, deception
Hnaska	frog	Occult powers, rain
Hogan	fish	Ablution, cleanliness, waters
Keya	turtle	Life, surgery

One notion that has taken root in the American psyche is that a native child was named after the first thing a woman saw after the baby's birth, which in turn delineated his character. Romantic, but untrue. Ohiyesa described the process by which an individual earned a name. "Indian names were either characteristic nicknames given in playful spirit, deed names, birth names or such as have religious and symbolic meaning. It has been said that when a child is born, some accident or unusual appearance determines his name. This is sometimes the case, but is not the rule. A man of forcible character, with a fine war record, usually bears the name of the buffalo or bear, lightning or some dread natural force. Another of more peaceful nature may be called Swift Bird or Blue Sky. A woman's name usually suggested something about the home, often with the adjective 'pretty' or 'good,' and a feminine termination. Names of any dignity or importance must be conferred by the old men, and especially so if they have spiritual significance, as Sacred Cloud, Mysterious Night, Spirit Woman, and the like. Such a name was sometimes borne by three generations, but each individual had to prove that he was worthy of it."[23]

In 1831, Sitting Bull was originally called Jumping Badger. Eventually, he earned the name *Hunkesni*, or "slow," for his resolute nature.[24] A child may also receive a name for the circumstances surrounding his or her birth. Thus, Charles Eastman (Ohiyesa) was first known as *Hakadah*, "the pitiful last," when he was born[25] because his mother died immediately after his birth, so he was the last to be born of that particular union.

Rarely did a person bear the same name throughout his or her life. Indeed, an individual could have several names. None necessarily supplanted the previous, but all had to be earned, at first by traits or characteristics, later, after some deed which typified or could be said to represent the individual. Not all names were animal, but many were. Another misconception was that all young men received a new name when they "cried for a vision" as part of a rite of passage from youth to adulthood. Not completely true. Some may not have had a vision, for not all such quests were successful and not all pleas to the Mysteries were heard. Or the individual may have received information on his life direction, but not necessarily a name. The name may come later.

Like their animal mentors, a person may have had more than one name. He or she may have had a "little name," usually one given at birth, subsequent names, having to do with physical attributes, acts or deeds, and a spirit name. The European mind may have a hard time with the idea of shifting names, but it reflected the concept of evolution where the name changed as the individual grew and developed. Names were rarely used in everyday speech except when discussing an absent third party.

The wolf dance pictured here is that of the Cheyenne who, at the time this photograph was taken, had long been allied to the plains Lakota. Both the Lakota and the Santee had a wolf dance; wolf was invoked before the war parties and before the hunt. For all aboriginal peoples, it was believed that the wearing of skins endowed the wearer with the animal's powers and its skills. From a photographic print c. 1927 by Edward S. Curtis. Part of the Library of Congress Edward S. Curtis Collection. Published in *The North American Indian,* Edward S. Curtis (Seattle, Wash.), Edward S. Curtis, 1907–30, v. 19, p. 136.

People received their animal mentors, and often their names, through waking visions or sleeping dreams. In a vision, the animal that appeared could be an animal essence, one that is envisioned, or it could be one that was physically present at that time — the eagle soaring overhead or the tiny ant that crawled across the ground at one's feet. Little distinction was made between the two. It was assumed if the real animal appeared, it was no coincidence. A spirit name may then given by the holy man which was never even spoken aloud. It was not shared with another besides the individual who bestowed it. The name was sacred, and the secret to be kept between the recipient and his maker.

The Dakota used the name as they used rituals and medicine bundles to invoke an animal's power. They were neither strange nor unique in this. Many cultures have endowed animals with godlike powers. The Egyptian gods had not only a human form, but a half-human form as they took on not only the characteristics, but also the appearance of the animal involved.

One has only to reach far enough back in time to find beliefs held and rites used similar to those of the Sioux in Old World culture. In ritual and rite, the green man of England revealed himself as a hart, or of a half-man, half-deer. The huntsman emulated the green man in order to solicit his power, or he dressed the part of the animal to gain supremacy over it. The Viking berserker is another example: he wore a bearskin shirt ("bear-sark") to take on the animal's strength in battle.

Even as late as post–Roman, Christian Europe, when the hunt was the privilege of the nobility and kings, prey animals were imbued with such mystical power that they found their way into Christian Mystery plays as symbols. The gentle hind represented virtuous women, just as buffalo embodied chastity for Dakota women. Heraldry, or the "rules of blazon" for coats of arms, also contain numerous animal representations. The definitions attributed to the species within the context of heraldry reflect the European views of the period, and probably evolved from the rites of old, which reveals a universality in human beliefs.

As always, the Dakota people exhibited a keen awareness of their surroundings, which included the various species that lived with them. They treated the animals upon whom they must depend for their livelihood with respect. Through observation, they learned their behaviors and their traits, and from these they surmised their powers. The Dakota did not divorce man from his environment; they embraced it and honored all who dwelled therein.

9. Politics and Trade

Long ago, the people of the plains ran short of arrowheads, and they could not hunt. Two young men, one thoughtful, the other brash, walked along a high hill discussing their plight. They heard the ringing of stone against rock in the distance and paused to investigate. Studying the horizon they spied a large spider who was busily breaking apart flint and fashioning arrowheads.

The young men approached the rock upon which the spider was perched. He took no notice of them and continued to work upon the stone. The impulsive warrior was incensed, for he did not like being ignored. "Let us kill him and take his arrowheads away."

"No," said the thoughtful one, "he is doing no harm. In fact, he is being quite industrious making the arrowheads we need so badly."

The first man scoffed and challenged the other. "You are afraid. Look. He cannot hurt you," said the first. "See what happens when I strike out against him." The brave took a stone and threw it at the spider. It smacked the creature hard against the side, and the spider spun onto its back.

Then as the young men watched, the spider rolled back onto its feet, got up and scowled at them. The impulsive brave laughed. "He does not seem to like us very much."

The cautious man considered the spider and his poisonous glance for a moment. Then he placed his hand on his friend's arm. "Come, friend, let us leave the animal in peace."

The men hurried down the hill. As they walked, the first man was taken with a fit of coughing and could not stop. Blood spattered from his mouth, coloring his lips red. He coughed and coughed until the blood came in great gushes, and he fell upon the ground dead.

The circumspect youth hastened back to the village and reported all that he had seen. Friends and relatives returned to the hillside and found the brash fellow's body, which they placed upon a travois and took home.

A council was called and they sent for the chief of spiders, Inktomi (Unktomi). The spider listened and then, after the chief had relayed the tale of the fallen soldier, Inktomi replied: "There is nothing I can do. The spider was just defending himself."

The chiefs nodded as the spider chief continued: "Friends, when I saw that your tribe was running short of arrowheads, I set my people to work making them so we could trade. When engaged in this work, the spiders do not wish to be disturbed, and your young man not only disturbed my man, but grossly insulted him by striking him with one of the arrowheads he had just fashioned. No man, not mine, not yours, will take such an insult lightly so he shot the braggart with tiny arrowheads that produced a hemorrhage."

The chiefs muttered among themselves, discussing the issue until they decided that the spider was well within his rights to defend himself. The Dakota had lost a fine warrior, but as a man he was rash and inconsiderate of others.

They announced their decision, and Inktomi replied: "There is much wisdom in your words. Now, if you will pass the pipe, we may part as friends, and my people will return to work fashioning arrowheads for you."

The woodland Dakota, like the Carolinian Santee, were canoe Indians. The canoe allowed them to travel great distances with relative ease, so the Dakota were able to attend trade fairs as far east as the St. Lawrence River. It was believed that the canoe allowed the eastern Siouan tribes to traverse the Great Lakes in the migration east and south. The photograph shows a family paddling a birch-bark canoe, similar to those used by some of the Dakota tribes. (Carl Gustav Linde photographic print, May 5, 1913.)

> *The pipe was smoked and the deal struck, and to this day whenever braves hear ticking in the grass they give it wide berth, for they would not disturb the creatures who perform a valuable service making arrowheads for their friends and allies, the Dakota.*[1]

This tale celebrates one of the cardinal virtues, *woksape* or wisdom, which must of necessity include caution and circumspection. Wisdom was of special import when meeting someone new, for who knew when a friend would become an enemy, or conversely when an enemy could be turned into a friend? In pre–European America trade meant alliance, so Inkotmi's promises of trade was more than an offer of friendship; it was a treaty which, once made, was sealed in the classic way: with the sacred pipe.

In *The Frontier Exchange Economy of the Lower Mississippi,* David H. Usner confirmed the connection between trade and alliance in the New World by describing the consequences of its lack: "For the Indians, exchanges of material goods represented political reciprocity between autonomous groups, while the absence of trade was synonymous with a state of war."[2]

The same can be said of modern times. Consider the trade embargo used as international sanction. Conflict versus trade alliance has been reflected by U.S. trade relations with the Middle East throughout the latter part of the twentieth century and the beginning of the twenty-first. The U.S. traded freely with Iraq in the 1980s and provided technology and intelligence to support its war against Iran. Later, when Iraq became viewed as a threat, sanctions were implemented against it in the form of a trade embargo until hostilities increased enough to precipitate a state of war.

The modern perspective of native trade tends to dismiss the first peoples of this continent as economically naïve and to incorrectly assume that trade before the arrival of the white man was a loose, haphazard, almost accidental affair of random encounters to which the white man brought order. Nothing could be further from the truth. Routes of international trade had been long established before white men arrived on this continent. The widespread use of the Clovis point across North America indicates not only interaction between peoples, but suggests the paleo–Indians of 14,000 years ago participated in a continent-wide exchange of ideas and materials.

The politics of each period was also shaped by territory, and an area's desirability was influenced by trade. One tribe would move into another's territory if it contained commodities that could be exchanged profitably elsewhere. Trade, along with the migration of language groups, was similarly affected by environment. The boundary map of the Americas was a fluid, mobile picture where cultures developed and devolved, and another would rush in to take the place of a fading one, just as it has been in the Europe of the past. Today modern borders continue to fluctuate, and one-time Yugoslavia has been broken into component parts, divided along former "national" lines.

Thus trade, territory and politics in the Old World and the New must be viewed not only against the backdrop of community and culture as a whole, but as a continuum developing from an ancient past. Consider the Tigris and Euphrates region which gave birth first to the Assyrian culture which was then replaced by the Babylonian and Sumerian civilizations. The land was overrun, becoming part of other empires until it became present-day Iraq. The Americas followed a similar pattern, outlined in the following chart.

> **Peru:** Caral 2600 to 1300 BCE → Chavin 1000 to 200 BCE → Nazca 200 BCE to 600 CE → Moche 100 to 800 CE → Wari (Huari) 700 to 1000 CE → Inca 1200 to 1500 CE
>
> **Mexico:** (Yucatan) Mayan culture 2600 BCE–1300 CE; (Plateau) Olmec 1200–500 BCE → Toltec 900–1200 CE → Aztec 1200–1600s
>
> **U.S.:** *Midwest*: Hopewell 100 BCE–500 CE → Oneota 500–1000 CE → Mississippi 900–1300 CE *Southeast*: Etowah 600–1600; Natchez 700–1730

Climate often dictated both the migration of nations and the movement of goods for exchange. It precipitated the rise and fall of civilizations. For example, the coastal Moche of northern Peru were destroyed by *El Niño* floods. The climate also provided the impetus for trade and influenced the items available to be traded. It motivated the formation of alliances to accomplish mutually beneficial goals. Climatic change usually coincided with transitional periods in Native American culture, often as a result of the gain or loss of local commodities.

Between 5000 and 3000 BCE average global temperatures reached their maximum level during the Holocene period, and were 1 to 2° Celsius warmer than they are today. Some of the first documented civilizations arose in this period. The ceremonial center found at Caral, Peru (circa 2600 BCE), dates from this period, while Mayan culture emerged farther north on the Yucatan peninsula.

Excavations in Nebraska indicate that, starting around 5000 BCE, the plains were predominantly agrarian, the landscape dotted with farms. Trade in corn established its cultivation further north. From 3000 to 2000 BCE a cooling trend occurred which caused large drops in sea level and an increase in coastal lands. The wetter weather inland continued to support farming and trading communities already present on the prairies.

A slight cooling trend from 1500 to 750 BCE caused renewed ice growth in continental and alpine glaciers. The sea level dropped two to three meters below present-day levels. The climate became dryer. The Olmec Empire, with their fine stoneworkers, developed in Mexico around 1200 BCE. Their civilization continued through 500 BCE. Further south in Peru, the Chavin culture emerged (1000 BCE to 200 BCE). They created a great stone temple complex and city with some three thousand people. Their artisans traded extensively. Goods from Chavin are found hundreds of miles north and south of the city.

The Nazca (200 BCE to 600 CE) filled the gap left by the fall of the Peruvian Chavin. Meanwhile the Mayan people and international trade continued to flourish. Textiles from the Nazca Indians, consider finer than anything produced in Europe at the same time, have been found in Mayan settlements, and items of Mayan manufacture have been located further north in New Mexico.

The mound-building cultures of both Egypt and the Americas appeared during the Halocene period. It is believed that temple building and pyramid mounds came to North America with Mayan and later Aztec trade. The south was the first affected. In the southeast the major mound-builders, the Etowah culture, rose in 600 BCE and continued through 700 CE. The more northern Hopewell mound-building culture appeared around 100 BCE and thrived to 500 CE, indicating stable communities based in trade and agriculture.

From the contents of North American mounds, the commodities traded and the routes followed can be traced. Deposits of copper in almost a pure state were mined in the Isle Royal region of Michigan and traded around Lake Superior in the north to the Gulf of Mexico in the south. Shells were brought from the Atlantic shore. Large conch shells from the Gulf region made their way up to an area that includes present-day Ohio and Illinois. Alligator teeth, fossil shark teeth and barracuda jaws from Florida and Louisiana were also found in Ohio mounds. From the far west (New Mexico and Wyoming), traders acquired obsidian, while grizzly bear teeth made their way east from the Rockies.[3] Thus, goods crisscrossed the continent.

In the west, the Anasazi culture of the American southwest developed around 500 BCE and continued to 1300 CE. The Mayan culture reached its peak in the classic period (200 to 950 CE) and declined thereafter, although remnants still existed when Columbus landed on Mexico's shore. Throughout this time, they continued to trade with tribes further north and along the coastal region. There are indicators that they made it as far east as Florida. Elsewhere, the Mississippi culture emerged from the ashes of the Hopewell, thriving through what is known as the Medieval Warm Period (900–1000 CE). Hopewell mounds are found in a territory from Arkansas to Wisconsin.

Later the Toltec civilization (900 CE–1200 CE) replaced the failing Mayan Empire, only to dwindle and vanish within three hundred years. The Aztec moved south around 1200 to fill the void. Their culture lasted until the sixteenth century. They were present when the first European explorers arrived and had developed thriving trade in the region. The Aztec traded with the Anasazi, who carried their goods to the Caddo of the southern plains region, who, in turn, traded further north. In the east, one branch of the Santee became firmly established in South Carolina by 1100 and were one of the many mound-building cultures. The Carolina Santee held trade fairs and attended those of others.

The next climatic transition, the Little Ice Age, began around 1300 CE and lasted until the mid–nineteenth century. The Little Ice Age would have placed pressures on the population, particularly in the northeast where it was believed its effects were most felt. The cooling trend may have caused the downfall of the Mississippi civilization and the Anasazi, for it was in the early fourteenth century that the Mississippi culture began to disintegrate and the Pueblo people replaced the Anasazi, when the Athapaskin-speaking tribes of northwestern Canada began arriving in the Four Corners region and took over the trade routes between Mexico and the north.

The profound influence of the Little Ice Age in the late period was well documented in the accounts of the European settlers, along with Lakota winter counts. The earliest references were found in the No Ears count of 1773: "when even dogs had sore eyes," indicating late snows. Extreme cold was mentioned again in 1784 and 1789. One authority ascribes the year when many pregnant women died (1799) to cold. The Big Missouri winter count described 1809 when

Lintrium conficiendorum ratio. XII.

Ea est in VIRGINIA cymbas fabricandi ratio: nam cum ferreis instrumentis aut aliis nostris similibus careant, eas tamen parant nostris non minus commodas ad nauigandum quo lubet per flumina & ad piscandum. Primum arbore aliqua crassa & alta delecta, pro cymba quam parare volunt magnitudine, ignem circa eius radices summa tellure in ambitu struunt ex arborum musco bene resiccato, & ligni assulis paulatim ignem excitantes, ne flamma altius ascendat, & arboris longitudinem minuat. Pane adusta & ruinam minante arbore, nouum suscitant ignem, quem flagrare sinunt, donec arbor sponte cadat. Adustis deinde arboris fastigio & ramis, vt truncus iustam longitudinem retineat, tignis transuersis supra furcas positis imponunt, ea altitudine vt commode laborare possint, tunc cortice conchis quibusdam adempto, integriorem trunci partem pro cymba inferiore parte seruant, in altera parte ignem secundum trunci longitudinem struunt, præterquam extremis, quod satis adustum illis videtur, restincto igne conchis scabunt, & nouo suscitato igne denuo adurunt, atque ita deinceps pergunt, subinde vrentes & scabentes, donec cymba necessarium alueum nacta sit. Sic Domini spiritus rudibus hominibus suggerit rationem, qua res in suum vsum necessarias conficere queant.

B 4

The Santee of the east were reputed to use the dugout canoe while the woodland Dakota used both the dugout and the birch-bark canoes. The type was dictated by the location of the tribe and the availability of materials. The print from White, titled *How they build boats*, shows native men of the east making dugout boats by burning and scraping. From the Library of Congress Rare Book Collection: Engraving by Theodor de Bry after a watercolor by John White in *Admiranda narratio, fida tamen, de commodis et incolarvm ritibvs Virginiæ*, Wecheli : svmtibvs T. de Bry, 1590, plate 12.

feed was so scarce, the horses had to eat bark, 1812 as the year when the snow was too deep to hunt buffalo and 1818 as the year ducks and geese froze in the sky.[4] No Ears recorded for the year 1822 an incident where a brave was forced to cut his leg off because of frostbite.[5] The following year, Big Missouri recounted a similar incident, and the year after that, the winter was so cold that they had to camp near a field of corn for food.[6] Further east, 1825 was recalled by the Europeans as "the year without a summer." In 1827 Iron Crow recounted the Winter of Deep Snow,[7] while the Big Missouri mentioned ice so thick that they couldn't use their horses to hunt.[8] In 1853, the Big Missouri winter count documented another winter where the snow was so deep and feed so scarce that nearly all the tribe's horses died.[9] The Little Ice Age lasted as late as the 1860s.

The dissolution of the Mississippi cultures during this mini-ice age created a vacuum. The Kansa, Osage, and Omaha tribes arrived in the plains/prairie border region during this time and absorbed some elements of the former Oneota tradition. Information gleaned in central Minnesota also suggests that the Yankton/Yanktonai Sioux were among the inheritors of Oneota traditions when they arrived in the region in the late 1600s. Climatic changes also drew the Dakota and Ojibwa south. The Quapaw and Ponca either followed or moved with the Osage, Kansa and Omaha into the area west of the Mississippi and settled around the Missouri River. Meanwhile the Illini inhabited a region that straddled the Mississippi.

Elsewhere other tribes jostled for position, migrating south and west even before the first Europeans hit the eastern seaboard. The drift would have increased bad relations between tribes. During this time the Dakota peoples would have bumped into different groups and formed opinions of them. As they migrated through other tribal lands they would have clashed over hunting rights, territory and commodities. By the time they settled around the Great Lakes, the Dakota would have developed trade partnerships, along with certain intertribal animosities.

Similarly the partitioning of the Siouan language often reflected both politics and trade of the period. Not all divisions were amicable and rifts often occurred. Many resulted in adversarial status between one-time allies, as found with both the Siouan Crow and the Assiniboin. Others were cordial as one band left with the blessing of the parent tribe in the search for territory and food, subsequently extending trade networks. Still, as time passed, differences in culture and tradition accrued until former linguistic cousins, friends and allies became foes.

At the time of the arrival of the white man on the continent, their neighbors included the Ojibwa (along the northern portion of the Great Lakes), the Menominee, the Potawatomi, the Mascouten, and the Winnebago (Wisconsin). The Sauk and Fox and Illini occupied a territory further south. The Dakota would have had interactions through trade with the Algonquin, Huron, Ottawa, Shawnee, Miami and Kickapoo. Meanwhile to their west lay the Cree, Crow, Hidatsa, Arikara, Mandan, Iowa, Ponca, Cheyenne and Omaha, with whom they also exchanged goods.

Their position between two great waterways, the Mississippi River and the Great Lakes, put the Dakota at a natural crossroads, turning them into middlemen in exchange between the tribes of the western plains and those of the woodlands further east. From the west, trade in obsidian and bear teeth continued. In 1766, Captain Jonathan Carver was amazed to see seashells adorning the clothes of the inland tribes.[10] The presence of dentalium shells—used as a medium of exchange by the Salish tribes of the Pacific Northwest—in the Midwest confirms an east-west trade route that led all the way to the coast. Meanwhile goods from the eastern seaboard made their way west.

Therefore, pre–European America can be seen as a vast network of interlocking trade routes and commerce in which the Dakota took an active part. Trade centers had been long established. In the 1500s Tadoussac, in present-day Quebec where the Saguenay and St. Lawrence Rivers meet, was an active trading center. The Cree held fairs near Lakes Winnipeg and Manitoba, exchanging goods from the lower Red and Saskatchewan Rivers eastward to the country of the Muskegon tribe around Hudson Bay, with whom the Dakota were familiar. Another trade center had been maintained for centuries before the arrival of the Europeans at Michilimakinac (Lake Superior) in present-day upper-peninsula Michigan. Michilimakinac was among the favorite of all the Dakota tribes, except the Wahpekute who traded at Prairie du Chien, along the Mississippi River in southern Wisconsin. The Dakota also held their own trade fairs at Blue Earth in Minnesota, as they attended those of other tribes.

Similar centers existed all across the continent, which often gave the resident tribe supremacy over others since they controlled a strategic intersection on the trade route. Such a point existed near the Congaree River in the Carolinas, where Siouan Occaneecchee and Cawtaba became the languages of commerce. In 1670, the Occaneechees dominated the region as they dominated an important ford on the main path between coastal Virginia and inland markets.[11]

During the first century of European exploration, the Spanish focused their efforts in South America. In 1546, Francisco Coronado came as far north as present-day Lindsborg, Kansas, meeting the Quivera, another trading people in the north-south exchange network of the plains. The first link in the southwest, the Athapaskin, became the Navajo and Apache. Pueblo and the plains Apache trade was established in 1601.[12] Further east the Natchez acted as intermediaries between the southern Gulf Coast, the eastern seaboard and tribes further west, and had done so for centuries. Present-day Mobile, Alabama, lying near the mounds of the Etowah, was another center that was still maintained long after the culture had vanished. At the time of early European settlers, Mobile lent its name to the trade language or *lingua franca* of the region, Mobilian.[13]

Trade Routes and Trade Centers—Indian trade routes crisscrossed the continent, allowing the movement of merchandise from one coast to another through a series of trade centers and intermediaries. The map above shows the major centers, where the Dakota (highlighted) and the Eastern Siouan peoples traded, along with the routes that linked them. Near the Great Lakes, the Dakota were well placed to act as intermediaries, and their connection to adjacent fairs and major trade routes allowed them access to coastal goods. The centers shown are by no means all that existed. Trade centers would have dotted the coastlines and the major waterways, the Mississippi and the Ohio River Valley. It is believed that the Aztecs traded along the Gulf Coast as far east as Florida. Their goods and ideas made their way up the Mississippi to the north. The Salish people of the west coast traded with the tribes of British Columbia up into Alaska, and they traded further south. The Shoshone and Ute also held fairs. Each provided a vital link in a north-south route between the Aztec and the tribes of the interior plains. Meanwhile the Shoshone also traded with the tribes of the Pacific Northwest and carried their goods east.

In the Pacific Northwest, along the Columbia River basin, Chinook became the Language of trade, until a mixture of "Indian, English, French and Spanish" replaced it.[14] The Algonquin-speaking Blackfoot became intermediaries between the tribes of the northern Pacific coast and those further east, as did the Assiniboin and the Crow in later periods. The Comanche eventually took over the network in the southwestern plains in Texas, with the Wichita Indians established as intermediaries further north. The Hidatsa, Mandan, and Arikara created trade centers along the Missouri River where the plains Lakota traded. In the southwest, the Pueblos of the Rio Grande held fairs in Arizona, New Mexico and Colorado.[15]

The allied Dakota tribes maintained their own trade network which operated both internally and "internationally." They held trade fairs and exchanged the acquired goods at Michilimakinac and at other centers along the St. Lawrence River. Before 1640, the Dakota Santee were happily placed, too far north to be of interest to the Spanish and far enough west to be beyond direct influence of the other European powers.

The later colonial powers—the British, French and Dutch—concentrated their efforts on the eastern coastal regions and along waterways via the Mississippi and the Great Lakes. As of 1700, only a few English traders had penetrated the Appalachian Mountains, and the Carolina Santee were numbered among the friendlier tribes.

However, white presence was felt by the woodland Dakota through the buffeting of tribes and through trade as they obtained European goods, mostly kettles and knives, through Indian intermediaries. The delay in contact left the Dakota technologically impoverished.

The Assiniboin broke away from the Yanktons some time before 1640 and found it impossible to remain neutral in the web of trade alliances that revolved around them. They quickly allied themselves with the gun-rich Cree over their gun-poor Nakota relations and went from allies to enemies in a relatively short time.[16] The Assiniboin remained the middlemen for European goods to the plains Algonquin, putting them at odds with their parent tribe, the Yankton. When the Cree lost their monopoly on the gun trade, the Assiniboin switched their allegiance to the Siouan Crow.

In the 1650s, the Great Lakes region became an asylum for many people displaced by the Iroquois, including the Fox, Potawatomi, Ottawa, Mascouten, Kickapoo, Miami and Huron. Without firearms, the Dakota and their territory were considered easy pickings. The Dakota saw their first guns in the hands of the Huron around this same time (1650),[17] as they struggled to break the Algonquins' domination over European trade in order to obtain this valuable resource.[18] Other tribes, such as the Ojibwa and the Cree, advanced quickly into the Dakota territory after acquiring European firearms and were unwilling to give up their monopoly on the gun trade to the Dakota without a fight.

The Menominee tribe, descendants of the "Copper Indians" of old, were also victims of immigration pressure before Europeans ever appeared in their villages. In Wisconsin, the Menominee and the Winnebago were subject to incursions from the Sauk and Fox and the Dakota as trade or its lack fueled animosities.

The Dakota first traded directly with the French, who approached them from the north. Indeed, by 1656, the Wisconsin and upper Michigan tribes (Ottawa, Wyandot, Ojibwa, Potawatomi, Fox, Sauk, Kickapoo, and Mascouten) were in a state of rebellion due to French trade with the Dakota. The Santee were among the participants of the Feast of the Dead trade fair, recorded by Pierre Radisson in 1660, along with some eighteen other Indian nations. Notably Dakota tribal elders asked for guns (thunder) from the French to be used against their avowed enemies, the Cree. "The Sioux made speeches, presented gifts of beaver skin, and promised to be faithful allies...."[19] But the French were more interested in maintaining the peace with the Cree than arming the Sioux against them. At the time, the Cree were largest and most important tribe in Canada, part of the Algonquin group and closely related to their southern neighbors the Ojibwa. Their territory included the Canadian provinces of Manitoba and Saskatchewan, making them direct competitors of the Santee, in both trade and territory.

The Illini also felt the bite of competition from the Dakota. Having discovered a rich source of fur in the Dakota homeland, the French remained indifferent to their former trade partners, the Illini, as they were beset by the many dispossessed tribes. As a result, the Illini turned and focused their aggression against the rival Dakota along the upper Mississippi in an attempt to recover lost trade.

In the 1600s, the medium of exchange with white traders was beaver. What a skin could purchase had been standardized by fur company policy, although the rate of exchange depended upon the size of the fort. At a large fort, twelve skins were traded to obtain a single gun. Ten skins bought a gun at a medium-sized fort and eight at the smallest. The size of an item also influenced price. For example: one beaver skin purchased a "pound" of kettle; however, since iron kettles weighed many pounds, they became costly items and the larger the kettle the greater the price. The following chart gives the "company standard" during Radisson's time.[20]

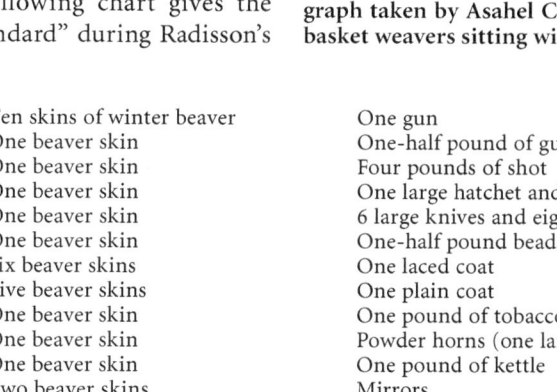

Skins were not the only things traded at the great trade fairs. Samuel Pond spoke of the artistry of the Dakota women, whose skills included basket making. Baskets of woven bark were used for storage of grain, and women also wove cloth from the bark of nettles or from basswood bark which was softened by boiling. This photograph taken by Asahel Curtis in 1910 shows two Indian basket weavers sitting with their ware.

Ten skins of winter beaver	One gun
One beaver skin	One-half pound of gunpowder
One beaver skin	Four pounds of shot
One beaver skin	One large hatchet and one small
One beaver skin	6 large knives and eight jackknives
One beaver skin	One-half pound beads
Six beaver skins	One laced coat
Five beaver skins	One plain coat
One beaver skin	One pound of tobacco
One beaver skin	Powder horns (one large and two small)
One beaver skin	One pound of kettle
Two beaver skins	Mirrors

When the Iroquois retreated east after the "beaver wars"—which was, in fact, the first American trade war—the many refugee tribes did not return to their homelands because the French fur traders refused to open new posts in the east and actively discouraged their allies from leaving Wisconsin for fear of losing their trade to the British. In so doing, they forced the refugees to look elsewhere for the beaver that the French demanded in exchange for goods, inadvertently focusing the competing tribes' attentions on the beaver-rich rice lakes of the Dakota in the west and the fertile soils of the Illini in the south.

Few realize that the move of the unmounted Lakota Titowan and Nakota Yanktonai onto the Minnesota plains was fueled not by the presence of buffalo, but by the region's abundant beaver population whose skins were so desired by the European traders. By 1685, the western Lakota and Nakota controlled an area from the Minnesota River in Minnesota to the head of the Yellowstone south to the Republican River. Lakota and Nakota beaver skins were traded to the Minnesota Santee in exchange for European goods. The Santee in turn acquired luxury goods from their Algonquin neighbors or directly from the French and took them back to the prairie tribes.

Dakota influence on trade was undervalued by their French "overlords." Writing in 1701, Pierre D'Iberville, governor of the Louisiana territories whose lands included the entire Mississippi Valley, viewed the Sioux as useless to them in trade and proposed moving them west to the Missouri River. To accomplish this goal, he said: "When they come to us, it will be necessary to bring them into subjection, make no presents, and compel them to do what we wish."[21]

By 1700, the Yankton monopolized the exchange of an extremely precious commodity, pipestone, from which came the sacred pipe or calumet. At this time, the Titowan had become the preeminent trappers of the prairies, a situation that lasted until 1796 when Jean Baptiste Truteau described them still as "primarily trappers and traders who also hunted."[22]

At that same time, the Lakota and Nakota had managed to break the Assiniboin-Cree monopoly on firearms. Still the Titowan, Yanktonai and the Yankton continued to trade their beaver pelts at fairs set up by the woodland Santee at Blue Earth, Minnesota. The efficiency of the Dakota distribution system is substantiated by trader Peter Pond, who spent the winter of 1775 among the Yankton, the people of the end. As the name suggests, the tribe lived in the most remote regions of Dakota territory and had limited direct interaction with Europeans, yet Pond found them using brass kettles and trade cloth.[23]

The Dakota devised a system of standardized units to calculate length, which they used in trade. Items were measured from ear to the longest finger, with the head turned sideways to ensure the maximum length. Poles and canoes were determined by the length of the arms fully extended to the sides. They also used the hand's breath as the Europeans had in the past. They shared with the Romans "the pace," which later became our yard. The Dakota, however, paced distance with legs extended wide, side to side, rather than the forward step used by the Romans. In 1834, Samuel Pond described as the process as laborious and rarely used.[24]

Thus, it can be seen that commerce among the tribes was sophisticated, an intricate affair in which the Dakota were one of the prime movers. Trade equaled politics and wars were fought to maintain trade with a specific trade partner.

Meanwhile, further south and west, the other plains tribes were taming another "technological marvel" left by the Spanish explorers, the pony. The Dakota exchanged goods with Mandan, Hidatsa and Arikaras in the west, who were well placed for the horse trade coming from the southwest and guns coming from the northeast. The Lakota traded with the Arikara, with whom they were often at war, which required a negotiated peace during the summer months; but they also remained true to their roots, using the Santee to obtain European luxury goods.

Trade based on family, friendship and alliance was motivated by a different set of values from profit. Samuel Pond described trade between the various bands in 1834: "The Dakota exchanged articles of property to a considerable extent among themselves.... All trade among them consisted in the exchange of goods, but nothing had a fixed value, and in bartering they did not always have regard to the relative value of goods exchanged."[25] He further observed, "There were few or none of the Dakota who made a practice of trading with their neighbors for the purpose of gain. The principle traffic of these Indians was with buffalo hunters, from whom they received tents, buffalo robes, and horses, in exchange for goods purchased from traders."[26]

The plains Lakota began trading for horses around 1707, an event important enough that it was noted in their winter count.[27] Prior to this time, horses had been acquired by stealing them from neighboring tribes, a fact also noted in their winter counts. The Lakota traded regularly with the Arikara for horses, although the Cheyenne claim to have been the tribe who introduced the western Titowan to horses. Still they were slow to adapt to their use. The first mounted war party recorded in Lakota winter counts did not occur until 1757, fifty years after their first trade.[28] The event initiated a cultural shift, particularly as the numbers of beaver found in the prairies began to decline in the last quarter of the eighteenth century. The Lakota had switched to hunting buffalo while the Yanktonai continued to trap beaver, abandoning buffalo grounds to move to places with an abundance of beaver.[29]

In the East the Dakota woodland Santee found themselves caught up the irresistible force of European conflict through trade. The Fox fought the French from 1701 through 1727, closing trade routes and many of forts,[30] which had a detrimental effect on the woodland Santee since it denied them access not only to trade, but to all-important ammunition and guns. The Dakota relationship with the Ojibwa was equally complex. Long-time enemies, on occasion the Santee fought side by side as allies of the Ojibwa, as they did against the United States during the Revolutionary War. They also traded with them, especially in the late period when the Santee adopted their style of dress. Intermarriage between the two groups must have been common, as evidenced by the shared genetic X-haplogroup found in few other tribes on the North American continent. Similarly, the woodland Dakota were friends of the Iowa until they began to compete for the same territory.

By the latter half of the 1700s, metal knives had replaced flint and bone, while the use of steel strikers was common. The United States entered the trade arena, competing with the British and Spanish further west, as early as 1791 when the No Ears winter count records: "They went around the country carrying flags." This event is interpreted by Flame's winter count as the first appearance of U.S. military troops, although other authorities attribute this entry to the arrival of British traders who continued to operate in the west after the Revolution.[31]

The fact that the western Lakota also lagged behind in the gun trade was documented by the Oglala Iron Crow in the 1799 winter count when he lists that year as the "first distribution of guns."[32] However, other Lakota tribes fared worse. One tribe did not see its first gun until 1814, as noted in the Big Missouri winter count.[33] Rifles that shot metal cartridges only made their way into the camps of the Hunkpapa in the 1870s.[34]

The increasing influence of white men on trade and their importance in Lakota and Nakota affairs can be traced by their appearance in tribal winter counts. While the plains Dakota continued to trade with other tribes, the number of entries dedicated to white men and women rose dramatically, from the first entries in the Big Missouri count, when they saw their first white women (1800) and the arrival of white missionaries, recorded in 1801.[35] Also in 1800, the Iron Crow count described the trading expedition of Regis Liosel to the upper Missouri with the pictorial representation of "nine white men." The 1802 No Ears winter count also mentions the arrival of Regis Liosel, who built a post on Cedar Island,[36] although the Big Missouri winter count gives the year as 1804 when a French trader known as Little Beaver "made his home upon an island in the Missouri River."[37]

That same year (1804) Meriwether Lewis and William Clark held their first meeting with the plains tribes. By the time of the expedition's arrival, the Lakota had taken over trade in the region. Trade routes on the northern plains had long been maintained that ran between the James River in present-day South Dakota to the plateau and on to the northwest coast, so the tribe stood upon the expedition's route. The timeline represented by the winter count, the Lakota year, began with the first snow and continued to the first snow of the following winter. Thus, it is the Iron Crow count for 1805 that records the meeting with Lewis and Clark at the mouth of the Bad River on September 25, 1804, when again: "the people came together with many flags."[38]

In 1805, Lewis and Clark witnessed and recorded an exchange between the Crow and the Mandan and Hidatsa, revealing much about the trade practices common among the plains peoples. The visiting Crow arrived with much pomp. After smoking the pipe, the Mandan and Hidatsa exchanged guns, ammunition, corn, kettles and axes for two hundred and fifty horses and large parcels of buffalo robes. In addition there were trade fairs held where women bartered for goods. In the Pacific Northwest, it was the women who did the trading, and they were considered shrewd, hard negotiators.

Often alliances attempted to block trade between competing tribes, in a form of trade embargo. Therefore, the Cheyenne who tried to establish trade with the Arikara found their overtures opposed by the Crow. When the Cheyenne were returned to the west, they were visited by the Shoshone and the mountain Crow, so the Cheyenne forced to trade with the Crow who, in turn, traded with those tribes further west such as the Nez Perce and Cayuse, and with the southern Ute.[39]

As Lewis and Clark met the Lakota of the west, the United States opened official relations with the woodland Dakota further east. They sent Lieutenant Zebulon Pike to Santee territory. As a soldier, he documented those things he felt would be of import to the government. He estimated the value of total trade, in terms of annual consumption, at $13,500 for the Mdewakanton, $12,500 for the Sisseton, $6000 for the Wahpeton and $2000 for the Wapekute.[40]

In 1806, the Big Missouri winter count tells of neighboring Mandan who were taken by Lewis and Clark to Washington, D.C.[41] Just four years later, it was recorded that the Liosel (Little Beaver's) house burned down.[42]

Back east, little by little the Dakota life was being eroded away through the trade which had once been the lifeblood of the community. By this time, the Dakota Santee had come to rely upon European goods, such as blankets, guns, kettles, axes, and hoes, which were adapted to their needs. Said Pond: "While their ancestors contrived to do without these things, they had now become indispensable. They [the Santee] understood their dependence on fur traders.... When their supply of ammunition was cut off they were not only unable to use fire-arms in hunting, but they were at the mercy of their enemies."[43] On September 23, 1805, the woodland tribes made their first treaty with the U.S. government. Liberally plied with alcohol by their hosts, the Santee relinquished a tract of land for an undisclosed amount.[44]

In 1808, Iron Crow noted that a trader (Little Beaver) and all his goods burned.[45] Elsewhere a white trader, John Potts, was murdered by a Blackfoot.[45] Trade with the whites also figured in the entries for 1810 and 1813 of the Big Missouri winter count. In the latter year, a "friendly white man came to peddle his goods."[46]

Dependence on white goods gave the Europeans power which they often used to interfere with the Dakota people. As the traders moved up the Missouri River in the eighteenth century, both the French and the Spanish sought to disrupt Dakota trading patterns by undercutting Santee prices in order to create a schism between the woodland tribes and those of the prairie. In 1815, the commercial value of buffalo was recognized.[47] Thus, white traders turned buffalo hunting into a lucrative business, distracting the plains tribes from trapping the beaver needed by their Santee cousins to maintain their place in the market.[48] The Titowan developed a prosperous business, dealing directly with the white traders.

The Dakota were shrewd, though, and not completely at the mercy of Europeans. As Pond explained. "In their dealing with each other, there was not much sharp practice, and they had a very careless way of making bargains; but in their dealings with the white men they were more particular and had no scruples about taking all they could get."[49] So they learned the concept of profit from the whites and displayed more materialism when dealing with them. Said Pond: "...sober Dakota were generally quite competent.... They obtained most of their goods in advance, and the majority of them were tolerably honest and paid their debts if they could; but some were sharp enough ... to take goods from one trader and sell their furs to another."[50]

Pottery was another product among the many things that would have been traded between the tribes before European contact. Later the more durable cast-iron kettle replaced clay pots. Although the woman pictured here firing pots is Siouan Crow, the Dakota also made pottery and would have used similar techniques to those pictured. Photographic print, Richard Throssel c. 1903. Library of Congress Prints and Photographs Division.

Many significant events went unremarked by their own counts. In July 1815, the representatives of the Dakota met with a delegation headed by William Clark at Portage des Sioux and signed treaties of allegiance to the United States government. During this period the Lakota tribe, the Oglalas, settled with the Arikara and adopted their horticultural economy supplemented by buffalo hunting, but the arrival of white traders with white man's diseases soon curtailed this experiment in agriculture.

As a result the Oglala remained "horse poor" in the latter half of the nineteenth century, like other agricultural tribes the Hidatsa and Mandan who maintained few horses, but carried on a profitable trade in them. The Oglala's more nomadic cousins, the Hunkpapa, boasted one horse for every two people while their enemy, the Crow, maintained more than two per person.[51]

By the 1800s, horses had become the primary medium of exchange among the plains tribes. The average buffalo robe was valued at $3.00, which means the horse, priced at ten robes, cost about $30.[52] The chart[53] below gives relative values.

Meanwhile the firmly entrenched Hidatsa and Mandan population resisted Lakota advances into their territory and maintained thriving trade centers. Later trade routes used by the Europeans can be traced by the appearance of smallpox among the trading nations, such as the Assiniboin, Arikara, Hidatsa and Mandan people, which weakened these tribes and brought about their eventual subjugation by the Lakota.

Tribe	Date	Item	No. Horses
Mandan	1830	Eagle feathered headdress	1–2
Assiniboin	1850	Quilled shirt and leggings trimmed with fur	1
Assiniboin	1850	War-eagle feather cap	2
Assiniboin	1850	Beaded scarlet blanket	1
Assiniboin	1850	Quilled shirt and leggings trimmed with ermine skins	2
Upper Missouri Tribes	1850	Fifteen eagle feathers	1
Crow	1850	Ten weasel skins	1
Crow	1850	One hundred elks' teeth	1
Crow	1850	Woman's dress of bighorn, decorated with 300 elks' teeth	3
Crow	1850	Carved pipe bowl	1 packhorse
Kiowa	1870	Muzzle-loading gun	1
Blackfeet	1870	Medicine pipes	9+
Blackfeet	1870	8 buffalo robes	1
Blackfeet	1870	Catlinite carved blackened pipe bowl with ash stem	1

White traders figured again in the Lakota's Lone Dog count of 1817 and 1819, when "another trading store was built." This event is also mentioned in No Ears and Kindle's winter counts, which stated that the Brule "made houses of rotten wood [yellow sumac]," apparently for white traders.[54]

Elsewhere Major Thomas Forsyth was sent from St. Louis in 1819 to provision a fort that was being built in Dakota territory as a part of a U.S. government drive to wrest trade in the west from the British. He pointed out that British success in trade with the Dakota was due to the superiority of British commodities. Thus, it can be seen that the Santee readily understood the value and quality of goods. Additionally the British chose agents who spoke the language and knew something of the culture. Forsyth recommended that the United States adopt this practice and apply the "golden rule" in trade as a way of ensuring Santee loyalty.[55]

The next Indian agent was sent in the summer of 1820. Major Lawrence Taliaferro's view was enlightened for his day. He condemned the influence of greedy white traders who exploited the Indians and defrauded the government of rightful taxes, and he maintained a running battle against those who provided alcohol to the Dakota.[56]

Lakota pictographs for 1820, 1821 and 1822 were devoted to the growing invasion of whites. The first describes trespass, "when a white man built his house on Sioux lands without permission." The following year, the tribe helped build a house for Joseph Gallineaux, who in a subsequent year brought whiskey to the Sioux, trading a single jug of whiskey for a mule.[57]

The Minneconjou also felt the arrival of a white trader was noteworthy. The winter count for 1828 mentions F.A. Chardon, who built an earth lodge on a creek north of the White River. This was a momentous enough occasion that it appeared in no less than seven tribal winter counts.

In 1830, the Indian Removal Act was passed by Congress. On July 15th of this same year, the Santee, along with the Sauk and Fox, signed a treaty giving the U.S. title to land in Minnesota, Missouri, and Iowa. The title included mining, timber and grazing rights.[58] Following this, white men and their doings appeared with increasing regularity. Vestal's Hunkpapa winter count mentions an accident that befell a trader called Yellow Eyes (Thomas Lestang Sarpy) in 1831 when his house blew up. This event was mentioned in ten different winter counts. Other 1831 accounts describe a fight between two white traders.

In Washington, proceedings were taking place that would change Dakota lives irrevocably. In 1834, the Indian Trade and Intercourse Act strengthened government control on Indian territory, defining it as "all that part of the United States west of the Mississippi, and not within the states of Missouri and Louisiana, or the territory of Arkansas, and also that part of the

United States east of the Mississippi River and not with in any state to which the Indian title has not been extinguished."[59]

Finally on September 29, 1837, the Santee ceded all their land east of the Mississippi to the U.S. in exchange for goods and annuities,[60] making the Minnesota tribes the first Sioux to become reservation Indians. Then the Santee began to trade extensively with the Ojibwa when, as Pond recorded, Dakota women began to purchase their rivals' beadwork rather than doing it themselves.

Two years later, the 1839 Big Missouri winter count commemorates when "white trader conducted his store in a tipi."[61] In 1847, the Yanktonai winter count marks the season when two white traders spent the winter with them and their allies the Hunkpapas. Their growing reliance on American trade was confirmed in 1850 when a Dakota killed a white trader and was put to death by his tribe for this transgression. The 1852 Big Missouri winter count mentioned the "big issue winter" which commemorates the first Fort Laramie treaty.[62] Then in 1857 Sioux Falls was established by traders from the Dubuque Iowa Company.[63]

Trade and alliance throughout the ages were formal occasions, although relationships could be tense even among trade partners if someone broke the rules of good conduct. Following the murder of a young man, Ohiyesa described the tension in the camp against the traders: "Every Indian in the camp, female as well as male, was intent on invading the camp of the *bois brule*[64] to destroy the murderer."[65]

Radisson gives the earliest account of trade negotiations with the Santee. Like many early European explorers, he was shocked by the Dakota tendency to approach traders, weeping and begging for guns and pity. What seemed like sign of weakness was, in fact, a mark of respect, for the Santee greeted them as supplicants, using the approach required during important ceremonial occasions, such as "crying for a vision."

The French, who had been dealing with tribes further east, fully understood the need for ritual. Radisson's text is difficult and contains much braggadocio; however, it remains the most accurate portrayal of the original Dakota ceremony for seeking alliance. During their introduction, the tribe arrived and set up camp. They held a banquet, inviting the French. The feast lasted five hours, during which they sat "without speaking one to another." After the meal, a representative of the trade company made speeches. The spokesman for the Santee shot an arrow into the air and then replied that he would discuss this with the rest of the tribe when they appeared tomorrow.[66]

The following day the Santee approached the French with incredible pageantry, and the "captayne made a speech of thanksgiving." The Santee called a council. "First they made a sacrifice to the french.... So said, they present us with castor [beaver] skins, adjuring us ... that the doors of their villages, the cottages of their wives and daughters were open at any time to receive us.... The second gift was, they would die in their alliance.... The third gift was that the doors of the forte opened if need required to keep them from the Christanos [the Cree] that come to destroy them.... The fourth gift was buffalo skins...." They asked in return for "thunder."[67]

The traders were invited to a second feast, with four boys to carry their guns and four women carrying bearskins upon which they would sit. A crier shot an arrow and announced the traders' presence. The French were given raised seats. The "calumet" was presented while an elder of the tribe "covered us with his vestments," an act which implied union. The pipe was smoked and the meal begun. The next day, the French presented their gifts. The negotiations took a full four days.

Little had changed centuries later in the process of trade, alliance and negotiation, as noted by Lewis and Clark. Such occasions were marked by pageantry and solemnity. Meanwhile the pipe remained integral to all contracts and oaths, and in particular, the formation of an alliance which was accompanied by feast and celebration.

Under close scrutiny, the common view of native trade has been proven erroneous. Trade in the Americas was extensive, crossing "national" boundaries. Trade routes had been established by Paleo-Indians and were maintained for millennia. These routes brought goods from the coast to America's heartland. Trade centers too had existed for centuries and possibly longer than that. Then as now trade was the lubricant that greased the axle of alliance.

The Dakota themselves were shrew tradesmen, particularly with outsiders, and had relied on trade between tribes long before their introduction to the whites. They used a system of units and measures which was consistent, fair and equitable. The Santee held fairs which drew tribes from hundreds of miles away. They understood not only their market, but the relative value of goods.

Gone is the image of the primitive who knew only how to steal or make war in order to acquire supplies, and that of the naïve native who needed the European to teach them about the concept of market forces in goods and exchange. In fact, the trading companies usually set up their forts near known trade centers and trade routes, taking over the territory claimed by Indian traders and supplanting them, and it was through trade, in guns and alcohol, along with the resultant diseases brought by the traders, as much as combat at arms that the white subdued the native peoples of America.

10. War and Peace

A long time ago when the people still lived in Minnesota, Chief Tawa Mackoce (meaning His Country) ruled over a band of Hunkpapa at Ble Wakan. He had three sons and a daughter. His sons battled the Crow, standing in the first rank, fighting hand to hand; but they were not to be the great warriors that their father had been in his youth, and they died in battle.

The chief's daughter loved her brothers dearly, and she swore she would not marry until she counted coup for each one of them. Her name was Makhta, and she was Winyan Ohitika (Brave Woman). Makhta was both beautiful and proud of her heritage, and there were many braves who would have had her as wife. One was the son of a chief. Called Red Horn, he could offer many gifts; the other was a poor man, but a valiant warrior, named Wanklee Cikala, Little Eagle.

The Crow people had moved into the area around the Missouri River, a land claimed by the Lakota, and the Hunkpapa could not allow this to continue. The chiefs called a council to discuss what must be done, sending out wands to elders and warriors alike. The elders spoke first. All listened in silence, learning from their experience and their wisdom. The warriors were called in to consult.

Outside the women set up their tipis under the watchful eye of the akitcita. The women moved soundlessly as they went about their business, for they did not wish to alert the rival Crow to their presence. The council lasted long into the night. As daughter of the chief, Brave Woman lived close to the great council chamber and she stood outside listening.

When all had had their say, the headman asked: "And who would go to war?"

A roar rose from many throats as the braves shouted their assent. Brave Woman raised her head, eyes shining. She would avenge her brothers' deaths at last. The men prepared for battle, and she went to the leader of the war party and informed him that she would ride with them. Her father grieved, but Brave Woman would not be swayed, and he could not deny her. The vow was made and must be fulfilled.

"Wear my war bonnet into battle," he said, "so all will know that you are my daughter and go with my blessing."

The young woman gathered her brothers' weapons, her father's war bonnet and his coup stick. She dressed in her best dress of white deerskin, selected the finest war pony from her father's herd and went to join the rest of the warriors. They rode in silence to the Crow camp, and when they arrived, they realized that it was larger than they had suspected. Tipis stretched as far as the eye could see. The Hunkpapa were greatly outnumbered. They dismounted, and the headman of the war party sent a scout to check the lay of the land.

Brave Woman strode to Red Horn's side and handed him her eldest brother's lance and his shield. She gave Little Eagle the younger brother's bow and arrow. To another warrior, she presented the youngest's war club, and to each she said: "Count coup for my brother."

The scouts returned and they made their plan of attack. When the braves rode out to fight, Brave Woman held back, singing songs and giving the trilling war cry of the Lakota

The Santee uprising marked the destruction of the woodland Dakota. The band was rounded up and three hundred warriors were sentenced to death. Some 270 were reprieved by President Lincoln, but thirty were hanged making it the biggest mass hanging in U.S. history. *The Siege of New Ulm in Minnesota* pictured the battle between Santee and settlers in August 1862 and was painted by Henry August Schwabe some forty years later (c. 1902).

women. The warriors were pushed steadily back by the Crow. When it appeared they would be overwhelmed, she rode forth alone. With her father's coup stick she touched one Crow warrior after another. Heartened by her courage, the Hunkpapa rallied. The battle raged around her as she counted coup for her brothers.

Suddenly her horse was hit by musket fire. It went down underneath her. She stood defenseless over her pony as the fighting continued around her. Red Horn rode past, averting his gaze from hers. Just then Little Eagle erupted from a cloud of battle dust, leapt down from his horse and offered it to her. Gratefully she mounted the pony, and she looked down at him, waiting for him to follow. Little Eagle shook his head. "The horse is wounded; it could not carry us both."

She did not move. Little Eagle took the bow that she had given him and slapped the pony's rump. It bolted. She returned to the edge of battle to find the Hunkpapa warriors in disarray. Brave Woman persuaded them to make a final charge.

Many died in the fight that drove the Crow from Hunkpapa territory and established them on the banks of the Missouri River, Little Eagle among them. After the dust of battle settled, she found his body and she rent her dress, cut her hair and gashed her arms, mourning him as if he had been her husband.

The war party's akitcita judged Red Horn harshly for his cowardice in abandoning Brave Woman in the fight. They broke his bow, took his eagle feathers, and sent him home to be with the other women. They erected a high scaffold where the Crow village once stood and placed Little Eagle upon it so he could guard the spot for all eternity.

Brave Woman became renowned among the people. Many men would have her, but she would have none of that; she refused to marry. No one could measure up to Little Eagle, who had given his life for hers. She lived a long time, as his widow, and was well respected among her people, for she had done a brave thing and helped to drive the Crow from Lakota lands, and her story is still told to this day.[1]

This tale taught about the cardinal virtues of bravery, *woohitika*, and fortitude, *wowacintanka*. It cautioned against cowardice, for in order to maintain the territory they needed to hunt, the Dakota had to fight any and all who sought to invade it. Thus, war for the Dakota was not a question of political or religious differences, it was a matter of survival.

In 1834, Samuel Pond gave a realistic assessment of the Dakotas' situation when he said: "The Indians did not make war on each other because they were Indians, but because they were men and like other men.... If they were to live at all, they must have a country to live in; and if they were to live by hunting, they must have a large country, from which all others were excluded. Such a country they had not because their enemies were willing that they should occupy it, but because they were able and willing to defend it by force of arms. If they had not resisted the encroachments of their enemies, they would soon have been deprived of the means of subsistence and must have perished."[2]

Ohiyesa (Charles Eastman) speaks of the life-and-death struggle the Wahpeton faced as they attempted to escape after the "Minnesota Massacre," the Santee Uprising of 1862. His voice is made all the more poignant because he speaks from the perspective of not only an observer, but an active participant and a survivor. "General Sibley pursued our people across the river.... In our flight, we little folks were strapped in the saddles or held in front of an older person, and in long night marches to get away from the soldiers, we suffered from loss of sleep and insufficient food.... We were compelled to trespass upon the country of hostile tribes and were harassed by them almost daily and nightly. Only the strictest vigilance saved us."[3] Still, "raids made upon our people by other tribes were frequent, and we had to be constantly on our guard. I remember one time a night attack was made upon our camp and all our ponies were stampeded. Only a few of them were recovered, and our journeys after this misfortune were effected mostly by means of dog travaux."[4]

As the Wahpeton moved west they found new enemies alongside the old. Besides the Ojibwa, Ohiyesa mentions battles with the Hidatsa and the Mandan. This pattern would be matched throughout their history, for the Dakota have had any number of ongoing wars on many fronts. As a nation of diverse tribes and dispersed bands, they commanded a wide territory. Their land abutted that of numerous other tribes and territorial claims were often disputed. The autonomy of the bands meant that one band may accept an alliance with a former enemy while another would continue the conflict, a continual source of confusion to the European, and later the American, negotiator.

While early explorers maintained accounts of events, particularly those that might influence trade, their interaction with the Dakota in the beginning was limited, and their view was narrowed by their perspective. Therefore, the best source of information comes from the Dakota themselves, the winter counts and the records of the neighboring tribes; although the winter counts run from winter to winter, thus their years overlap our own, which creates some confusion in dates.

According to another tribe's tradition an early conflict between the Dakota and the Algonquin was instrumental in the destruction of the mound-building culture of the Oneota in Iowa. The Algonquin traveled west by way of the St. Lawrence River to the Great Lakes and south into the Mississippi Valley, where they met the Dakota. The two clashed, and the mound builders were crushed between them.

Later in the 1600s, at the time of European contact, the Omaha appear to have been the principal occupants of this region around Bull Run, not apparently the descendents of mound-building peoples, but replacing them. The Ponca may have been present too, still a part of the parent tribe. The Iowa and, probably, the Oto lived on the site intermittently. When the Omaha met the Dakota speakers later during this time, they immediately became allies, perhaps recognizing their common roots.

Further east, around 1656, the Iroquois had successfully subdued the Erie. Then the Iroquois war parties swept into lower Michigan and finished expelling what remained of its resident tribes. This resulted in a sudden influx of refugees, with the Miami being pushed into northern Illinois and eastern Iowa, thus into the lands of the Nakota. Meanwhile groups of Shawnee relocated to central Illinois, invading Illini territory.

Previously the Osage, Quapaw and Kansa had been forced by the Iroquois to leave their original homes along the lower Ohio and Wabash Rivers to an area west of the Mississippi. The second influx caused the Omaha, Ponca, and Kansa to continue up the Missouri River. The Osage, however, settled along the lower river, placing them in direct competition of the Illini west of the Mississippi. The Quapaw moved into Arkansas and would eventually force the Chepoussa and Michigamea to abandon the area. When the fighting began in Illini country, the French at Green Bay and Sault Sainte Marie made no effort to intervene and not-so-secretly hoped the Iroquois would defeat rival traders Sieur de La Salle and Tonti and their allies, the Illini.

By this time, Dakota territory had become a rich source of furs for the French. The other area tribes, the Ottawa, Wyandot, Ojibwa, Potawatomi, Fox, Sauk, Kickapoo, and Mascouten,

The start of a war party shows several Dakota men on horseback riding in a circle around a tipi. The men would gather and sing sacred songs. Wolf medicine would be invoked to ensure the success of the war party. Women and children would have turned out to cheer their men on. Photographic print taken by Edward S. Curtis, c. December 26, 1907, as part of a series. From the Edward S. Curtis Collection (Library of Congress). The picture was published in *The North American Indian* by Edward S. Curtis (Seattle, Wash.), 1907–30, v. 3, p. 12.

rebelled because they had lost French trade and turned hostile gazes at the Dakota. The French did not want another war with the Iroquois for defending the Illini. They remained neutral and concentrated their attentions on the Dakota. The competition over furs, trade and territory eventually led to war among the adjacent tribes.

In 1658, following his introduction to the Dakota, Pierre Radisson recorded the ongoing war between the Dakota and the Cree: "...the Christinos [Cree] that come to destroy them; being allways men, and the heavens made them so, that they were obliged to goe before to defend their country and their wives, wch is ye dearest thing that they had in the world, & in all times they weare esteemed stout & true soldiers...."[5]

When the displaced Huron first arrived on Isle Pelee (Prairies Island, just above Red Wing) in the Mississippi around 1656, the Dakota welcomed them, but the Huron, seeing they lacked firearms, treated the Santee contemptuously. The latter rose up against these intruders who had migrated into their hunting grounds in 1659. The Huron numbered fewer than 500. Despite the odds, they fought to maintain their position against the more powerful Dakota. After the defeat of the Huron, the Santee revealed a great deal of forbearance and circumspection, along with subtle strategy. When the Huron became lost in the marshes after battle, the Dakota defenders stretched beaver nets across all paths and attached bells to them. When the Huron stumbled into the nets, thereby alerting the Dakota to their presence, the Santee fell upon them. A few were killed to warn other tribes against making incursions into Dakota soil. The rest were set free to carry this message back to the Huron camp.[6]

In 1662 Ojibwa, Ottawa and Mipissing warriors inflicted a major defeat on the Iroquois at the southeastern tip of Lake Superior. However, other Iroquois warriors arrived from the east. As the Algonquin tribes tried to escape the marauding Iroquois, they ran into the Santee, whom the Jesuits called the Iroquois of the west.

Meanwhile the Illini had been evicted from their homeland. Said Father Claude-Jean Allouez in the 1660s: "They used to be a populous nation, divided into ten large Villages, but now they are reduced to two, continual wars with the Nadouessi [Sioux] on one side and the Iroquois on the other having well-nigh exterminated them."[7]

The Dakota finally drove the Huron and Ottawa refugees back east to the Michilimackinac in 1670. Two years later they defeated a large war party of Huron, Ottawas, Foxes and Potowatomis who had invaded their land and "slew them in great numbers," said Nicolas Perrot. As a result the other refugee tribes came to view the Dakota with fear. "The Nadoussious and the Iroquoise are eating us," a Miami chief told Allouez. "Take pity on us. We are often ill, our children are dying, we are hungry."[8] Wars between the Fox and the Dakota also occupied the Santee during this period (circa 1660s), and hostilities increased with the arrival of more refugees from the east as each tribe attempted to hold onto vital hunting lands.

Animosities had existed for a long time between the Dakota Santee and the neighboring Ojibwa. Native statements, documented by William W. Warren in *The History of the Ojibway Nation*, asserted that rivalry began due to "personal differences,"[9] although territory was at the heart of the conflict. For much of their history, even when the Santee lived further north, their land lay next to the Ojibwa, and as the two tribes drifted south, they followed parallel paths. Clashes over hunting grounds and boundary disputes would have caused deep-rooted animosity and grievances accumulated. Certainly hostilities predated the flood of refugees and the political machinations of the rival trade companies. The disputes between the Ojibwa and the Santee were to have far-reaching consequences for the Dakota, and, defending as they were their sacred land (*Mde/Ble Wakan*), the conflict became, for the Santee, something of a holy war.

Thus, during the 1600s the Sioux were locked in life-and-death struggles with ten different tribes, with battles recorded between them and the Fox, the Huron, the Ottawa, the Potowatomis, the Menominee, the Mascouten, the Illini, the Miami, the Ojibwa and the Cree. In 1670, the Menominee made peace with both the Dakota and the Ojibwa. With skill and political adroitness, the Menominee remained neutral and did not take part in the conflicts that were to follow. Meanwhile there were battles between the French and Dakota, documented in French scalp records.

Elsewhere the Iowa and Mascouten vied for the same territory. At this time, the Dakota and Iowa were allies, and the Santee and the Nakota tribes may have been drawn into the conflict. Dakota battles with Illini continued until 1683. This conflagration grew until 1690 when the Fox, Kickapoo, Mascouten, Miami and Illini joined together to fight the allied Dakota and Iowa. In 1692, hostilities began between the English and the French (King William's War, 1687–1697), into which the tribes were inevitably drawn as the various bands sided with their trade partners.

Spurred by the French, the final Ojibwa conquest of Santee lands started around 1695.[10] However, clashes between the two tribes were longstanding, with Sieur Du Luth, who met the Santee in 1679, among the first white men who tried unsuccessfully to negotiate a peace between them.[11] According to some writers, the conflict had already lasted some 300 years. Conservative estimates say 200 years, or sometime between the 1380s and the late 1400s.

The War of Spanish Succession or Queen Anne's War (1701–1713) continued the trend of native participation in European conflict. Only a year after French governor D'Iberville referred to them as useless, the Dakota proved their worth in war as well as trade by aligning themselves with the French. The Iroquois sided with the British.

Also during this time, 1712, the Fox and Sauk combined into a single fighting unit which was going to have a profound influence on Dakota history. Continuing warfare between Kansa, Pawnee, Comanche, Nakota, Osage, Missouri and Oto, Iowa, Fox and Dakota resulted in a peace referendum in 1723, when the Dakota and Fox and Sauk became allies. Two years later, the Huron, who had attempted a return to their homeland, were forced to seek refuge in the Midwest again.

The Fox had long been considered agitators by the French. They repeatedly attacked and disrupted French trade, closing trade routes and causing the French to abandon forts. The Dakota allied themselves with the Sauk and Fox and joined their fight against the French in 1727,[12] inadvertently cutting off their own supply of firearms. This conflict resulted in further warfare between the Santee and French allies, the Ojibwa. When the latter turned their attention to the *Oceti Sakawin,* the Dakota — armed only with bows and arrows, clubs and spears — had to fight an opponent with far superior weaponry.

Within 15 years (1743), the Ojibwa had driven the Dakota from northern Minnesota into territory belonging to the Iowa, and the one-time allies became bitter enemies, although some believe the enmity occurred because the Wahpekute killed an Iowa chief. By this time, the Dakota had become friendly with the Osage, and the Iowa found themselves trapped between two important tribes. To combat this, the Iowa formed an alliance with the Sauk and Fox, which would have revoked any previous alliance they had made with the Dakota.

In 1744 King George's War, or the War of Austrian Succession, erupted and lasted until 1748, again involving the Europeans' Indian allies. As the conflict continued, the Ojibwa, who had absorbed the Ottawa, the Potowatami, Menominee and Mascouten, united to force the Illini from Wisconsin in 1746. Perhaps as an indirect result of King George's War, the Hurons, Ottawa, Abnaki, Potawatomi, "Ouabash," Sauteurs, Missisauga, Fox, Sioux, Sauk, "Sarastau," Loups, Shawnee and Miami joined forces to attack the French living in Detroit (August 1747).

Ojibwa aggression against the Santee culminated during the three-day battle of *Kathio* in 1750 when the woodland Dakota were forced from their homeland. The strategy used during the assault included the use of primitive bombs. The Ojibwa threw bags of gunpowder through smoke holes of the Dakota lodges into the fire below. Their tactics have given rise to the conjecture that the French were involved in the Santee expulsion, for this type of warfare was unprecedented among the tribes.[13]

The Dakota lost land that was considered sacred to them, so the enmity that resulted would have attained the status of a crusade. Viewed from this perspective, it's not surprising that some five attempts by successive "overlords," including the French, the British and the U.S. governments, to get the Chippewa (Ojibwa) and the Dakota to make peace failed.

Through trade, the Native American people were repeatedly drawn into European politics, as different tribes sided with their trade partners, either the French or the English. The War of Spanish Succession, the War of Austrian Succession and the Seven Years' War (French and Indian War) were fought upon both sides of the Atlantic, making them the first truly global conflicts. At first the Dakota were allied to the French later they allied themselves with the British.

The French and Indian War (the American theater of the Seven Years' War) began in 1754 with dire consequences for the native tribes and lasted until 1763. At this time the Dakota fought beside the French against British. In 1763, the Ottawa chief Pontiac led an attack against the British at the former French redoubt of Fort Detroit.

When not at war with their Indian neighbors, the Santee maintained strained relations with the Algonquin tribes, the Ottawa, Huron, and Potawatomi. The Santee would lay animosity aside and become allied with a traditional enemy if the cause was considered important enough. Therefore, the first Santee chief, named Red Wing, attended Pontiac's council on April 27, 1762, and joined the battle against a common enemy, the European, taking an active part in the siege of Detroit.[14]

The Attack, painted by Frederic Remington in 1907, pictures the start of a lightning raid for which the Dakota were greatly feared; however, many battles were defensive. The Dakota of the east and the Lakota of the west could raise thousands of braves with ease. From the Library of Congress Prints and Photographs Division.

At this time the Lakota and Nakota winter counts become an invaluable source of information. The winter counts, pictorial accounts of their history sketched on a buffalo hide, succeed the former method of record keeping, counting sticks, without entirely supplanting them. Thus the two methods of record keeping went on concurrently until the late 1800s. In winter counts, a single pictograph documents the most important event of the year. They were meant as mnemonic devices. The event, often a battle, would act as a reminder for the record keeper from which he could relay verbal tradition. Therefore, the single battle depicted could symbolize a whole series of encounters in an ongoing war. Likewise, the absence of battle in the pictograph did not mean the absence of war. Rather it indicated other events took precedence.

The No Ears winter count began in 1759, and in the years between 1760 and 1766, it recorded the deaths of significant members of the tribe, sometimes at the hand of an enemy. Unfortunately, it often does not mention which enemy since the tribe members would have known. From this distance, the historian can only guess. In 1767, the No Ears count recorded an event which would have shaken Dakota society to its roots: "They divided themselves into two sides," signifying an argument within Dakota ranks. A year later, the winter count indicates: "Those who speak the same language fought one another," suggesting civil war.[15]

Elsewhere the Europeans continued to make their influence felt. Around 1767 or 1768, a trader who had settled at Leech Lake was attacked by local tribes and died. The fur company at Mackinac told the Leech Lake Indians to come to Mackinac and make reparation for the goods they had taken, by a payment of furs. At the same time, they threatened punishment in case of a refusal. A tribal delegation responding to the summons arrived at Mackinac in the spring of 1770. They brought furs, which they saw as fair exchange for the goods taken. The company representatives took their furs and gave them a cask of liquor and a closely rolled flag. They were instructed to wait until they returned home before they broke the seal, but the delegation opened it during a feast with a band based near Fond du Lac on Lake Superior. Many of the band and delegation died. Smallpox killed nearly all of the three-hundred-strong band at Fond du Lac. The epidemic swept through other tribes, although the Chippewas (Ojibwa) north and west of the lake escaped its ravages. A band near Cass Lake, however, was wiped out completely. Only one child survived.[16] The Dakota would also have felt the effects of this epidemic since they were living in the area at the time.

A member of the tribe recognized the disease, smallpox, and suspected the spread of the infection was a direct result of the gifts. Germ warfare did have historical precedent during the French and Indian War. When an epidemic of smallpox swept through a fort, the British removed the blankets from the dead and sent them to the hostile tribes hoping to infect them.

The Santee did not fare well against the better-armed Ojibwa, who eventually acquired the Dakota villages established at Sandy, Cass, Winnibigosh, Leech and Red Lakes. In 1769, the Santee seized the offensive and attempted to retake their home, but the campaign failed, although they continued the fight with lightning assaults and sorties into their one-time territory throughout much of the 1800s.[17]

Further west, the Lakota were becoming embroiled in the politics of the plains. In 1771, according to the No Ears winter count, the plains tribes were at war with the Mandan and burned one of their villages. Four years later, according to No Ears, two scouts were killed. The Assiniboin, who had separated from the parent Nakota early in the 1700s, battled intermittently with the various tribes of the Dakota nation and the Algonquin Blackfoot. Yet it would appear that truces did occur in this continuing conflict, for the No Ears winter count for 1777 relays: "Assiniboines arrived," either for trade or peace talks.[18]

When the British took over French territory, both the Santee and the Menominee became British allies, fighting alongside them against the Americans in the Revolutionary War, which also placed them on the same side as the Iroquois. In *One Vast Winter Count: The West before*

Lewis and Clark, Colin Calloway said: "British agents recruited Indian warriors from the western Great Lakes to fight in Eastern campaigns. The Mdewakanton Santee chief Wabasha visited the British in Quebec (1776) and was given a general's commission in 1778."[19] Wabasha was honored when he visited Mackinac, then a British fort, in July 1779, when he was greeted with a special artillery salute.[20] Later "Sauk and Fox warriors joined one thousand British and Indians—mainly Sioux under Wabasha and Ojibwas—who attacked St. Louis in May 1780...."[21] Thus, one-time enemies were brought together under the British flag.

Internal conflicts between the various Indian nations continued alongside the American Revolution. The first year of the Iron Crow's winter count (1785) tells that Bear Ears was killed by an enemy without specifying which one. The next year Metal Ornament entered an enemy camp while away at war, although it does not say whose camp, and Broken Leg Bird was killed by an enemy. The following year must have seen a halt in hostilities with the Mandan, since the Oglala made winter camp with them. In 1788, Iron Crow mentions the death of *Sluke Raka* at the hands of an enemy. In 1790, the Lakota winter count noted a battle between the Mandan and the Sioux: "They killed two Mandan on the middle of the ice."[22] The pictograph rather understates the events of that year, when some two thousand Lakota warriors attacked the Mandan and the Hidatsa. The entire Mandan Deer Creek camp was captured and all the lodges destroyed. These were no horse raids or mere revenge killings reputed to be the Indian way of war, but a concerted effort to push other tribes from valuable territory.[23]

Yet according to No Ears, two years later the Oglala again camped with the Mandan. 1796 marks the year when "they came home victorious with scalps," but again which tribe is attacked is not mentioned. This happens throughout the text, but then the band would have been aware with whom they had ongoing battles and would not necessarily have to mention it since it was part of common knowledge. This happens most often when a tribe member is killed: it's the death, the loss of an important member of the tribe, that would have been considered significant and not the name of the enemy. For example, the following year, a "war bonnet wearer was killed."[24]

After the Revolutionary War the Dakota peoples were bemused to learn that they had to change allegiance to yet another foreign power, the Americans. Nearly a century after the British surrendered to the Americans, many Dakota still claimed loyalty to the Great Mother of England (Queen Victoria) rather than the Great Father in Washington, so Sitting Bull sought sanctuary in British Canada after the Battle of Greasy Grass (Little Bighorn).

The successive administrations, whether French, English or U.S., also didn't understand Indian strategy. Most people believe that the native peoples did not have pitched battles where hundreds or thousands were pitted again one another. White historians contend that the native people preferred the swift raid, often with a specific intent, for example, to get horses, not unlike the cattle raids described in the legends of Celtic Ireland, or sometimes to capture women as a means to invigorate the bloodline of a village.

However, history asserts otherwise. For example, during Little Bighorn, the combined forces of the Lakota and Cheyenne warriors numbered in the thousands. Henry Schoolcraft relayed a story of pitched battle between the Siouan tribes of the east and the Cherokee with thousands of combatants. "The Catawbas as invaders of their soil and freehold, marched in great force to meet them at, or near, the Old Nation Ford, and a battle ensued.... It was said that the Cherokees lost 1100 men and the Catawbas about 1000."[25] Later, during the war with the Huron, the woodland Santee, whose lands were sparsely populated, were able to assemble three thousand warriors to defend their territory against the invading Huron and Ottawa. Thus, random raids does not adequately describe Dakota warfare and the Dakota were perfectly capable of gathering forces of thousands.

Meanwhile the Titowan and the Nakota, Yankton and Yanktonai, migrated across the

Once battle was joined, it relied on individual heroism with two men pitted in conflict, often to the death. The painting by Frederic Remington shows the weapons in common use in warfare, the axe and the club. Part of the Library of Congress Prints and Photographs Division, it was painted in 1903.

prairies, and the jostling that had taken place in the Great Lakes continued further west. As they marched across the plains, the combined Dakota tribes waged a war of conquest, contesting the concept of "lightning strikes and inconsequential raids." In "The Winning of the West," Richard White said: "This [the Dakota's] advance westward took place in three identifiable stages.... Each of these stages possessed its own impetus and rationale. Taken together ... they resulted in the dispossession of numerous tribes and made the Sioux a major Indian power on the Great Plains during the nineteenth century."[26] The different tribes and bands expanded for similar reasons which gave unity to their wars. They fought over both trapping and trade rights; hence over territory and the right to hunt in a particular region.

The Lakota and Nakota victories on the plains were assisted by repeated epidemics of smallpox recorded in Brule winter counts in 1779 through 1781 and 1801 and 1802, which had sufficiently weakened the Arikara, Hidatsa, Mandan and Omaha to make them vulnerable to Titowan attack.[27] These epidemics also ended the Oglala's early experiment in horticulture. The Oglala of Standing Bull reached the Black Hills in 1776.[28] That other hostilities continued at the same time as these events is noted in No Ears's entry for 1801 when "they came home victorious."[29]

Before 1802, the Siouan Missouri were driven from Missouri River region of Nebraska by the Sauk. The Missouri headed west to live with the Oto along the Platt, and the Dakota presence began to be felt by tribes other than the Mandan. The 1803 Battiste Good winter count tells of a horse raid against the Pawnee, when they brought home iron-shod horses.[30] The Pawnee were among the last of the agricultural tribes left on the plains and late contenders against the Lakota. Originally, Pawnee aggression was targeted against the Arapaho and the Cheyenne while the Lakota and Nakota horse raids remained mere inconveniences. When the allied Dakota tribes wrested control of the gun trade from their then competitors, the Cree-Assiniboin, then the Sioux became perceived as a threat by the rival Pawnee.

Meanwhile the Big Missouri count records another conflict with the Crow.[31] The Crow too were long-term foes, with warfare between the Titowan and the Crow dating back to the old trade rivalry of the early trapping days in the 1700s. Also in 1803, the Omaha and Ponca sued for peace with the Lakota Brule. While one band agreed, another continued the war. The Ponca retaliated against the wrong band and the peace initiative ended.[32] The Brule struck back against the Omaha, at which time the Omaha and Ponca abandoned their villages to become nomadic tribes, cutting themselves off from normal trade routes. Ultimately the strategy failed since they were no longer able to obtain guns. The Iron Crow winter count is probably referring to this series of battles when they recorded that they had killed an Omaha woman at night (c. 1804).[33]

In the eighteenth century the control of trapping grounds was the primary reason for war. In 1804, buffalo robes and hides had begun to replace beaver pelts as commodities, and hence as a basis for conflict. In this same year further east, the Sauk, Iowa and Dakota did battle against the Osage, revealing the shifting alliances of the times from 1743, when Dakota and Osage fought against combined forces of Iowa, Sauk and Fox.

In the west, the Lakota feared an alliance of Arikara with the Mandan and Hidatsa, and formed an effective use of the blockade to prevent this from happening. This cut the Arikara off not only from the buffalo but from trade. White merchants were stopped along the Missouri River. In defense, the Arikara and Mandan united and sent out war parties to attack their common enemy, but differences between the two tribes eventually caused the alliance to dissolve.[34]

By the time of the arrival of Meriwether Lewis and William Clark in 1805, the Lakota dominated the region, and the strength of the Mandan, Hidatsas, Arikara and Omaha had been reduced considerably. The American explorers left the Mandan camp in April and had several encounters with the Lakota as they tried to prevent the expedition's advance up the river. Yet the appearance remained unremarked in any of the Dakota counts, except Iron Crow's. The other documented local affairs of import and the only reference to warfare this year comes from the Big Missouri winter count which spoke of killing an Omaha as he ventured into one of their camps.[35]

In September of 1805, the Santee took a fatal step by signing their first treaty with the U.S. government. Lieutenant Zebulon Pike headed an expedition meant to establish U.S. sovereignty in an area where the British still traded freely. The Dakota exchanged a tract of land (about 100,000 acres, estimated by Pike at a value of $200,000) for an undisclosed amount. The Santee received $200 worth of gifts[36] and were liberally plied with alcohol. Interestingly enough, the treaty, ratified in 1808, was never proclaimed[37] and the "undisclosed amount" was finally set by the Senate at $2000, or a penny an acre, which was never paid.[38]

No Ears mentioned an attack where eight were killed by an unrecorded enemy in 1806, while Iron Crow refers to the death of Black Rock either in this or an unrelated attack.[39] In 1807, the Big Missouri winter count described an encounter with the Crow when an enemy warrior entered a Lakota camp and was killed by the tribe.[40] In the north, the Oglala were contesting the region between the Missouri River and the mountains, unsettling the Kiowa, Arapaho, Crow and Cheyenne.

Although their impression was not favorable, Lewis and Clark recognized the Lakota as the preeminent power in the region, and because of Lakota opposition to the expedition, their records referred to the tribe as "the vilest miscreants of the savage race."[41] Yet American power could not subdue them; thus, the fledgling U.S. was forced to pay tribute to the Lakota. Around 1809, Lewis sent a force of 150 men to recruit Indian auxiliaries from among the Teton tribes and was rebuffed. However, the Lakota found the Americans useful allies as long as their ambitions coincided,[42] for later the Lakota joined the white soldiers in an expedition against the their tribal enemies the Arikara.

Influenced by trade, again the woodland Dakota rallied to the British during the War of 1812 when trader Robert Dickson brought a contingent of 130 Dakota, Ho-Chunk (Winnebago), and Menominee to Mackinac. The participation of these tribes was instrumental in wresting the fort from American hands, but when the opportunity to fight their enemies the Ojibwa appeared, many Santee braves deserted the British cause to turn their attentions to their long-term adversaries, and toward the end of the conflict at least one band of Wahpekute changed allegiance completely, siding with the Americans.[43]

The Lakota winter counts of 1809, 1812 and 1813 record the continuing conflict with the Arikara. In the last year, "Big Road's father was killed" by the Arikara. Meanwhile Iron Crow's winter count for 1810 recounts that "a man wearing a red shirt was killed by an enemy," and 1813 mentions a battle with the Gros Ventre in which they killed six members of that band. The Kiowa figured in the No Ears account for 1814 when they crushed a Kiowa's skull. The event took place when the Lakota went to a Kiowa village near the head of Horse Creek to sue for peace.[44]

Indirectly the U.S. government assisted the Lakota and Nakota people in their conquest of the prairies by saving the then-united Saone, which consisted of the Sihasapa or Black Foot, Oohenunpa (Two Kettle) and Itazipco (Without Bows), along with the Yankton and Yanktonai, from the most devastating effects of the epidemics that were running rampant across the plains. The Lakota and Nakota people controlled vital trade routes. To ensure that trade was not interrupted, the U.S. government provided them with vaccinations that protected them against smallpox.[45] Meanwhile climatic change in the plains caused a shrinking in the size of the buffalo

This series of photos was staged for Edward Curtis in 1907, at time when such warfare would have become a thing of the past. This picture shows men on horseback gathering to plan before the upcoming raid. Many enemies were distant, requiring days-long rides before battle. The war party would stop, particularly when they neared the enemy camp, and call upon the spirits to bless their endeavor. Photographic print, Edward S. Curtis, c. 1907, published in *The North American Indian*, Edward S. Curtis (Seattle, Wash.): Edward S. Curtis, 1907–30, Suppl. vol. 3, pl. 98. Edward S. Curtis Collection (Library of Congress).

herds which, in turn, fueled further Lakota expansion as the plains Titowan required more territory to feed their growing populations. As Lakota and Nakota power in the region increased, they were further able to restrict enemy tribes' access to European goods.

Throughout 1813 and 1814, conflict between the Santee and the Ojibwa continued. When the news of the Treaty of Ghent, which marked the end of the War of 1812, reached Minnesota in 1815, the Americans took advantage by negotiating a series of treaties between various warring parties. Thus, the combined Dakota tribes met with the Ojibwa for peace talks at Portage des Sioux. The delegation was headed by William Clark. On July 19, the different bands signed the first of several treaties with the U.S. One delineated the boundary between the Dakota and the Ojibwa.[46] Winter counts record that "They died in the city," possibly referring to the death of Black Buffalo during this meeting at the confluence of the Missouri and Mississippi Rivers.[47]

In 1816, Iron Crow recorded another form of treaty when "angrily they took hold of each other's hands," which Wissler interpreted as a peace settlement, albeit a reluctant one, with the Crow. The American Horse count for that year confirmed: "They made peace with the Crow at Pine Bluffs."[48]

Among the duties assigned to Indian Agent Major Lawrence Taliaffero was to broker a final peace between the Dakota and the Ojibwa. During the first seven years of his tenure (1820–1827) he brought the tribes together ten times. In 1823 he recommended a geographical line of separation to accomplish this goal. Next year, he took parties of Dakota, Ojibwa and Menominee on a series of trips to Washington to show them the strength and might of the Americans. Some members of the delegation dropped out of the group at Prairie du Chien and more took flight in Ohio. No treaty was signed, but it set the stage for an intertribal council held in 1825.[49]

Strife remained a constant in both east and west. The Fox and Sauk attacked the Iowa in 1823. The result was a massacre. Elsewhere the Great Man, No Ears and Iron Crow winter counts record a major battle with the Arikara.[50] To combat their total subjugation, the Arikara attacked the American Fur Company with whom the Lakota had formed a loose trade agreement. The Lakota struck back with a force of 1500 warriors accompanied by U.S. soldiers under the command of Colonel Henry Leavenworth. While the expedition proved successful, it did not lead to the total annihilation of the Arikara. The Lakota blamed the Americans for letting the enemy escape. The campaign continued, and the Arikara were forced to move south to territory occupied by the Skidi Pawnee. The Nakota Yanktonai took over the area abandoned by the Arikara.[51]

The Yanktonai meanwhile recorded a fight between themselves and the Ojibwa near present-day Bismarck, North Dakota, after finding their enemies had built a fort in Nakota territory. The Yanktonai attacked and defeated the plains Ojibwa and razed their fort.

In their march across America's heartland, the Lakota and Nakota people had already overrun the Omaha, Oto, Cheyenne, Missouri and Iowa.[52] The year 1825 saw the final phase of western expansion toward the Platte, motivated by trade as the number of fur-bearing animals dwindled along the Missouri. Their advance ousted the Arapahoe, the Kiowa, the Crow, from their traditional lands and dispossessed the Cheyenne a second time. First the Arikara and later the Arapaho and Cheyenne succumbed, allying themselves to their conquerors, although this process would take decades.[53]

According to U.S. treaties, the Dakota tribes were the sole possessors of Iowa north of the Upper Iowa River and the northwest portion near the mouth of the Big Sioux. In 1825 a second council of all the tribes was called by Indian Agent Major Lawrence Taliaferro at Prairie du Chien. The chiefs gathered, decked in paint and feathers, each tribe striving to outdo the others. The Sioux came on horseback; the Sauk and Fox dashed up the river in their war canoes, singing their war songs. The Ojibwa, Menominee, Winnebago, Iowa, Patowatonmi and Ottawa also attended.[54]

On June 22, 1825, the Lakota and Nakota bands signed a treaty with the U.S. which created a new set of boundaries. The Hunkpapa followed suit on July 16th. As with the Dakota, the first treaties marked the beginning of the end for the Lakota/Nakota people. It also represented U.S. recognition not only of the tribes' political significance, but also of their status as a nation-state and the primary power on the American prairie. The initiative culminated on August 19th when the Santee signed a peace treaty with the Sauk, Fox, Menominee, Iowa and Winnebago.[55]

According to the treaties, the Dakota were to hunt north of a line passing from the mouth of the Upper Iowa River through the upper fork of the Des Moines River to the fork of the Big Sioux, and down the Big Sioux to the Missouri. The Sauk and Fox were to keep south of this line. The Fox gave permission to the Iowa and the Oto, both of the Siouan-language family, to live in this territory with them.

The conference that began festively ended in tragedy. Several members of the attending tribes died on their way home as a result of drinking whiskey provided by the Americans, giving rise to rumors of poisoning which persist to this day. The line drawn between the warring bands in 1825 was not surveyed until 1835, although the tenuous peace reduced the number of raids.[57] By 1827 the war between the Santee and the Ojibwa flared again when a band of Dakota attacked a party of Ojibwa visiting Fort Snelling. The culprits were seized and turned over to the Ojibwa, who forced them to run the gantlet. The conflict between the two tribes persisted until the reservation era in the late 1800s.

Warfare was again important in the No Ears entry for 1826 when young warriors returned home from an ambush and died after eating bad meat. The No Ears and Short Man winter counts of 1828 both recount battles with the Mandan. Next year the Yanktonai winter counts describe hand-to-hand combat between the Mandan and the Titowan Minneconjou. By 1829, another rival of the Lakota, the Ponca, had been driven from their lands. That same year, the winter counts recorded the death of a Yanktonai who had been killed by the Bad Arrows, a band of Shoshone. Elsewhere, Striped Face decided to keep captives from a previous battle with an unspecified enemy.[57]

The winter counts of 1830 were full of major battles. White Bull mentions one between the Lakota and the Arikara. Elsewhere, the Lakota fought with Bad Arrows (Shoshone) and the Crow. At this same time, the Mandan were also fighting the Crow, which made the one-time enemies, the Mandan and the Lakota, indirect allies. Meanwhile the Oglala began an offensive against the Gros Ventre and the Pawnee.

Along the Mississippi, the tribes who had signed treaties of peace—the Sauk, Fox, Santee and Iowa—sent war parties across the boundary drawn by the United States. As a result, in 1830, the government secured territories on either side of the line around twenty miles wide, extending from the Mississippi to the Des Moines. This strip, forty miles wide, was termed the Neutral Ground. Any tribe could hunt and fish without being charged with trespass. In that same year, Andrew Jackson's Indian Removal Act was passed by Congress, moving all tribes east of the Mississippi to the land beyond its western banks, stirring further conflict among the resident population.[58]

In the west the conflict between the Lakota and the Gros Ventre persisted, with at least one battle mentioned in Dakota winter counts, but most of the action was concentrated in the east. Black Hawk's war began this same year. While the U.S. government paid lip service to peace initiatives between the Ojibwa and the Santee, at other times the U.S. government had a more pragmatic approach, taking advantage of age-old enmities, as they did when they informed the Dakota chiefs of Black Hawk's return to Iowa following the 1832 conflict. The Dakota lay in wait at the ford and ambushed Black Hawk, exacting revenge on the Sauk and Fox peoples for age-old arguments and inadvertently doing the government's work for it by ridding the U.S. of a potential source of unrest.[59]

In 1833, Potawatami, Ojibwa and Ottawa were forcibly removed by the U.S. government to Michigan. The following year found the Lakota at war with the Cheyenne. During the period from autumn 1835 through autumn of 1836, the plains Dakota were fighting on several fronts. The winter count for 1835 of Minneconjou Lone Dog mentions an Arikara killed by a Sioux. The Yanktonai Blue Thunder winter count describes a battle when the combined Dakota, Nakota and Lakota Blackfoot fought against the Mandan and the Arikara. At the same time, the Hunkpapa winter count recounts a Sioux peace party destroyed by Mandan and Arikara. The Yanktonai must have been participants in this parley, for the Yanktonai winter count relayed that many of its warriors were killed too. The Big Missouri winter count talks of strained relations with Cheyenne and subsequent battles with them.[60] The following year, the Oglala No Ears, Iron Crow, Short Man and Brule winter counts all tell of a battle where they "fought across the ice." Both American Horse and Battiste Good identified the tribe as the Pawnee.[61] Two years later (1839) the Lakota retaliated, killing one hundred Pawnee, but nearly died of starvation as a result of the expedition.[62]

The Mandan and Hidatsa clung tenaciously to their tribal lands. In 1836, famine caused the Yanktonai to start a series of raids against these agrarian tribes, who retaliated, killing more than 150 people and taking fifteen captive. The following year, one of the worst smallpox epidemics hit the sedentary tribes. Completely hemmed in by Yanktonai, the Mandan-Hidatsa bands were unable to relocate. The Mandan were ruined; the Hidatsa lost 50 percent of their population, along with the Arikara, who had chosen this inopportune time to return to their old lands. From that time, the Nakota blocked the survivors from the bison herds that could have provided them with food.[63]

Curtis followed the men throughout the stages of warfare. Here they have achieved their goal, arriving at the enemy village, and are shown riding across the plains toward their adversary in the early morning light. Many raids began at dawn, with the men approaching under the cover of darkness in order to retain an element of surprise. Photograph by Edward S. Curtis, c. 1907. Edward S. Curtis Collection (Library of Congress). Published in *The North American Indian,* Edward S. Curtis (Seattle, Wash.): Edward S. Curtis, 1907–30, suppl. v. 3, pl. 99.

Back east, the Dakota clashed with the Ojibwa in 1835 and 1836. Fighting reached a peak in 1839 when a party of Ojibwa asked for and received hospitality from the Dakota, and then killed their hosts. The Dakota retaliated. The following summer a famous chief, Cloud Man, was murdered, and the Dakota ambushed several bands of Chippewa (Ojibwa) traveling from Fort Snelling and killed over 100 men, losing 23 warriors themselves.[64]

The year 1837 marked a time of further unrest between the Lakota and the Pawnee, when again "the Pawnees and the Sioux fought across the frozen Platte with arrows." In Minnesota, the Santee ceded all their lands east of the Mississippi to the United States[65] for a sum of $300,000, which would be invested "to pay the chiefs and the braves annually forever an income of not less than five percent...." In addition, a portion of the interest would be applied to an education fund and the rest to be paid in specie or goods that the tribe could specify. The traders also profited from this agreement, receiving $90,000 in payment for the "just debts of the tribe."[66]

Meanwhile 1840 brought peace between Ojibwa and the Yankton Nakota over territories in North Dakota.[67] Under Bull Bear, the Lakota Oglala began a concerted campaign against the Pawnee, who turned to the Americans for help. Simultaneously the smallpox epidemic that destroyed the horticultural Mandan and Hidatsa also ran unchecked against the agrarian Pawnee. The weakened tribe was unable to combat the Oglala advance and surrendered their hunting grounds the following year. By 1841 the Kayaksi (Bull Bear's former band) pushed down to the Smoky Hill River in Kansas while other bands moved west and the Hunkpapa and Yanktonai pressed north into Canada. During this period, the Lakota forces continued to fight the Crow, the Shoshone, and the Pawnee.[68]

The presence of the neutral zone in Iowa established in the previous peace treaty decreased the number of encounters between Algonquin, Iowa and Oto on one side and the Dakota on the other. In 1841, everything south of the forty-sixth parallel and north of the present Iowa-Minnesota border was incorporated into Indian Territory to house the tribes displaced by the Indian Removal Act. Then, the U.S. government moved the Winnebago (Ho-Chunk) onto the strip of neutral territory. Of Siouan stock, the Ho-Chunk claimed to be the people from whom sprang the Iowa, Oto, Ponca and Osage. Elsewhere, the Dakota were involved in their own internal disputes, and the Oglala were feuding among themselves when the Oglala band the Kiyuksas ("cut-offs") split off from rest of tribe.

The following year (1842), the plains Lakota concentrated on winning horses from other tribes for a strategic purpose, for the next year they met with the Pawnee to exchange the horses for one of the sacred arrows of the Cheyenne. However, two of the winter counts mention continuing warfare in 1843 when both No Ears and Short Ears said: "They brought home captives" following a battle with the Pawnee, and Iron Crow recorded the fact that "they brought home a sacred arrow,"[69] which suggests that the arrow was captured rather than a part of an exchange. The arrow was reputed to predict the future and foretell the outcome of battles. If its blade was marked by blood it presaged defeat while a clean blade indicated victory.[70] In 1844, the Oglala, No Ears and Short Man counts relayed the death of He Crow by an enemy, while Iron Crow indicated the death of thirty warriors at the hand an enemy, but none recount which one.[71]

In Iowa, the Ho-chunk position between the Sauk and Fox in the south and the Dakota in the north became untenable, leaving them in the direct line of fire between warring tribes, but in 1844 a treaty was finally signed between Sauk, Fox and the Dakota which all parties observed and continue to observe to this day.

By this time, the northern Lakota tribes, the Oglala and the Brule, had completely displaced the Kiowa and pushed the Crow west to the Powder River. The Cheyenne and the Arapaho, perhaps observing the hardships of the tribes who attempted to contest the Nakota advance, formed an alliance with the Lakota. The idea of alliance was sweetened for the Cheyenne by the return of their sacred arrow. After the alliance of the Arapaho, Cheyenne and Lakota, the balance of power in shifted in their favor. Together the three tribes dominated the north central prairies for the next fifty years.

Still the Lakota/Nakota had to fight to maintain their hold on the prairie throughout the latter half of the 1800s, although there was a shift in fronts and emphasis. The 1848 Yanktonai winter count documents continued strained relations between Arikara and Yanktonai when two warriors from each tribe were killed in hand-to-hand combat. The 1849 Short Man count documents the killing of a Pawnee warrior.[72]

Another treaty was hammered out between the Santee and the U.S. in 1851 at Traverse des Sioux. The Santee ceded some million and one-half acres in western Minnesota and eastern South Dakota, for about ten cents an acre.[73] By this time, the Dakota had become jaded by previous dealings with the Americans. A Sisseton warrior requested that the terms of the agreement not be changed after the treaty had been signed and later commented bitterly: "You think this is a great deal of money, but you must well understand that the money will all go back to the whites again, and the country will remain theirs."[74]

In 1853, the Hunkpapa did battle against the Crow, killing a man wearing a four-horned war bonnet — a fact commemorated in both Yanktonai and Hunkpapa winter counts. Their old enemies, the Assiniboin, also plagued them. The next year, the Yanktonai fought the Assiniboin on White Earth Creek and five Assiniboin were killed. Battles between the Oglala and the Pawnee continued in 1854.

It was only toward the end of the 1850s, with the beginning of mass migration of American settlers through the plains to the west coast and its subsequent disruption of the herds, that the combined Dakota tribes began to understand their real adversary, the white man, and then, as they had in the past, they combined to form a united front against their foes. This decision may have been thrust on them by the renegade Wahpakute band, the Inkpaduta who had not signed the 1851 treaties. The brother of the Inkpaduta band leader was killed by a white whiskey trader in 1854. On March 8 and 9 in 1857 the tribe attacked the white settlement near Okoboji Lake in Iowa, killed thirty-four people and took three women prisoner. Their campaign continued at Spirit Lake, Iowa (not to be confused with Spirit Lake or *Mde Wakan* in Minnesota), and a place called Springfield, near present-day Jackson, in southern Minnesota.[75]

The first skirmish between the Lakota Brule and the whites was recorded in the No Ears, Short Man, Iron Crow and Big Missouri winter counts for 1854, after Conquering Bear was killed by Lieutenant G.L. Grattan's command. The Lakota retaliated in what is now called the Grattan Massacre, where thirty white men were killed. The following year, Colonel William S. Harney (White Beard) came to punish the Lakotas for the Grattan Massacre, attacking the first camp he found. It was destroyed, and eighty-six people were killed. A total of seventy women and children were captured and held hostage.[76]

Both 1856 and 1857 saw warfare with the Crow continue, when "a war bonnet was cut in two in battle," and, later, "when ten Crow were killed."[77] That same year, the exploits of a young Sitting Bull were recorded when he participated in a raid on an Assiniboin (Hohe) camp. Swift Cloud had chased a Hohe child onto the ice. The boy attempted to defend himself with his bow and arrow, but the arrow slipped from his bowstring. Sitting Bull intervened. He adopted the youth, who became known by the name Jumping Bull. He remained loyal to Sitting Bull for the rest of his life, fighting beside him at the Battle of Greasy Grass.[78]

The winter counts for the year of 1858 were marked by the deaths of two notable warriors — Blunt Horn and Brown Robe — at enemy hands, but neither gave of the name of the enemy.[79] Elsewhere, the Yanktonai winter count describes an attack by a war party of Crow, but the tribe sustained no injuries as a result of the assault.

As a result of the conflict with the Inkpaduta, a treaty was signed on June 19, 1858, following four months of negotiation in Washington, D.C., with selected Santee chiefs; the treaty reduced their land allotment. The document left not only the amount of compensation but also the right to title up to the discretion of the president. The Mdewakanton Little Crow was reluctant to sign. He explained his position: "We have been so often cheated that I wished to be cautious, and not sign any more papers without having them explained so that we may know what we are doing."[80]

The Yankton, who had been angered by the 1851 treaty that ceded lands they believed were theirs and subsequently attacked white settlers in the region, were somewhat mollified to have their rights to mine pipestone confirmed by the United States government. The Senate ratified the treaty in 1859, and a year later they assessed the value of the land relinquished by the Santee at thirty cents an acre.[81]

In that same year (1859), Big Crow was killed.[82] Elsewhere, the Hunkpapa and Minneconjou winter counts recorded further fights with the Crow while the Big Missouri winter count describes further conflict with Pawnee.[83] Meanwhile the Nakota Yanktonai struck out at the Assiniboin.

Two years later (1861), the warrior Red Feather was killed by an Assiniboin who attacked a war party. The war party had successfully vanquished their assailant, but when Red Feather tried to count coup against the fallen soldier, he was stabbed. The Hunkpapa leader Red Weasel was also killed that year during a horse raid on an Assiniboin camp. Similarly, Spider-like was killed by an enemy. The winter counts for the year 1862 commemorate the taking of a scalp which Wissler believed was Pawnee.[84]

That same year saw the fatal confrontation between the Dakota Santee and the whites which

The return of the triumphal war party was painted by Frederic Remington (c. 1916). The party would have been greeted by the women, singing their distinctive ululation, and their protectors. Dakota women would dance the scalp dance to commemorate their victory, where one respected grandmother would hold a stick from which all the scalps taken would be hung while the rest circled around her.

heralded their downfall. After that, the white man became the primary enemy of the Lakota. These later battles of the Indian Wars have been well documented and are outside the period recorded in this book. However, disputes over possession of the northern territory with the Crow and the Shoshone were common during this period while the southern portion of Lakota land continued to be contested by the Pawnee. Further west, the Lakota battled the Ute, and so it remained until the plains tribes were forced by the U.S. government onto the reservations.

Often, though, territorial invasion did not develop into open warfare. Instead, the tribes would move into an area to hunt and then escape undetected and unscathed, which was their goal, after all, to gain access to the herds and to the territory. According to Richard White, for the Lakota: "Their ability to hunt in safety without striking a blow comprised a strategic victory...."[85] American confusion about the target and logic of such expeditions and their motives explains why so much of intertribal warfare is so often dismissed as random raids.

Richard White summarized the conquest of the plains. "It is ironic that historians, far more than anthropologists, have been guilty of viewing intertribal history as essentially ahistoric and static, of refusing to examine critically the conditions that prompted Indian action. In too much Indian history, tribes fight only 'ancient' enemies, as if each group were tolled out an allotted number of adversaries at creation with whom they battled mindlessly through eternity. Historians have been too easily mystified by intertribal warfare, too willing to see it as the result of ingrained cultural pugnacity."[86]

Studies of Dakota history, however, reveal that their conflicts were neither a frivolous means for the warrior to gain recognition nor were they gratuitous. The natives fought as mankind has always fought: for dominance over a certain region and the wealth it contained, and for survival. Hence, the tribes would often fight the same tribe, their nearest neighbor who also would lay claim to the precious hunting grounds and eventually attained the status of a "traditional enemy."

Similarly, in modern times the Europeans and their allies have battled continually against their nearest neighbors. The French fought the British, the British fought the Spanish, and so on. Sometimes European powers banded together to fight a common foe, also neighbors, the people of the Middle East. Viewed from the inverted telescope of time, and since these wars date back to the 1100s, the later historian could easily be justified in describing Christians and Moslems as traditional enemies, and such wars as nonsensical since they have often been conducted in the name of religion or under the guise of a "just war." The truth is that the reason for war has almost always been economic. In medieval times, the Crusades were as much about the control of the spice trade and the trade routes east as they were about religion, just as now we fight over control of another precious resource, oil.

Close examination of the Dakotas reveals a people who presented a unified policy of expansion driven by economic necessity, along with an integrated defense against all those who invaded their homeland. Their warfare was systematic, with a specific goal in mind, which they were able to coordinate on several fronts. Their battles were not limited to the lightning strike or raids of small, inconsequential war parties, with no greater objective than to thumb their noses at their traditional enemies. On the contrary, the Dakota commanded hundreds, even thousands of warriors into purposeful campaigns with specific goals in mind. During their history, the Dakota used the full gamut of tactics and stratagems, including subterfuge, embargo and blockade, and were wise enough to cherish any victory that could be accomplished without bloodshed.

11. The Way of the Warrior

Once many winters long gone, a young Dakota warrior crept quietly with his friends through enemy territory. They traveled light, carrying only their weapons and no food, for they were here on a deadly quest to find the remains of a war party long overdue at their camp. They moved swiftly, making soft animal sounds to fool the enemy, lest the slap of branch against thigh or snap of twig under foot betray their presence.

It was late in the day when they came across their fallen brethren, with Ojibwa arrows sticking from their breasts, and the young men were horrified to see the warriors skinned like animals. But night was closing in on the search party, and the braves must return to their village to report what they had found. Vowing vengeance, they left the dead behind and slipped into darkness. As they headed back into their own territory, they heard an enemy war party approach. The Dakota braves faded into the forest, except one young man who climbed quickly up a tree.

The Ojibwa settled under the very branch upon which he sat. He was in desperate straits. He prayed to the spirits of the forest, and his prayers were answered when he was transformed into an owl. He spoke to the warriors in the language of the owls, telling them of the great Dakota war party that advanced even as they sat comfortably next to their fire. The Ojibwa extinguished the flames and fled into the night.

The young brave flew down to the forest floor and changed back to his old form. He returned to his village and met his friends, who already met in a great war council. He told all that he had done and all he had seen, and he became known from that day forth as Owl, for surely he had owl medicine within him.

Young Owl was named as the head akitcita of the war party that would avenge their fallen comrades who had been treated so ignominiously. The warriors prepared for battle, making arrowheads and fletching arrows, and every fourth night, they danced the war dance and sang to the spirits to guide them.

When the preparations were complete, a war party of twenty braves left the village. At first they hunted freely, for they were well within Dakota lands. On the fourth day, they assembled to listen to Owl sing his war song. The men were confident in their new leader who carried great magic within him. They entered enemy territory the next day and Owl ordered that no man shoot a gun. Until their venture succeeded or they died in the trying, the braves would fast, for theirs was a sacred trust; but the young can be forgetful, and when a youth discharged his firearm, the akitcita Owl broke his gun and sent him away.

They had advanced far into the woods that once had been their home when one night Owl decided to call upon the spirits. He dug a hole into the ground and filled it with water. Next to this he placed the hoop that was the symbol of the Dakota people and his weapons, and he sang, asking where his enemy might be found. Then he called upon the spirit of the bear, protector of the Ojibwa people. When the spirit came close to the hole, Owl struck it with his rattle and killed it. Since it had been vulnerable to his magic and his strike, Owl knew the expedition would be successful.

11. The Way of the Warrior   149

The scalp shirt came into use around 1850. It was among the most important pieces of regalia for the Chiefs' Society. The hair was clipped from a horse's tail or contributed by members of the tribe. Only two men were elected to become "shirt wearers." Sitting Bull was not only a member of the Chiefs' Society, he was a shirt wearer and pipe bearer. The above picture shows two long-sleeved buckskin shirts attached to background. The photograph was taken by Edward Curtis c. 1908 and published in *The North American Indian*, Edward S. Curtis (Seattle, Wash.): Edward S. Curtis, 1907–30, v. 3, p. 30. Edward S. Curtis Collection (Library of Congress).

> *In the morning, Owl sent four scouts ahead; but their Ojibwa adversary was not far and it was the war party rather than the scouts who came upon the village first. Inside the camp, the people went about their business, unaware of Owl's band.*
>
> *The warriors did not tarry. Who knew when an enemy war party would return home? The Dakota braves fell upon the village, killing and scalping everyone. They loaded their horses; the war prizes would be divided fairly among the party later, but here, deep inside enemy lands, they moved quickly and quietly. They did not rest until they'd crossed the river once again.*
>
> *When the war party saw the distant tipis of their village, Owl raised his voice in the victory song. Triumphant, he entered the village, for he knew his wife would rejoice as she carried the scalps he had taken and dance the scalp dance to celebrate his great triumph.*[1]

―⁂―

Like the story in Chapter 10, this tale story honors the cardinal virtues of bravery and fortitude, for it took courage to strike deep in the heart of enemy territory and strength to endure the days-long fast necessitated by the endeavor. It illustrates the Dakota way of war, from its onset in council to the strike through the division of spoils and celebration that follows.

Early in their history, the Dakota were described by friend and foe alike as gentlemen warriors who would not dream of desecrating the bodies of their enemies by flaying them. The Dakota honored fallen enemy soldiers and mourned their deaths in sacred rite. The scalp lock, not the scalp, was taken, as Wahpeton Charles Eastman explained: "It [the scalp lock] was a small lock not more than three inches square, which was carried only during the thirty days' celebration of a victory, and afterward given religious burial."[2]

In sign language, the gesture for Dakota was a single slicing motion across the throat, or "cut throat," which was comparatively speaking a quick and clean form of death. They were efficient, businesslike, using a surgical incision to make their point, and then showing good will to the vanquished.

The European reporters of the period agreed. Writing in 1660, Radisson commented upon the esteem with which they were held among the warring tribes of the Great Lakes region. "Those men were Nadonsoron [Sioux]. They weare much respected that no body durst not offend them...."[3]

Father Jacques Marquette found the woodland Santee "less perfidious than they [the Iroquois], [the Dakota] who never attack unless they have been attacked."[4]

Later Jesuit priest Father Louis Hennepin was captured by the Santee in 1680. He spent three months as their prisoner and had the opportunity to observe them close at hand. At the end of his captivity, he viewed the woodland Dakota as morally superior to the other tribes. As warriors, they were admired even by their adversaries. Said Hennepin: "They also make all the surrounding tribes tremble even though they have only bow and arrow. These Indians run faster than the Iroquois but they are not so brutal and do not eat the flesh of their enemies...."[5]

During the Revolutionary War, Lieutenant-Governor Patrick Sinclair also thought highly of his Dakota allies and applauded their military prowess and the bravery of their warriors. "A warlike people, undebauched, under the authority of a chief named Wabasha of very singular and uncommon abilities, who can raise 200 men with ease and is accustomed to all the attention and obedience required by discipline."[6]

Few deny that European influence on the art of war was profound. Nowhere is this better illustrated than in the practice of scalping. The origin of scalping has long been debated, but evidence suggests that it originated in medieval Europe. The first recorded use of scalping comes from France in 1350 after the Black Death had depleted the population. Peasants found themselves freed from the land and from landlords, now absent or deceased, able to move and charge a fee for their services. In an attempt to force the workers to return to the land, the nobility turned upon their own people, scalping selected victims to instill terror and compliance among the survivors.

Scalping as a European import to the Americas is confirmed by early colonial records which document the bounty paid to Indian warriors by the fur companies for the scalps of any tribe who had been designated as "troublesome" in the arena of trade. The scalp lock described by Eastman was already common among many tribes as a trophy of war. With the arrival of the Europeans into Indian affairs, the scalp lock was replaced by full scalps.

Charles Eastman (Ohiyesa) concurred: "Wanton cruelties and the more barbarous customs of war were greatly intensified with the coming of the white man, who brought with him fiery liquor and deadly weapons, aroused the Indian's worst passions, provoking in him revenge and cupidity, and even offered bounties for the scalps of innocent men, women, and children."[7]

In the New World, first the French, then the British—both the colonial government and the traders—and later the Americans paid for scalps of tribe members whose tribes were deemed dangerous. During the American Revolution, the British governor of Detroit, Henry Hamilton, bought the scalps of white settlers in frontier homes and villages. The following excerpt from the state papers of Virginia, *In Council*, June 18, 1779, relayed the growing concern on the American side. "It appears that Governor Hamilton gave standing rewards for scalps, but offered none for prisoners, which induced the Indians, after making their captives carry their baggage into the neighborhood of the fort, there to put them to death and carry in their scalps to the Governor, who welcomed their return and success by a discharge of cannon."[8]

Scalping had its propaganda value which was exploited by Ben Franklin during the Revolutionary War in a letter about a shipment of scalps "captured" around Tyron County, New York, and taken to Albany in spring of 1782. Although the letter describes a fictitious event, it accurately portrays the trafficking of a gruesome cargo. The scalps had been "cured, dried, hooped, and painted with all the Indian triumphal marks."

Bounties placed on scalps made them a big business. Scalps of different age groups and genders brought different prices. Bundles were shipped in lots of eight to twenty, each bundle containing eighty-eight to one hundred scalps. Each scalp was stretched on a painted willow hoop and further painted on the inside of the skin. The colors and markings were used in a wide combination so that all of the necessary information about any particular scalp could be had at a glance.

The special preparations were required by the European powers in order for the tribe to receive payment. For example, Franklin itemized the following package: "88 scalps of women; hair long, braided in the Indian fashion, to show they were mothers; hoops blue; skin yellow background, with little red tadpoles, to represent, by way of triumph, the tears of grief occasioned to their relations; a black scalping-knife or hatchet at the bottom, to mark their being killed with those instruments."⁹

Son of the noted Oglala warrior Red Cloud, Jack Red Cloud posed for this portrait taken by Herman Heyn c. 1899. He wears an eagle headdress made from the tail feathers of "spotted eagle," the immature bald eagle. The headdress was part of the regalia of the warrior societies and was awarded to men of proven bravery. According to Wahpeton Ohiyesa, a man had to have been successful in ten battles to be entitled to a war bonnet, although the traditions varied from tribe to tribe.

> Package 1— 43 scalps of Congressional soldiers, 62 scalps of farmers
> Package 2 — 98 scalps of farmers
> Package 5 — 88 scalps of women hair braided, 17 grey-haired women
> Package 7 — 211 scalps of girls, big and small
> Package 8 —122 scalps, a mix of the above, including 29 infants' scalps

For the Dakota, war was a way of life. In 130 years of the No Ears winter counts (from 1759 through 1889), war figured in fifty-five entries, and then only if one omits all the times notable people were killed, without the qualifier "by an enemy." This, however, does not mean that the individual did not die as a consequence of warfare. For example: the pictograph for the 1834 No Ears winter count was translated as: "A Cheyenne was killed when he arrived home." According to Battiste Good and American Horse, the tribe was at war with the Cheyenne at the time, which suggests that the death was at the hands of the Sioux, and Wissler contends that the incident occurred as the Cheyenne warrior entered a Lakota encampment.[10] Likewise no mention does not mean that battles did not occur in a specific year, only that it was not the most notable event. Thus, the death of many pregnant women (1799) or the repeated appearance of smallpox in 1819 and 1851 took precedence over any mention of battle.

Since it was essential to the survival of the people, war became a sacred function. Without deeds of honor, a man did not advance far within the tribal structure, and without proving his worth in war, a boy did not become a man. Training as a warrior began early in life, through tales of courage and through the games children played. Archery contests and horseback races were aimed at honing those skills required by a warrior.

Young Ohiyesa's uncle subjected him to a series of mock raids at night to teach him how to awaken alert and ready for battle. He would be aroused by the sound of gunfire and "warwhoops" and, considering the period, never knew when it might be a genuine attack.

His uncle would also challenge Ohiyesa to fast with him, a valuable part of the warriors' arsenal. "All boys were expected to endure hardship without complaint. In savage warfare, a young man must ... be able to go without food and water for two or three days without displaying any weakness, or to run for a day and night without any rest."[11]

Ohiyesa also described a game he called "war on bees,"[12] which allowed boys to practice many of the arts of war. They painted themselves, as they had seen their fathers do, and then proceeded to attack a beehive, using all the skills that would be required by them later in life. They learned stealth as they crept as close as they could to the hive without alerting the bees. They learned bravery when the young boys would leap up and face a "warrior" that could strike back. Shrieking war cries, they beat the hive with sticks. By accepting the stings of battle in silence, they learned fortitude, *wowacintanka*, the stoicism required of a warrior. The child who shouted or cried out in pain was shamed and shunned by his friends.

War, as fought by the Dakota, was ruled by regulations even more rigorous than those of the hunt. War could not be made against a friendly tribe. War parties had to be approved by a holy man, then by the camp council, and an *akitcita*, or *zuya wikasa*, would then be nominated to lead the party and those who had elected to participate would prepare for battle. The rules of war even extended into the tipi, with men forbidden to have sex with their wives the night before battle, for it was believed that female power, which nurtured, would weaken the warrior.[13]

The warriors danced the war dance before each battle. Normally dispassionate, Pond revealed a measure of distaste when he described it. "Performers in the war dance painted their faces in such a manner as to render their appearance most frightful, and each held some weapon in his hand. They stood with their knees bent and kept time to the drum and rattle by short, quick jumps, lifting both feet from the ground at the same time. Whey they stopped to breathe, someone would recount, in loud voice and with appropriate gestures, his exploits in war.... Their main objective in the war dance seemed to be to render themselves as hideous as possible."[14]

The Dakota preferred open attack. However, other strategies, including embargo, siege and blockade, were used. Ambush too was not only considered acceptable, but at times was expedient, particularly in a defensive position. If the Dakota were outnumbered, then their job became to harass and harry their opponent until the trespasser was driven from the territory.[15]

In a defensive situation, the elected *zuya wikasa* took charge of the village, replacing the camp *akitcita*. The people would be quickly led to a more secure location and every able-bodied man sent to confront the intruder. If the opposing tribe outnumbered the band, then the women, children and their protectors would leave the area as quickly as possible to join another Dakota band. They would be guarded by their strongest and their best, the Chiefs' and the Brave Hearts Societies. The young warriors were left behind to delay hostile pursuit and await assistance from an allied band.

While the Dakota overall strategy was determined collectively, the actual fighting was a solitary affair, similar to the great buffalo hunts where participants were positioned and told when to start, but once the signal was given each hunter acted alone, selecting an animal and pursuing it to the best of his abilities. So too in battle each warrior fought on his own, and he won or lost based solely on his skill. Often an individual warrior followed certain precepts, or limitations, taken as result of a vow or because he was a member of a specific society. Thus, a brave might dismount, tack himself down to the ground by a sash and fight until he was killed or the battle won.

Many strictures also surrounded the division of property acquired as the result of battle. If a man killed an enemy then he was allowed to keep whatever was on that person's body, including his weapons and his horses. If a war party captured a camp, then the property was divided equally. If a child was found in the camp, then he or she went to any individual who had been approved by other members of the war party. If a single warrior captured horses, women, and children, they then become his responsibility.

As gentlemen warriors, their treatment of prisoners was exemplary. The early Jesuit view was unanimous on this account. The Santee were "content to win a victory, sending back free and uninjured prisoners taken by them in battle."[16] In 1687 Father Joseph Marest agreed, stating that they "did not wreak on their prisoners those horrors which disgrace most of the other nations in this continent."[17]

The Iroquois and the Algonquin tribes of the east often subjected their captives to torture. The prisoner could be held among the lucky if he successfully ran the gantlet, where he would be forced between two columns of flailing sticks and tomahawks. If he proved his bravery by not flinching under the assault, he may be allowed to survive. Those who did had little hope of escape. They would be kept as slaves or sold to white traders for slaves. The Seneca would cut off the toes and a portion of the foot to ensure captives could not run away.

In the Carolinas, many prisoners were condemned to death were burned at the stake, or by a means described by John Lawson in the 1700s: "...whilst others split the Pitch-Pine into Splinters, and stick them into the Prisoners Body yet alive. Thus they light them, which they burn like so many Torches, and in this manner, they make him dance round the great Fire, everyone deriding and buffeting him until he expires...."[18]

The treatment of prisoners after the siege of Detroit by the Algonquin Ottowa on May 9, 1763, illustrates the point. Said Francis Parkman in *The Conspiracy of Pontiac*: "The Indians ... made them strip themselves, and then sent arrows into different parts of their bodies. These unfortunate men wished sometimes to throw themselves on the ground to avoid the arrows; but they were beaten with sticks and forced to stand up until they fell dead; after which those who had not fired fell upon their bodies, cut them in pieces, cooked, and ate them. On others they exercised different modes of torment by cutting their flesh with flints, and piercing them with lances. They would then cut their feet and hands off, and leave them weltering in their blood till they were dead. Others were fastened to stakes, and children employed in burning them with a slow fire. No kind of torment was left untried...."[19]

In contrast, Dakota treated their prisoners humanely, even with respect. Many were returned to their parent tribe, as happened with the Huron after the 1659 battle described in Chapter 10. Their European captives were also dealt with fairly, so after three months' captivity, Hennepin was returned to Duluth unharmed.

In *Indian Boyhood*, Ohiyesa described the farewell given by a female prisoner of war to his grandmother as she prepared to return to her people. "I understand why your son took my sister and myself captive. I hated him at first, but now I admire him, because he did just what my father, my brother or my husband would have done had they the opportunity. He did even more. He saved us from the tomahawks of his fellow warriors, and brought us to his home to know a noble and brave woman.

The shield was an important part of the warrior's regalia. Thomas No Water, pictured here, carries a shield which was mistakenly identified by the photographer as a "tambourine." The shield is painted with the image of a horse. Made of rawhide, the shield could not stop bullets; the protection it provided was spiritual, endowing the warrior with the animal's power. The horse, called *sunkmanitu*, combined the Dakota word for dog and the Algonquin word for god, suggesting an animal that was sent from the divine. No Water also wears a single upright feather, which, according to Oglala tradition, indicated that he had either counted coup, struck an enemy with a club or a stick, or led a war party. Photographic print, c. 1899, by Herman Heyn.

"I shall never forget your many favors. But I must go. I belong to my tribe and I shall return to them. I will endeavor to be a pure woman also, and to teach my boys to be generous warriors like your son."[20]

The rules of combat among the warrior societies of the plains Lakota clearly outlined the correct treatment of prisoners. If the Lakota captured a group of people from another tribe, a member of the Chiefs' Society would present a horse to the youngest prisoner. Similarly a female captive was treated as well as her captor's wife, and the children treated as his children. In fact, Lakota warriors looked down upon the Cheyenne, who purportedly raped their female captives.

If a captive chose to stay with the Dakota — and many did — he would be welcomed into the tribe as soon as he learned the language. Some would be adopted as a member of the family. Ohiyesa explained what became of the previous woman's sister who "chose to remain among the Sioux all her life, and she married one of our young men. 'I shall make the Sioux and the Ojibways,' she said, 'to be as brothers.'

"There are many other instances of intermarriage with captive women. The mother of the well-known Sioux chieftain, Wabasha, was an Ojibway woman. I once knew a woman who was said to be a white captive. She was married to a noted warrior and had a fine family of five boys. She was well accustomed to the Indian ways...."[21]

Another example of a captive who changed allegiance was Jumping Bull, who was saved by Sitting Bull during a battle. Jumping Bull was adopted by Sitting Bull as his brother and remained with the Hunkpapa for the rest of his life.[22]

This did not mean that Dakota prisoners never feared for their lives, and rightly so, since the leaders of rival tribes were often sacrificed in order to ensure the compliance of their respective bands. In her book *Six Weeks in Sioux Tepees*, written about the 1862 uprising, Sarah Wakefield described her treatment by Shakopee's Mdewakanton. The one to rescue her and the runaway horse, and the first to lay hands on her, was Chaska (meaning "oldest brother"). His companion Hapa wanted to kill both her and her children. The eldest said: "No, I am going to take care of them; you must kill me before you can any of them."[23]

Wakefield attributed the charity of the oldest brother to the fact that he was a "Christianized Indian." In truth, he was following Dakota traditions regarding the treatment of prisoners, which stated that a captive female belonged to the first man to touch her, which in turn made him her protector. Throughout the 1862 conflict, Chaska and his family guarded Wakefield and her children from the wrath of the tribe, disguising them by dressing them in native clothes and darkening their skin so they would blend with the rest of the band. At the end of six weeks, she and her children were returned to her husband. She repaid their generosity when she became the only captive to defend the Mdewakanton during the Mankato trial of 1862, despite the ridicule she received from others, and later in her book, she defended not only them but the justice of their cause again.

Protocols of Dakota warfare varied between the different sodalities. Many of war societies were also *akitcita* societies, including the *Tokala* (Fox), *Wikin ska* (white marked), *Sotka yaha* (Wand carriers), *Kangi yuha* (Crow owners), and *Ihoka* (Badgers). *Akitcita* society, *Cante Tinza* or Brave Hearts,[24] meanwhile were sworn specifically to defense. In addition to the *akitcita* societies, there were other warrior societies: the *Miwatani* (no-flight or Mandan) society, the Owl Society, the Omaha Society, the Otter (*Ptan*) Society and the *Heyoka* warriors.

Much of the information about societies comes from James R. Walker. Many of those described were founded in the second half of the 1800s. Yet warrior societies had long been part of Dakota life, and although information about the earlier societies remains scarce, many of the rudiments would have been the same. Each sodality had its own regalia, specific insignia, oaths and mode of dress. Regalia were the most important. As symbols of the society, regalia belonged to the group as a whole and were bestowed on their most honored members. Said Thomas Tyon in an interview for Walker: "Only those who had been scouts in war a had right to regalia."[25] Insignia consisted of the awards given to individuals for acts of bravery, while the mode of dress included specific paints, marks or attire worn by a society's members.

The *Tokala* or Kit Fox society dated from the time of the alliance with the Cheyenne and the Arapaho, around 1844. It had been created to maintain unity between the tribes.[26] The *Tokala* warrior swore to undergo hardship and punishment with fortitude. He wasn't to lie, except to an enemy, or to steal, unless it was from an enemy. The warrior agreed to help the needy, women, children and the elderly, to make sure that no widow of any other Kit Fox member went hungry. Like a Chiefs' Society member, the *Tokala* swore to treat captured women as well as he did his wives, and if he had children by her to accept them as he accepted any other child.

Members of the *Tokala* painted their bodies yellow. Pictures which portray the exploits of Crazy Horse show him with his body painted yellow, indicating that he was a *Tokala* warrior. Red hands allowed one to handle sacred objects, while red painted on legs, thighs and feet meant the warrior had danced in the sun dance. Members wore a yellow fox skin, hanging from their right wrist. They would further be adorned with otter-fur wristlets, armlets of sweet grass, red plumes for bravery and a red dangle of tanned skin if wounded in battle. Regalia included kit fox skin, spears, feathered staffs, swords, rattles, whips, a drum and drumsticks.

The Omaha Society, another recent innovation, was created sometime after the Kit Fox Society, hence after 1845. Thomas Tyon listed the regalia of the Omaha as two crow skins, two whistles, two whips and six drumsticks. Two of the drumstick owners were also the leaders. Other regalia included a serving stick and a spoon. According to Tyon, they were one of the most complex societies: "The Omaha have many rules, very many rules."[27]

The Brave Hearts Society was charged with the defense of the helpless in times of danger. If any child or woman was threatened, a member of the Brave Hearts was obliged by sacred law to rescue them. Sitting Bull became a member of the Brave Hearts Society as a young man. Since he was born around 1831 and he won his first feathers in 1845 and 1846, at which time he would have become eligible to join, one can surmise that the society had been established before this time, and thus predates the Kit Fox society.

As a Brave Heart, Sitting Bull became one of the two war bonnet and two sash wearers, who carried among his regalia a string and stick with which he was supposed to pin himself to position during battle. The Brave Hearts wore the horned headdress with eagle feathers gathered together so they lay flat. Within this group was an elite core, the Midnight Strong Hearts, whose regalia consisted of a buffalo cap with four eagle feathers, a weasel skin and feathered lance.[28]

Another photograph from Herman Heyn shows Oglala warrior John Comes Again. The roach, pictured here, was first adopted by the woodland Dakota from their Algonquin neighbors. It became part of the Lakota regalia with the Omaha Warrior Society, which was formed after 1845, and suggests that John Comes Again was a member. Photographic print, c. 1899 by Herman Heyn.

At the time of writing — around the turn of the 19th century — Thomas Tyon and John Blunt Horn stated that the White Badge Society had originated five generations ago, about 100 years or in the late 1700s, although they relayed little else about the group The White Badges wore a white sash. They also bore a white stripe on their shield and painted a white stripe on their bodies and on their arms.[29]

According to Utley, the Silent Eaters (another name for the Chiefs' Society) was formed in 1869. It was dedicated to the protection of the group rather than the advancement of the individual.[30] Thomas Tyon said the sodality had no regalia and performed no dances. However, the society had nominated shirt wearers and pipe bearers, which suggests regalia, along with the buffalo headdress. Only those who wore the buffalo headdress could perform the buffalo dance, which means the wearers of the buffalo headdress must have had specific dances and ceremonies. Silent Eaters painted their bodies white was a mark of membership.

Sitting Bull himself formed the White Horse Owners Society in late 1875 or early 1876, who primarily acted as *akitcita*.[31] Thus, many of the groups recorded by Walker were of later formation. Still societies such as the Wolf and Bear Societies had existed since earliest times and were common to both the Lakota and the Dakota. Information on these other societies is limited. The lance bearer of the Ptan (otter warrior) wore a headdress with a plain headband. If he had killed an enemy he dangled a scalp from his horse. Members of the Owl Society painted dark rings around their eyes. A red roach worn at the parting on one's hair indicated the Owl warrior had attacked an enemy who was in a protected position. A black horizontal line across the cheek marked a warrior who had killed an enemy. Black around the mouth and chin indicated the warrior who returned with a war party where scalps had been taken.

Some insignia or marks were shared between groups. Irregular red stripes painted on the forearms indicated a man who had escaped captivity. Red dots, stripes or marks on a particular part of the body indicated knife wounds. Horizontal lines indicated the number of battles a warrior had been in — one for each encounter — and they could paint these same black stripes on arms, legs or radiating from the neck. So Crazy Horse appeared not only with body painted yellow as a *Tokala*, but also with the red marks and stripes on arms, legs, and torso, which signified his many wounds and battles. Black diagonal stripes meant a warrior had done battle on foot while black crosses indicated battle on horseback. Otter fur worn around the ankles was the mark of a successful scout.

Colors had specific meanings. Yellow meant a willingness to do dangerous deeds. Red not only meant the spilling of blood, it meant compliance with tribal customs. The headman of a war party would paint his forehead red with the black radiating stripes. The number of stripes indicated the number of encounters, thereby combining two different symbols to mean something new. Blue, the color of sky and wind, referred to spirit. Green meant fertility. In addition to the colors, a man could also paint specific emblems on his body if he had seen them in a vision. One often saw animal forms or figures of the sun and moon on the *Heyoka* warrior.

The eagle feather was one of the most important badges of courage and, as such, became a medium of exchange between tribes. The symbolism of the feather was quite complex. The type of feather — tail or wing — its color and cut, and the way it was worn indicated certain heroic deeds. However, this varied not only between the Dakota tribes, but between bands within a single tribe. According to Walker's *Lakota Society*,[32] the following rules were recorded for the Oglala. A man received a tail feather of an eagle which was worn upright if he:

- counted coup.
- struck an enemy with a club or a stick.
- led a war party.

The feather could be dyed:

- blue if he had been the leader of a successful war party.
- red if the warrior was wounded in war.
- yellow if the man had survived an encounter with an enemy, escaped captivity or had his horse shot out from under him.

The yellow feather could be painted with blue stripes if a man had been wounded on his body, to symbolize the protection of *Skan* (wind) who saved his life. If wounded on his legs or arms, the stripes were red to symbolize the protection of *Wi* (sun).

The feather was tied in the hair if he:

- was a successful scout, who also received a wing feather for each scouting party.
- fought an enemy.
- had taken a horse, thereby enriching the tribe, and the feather was dyed green.

If a man killed an enemy then he could wear a feather from a pieced ear. The warrior with many honors could hang his feathers from his clothes, staff or weapons. Anyone who had done great deeds in war notched the feather, which he hung from a forelock or from an ear, and any man who struck coup after injury wore a red tail feather split halfway down the quill.

Other tribes had different rules. The Wahpeton system was recorded by Ohiyesa. "It is not true that when a man wears a feather bonnet, each one of the feathers represents the killing of a foe or even a *coup*. When a man wears an eagle feather upright upon his head, he is supposed to have counted one of four coups upon his enemy."[33] Even the meaning of coup varied depending upon the tribe. The coup described in the Lakota story of Brave Woman was a strike made upon a living foe. However, according to the Wahpeton Eastman, the coup was defined as the after stroke, or touching of the body of the fallen. "It is so ordered, because often-times the touching of an enemy is much more difficult to accomplish than the shooting of one from a distance. It requires a strong heart to face the whole body of the enemy, in order to count coup on the fallen one, who lies under cover of his kinsmen's fire."[34]

The Wahpeton brave wore his eagle feather hanging down if he was wounded in the same battle where he counted coup. When wounded but not able to count coup, he trimmed the feather, and the feather awarded may not be an eagle feather. When a warrior wore a feather with a round mark, it meant that he slew his enemy. When the mark was cut into the feather and painted red, it meant he had taken a scalp. A man must have been successful in ten battles to be entitled to a war bonnet, and if he was recognized as a leader, then he could wear a war bonnet with trailing plumes. Those who have counted many coups tipped the ends of the feather with bits of white down. Sometime the eagle feather would be tied with a strip of weasel skin, which indicated the wearer had the honor of killing, scalping and counting the first coup upon the enemy all at the same time.[35]

The Sisseton warrior received the war bonnet if he went in and out of an enemy's camp circle. Elsewhere refinements of tradition created an elaborate system of dots. The number of red dots relayed the number of men killed in a single battle, so a man could have several dots painted on his feather. A feather painted with a red triangle indicated that the warrior had both cut an enemy's throat and scalped him, while the tip would be taken off the feather if he had only cut the man's throat. A notch along the top meant that the man was the third to wound an enemy; notches on either side, the fourth; while if the down was stripped away from a portion of the shaft, then the man was fifth to wound an enemy. The feather split along the shaft signified that the warrior had been wounded many times, and beads were added along the shaft for multiple kills, the number of beads revealing the number of men killed.[36]

Other items also could become a form of insignia that explained a man's position or success as a warrior. For example, if a man were shot, then he was allowed to wear a bullet on a string around his neck. The Lakota who had taken a scalp carried a red staff. One who had counted coup was entitled to wear a miniature red bow in his hair, while one who was injured wore a red arrow.

Before the arrival of the gun, weapons included the axe or tomahawk, the club, and bow and arrows. Both Pond and Eastman believed that the stone arrowhead was never used by the woodland Dakota. Said Eastman: "...people have always claimed that the stone arrows which are found so generally throughout the country are the ones that the first man used in his battle with the animals. It is not recorded in our traditions, much less is it within the memory of

The buffalo headdress indicated a member of the Silent Eaters or Chiefs' Society. The bravest of the brave, members of the society were those men who had given up a warrior's lifestyle to protect the women and children of the camp. Only those who had strong magic were allowed to wear the buffalo headdress and could perform the buffalo dance. This portrait of No Heart was taken by Frank Bennett Fiske in Fort Yates, North Dakota, and appeared on a cabinet card published in 1906.

our old men, that we have ever made or used similar arrow-heads. Some have tried to make use of them for shooting fish under water, but with little success, and they are absolutely useless with the Indian bow which was in use when America was discovered."[37] However, the Lakota legend, relayed in Chapter 9, where Inktomi sets his spiders to work making arrowheads seems to indicate that the plains tribes did use stone-tipped arrows.

Victories were celebrated with the scalp dance, described by Pond. Woman led the dance holding their husbands', their sons' and their brothers' trophies. An old woman carried the staff with the scalps while the others formed a circle around her. Clothed in their best, they stood side by side, their blankets wrapped around them, facing the center. They progressed around the circle by jumping sideways a few inches. They stayed perfectly straight and in close order and so passed slowly around the circle. Meanwhile the men sang the scalp song and beat the drum. Periodically men and women would form two lines facing each other and dance forward and back. The song was repeated and women responded with the ululation. The ceremony lasted all night. Men danced wildly if they danced at all, in marked contrast to the measured step of the women which, Pond believed, added a gruesome aspect to the proceedings.[38]

Peace and alliance were formal affairs which respected divergent traditions, some unique to a particular group and some shared between them. Most of the eastern woodland tribes "buried the tomahawk," as a symbol of peace between the two nations, which has become adopted into the English language in the familiar expression "bury the hatchet." While no documentation was found to indicate this was part of the Dakota ceremony, they would have respected the other tribe's customs.

Meanwhile the use of the calumet, or peace pipe, was common to all tribes, including the Dakota. Alliance with them followed prescribed steps. The representatives of the tribe who came to sue for peace would enter the camp from the east to signify their peaceful intent. They would come to the council lodge in the center of the village where the head chief would meet the visitors. Others would be summoned to attend, the headmen, the *akitcita*, the war chiefs and the braves. The pipe would be smoked. The representative would submit their proposal and gifts were presented. Terms would be discussed; agreements arranged for the release or exchange of prisoners. The pipe would be smoked with each oath made. Feasts would punctuate the negotiations, which could take a full four days. In fact, the proceedings would have resembled the ceremony of a trade alliance described in *The Voyages of Peter Esprit Radisson*.

The formalities of the Dakota find their reflection in treaties of the present day. Indeed, the Dakota system shows a logic and a reason that sometimes seems to be lacking today. Their protocols were clearly defined, eliminating the months spent agonizing over the seating arrangement and the shape of table before international representatives ever reached the negotiating stage, as happened in the Paris peace talks during the Vietnam War.

An important alliance between tribes was often solemnized with the *Hunka* (adoption) ceremony. Once the ritual was completed, the tribes became as one family, which gave them the same protection and defense afforded any other Dakota band. Samuel Pond described the *Hunka* covenant: "The two ... thus bound to each other by the mutual promise of friendship were expected to have a particular regard for each other's welfare, and each was bound to stand by his friend and aid him in all times of necessity."[39]

Again history discredits those who would view the Dakota way of war as disordered, confused or in any way an *ad hoc* series of inconsequential raids and personal vendettas, although retaliatory strikes did occur. The Dakota warrior worked within a unified policy, according to set rules of gentlemanly conduct.

Just as their boundary disputes and their changes in alliances were not arbitrary, so too, the paint and feathers worn by a warrior were neither arbitrary nor simple adornments. The societies each had an identifying mark or insignia, similar to uniforms. They also had awards, symbols of achievements, which could be compared to the medals and the insignia of rank in present-day armies. The red slashes on legs and arms, like the American Purple Heart, were worn by those who had been wounded in battle. The eagle feather was awarded to those who had achieved excellence in the art of war.

Dakota campaigns were well organized with specific goals in mind. Whether it was to avenge a wrong done to their people or to defend their home, they had a strict code of conduct in warfare which did not include rape, torture or mutilation, until the late period when they learned to respond in kind to white atrocities. Their form of death was swift and expedient—hence merciful—and in their quest to prove their courage, the coup counted as much as the killing stroke.

The Dakota had a form of "Geneva Convention" which outlined the humane treatment of prisoners long before the Europeans had conceived of the idea. They showed charity to the enemy and were renowned for their humanitarian treatment of prisoners. Compare the release of the Huron to their camp, against the U.S. handling of the Dakota after the Santee rebellion in Minnesota in 1862, with mass hangings and thousands of noncombatants herded onto a desolate reservation to die. Weigh the treatment of Sarah Wakefield, who was fed and protected by her Dakota captors, against the conduct on both sides during the Civil War towards enemy prisoners. In the final analysis, the Dakota way of war shows an enlightenment, with mercy for the vanquished both living and dead, that the U.S. government in the 1800s had yet to achieve.

12. Social Graces

As the family broke fast on a bright sunny morning, the Yamaha[1] rode his pony around the camp, announcing the news. The daughter of White Eagle invited all pure maidens to a feast. The young men were also invited to make sure that no unworthy women attended. The event would be held in the Wahpeton village.

The camp buzzed with activity as the herald left to give the other bands the message. The girls prepared their finery, bright calicos or beaded buckskins. Some painted vermilion on their cheeks and if they had earned the privilege by becoming a buffalo woman, they painted the part of their hair bright red.

The day of the feast, the young women came from far and wide. Some walked sedately, accompanied by their grandmothers. Some rode on horseback. All came to enter the maidens' circle where two arrows pierced the ground next to a conical rock. Under the watchful eye of the spectators, the girls approached this altar one by one to touch the stone and the arrows and each to declare her virtue.

Beyond the maidens' circle, sage grandmothers gathered to watch those girls who had been given into their care. The day was sunny and beautiful. The entire population turned out, men and women alike, representing the many different tribes and bands, for what better way for a man to find a chaste wife?

Food was being served to the women inside the circle when a young man interrupted the proceedings. The disturbance rippled throughout the crowd as he advanced to the edge of the circle and stopped behind one of the women.

"You do not belong here," he said.

The young woman stood up, back straight and head proud. "What do you mean?" she said. "Three times you have approached me, and three times I have sent you away. Twice I was not alone and others can attest to my behavior. Only once when I carried water from the stream was I alone, and then my grandmother can tell you that I was gone only a few moments."

His lie exposed, the youth stared mute at the ground. The akitcita moved in, shouting for the man to be removed from the circle, and the maidens feasted, the betrayed woman among them. Then the women rose to dance the maiden dance, four times around the altar, and as they left the sacred circle each swore an oath to remain virtuous until she became a wife.

But not all the stories have such happy endings, for many moons ago when the people still lived in the land of the sacred lake, a maid grieved. A great chief had left presents outside her family's tipi, and they had been accepted.

"Why did you take them?" she asked her sister-in-law. "I do not love him."

"He is a brave warrior who has won many feathers. You would be lucky to marry him."

The chief came to visit often and he boasted of his valor, but she turned her face from him. The maiden's brother saw her sorrow and relented. "I thought such a staunch warrior would make you happy, but I will not force you to marry one you do not love."

The chief's gifts were returned, and the chief smarted over this refusal. One night northern lights danced across the heavens. People emerged from their tipis to gaze at the sky, for it was a sign of great evil.

The day of the maiden feast fast approached, and the chief devised a plan to avenge the insult done him. When the women sat inside the circle, he declared that the young woman who had rebuffed him was no maid, and he led her from the sacred space.

Stunned, she did not think to protest her innocence. Instead she turned to find her brother among the crowd. His angry countenance and the silence of her chaperone condemned more than the chief's words, for she knew she would find no solace there. Without support, she had no defense against this accusation. Who would believe her word over that of the great chief if her own family did not?

Friendless and betrayed, shamed and shunned, the girl took the only refuge left to her: death. They found her lifeless body the next day, a knife protruding from her breast. However, the chief's evil deed did not go unpunished. Within six weeks he was dead, killed not in noble, glorious battle, but a victim of the smallest of enemies, smallpox.[2]

The flute was integral to courtship. The hopeful man would play it outside the door of his intended. The blanket was drawn over the face to indicate the man's respect. The flute was made of either wood or bone, and called the *cotanka*. This picture was painted in 1909 by Frederic Remington, who called it *The Love Call*.

The Dakota placed great importance on fidelity and virtue. The trial represented by the maidens' feast was not confined only to women or to singles. Samuel Pond attended a similar rite held for the married people who remained true to each other. Married women celebrated their devotion in the *isnala kic'un*, the "being alone" ceremony, which affirmed they had remained faithful to their husbands throughout their marriage. Additionally women over forty or fifty were honored if they had only had a single spouse.

According to Eastman (Ohiyesa), there was also a feast for eligible males who avowed they had never courted a woman,[3] "for whom the rules were even more strict, since no young man might attend this feast who had so much as spoken of love to a maiden. It was considered a high honor among us to have won some distinction in war and the chase, and above all to have been invited to a seat in the council, before one had spoken to any girl save his own sister."[4]

If a man wished to challenge a woman's virtue, he could throw her bowl away, but he had

Among the Dakota woman's many chores were the tanning of hides and the making of the tipi, along with clothes. She gathered food, such as the prairie turnip, *mdo*, and roots of the water lily, and often grew the corn. She was responsible for the maintenance and upkeep of the home. The photograph, *When winter comes*, shows a Dakota woman, going about her duties carrying firewood toward the winter lodge. Curtis Collection (Library of Congress). The photograph was taken by Edward Curtis on July 6, 1908, and published in *The North American Indian*, Seattle, Wash. 1907–30, Suppl., v. 3, pl. 105. (Part of the Edward S. Curtis Collection, Library of Congress.)

to be prepared to "bite the knife," taking the weapon into his mouth. If he lied, it was believed the knife would kill him. Many men were unwilling to take the risk.[5]

Ceremonies for men, women and couples—and the means to challenge deception in both the accuser and the accused—stress the value the Dakota placed on chastity, fidelity and honesty in both men and women. While young girls had much more freedom than their European counterparts, this was curtailed when they reached a marriageable age.

Unlike the Santee of the Carolinas, Dakota women were expected to maintain their virginity until they wed. In his book, Pond explained the extent to which this was taken. "Mothers took great pains in training their daughters in the habits of decorum. They were taught to assume the correct posture, and to gather garments close around their feet."[6] To further protect young women of marriageable age, they were instructed to sleep with their feet pointed toward the fire and rarely were they allowed out unescorted, especially if they may encounter a white man. As a result Pond found the Dakota women "chaste in their conversation and modest in their behavior, both at home and abroad."[7]

Modesty and civility seemed to be characteristic of most their interactions with each other and even with the unwelcome outsider. Pond described the Dakota as affable and courteous. He said they were quiet in manners, although animated in speech, seldom rude or boisterous. Men spoke in hushed tones even when their passions were aroused. Often subject to impertinent questions of white men who came to visit them in their tipis, they were too polite to mention their resentment openly.[8]

Eastman concurred, stating that courtesy and consideration were necessary when living in close quarters for prolonged periods. As many as four families from two generations could sleep in the Wahpeton summer house.

Their myths encapsulate the morality of the Dakota people as much as the mystery plays of old relate Christian virtues. The stories of the divine relay tales of deception, deceit, incest, infidelity, adultery and their subsequent punishments. Anything that challenges the established order and public peace has ramifications. The birth of *Ksa* illustrates. This mystery is brought forth fully formed, an unnatural act and, as such, not without its repercussions. The creature hatched by *Wakinyan*, despite all his intelligence, develops a spiteful and vengeful spirit that proves his undoing.

The legends have many of the same ingredients of the Greek or the Roman mythos, but the Lakota pantheon actually has a constancy not found in their European counterparts. It reveals none of its caprice where Zeus/Jupiter castigated a human simply because the god was having a bad day. Instead each Dakota divinity is punished for a real crime — *Unk* for creating contention amongst the others; the mortal *Ite* for her vanity; *Ksa* for abuse of wisdom and power; and *Wa* and *Ka* for causing pain to another.

Even the duped *Wi* does not escape unscathed for his adulterous glance, suggesting an equality between the sexes lacking in Europe of the time. It's not only the women who get punished for a breach of faith while the male god goes larking about as a bull, a swan or whatever else suits his purpose and his fancy. *Wi*, son of the great *Skan*, must give up his wife whom he has wronged with this look.

The tales reflect a kind of justice unknown to the Europeans of the time. The Dakota defines infidelity as something as insignificant as a look while at the time of America's "discovery" Elizabethan Europe still applauded "gallant love," which by its definition could only take place with someone other than one's spouse. For the Native American fostering strife or any conspiracy against the collective good is punishable by banishment. Even the abuse of talent or power, which is *Ksa's* crime, leads to misfortune for the perpetrator while those who have been victimized must be compensated.

In most cases the punishment fits the crime. So *Ite* the vain has her face twisted out of true and the faithless *Wi* loses his wife. Reprisals also show a certain element of compassion. Thus, *Skan* permits *Tate* to leave the hallowed halls of the divines to join *Ite* on earth. *Tate* follows her by choice for the love of the woman who betrayed him, so he shows forgiveness.

From this we can surmise that love and fidelity were not the alien concepts the historians, shocked by multiple marriages, would have us believe. Men could mark or disfigure a promiscuous wife, but the wronged woman could likewise dictate retribution. Said Eastman: "A marriage might be honorably dissolved for cause, but there was very little infidelity or immorality, either open or secret."[9] And barrenness, according to Eastman, was not considered sufficient reason for divorce, while European nobility of the period felt no qualms about setting aside a fruitless union.

In Lakota legends, faith is rewarded, just as its breach is penalized. Marriage is an important state while love is a powerful emotion, a cause worthy of self-imposed exile, even death. Gone is the image of the native brave with many wives who are little better than slaves.

Likewise, the stories reveal a real concept of democracy, one not known to the colonizing English, one that stressed the collective good over that of the individual. The public weal is more important than a single person's desires. Even one of the chief deities, who could be likened to the European aristocracy, were not exempt from its rules. Petty jealousies are not permitted to disturb the tribe's tranquility, and if they do, the discipline is not only swift, it is appropriate.

The creation mythology reiterates the principle that something must be sacrificed in order for creation to take place. So each of the major divinities has to give up something of him or herself to get a companion. As in heaven, so on earth: so the Grandmother of the young Ohiyesa explained the importance of sacrifice to the divine. "You must remember in this offering you will call upon him who looks at you from every creation. In the wind you hear him whisper to you. He gives his war-whoop in the thunder. He watches you by day with his eye, the sun; at night, He gazes upon your sleeping countenance through the moon. In short it is the Mystery of Mysteries who control all things to whom you will make your first offering."[10] The gift must be worthy, the most precious possession, the most loved, the most valued, and Ohiyesa was asked to sacrifice his beloved dog to ensure he found favor in the Creator's eyes.

Women also did all the cooking. This picture, staged for Herman Heyn, shows two women and a child seated on ground. They use an iron kettle, a luxury brought by the white man. Before that time, the woodland Dakota used clay pots. Photo by Herman Heyn, c. 1899.

Like the Christian of that day, the Dakota believed in providence. Evil deeds provoked powers to anger which reverberated beyond the "sinner" to the family, band or tribe. The Dakota held up the example of the Wahpetuke. Hospitality was considered a sacred trust. Yet long ago when the Iowa wanted to return home from Canada through Dakota territories, they were given leave to travel through Dakota territory by the Mdewakanton who asked their kinsmen the Wahpetuke to let them pass. The latter agreed, admitting the Iowa into their camp for a feast and then falling upon them and killing them as they ate. The story is confirmed by Iowa tribal history which describes the same incident where one of their chiefs had been treacherously slain on the Iowa River by a band of Sioux.[11] After this time, it was said, the Wahpetuke never prospered, and so retribution was meted against an entire tribe for their breach of sacred trust. The Sauk killed many of them in a battle some 100 years after the original massacre.

The observer Pond explained: "The punishment of the wicked was ascribed to *Takuwakan*."[12] Daily prohibitions, though, were simply described as *wakan*. Although *Wakan* is defined overall as anything that is mysterious or sacred, it had other usages. To say something was *wakan* meant that it should not be done. So it was *wakan* to point a loaded gun at a friend, meaning it should not be done. Likewise, it was *wakan* to tempt fate by threatening death even in jest, and there were stories to illustrate such points. One such included a young man who threatened to kill his brother when he refused to join a hunt and then accidentally shot him when he returned to camp. According to Pond, these strictures had more influence in their daily affairs than their rites and rituals.[13]

In truth, laws governing morality varied little from those of the Europeans. Eastman agreed. "Murder within the tribe was a grave offense, to be atoned for as the council might decree, and it often happened that the slayer was called upon to pay the penalty with his own life. He made no attempt to escape or to evade justice.... Hence did not hesitate to give himself up, to stand his trial by the old and wise men of the victim's clan. His own family and clan might by no means attempt to excuse or to defend him, although the powerfully placed could exert influence. Still the judges took all the known circumstances into consideration, and if it appeared that he slew in self-defense, or that the provocation was severe, the lawbreaker might be set free after a thirty days' period of mourning in solitude. Otherwise, the murdered man's next of kin were authorized to take his life; and if they refrained from doing so, as often happened, the killer often remained an outcast from the clan."[14]

Morality also found reflection in their ceremonies, other than the maiden feasts to celebrate virtue. "There were many ceremonial customs which had a distinct moral influence; the woman was rigidly secluded at certain periods, and the young husband was forbidden to approach his own wife when preparing for war or for any religious event."[15] Only the chaste and pure of body and spirit could handle religious objects.

Each society had its rites of initiation where men swore to uphold certain ethical virtues, with prohibitions against stealing and lying. However, the beliefs on the latter two appear to be flexible, as they are in the present day. Consider the Fox Society vow that averred stealing from a friend, but condoned it against an enemy, and whites soon proved themselves to be enemies. So it is in no way a surprise that in 1834, Pond said: "The thievish propensities of the Dakota were pretty strong. Property was seldom safe when so exposed that they could take it with little danger of detection ... but it was deemed less disgraceful to pilfer from the whites than from their own people."[16] Pond compared the Dakotas with ancient Spartans, where detection of crime was a greater sin than the deed itself.

Yet with their custom of generosity where one gave to those less fortunate, they may not have always viewed the use or removal of goods as theft. Particularly food: if the individual was a friend, the native may have assumed that the person would have given it freely. This happened in Lawson's time when he and his Indian guide entered home of a relative while he was absent and took what they needed from the man's stores. Therefore the Dakota made a distinction between theft, and the taking what may have been a gift, that the white man did not grasp.

Stealing within the tribal environment was forbidden so their behavior within the confines of the village was more circumspect. The Carolina Santee shared this view. "Thief is held in Disgrace, that steals from his country folk."[17] This fact was also acknowledged by Eastman in *The Soul of the Indian*. "To steal from one of his own tribe would be indeed disgrace, and if discovered, the name of '*Wamanon*,' or Thief, is fixed upon him forever as an unalterable stigma. The only exception to the rule is in the case of food, which is always free to the hungry if there is none by to offer it. Other protection than the moral law there could not be in an Indian community, where there were neither locks nor doors, and everything was open and easy of access to all comers." Meanwhile: "The property of an enemy is spoil of war...."[18]

A similar disparity governed honesty. As a trait, it was much esteemed, and yet a man might also be honored for artifice or sleight of hand. Then as now, honesty, like so much in life, was situational. To deceive an enemy was laudable. To hide an unpleasant truth from exposure was expedient. Honesty, however, was valued enough that it could mediate punishment. Therefore, the man who confessed his crime was more likely to be forgiven than those who clung to deception.

Still the punishment for lying could be severe. Eastman conveyed the traditional teachings.

Before the arrival of the kettle, the nomadic plains tribes used a buffalo paunch as a cooking vessel. The bag would have been suspended on a tripod next to a fire, rather than over it. Stones were placed in the fire and the superheated stones put in the paunch to boil the water and cook the food. Entitled *Primitive Cooking*, the picture shows High Bear, a Brulé Sioux man, cooking in a paunch. The photograph was taken by J.A. Anderson in 1911.

"It is said that, in very early days, lying was a capital offense among us. Believing that the deliberate liar is capable of committing any crime behind the screen of cowardly untruth and double-dealing, the destroyer of mutual confidence was summarily put to death, that the evil might go no further."[19]

This appears to be confirmed by the experience of Wi Jun Jon, a member of the Yankton offshoot, the Assiniboin. In 1832, he was sent to Washington to represent his people. On his return he told incredible stories of great houses of stone and a land overrun by the white man. He was condemned as a liar and later put to death, shot in the head for describing what he had seen in the east.[20]

Despite the flexibility, Pond asserted: "The Dakota were quick to discern between right and wrong, and knew very well what to approve and what to condemn."[21] Meanwhile, he said: "Theft and falsehood had no open advocates, and no one spoke well of notorious thieves and liars."[22] The image that emerges is that probity, like fidelity, was valued, but humankind — as imperfect beings — did not always live up to the ideal, and some had a harder time of it than others.

In fact, oaths and vows were integral to Dakota society and taken much more seriously by them than by European society, as witnessed by the litter of treaties discarded by the whites when it was deemed expedient. Once word was given and sealed with the pipe by the Dakota, it was inviolate and those who broke vows were never trusted again. They were shunned or exiled from the tribe. Imagine, then, the confusion for the Dakota when they became embroiled in a world of ever-shifting alliances— French, British and later the United States— where a treaty, an oath, was not as good as the paper upon which it was written and about as durable.

Inside the tribal setting, an oath or a pledge often took the form of a taboo (*tehila*) which could be seen as another form of individual sacrifice. It was customary for men to abstain from a certain type of meat, or a specific cut of a particular animal. Taboos were usually voluntary. They could be temporary or permanent. Cheyenne Roman Nose provides an example of the latter, with a permanent prohibition against the use of metal, meaning he could not eat if the meal had been cooked in the standard kettle.

A temporary taboo was exemplified by the Keeper of the Soul ceremony. Along with his other duties the avowed Keeper was prohibited from handling metal — not knife, pot or kettle — and he was barred from hunting for a period of a year, which involved considerable sacrifice.

Fasts were common, often as part of a ceremony or as an individual vow. Ohiyesa's grandmother admonished her grandson: "Only those who seek him (the Great Mystery) in fasting and in solitude will receive his signs."[23] To take part in the *Hablenchya* (which Ohiyesa called Hambeday, revealing one of the many dialectic differences between the tribes) a man had to fast for four days. The ceremony itself lasted for a further four days during which time the supplicant did not eat. Similar cleansing fasts were common with other ceremonies, such as the sun dance. Even today the rule remains, with fasting and abstaining from alcohol — the latter for a period of up to one year — essential to participate in the sun dance ceremony.

An individual may also foreswear food as part of a blood oath. Likewise, someone might refuse to eat until he or she had accomplished a certain feat. Fasting was also an essential part of mourning. Meanwhile, limiting food consumption was often a harsh reality of life, or a necessity as the war party that must, of necessity, travel light. Eastman (Ohiyesa) believed such fasts strengthened his people. "Even if there were plenty to eat, it was thought better for us to practice fasting sometimes; and hard exercise was kept up continually, both for the sake of the health and to prepare the body for the hard exertions that it might be required to undergo."[24] He continues, "In times of famine, adults often denied themselves in order to make the food last as long as possible for the children.... As a people they can live without food for longer than any other nation."[25] However, "the usual custom was to eat only two meals a day, and

Boys were considered the future defenders of the people and were trained the arts of war from birth when they were met by lullabies that spoke of the exploits of war. A boy was taught by his father and his grandfather to shoot and hunt. The photograph from the Heyn and Matzen studio is a portrait of John Lone Bull, wearing a beaded vest and holding traditional bow and arrows. Photograph by Heyn & Matzen, May 24, 1900.

these were served at each end of the day. This rule was not invariable, however, for if there should be any callers, it was Indian etiquette to offer either tobacco or food, or both."[26]

Food was shared equally among all the people. Eastman elaborated on their values in a later book. "The native American has been generally despised by his white conquerors for his poverty and simplicity. They forget, perhaps, that his religion forbade the accumulation of wealth and the enjoyment of luxury.... the love of possession has appeared a snare, and the burdens of a complex society a source of needless peril and temptation. Furthermore, it was the rule of his life to share the fruits of his skill and success with his less fortunate bothers."[27]

If any maxim illustrates the morality of a nation, then it is the Dakota views on the treatment of the weak, vulnerable or helpless. All chiefs and headmen swore not to eat until everyone was fed. They were to give a horse to any elder who might fall behind and to the youngest child of any prisoner. These vows were taken seriously, and it puzzled white traders to find the chief was often the poorest person in the tribe. Likewise, each new member of the warrior societies were enjoined not to eat until every child and every elder had been fed.

The custom of giving away one's possessions to another — now referred to by the Crow term *Pot latch* — was shared by the Siouan tribes of east and west. The practice bewildered acquisitive whites, like Lawson, who was present when a man lost his home to a "great wind." Each member of the tribe gave the victim something to replace what had been destroyed until, by the end of the ceremony, the man was better off than he had been before the storm and better off than many who had given him gifts. Similarly, the Carolina Santee would let no one go hungry as long as it was in their capacity to give assistance. "It often happens that a Woman is destitute of her Husband and has a great many Children to maintain; such a Person they always help."[28]

For the Dakota, Generosity (*wacantognaka*) was a highly prized trait and was considered one of the four cardinal virtues. Ohiyesa described the practice of gifting. "Public giving is a part of every important ceremony. It properly belongs to the celebration of birth, marriage, and death, and is observed whenever it is desired to do special honor to any person or event. Upon such occasions it is common to give to the point of utter impoverishment. The Indian in his simplicity literally gives away all that he has, to relatives, to guests of another tribe or clan, but above all to the poor and the aged, from whom he can hope for no return.... Orphans and the aged are invariably cared for, not only by their next of kin, but by the whole clan."[29]

Eastman continued in the same vein: "The true Indian sets no price upon either his property or his labor. His generosity is only limited by his strength and his ability."[30] Pond described the rite that surrounded gifting. When a person received something, the act was formally celebrated. The recipient would walk around the camp, singing a song designed for the occasion. When he got the people's attention, the name of the giver and the type of present was announced. "There was also much given to the poor, such as widows and orphans, especially of food, for none were ever suffered to starve if there were provisions in the camp. When a woman fed her own family, she also fed all who were present; and when game was brought in, a portion was sent to those who had none."[31]

Pierre Radisson first met the Dakota after a particularly harsh winter. The traders were unable to hunt and near to starvation until the spring thaw. The Santee had heard of his plight and arrived as soon as spring released the land from winter's thrall, bearing gifts of food. Radisson said with typical European asperity and ingratitude: "...it would have been welcomed if they had brought it a month or two before."[32]

Meanwhile the American tribes viewed the Europeans as parsimonious and inhospitable. For in all Indian nations the sharing of goods was commended. The French in an attempt to impress the natives in their region took representatives to France. Their reaction was not favorable. Different reports written at the time record the same sentiment.

Writing in 1636, Gabriel Sagard said: "Those of their Nation, who offer reciprocal hospitality, and help each other so much that there is no poor beggar at all in their towns ... so that they found it very bad hearing that there were in France a great number of needy and beggars and thought it was due to a lack of charity and blamed us greatly, saying that if we had some intelligence we could set some order in the matter, the remedies being simple."[33]

Father Christien LeClercq wrote: "Thou sayest of us also that we are the most miserable and unhappy of all men, living without religion, without manners, without honor, without social order, in a word, without rules like the beasts...."[34]

Dakota women would give food, clothing, medicine and succor to those in need, as illustrated by Sarah Wakefield in her book, *Six Weeks in Sioux Tepees*. The entire family became involved in the protection of the captive Wakefield and her children once their father had brought them into his home. She and her children were disguised and hidden when necessary to keep them safe from those who would wreak vengeance upon her for their ill treatment at the hands of the white man. In one incident, a warrior demanded the death of all whites inside the camp, and the wife of her captor tucked Wakefield inside some buffalo robes and then stood guard over both mother and children against any who might approach.[35]

Meanwhile the girl was the future mother of a noble race. Much care and attention was paid to the dress of the young as revealed by a portrait of Two Shawl. The child sits on a log and wears a miraculous medal on a necklace for protection. The leggings are beaded, as are the moccasins. Photo by Herman Heyn & Matzen, May 24, 1900.

Children too were considered sacred, as illustrated by the Lakota word for child *wakan-heja* or *wakan-jeya*. Dakota babies were well tended. Children under four slept with their parents or grandparents. The extended family unit as revealed by their relationship names meant that one's father's brothers were also fathers, while his mother's sisters were additional mothers. Thus a child was not orphaned if both parents died since alternate parents already existed. The extended family structure to a certain extent explains polygamy within the culture, for if a man's brother died, he would be expected to marry the widow and take care of her children.

To the outside observer, Dakota parents often seemed indulgent of their children. Back in the 1700s, explorer John Lederer found the Siouan children of the east coast particularly undisciplined. "These Indians are so indiscreetly fond of their children that they will not chastise them for any mischief or insolence."[36]

Indeed physical punishments were rare when a sharp word or a stern look would do. Children were taught to be deferential to their parents, especially when instant obedience to a command may be a necessary survival skill when the tribe was under attack. The Dakota peoples while patient with their offspring reprimanded them for impertinence.

While they appeared carefree to others, Dakota children had responsibilities. They had specific chores—such as taking the horses to water—but once such duties were completed, they were free to entertain themselves without interference and until the age of eight girls could roam freely with their brothers.

In both his books, *Indian Boyhood* and *Soul of an Indian,* Charles Eastman discussed the difference in training between genders. "Scarcely was the embryo warrior ushered into the world, when he was met by lullabies that speak of the wonderful exploits of war.... He is called the future defender of the people whose lives may depend upon his courage and his skill. If the child is a girl, she is at once addressed as the future mother of a noble race."[37] He continues: "At the age of about eight years, if he is a boy, she [the mother] turns him over to his father for more Spartan training. If a girl, she is from this time much under the guardianship of her grandmother, who is considered the most dignified protector for the maiden. Indeed, the distinctive work of both grandparents is that of acquainting the youth with the national traditions and beliefs."[38]

Grandparents told stories of the past and imparted to the young manners and morals through the traditions and history of the tribe. Grandparents and elders were treated with respect. Ohiyesa mentions the attention afforded an elder. "In short, the old men and women are privileged to say what they please and how they please, without contradiction, while the hardships and bodily infirmities that of necessity fall to their lot are softened so far as may be by universal consideration and attention."[39]

Reverence for elders was found in the Siouan tribes of both east and west. Speaking of the Catawba, Lawson said: "Whensoever an Aged Man is speaking, none ever interrupt him (the contrary Practice the *English*, and other *European*, too much use) the Company yielding a great deal of Attention to his Tale, with a continued Silence, and an exact Demeanour, during the oration."[40]

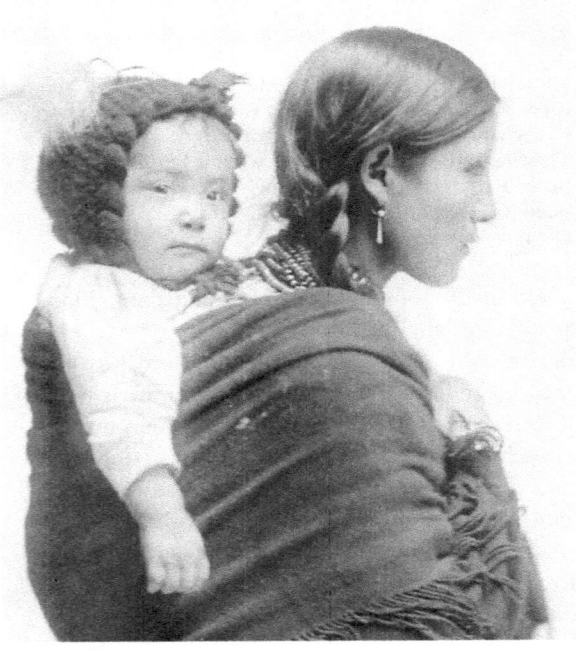

The Dakota woman had the ultimate say in the upbringing of the children, which were hers even if a couple should split up. At the age of eight, children of both sexes were turned over to their grandparents for education, daughters to the grandmother and sons to the grandfather; but the mother still had a voice in their affairs. Photographic print taken in 1901 by Howard D. Beach of Buffalo, N.Y.

Elders were often invited to counsel, and when unable to attend, their advice otherwise sought. The Siouan culture was not unique in this; it appears to be have been a universal for all Native American peoples. It is perhaps their treatment of the elderly, the weak, the sick and the helpless that is their most enduring and endearing trait, one for which they must be respected and from which Western culture could learn a great deal.

In review, the Dakota people had a strong belief in right and wrong which were contained in their four cardinal virtues—wisdom, bravery, fortitude and generosity. They honored the common good over that of the individual and held many same of the values dear that the Europeans professed to value, such as fidelity, probity, honesty, chastity, charity, courtesy and modesty. Unlike many of their white counterparts, the Dakota acted on them. They upheld these beliefs in their rituals and in their treatment of others. They rewarded the virtuous, the faithful and the honorable. Their word once sealed with the pipe of peace was sacrosanct. They not only scorned the habitual liar and the thief, they censured them. In a culture when one must rely on the veracity of another tribe member to survive, the punishments could be severe, ranging from simple shunning to expulsion or even death.

Likewise, settlers' tales of theft and cupidity date from the period when the Dakota and the white man were at odds. Once white settlers and traders attained the status of adversary, they would have become exempt from the rules that dealt with theft and honesty within the tribe and among allies. Other such stories date from the post-reservation era when the people — deprived of their land, their traditions and their livelihood — were forced to abandon the values of the past in order to survive.

13. Within the Tipi

Tate and his sons lived in a tipi on the earth in the land beyond the pines. He sat in the place of honor opposite the door. His first-born, Yata, sat beside him. Eya, the second, sat on his father's right. The third son, Yampa, sat to his left, and Okaga sat beside the door facing Tate. Yum took the woman's place next to the fire.

Tate did the woman's work when his sons went to hunt. He knew where his wife Anog Ite dwelled and sometimes he would go watch her, for he still remembered her as Ite of the beautiful face, and he would protect her from harm as long as they lived. His promises to her and his love for her were undiminished by the years.

One day when his sons were away, a star fell from the sky outside his lodge. Tate went outside to look, and he found a young woman as fair as Ite once had been. She wore a dress of white. Curious, Tate he asked her why she had come.

"My father has sent me to you."

Tate smiled, for he knew her as Wohpe of the bright star. "I am your father's friend, and you are welcome in my home. As my brother's daughter, you are my daughter also. Come live in my tipi with me and my sons."

Tate led her by the hand to his lodge and then moved to return to work on the hide he was scraping. Wohpe took the tool from him and said: "Let me do the woman's work." And she finished a buffalo robe for him as fine as any he had ever seen.

As the sun sank low in the sky, the eldest, Yata, entered to the tipi. His gaze fell upon the beautiful face and he retreated to sit outside alone. Eya peeked inside the door and, seeing his father and some strange woman, he went to sit beside his brother. Yanpa did the same. At last, Okaga arrived with Yum by his side. The youthful Yum ran to the door to gape at the stranger. She smiled at him, and he went inside and snuggled up beside her. She put her arm around him while Okaga took his assigned place just inside the door.

"There is no food prepared," Yanpa complained to his brothers.

"She has bewitched him," said Yata, and Eya agreed.

Hearing the conversation beyond the door, Tate said: "I must make dinner."

"No," Wohpe reminded him gently, "I shall do the woman's work." No sooner had she spoken than a cheery fire blazed in the hearth, and stones sizzled and hissed next to the glowing coals. She placed the heated stones in the cooking bag.

Tate called to his sons. "Dinner is cooking. Come in."

Yanpa relented. "I am hungry." And he went inside and sat in his assigned place.

Again, Tate called to his sons, and Eya joined them inside the lodge.

"You are keeping everyone waiting," Tate shouted to the stubborn last. "Come eat."

The ever-suspicious Yata entered. He would watch this witch and see what sort of spell she had placed on his father.

When all were gathered, Wohpe served each according to their station, giving to each son his favorite dish. To Tate she provided thick soup and liver. For Yata she produced wild rice and flesh, both lean and fat. To Eya, she gave duck and wild turnips. Yanpa wanted everything she had given to his brothers, so she plucked liver, flesh, rice and turnips from her magic bag. She put a little food in a bowl and placed it in front of Okaga. It smelled of fruit, flowers and sweet grass. Okaga stared at the dish, tasted the food. It was good. He ate heartily until he was sated. Wohpe fed tidbits to Yum, and he too was content.

When night fell, Okaga could not sleep. He sat outside the tipi, covered his face with his blanket and began to play his flute. Inside, Wohpe listened intently.

"Why do you listen so?" asked the youthful Yum.

"I listen to the song of my beloved," she said.

The next day after his restless night, Okaga snapped at his younger brother for the first time. Yum ran to kind Wohpe for comfort. "Why is Okaga angry with me?"

"He is not angry. Leave him alone and do not worry. He suffers from love sickness now, but someday you, I and he shall live happily together."

That night they ate in silence, but Okaga was troubled, for he was heartsick. When it was time to sleep, he remained restless. He sat and played his flute. In this way, he showed his love for her, but before he could woo the fair Wohpe he must perform some great deed, some act of bravery to show himself worthy of her affection, for no man could approach a woman until he had become a warrior.

―⌇⌇―

Children were *wakan*, as revealed by the Lakota word for child, *wakanheja*. They were both treasured and protected by their Dakota parents. White settlers often viewed the Dakota as overly indulgent with them. The portrait of White Bull shows a baby in a beaded cradleboard propped up against a studio prop tree trunk. Lakota women prided themselves on their beadwork and lavished particular care and attention on the cradles used to carry their babies. Photo by Herman Heyn and Matzen, May 24, 1900.

At the time of contact, the condition of Dakota women was better than that of their European counterparts. The importance of women and their place in the community was reflected by the fact that they and significant events in which they participated were mentioned in numerous winter counts, such as the Big Missouri winter count, for the years of 1799, 1800, 1828, 1874, 1888 and 1905. In the No Ears and Iron Crow counts, their activities were commemorated in 1770, 1792, 1793, 1798, 1799, 1804, 1853, 1856, and 1857. It is interesting to note as references to white men increased, references to women decreased, indicating that women lost some of their esteem among the Lakota after the arrival of Lewis and Clark.

Their position and their subsequent treatment declined in the late period after the introduction of alcohol. Still, the women of the Dakota held status and authority unknown to white women at the time of contact. A Dakota woman could act as *akitcita* and police the tribe. Once nominated, she took the office with all its powers, duties and responsibilities. As *akitcita*, her voice was heard and her rulings absolute.

Women elders spoke at council and could become council members. Eastman (Ohiyesa) said in *Soul of the Indian*: "...a woman who had attained to ripeness of years and wisdom, or who had displayed notable courage in some emergency, was sometimes invited to a seat in the council." This privilege was not extended to the young wife who was still sovereign in her own home, where "she ruled undisputed within her own domain, and was to us a tower of moral and physical strength...."[1]

Women's participation in ceremonies, such as the sun dance and the inipi (sweat lodge), was essential; therefore, they often became members of important warrior and *akitcita* societies. The medicine lodge, unique to the woodland Santee, was also open to her and Eastman noted: "Women were admitted to membership upon equal terms, with the possibility of attaining its highest honors."[2]

Women owned property. In truth they were the only property owners. This custom was well established and in operation at the time when the Dakota first met Pierre Radisson in 1660, as evidenced by the Dakota warriors' promise to the French traders that "the cottages of their wives and daughters were open at any time to receive us."[3] Thus, the warriors did not claim ownership of their homes when they offered hospitality to the traders, but acknowledged their wives' possession.

Two hundred years later Eastman records the estate of the Dakota women as little changed. "All the family property was held by her, descent was traced in the maternal line, and the honor of the house was in her hands."[4] Women owned the lodge and all it contents, along with all the tools required to maintain it. A warrior may paint the story of his exploits on the outside of the tipi, but his wife owned the physical structure, and she could choose, if she so desired, to throw her husband out.

Women not only attended, but participated in trade fairs, purchasing luxury items that they could not get anywhere else. The women of the Chinook conducted their fairs and were considered shrewd bargainers and skilled traders. The economic value of Indian women in the fur trade was recognized even by white traders of the time. As Edwin Denig noted in 1850, "The raw hide of the animal has no value. It is the labor of putting it in the form of a robe or skin fit for sale or use that makes its worth."[5] Only after the buffalo hide was scraped, tanned and worked by the women into something useful like a blanket or a robe did it acquire value.

Meanwhile the man's only belongings were his weapons, his horses and his clothes. In other words, the shirt on his back. The father was the hunter and warrior. Men fashioned weapons, the tools of their trade, and women did not touch these articles which were his possessions. This did not mean she did not know how to shoot a bow — legends are rife with examples of a woman taking over the hunting duties when men were absent — rather it suggests that she maintained weapons of her own, and when necessary, she would fight to defend herself, her family and her band.

The warrior did not accumulate wealth, for it was believed he could always replace it, but hearth and home were necessary to sustaining a family; thus property was the domain of women. Eastman described men's attitude in *Soul of an Indian*: "It is believed that the love of possessions is a weakness to be overcome. Its appeal to the material part, and if allowed its it will in time disturb the way the spiritual balance of the man."[6]

Not only was divorce possible for the Dakota woman, but she could instigate it, as long as she had the manpower to back it up. If a marriage was dissolved, the woman kept the property, the tipi and its contents, unless the wife had participated in the most heinous of marital crimes—adultery. She also maintained the custody of the children unless there was some compelling reason why she should not, as would be the case of the adulteress. Her punishment included the loss of all her possessions, making her incapable of providing a home for her family.

Comparatively speaking, European women of the time fared less well than their Dakota sisters. Divorce in some Catholic countries was still illegal as late as the 1970s. In England, a divorced woman had no right to a share of the couple's community property. Often she forfeited the custody of her children if she filed for divorce, and the laws denying women joint access to children and property were not repealed in the United Kingdom until the 1950s.

Although marriages were arranged, Dakota women had a voice in the choice of partner. However, the reality did not always live up to the ideal. The book *Dahcotah: The Life and Legends of the Sioux Around Fort Snelling* contains several stories about young women each forced into a loveless marriage to a brave not of her choosing, if he were important or powerful enough, or if the family liked the gifts that the suitor provided. The number of legends on this subject suggest that a woman's choice was often overlooked. The tale of Winona's Leap, where a young woman kills herself rather than marry the wrong man, is a classic which is shared among the all the Dakota tribes.

One of a woman's most sacred duties was as a mother; as such she was considered a co-participant to the creator. The Dakota mother was charged with teaching her children the religion and the traditions of the tribe. Pictured here, an Oglala woman with a baby on her back. Photogravure by E.S. Curtis, used as an illustration in *The North American Indian*, v. 3, opp. p. 18, published in 1905.

The European recorders of the period viewed the custom of gifts for the bride's family with disapproval. They saw it as a purchase, buying a bride, little better than slavery. However, the tradition that helped to prove a man's worth was not unique to Indians. Even in twentieth-century America, a suitor was expected to demonstrate to his prospective bride's parents that he would be a good provider.

The custom of gifting provided proof positive in a simple, straightforward way that the man would be able to support a family. In the early period, before the horse, gifts of weapons, hides, pelts and porcupine quills would have been common. In the later period, the bride's price was expensive, about 3 horses. Horses, which were the medium of exchange, were valued at 10 skins apiece, so the wife was highly prized. James Walker, who lived among the Lakota between 1896 and 1914, said that the standard price was six buffalo skins.[7] By his time, the buffalo had been nearly exterminated upon the plains, making skins a precious and rare commodity. Gifts of skins were eventually replaced by gifts of guns, cloth and blankets. The poor man could prove his worth by living with the girl's parents for a year and providing for them. Women supported the custom. It was considered shameful for a woman to wed without an adequate bride's price. Said Pond: "The better the price paid, the better they were pleased, for the payment of a great price proved that they were esteemed valuable."[8]

Marriage was called *ikiciyuze*, "to join together." Lineage and how one traced the line of descent varied from tribe to tribe. The woodland Dakota male would take up residence in his wife's tipi, and the lineage was traced through the matrilineal line. Said Eastman: "The wife did not take the name of her husband nor enter his clan, and the children belonged to the clan of the mother."[9]

Tradition changed with the prairie Lakota. The Oglala woman joined their husband's band or *tiyospi*, and mothers mourned the loss of their daughters. It was said when your daughter married, you lost her, but when your son married you gained a daughter, who was a valuable commodity. For the parents, a daughter moving from home meant a loss of a pair of important hands and an essential helpmate in perpetuity, and for an aging couple without sons, this could spell economic disaster unless they joined their daughter in his husband's band. Only if a man could not provide a bride's price would he enter his wife's tipi, becoming a "buried man."[10]

Courtship usually followed a set course. The young man must have earned his adult name before he paid suit. To avoid embarrassment and public rejection, a potential suitor usually approached his intended as she moved about the camp to see if she would welcome his advances. If he met with a positive reception, he then visited her in her family tent or he met her as she carried water from a brook, one of the few times when she might be alone. If she were carrying water, he would offer to help. Throughout this time, the woman had ample opportunity to rebuff him if she felt so inclined.

The official courtship began when the man covered his face, as a sign of respect, placed himself outside his intended's lodge and played his flute, as illustrated in the love story of Okaga and Wohpe. The instrument was made from the wing bone of a bird or some kind of wood. It was called a *cotanka*. He played his flute to impress her. The process could continue for a long time as the woman considered the man's suit.

If interested, the woman would step outside her lodge. If not, she ignored him. Once she left her lodge, she may or may not choose to speak with the young man at that time. As the courtship continued, the brave would don his best attire and a courting robe and march back and forth in front of her lodge. If favorably impressed, she would again exit the tipi and stand while her suitor drew closer to the lodge with each pass. Eventually he would take his place beside her and drape his robe over her shoulders. Said Walker: "This was the equivalent to a public announcement of betrothal."[11]

The parents then would invite him inside. If she smiled at him, offered him food or water, this confirmed her choice. She would then make moccasins for her affianced and gave them to him. If he put them on in her presence, then he likewise confirmed his choice.

Finally the suitor would approach the woman's brother to negotiate the terms of the agreement. If the woman had a married sister, then her husband would speak for the family, and if neither brother nor brother-in-law existed, the parents acted as intermediaries. Sometimes a *Wikte*[12] would perform this vital function. The negotiations usually took several sittings. Meanwhile the courtship continued with the man playing his flute outside her door. The maiden's female friends would burn wood chips from the cottonwood tree next to the lodge during the process of negotiation to drive *Anog Ite* (the Two-faced Woman) away and ensure a happy union.

Once established, the bride's price would be left outside the door, and if there was any question about the agreement, the items would stay where placed until the final decision was made. During these discussions, the value of the gifts carried less weight than the value of the man.

The wife's family also provided goods for the new couple. The conventional dowry included an awl, a tipi, robes, sinew thread, cooking pot and utensils. Her trousseau, though, depended upon the generosity of family and friends, but might include dresses, leggings, decorated bodice, moccasins.

At the appointed time, the suitor and his kin would bring his gifts to her lodge. Female family members carried food for the wedding feast, as did the woman's family members. Once the price was delivered and finally accepted, the woman would then lead the man to her tipi and offer him the position of honor. However, traditions do vary: with Sisseton and Wahpeton, it was said that the man led the woman to their shared home. However the basic principles remained the same. After they arrived at the lodge, he settled opposite the door, and she would put moccasins on his feet and take her place next to the fire.

It's interesting to note the different perspectives of the two authorities who documented the Dakota marital relationships and what their opinions say about social change in the period. Writing in 1834, before reservations, Pond said: "They [women] had their acknowledged rights, and the spirit to maintain them. In many respects they were treated by the men as equals, and participated with them in their most sacred religious festivals.... Indeed, Dakota women, old or young, are not the right material to be made slaves.... the difference in habits and disposition, between man and women, was as great among Indians as among us. But though the women differed from the men, they were not held in subjection by them."[13] Their status had changed considerably as time progressed, and not for the better. In the post-reservation era, Walker, who had observed the Lakota at the turn of the 19th century, said that a man's "woman was his property."[14]

Overall, though, the traditions of courtship and marriage seem reasonable. They gave the couple ample opportunities to change their minds—during the first tenuous overtures, as the man played his flute outside her tipi and after the declaration of intent. The woman could reject him as he strode outside her tipi, when he "covered her with the blanket." The process could break down during subsequent negotiation between the man and the family of the betrothed. Likewise the man could reject her as she made her gift of moccasins or quite simply by not following suit.

Once married, the husband had a say in the affairs of his wife's sisters. When they reached marriageable age, he had first choice. If he wished, he could marry them himself, and if he did not, he still had a voice in the selection of the groom. If he married his wife's sisters, they would usually be welcomed as someone with whom the first wife could share household duties. Many multiple marriages of this type did not include connubial rights. It was an arrangement of convenience for the husband and the wife and the sisters, particularly if they had lost their parents. They then gained protection, support and acceptance into a new family group, a vital part of the Dakota life.

Not all polygamous marriages remained within the family. A man could choose any woman he pleased. In theory the first wife, or wives, had a say in the matter; however, whether her voice was heard is hard to tell. The tales recorded by Mary Henderson Eastman of unhappy, displaced first wives suggest that was not always the case. Instead the original wife would be replaced by the second, which became a source of continual turmoil that did not make for a happy family. If later marriages created unrest within the household, the man was held as an object of mirth, and many braves agreed that keeping one's wives within a family unit, in other words sisters, was the best way to ensure peace. Familial obligations often required a man to take a second wife. If, for example, a man's brother died, he then was expected to take his brother's wife as his own and provide for her.

Both Pond and Wahpeton author Charles Eastman agreed that polygamy was the exception rather than the rule. Inside observer Eastman said: "There were, indeed, few plural marriages except among the older and leading men, and plural wives were usually, though not always, sisters."[15] The number of multiple marriages usually depended upon the ratio of men

This picture was drawn by John White in the 1500s. It shows men and women dancing around a circle defined by posts with carved faces. Two women stand in the center, at the heart of the ceremony. Analogies can be drawn between the tribes of the east and those of the west. For example: Dakota women stood at the center of many of the most important rituals and rites, such as the sacred ball game. Women marked not only the center, but also the four directions in the horse dance. From the Library of Congress Rare Book Collection: engraving by Theodor de Bry after a watercolor by John White appeared in *Admiranda narratio, fida tamen, de commodis et incolarvm ritibvs Virginiæ*, Wecheli: svmtibvs T. de Bry, 1590, plate 18.

to women. If, through warfare, death or disease, there were more women than men, then a man would take more than one woman under his protection. Pond estimated the figures were less than one in ten, and conjectured that they might not be "more than one-twentieth." Furthermore, he stated: "Polygamy was not popular with the Dakota, and they generally spoke of it as undesirable, but it existed...."[16]

Suicide rates among Dakota women indicate that a woman's life was not always a happy one. According to Pond, suicide among women was common while rare among men. During his twenty years with the Dakota he knew of only one incident where a man shot himself, but he lists several women who chose to die by their own hand. He personally cut down two women who had hanged themselves.[17]

Women were more often the recipient of physical discipline than children, and it was not unknown for a woman to respond in kind. Violent reprisal was not exclusively directed by husbands against wives; it could also cross other familial lines. The captive Sarah Wakefield had particular problems with Caska's sister. As Wakefield's captor Caska was also her provider and her protector. One day she asked for a "sacque" to replace hers. Caska asked his sister to provide one. She gave Wakefield cloth, and during the next rain, the color faded; then: "He caught her by the hair, slapped her in the face, and abused her shamefully"[18] for her lack of generosity.

Evidence recorded by eyewitnesses seems to indicate that violence in the family was a later manifestation, another result of the introduction of alcohol. It is recorded in the accounts by Mary Henderson-Eastman, Pond, and Wakefield, all written after the 1830s. Little mention is made about domestic violence among the Plains tribes until after the "Indian Wars" or the "post-reservation" era, after which time the culture had been irrevocably damaged. Tribal members who recalled the pre-reservation period all agreed that quarreling within the family was rare, which suggests that violence in the home escalated as their society disintegrated.

In a marriage, if the situation became unbearable for either partner, then separation was a viable option. A woman kept her children and her property. A woman as well as a man could demand separation. She obtained a divorce by the simple expediency of placing his possessions outside her door. However, the woman had to have the means to back her up if her spouse chose to protest. This means her brothers, father or other male members of her extended family were to defend her, should her spouse choose to retaliate. The Big Missouri winter count for 1828 documents just such a case where an abused wife fled to her father's tipi. The husband refused to accept her decision, attacking her in her father's home, and was himself killed.[19] The fact that it was a notable enough event to document in the winter count suggests such incidents were rare.

However, the fact that most warrior bands had, as a part of the initial oaths, a prohibition against seeking revenge against an estranged spouse seems to indicate that such conflicts were not unknown and were generally frowned upon. If connubial strife threatened the tranquility of the village, then the *akitcita* were called upon to make a ruling.

A man could divorce his wife by announcing at a public ceremony that he was going to *wiihpeye*, "throw her away." At an appropriate time, he would approach the drum and hit it with a drumstick. Then he would toss the stick over his shoulder, "throwing it away." The custom originated with the *Miwatani* (Owl) society and the other warrior societies adopted it including the *Tokala, Ihoka,* and *Omaha.*[20] Or the man could divorce his wife by simply giving her away to another man.

While many marriages did not last, reconciliations were also common, and if the couple made it beyond the stormy first years of adjustment, the marriage usually lasted a lifetime. Indeed, Dakota men could be among the most devoted of husbands.

With possessions came responsibilities. In Dakota society, the difference between women's duties and those of man seem to confirm the old adage: "A man works from sun to sun, but a woman's work is never done." The women cooked, cleaned, hauled water, collected firewood, scraped and tanned hides, and made the clothing, moccasins and snowshoes. Women wove mats, pulled the rushes, cut grasses, leveled the ground for the tipi. They were also expected to bring in their share of the food, so they gathered the berries and roots that supplemented the meat brought in by their husbands. They dug the turnips, gathered wild rice, dried the grain and packaged it, and made the *wasna* that was a staple of the tribe. In addition, with the more agrarian Santee, the women also planted the corn, harvested the maple sugar and built the canoes.

Likewise, it was the woman's job to cut down the trees to make the lodge poles needed for the tipi. When the camp moved, women took down the tipi and packed it, and when they arrived at a new location, women put it back up again. If a woman did not have enough horses or dogs to haul the tipi, then she could either abandon the poles and replace them, or the woman could drag them herself and did if necessity dictated. The woodland Santee woman built the wooden structure, the *tipi tonka,* that was their summer home.

A legend from another plains tribe, the Algonquin Blackfeet, explains the division of labor. When the world began, men and women emerged from different lakes and for a while they lived separately. The men could hunt, but they could not tan hides. Meanwhile the women had difficulty obtaining hides, for they could not hunt; but had great skill creating fine robes. So, the tribe of women and the tribe of men lived in poverty. *Napi* the "creator" saw this and introduced the two tribes to each other. The union proved so successful that *Napi* decided to make it permanent. He decreed that man would hunt and protect, and women would do everything else. Blackfeet women complained bitterly to the missionary Pierre De Smet in 1846, declaring their anger that their mothers had accepted this arrangement.[21]

Europeans observers were shocked to watch the man sitting smoking tobacco while his wife erected the tipi. However, many of the wives believed that the dangers their husbands faced each day in warfare and on the hunt while women and children remained in the protected village environment more than balanced the hours of toil women invested in their homes. In *The Lance and the Shield, the Life and Times of Sitting Bull*, Robert Utley explained the relationship between man and women. "The simple fact is that woman had her own place and man his; they were not the same and neither inferior nor superior."[22]

Pond defended the Dakota division of labor by comparing it with our own. "The white man sits idly by and sees his wife or mother laboring, perhaps beyond her strength in cooking or washing for him, not because she does not need his aid nor because he is unable to help her, but because it is work to which he is unaccustomed. He does not put his hands in the wash tub, because it is not his business; and the Indian hunter does not help his wife or mother carry her

This photograph, called *The Squaw Dance*, does not indicate the ceremony being celebrated. In fact, there were a number of dances which were exclusively women's domain, such as those celebrated at the maiden feast and the scalp dance. The photograph, taken at Pine Ridge, South Dakota, by Butcher & Son of Kearney, Neb. (May 15, 1908), shows a group of women, standing in the background, facing front, wearing headdresses, and a group of women sitting in the foreground turned away from the viewer; in the middle distance a group of men are crouched in a circle. The positions indicate that this may have been a dance held by the *Katela*, or "Strike Dead" Society. Also pictured here is the Oglala Chief American Horse; he stands on the left, facing front.

load because it is not his business. Very likely the white woman needs as much help as the Indian woman, but her husband lets her do her own work. Because the Indian man lets his wife do her own work, the white man calls him a brute."[23]

The division of labor was not always rigid. During a move, the women took charge of the baggage to allow the men a chance to hunt for game, although men would often assist with carrying if the women could not handle it all. Men who were too old to hunt helped with taking down and erecting the tipi, and when they had returned from the hunt, many men would haul water, gather and cut wood, entertain the baby and make repairs to the saddles. The men would also take part in the construction of the more permanent *tipi tonka* of the woodland Santee, even though it was considered a woman's responsibility. In one band, it was considered the man's duty to roof the wooden summer home. Some other chores were also shared, such as making cradles, paddles, canoes, bowls and spoons. When not hunting, Santee men as well as women gathered food. They would dig up *psinchincha* and the fleshy roots of the water lily. Certain events, such as the wild rice harvest, were community affairs in which both genders participated.

Inside the tipi, the man was the head of the family and treated with respect, but the wife as the owner of the lodge was its head, and she had the last word on everything that had to do with its maintenance and upkeep. A woman's children were hers. Even after they reached adolescence and they had been committed to the care of their elders, the woman still made the decisions concerning their upbringing. If there was a difference of opinion, her voice took precedence over that of her husband. After they reached a certain age, the grandparents would train the young in their respective roles. When the son was old enough, he would join his father in the hunt, but once they stepped back into the tipi, both husband and son became subordinate to her.[24]

Childbirth was likewise women's work. The husband would absent himself from the village when his wife was having her first baby. He would hunt or go to stay with his father's people until the baby was born. Older female relatives cared for the wife. Often midwives were called upon to attend the birth. The new-born (*hoksiyopa*) was wrapped in swaddling bands and placed on a cradle board, and the child named according to its birth order.

However, Ohiyesa gives an altogether different and a more naive impression: "...she seeks no human aid.... The ordeal is best met alone, where no curious or pitying eyes could embarrass her."[25] He describes a process whereby the woman retreated from the tribe without assistants, disappearing to return with a child in hands. But Eastman was writing from the perspective of a ten-year-old boy at a time when he would have been protected from all the nuances of childbirth and labor. His grandmother was a medicine woman, and he acknowledged she was a midwife. There would have been no midwives if there had been no need. Thus, one must assume that if the pregnant woman left the village she did not do so alone, but attended by a midwife and a number of female relatives.

Ideally, a woman would have five or six children; however, many had fewer since women tended to nurse their children until the age of two. A large family was valued because it provided many working hands. The tipi weighed several hundred pounds and the woman needed help dismantling, transporting and erecting it. Children provided the additional manpower. Older children took care of the younger as soon as they learned to walk. Children shared in hunting and gathering of food. They watered and fed the horses.

The worst indictment of women's position of Dakota society in the pre-reservation era comes from Mary Henderson Eastman. In *Dahcotah: The Life and Legends of the Sioux Around Fort Snelling*, Henderson Eastman espoused many feminist views, although she never openly advocated the Women's Rights Movement developed by Susan B. Anthony and Elizabeth Cady Stanton. Still her book contains numerous real-life examples of women wronged by family, friends and spouses, or women who had their lives destroyed by rumors, lies and innuendo. Her records of the tribe are an invaluable resource, albeit slanted. Her primary source of information about the tribe came from the alienated and disaffected. As a woman herself, Eastman would probably not have talked to the men of the village and the contented Dakota wife would have been reticent about what happened within the tipi; therefore, the view which she presented would have been a jaundiced one.

Additionally, her rather nebulous relationship with her husband's (Seth Eastman) daughter from a previous union with a Dakota woman probably colored her perspective. The only mention of their relationship included an indirect reference by army surgeon George Turner. When writing to William C. Baker about a recent smallpox epidemic, he said that Henderson Eastman was forced to consign herself and her children to her "enemy's care." The use of the term "enemy" in the context of Eastman's half-blood daughter suggests that their association was a troubled one.[26] The grandson of this union was the noted author and doctor Charles Eastman, Ohiyesa.

Despite this dissenting voice, most authorities agree that the woman in Dakota society was a force to be reckoned with. She had a say in tribal affairs through election to prominent posts or through the force of public opinion. She held the economic power not only within the family, but within the community, and as the producer of children she held its future in her hands. She was fully capable of defending herself, in battle and within the tipi. Her word concerning the upbringing of the children was law. Quite often as its eldest member, a woman was the head not only of her own lodge, but also of the entire household, as noted in 1880 Red Cloud census.[27] The reality thus presented belies the image of the Dakota woman as a victim of a male-oriented system, revealing a individual who knew her worth and operated with considerable independence when her husband was gone on either the hunt or the warpath.

14. The Power of Women

Long, long ago, two Lakota braves lay on a hill watching for signs. From their vantage point along the ridge, they saw a lone figure on the horizon. Surprised, the men moved to the next hill to see if it was an enemy, but as the person drew near, they realized the traveler was a woman. She wore no clothes, and one young man declared he would go meet her, embrace her and if he liked her, he would hold her in his tipi.

His companion warned against it. Such things were wakan and not to be done, but the first brave was not to be dissuaded. Wisely the second man withdrew while the first waited on the hill for her arrival. When he tried to embrace her, a cloud of dust rose around the two of them. When it had dispersed, the woman was alone again.

She noticed the first man's companion where he lingered not far away and beckoned for him to come. He hung back, but she assured him that he would not be hurt. When he approached, he saw a pile of bones that had once been his companion. The woman explained that madness had made the young man try to harm her. For his temerity, he had been punished and she had picked his bones clean.

He drew his bow against this destroyer of men, but she said: "If you do as I ask, you may have any woman you please as wife, for I am wakan. But if you hurt me, then you will meet the same fate as your friend."

The brave agreed to help her. She directed him to return to his camp and call council. In a short time, they would see four puffs of smoke in the sky. They must prepare a feast. As they sat down to eat, she would come to the village. The men must keep their heads bowed until she had entered the circle and was among them. She would serve the feast to them, and they must obey everything she said. If they did, then their prayers to Wakan Tanka would be answered. They would find prosperity and happiness. If they disobeyed, then Wakan Tanka would turn his face from them and they would be punished.

The brave did as instructed. The village prepared a great feast to welcome the wakan woman. A few days later, four puffs of smoke rose into the heaven. They finished their preparations and then took their places in the circle. The men kept their heads down, while around them, they heard low murmur of the women expressing their admiration. One young man glanced up, and a puff of black smoke blew into his eyes.

"You have defied me," the wakan woman said. "From this day forth your eyes will burn as if you had smoke in them."

Then the woman took the food and served it first to the children, then to the women and finally the men. After she had done so she invited the men to look up. What they saw was a woman of unsurpassing beauty who was dressed in the softest deerskin robes.

She told them that they had seen her first as smoke and so they would always see her as smoke. She placed the bundle on the ground, taking out a pipe and a rock. Then she said: "With this sacred pipe you will walk upon the earth; for the earth is both mother and grandmother, and She is sacred. Every step that is taken upon Her should be as a prayer.

"The bowl of the pipe is red stone; it is the Earth. Carved in the stone is the buffalo calf who represents the four-leggeds who live upon your Mother. The stem of the pipe is of

The Assiniboin chief Wi-Jun-Jon ("Pigeon's Egg Head") went to Washington to represent his people. Upon his return, he told of buildings large enough to house an entire tribe and white men as numerous as the grasses on the prairie. He was branded as a liar and eventually was shot by a member of the tribe. The Assiniboin were a Siouan tribe that separated from the Nakota in the 1700s. Both tribes valued honesty so much that punishment for the convicted liar could be death. This lithograph gives two views of Wi-jun-jon — on his way to Washington wearing traditional Native American dress and carrying a calumet, and then, during his return to his village, when he was pictured wearing a uniform with top hat, carrying a fan and an umbrella. George Caitlin, artist, published by Currier & Ives, New York, between 1837 and 1839.

wood, and stood for all that grows upon Her. And these twelve feathers which hang here where the stem fits into the bowl are from Wanbli Gleska, the spotted eagle, and they embody the winged ones who fly in the heavens. All these people and all the things of the universe are joined to you who smoke the pipe; all send their voices to Wakan Tanka, the Great Spirit." She touched the pipe to the stone and said: "With this pipe you will be bound to all your relatives — the four-legged and the winged ones — as you are bound to Grandfather and Father Sky, Grandmother and Mother Earth.

"The rock has seven circles which are the seven rites that I shall teach to you." Then she filled the pipe and passed it to the chief. Later she instructed the people in the making of tobacco and the care of the pipe. She told them that this breath, this smoke, was sacred, and when they made an oath by the pipe, it too became sacred. If they prayed with the pipe, she would hear them and take their prayers to Wakan Tanka, who would look kindly on the people that had prayed in this Wakan way and their prayers would be answered.

After the feast, the woman stayed in the camp to teach the Oyate some of their most sacred rituals. When it was time for her to go, she called the people together and she directed them to sit in a circle around the fire. She told the shaman to place sweetgrass on the fire. Smoke surrounded her and she vanished as she had promised — as smoke. Some of the children ran to the edge of the village where they saw her turn into a white buffalo, and they knew then that she was Wohpe, Falling Star, who wed the south wind, the mighty Okaga.[1]

A woman's life may not have been a joyous one, yet as the story illustrates, women were held in high esteem in Dakota religion. The messenger of the divine is a woman. Women and children were served first at the banquet. The White Buffalo Woman brought the *canupa wakan* (sacred pipe) to the Dakota nation. When the pipe was smoked in a *wakan* manner, it is this same woman who takes their messages to the Great Spirit. It was through a woman that their voices were heard in the heavens and through her that the Dakota people were made strong.

She brought them the seven sacred rites and instructed them how best to please the divine. In at least one of the winter counts, the arrival of the White Buffalo Woman is documented, suggesting that she was, in fact, a historical personage rather than a myth. The No Ears count for 1798 said: *Wakan Tanka winyan wan iyeypi* (They found a female Wakan Tanka).[2]

There are several versions of this tale. In one, the White Buffalo woman transforms herself into snakes and devours the young brave who would lay hands on her person. In another, the snakes descend after the man is dead to feast upon his bones. In yet another, she transforms herself into a buffalo and rebukes him for his lustful thoughts, but does not kill him. In other variations she does not stay in the village, but returns, each time teaching them more of the sacred rites. In none is *Wohpe* considered weak or subservient to men. Any who would treat her badly are punished, and so the women of the Dakota should also be treated with honor and respect.

In the village environment, Ohiyesa described women as the primary instructors of the morals and values of the people. She taught through action, hence by example: "...she (the Indian mother) humbly seeks to learn a lesson from ants, bees, spiders, beavers, and badgers. She studies the family life of the birds, so exquisite in its emotional intensity and its patient devotion.... In due time the child takes of his own accord the attitude of the prayer, and speaks reverently of the Powers. He thinks that he is a blood brother to all living creatures, and the storm wind is to him a messenger of the 'Great Mystery.'"[3] Within the family, the wife and mother taught her children the ways of the pipe and instructed them on the sacred ceremonies. An individual's line of descent was traced through her mother and her mother before her, hence, animal totems were received from their great-grandmother's clan.[4]

Women as a gender were considered co-participants with the Creator. In giving birth to a child, the woman contributes in the creation of new life for the family and the community. "A child is the greatest gift from *Wakantanka* ... in response to many devout prayers, sacrifices and promises."[5] For their part in the creation cycle, women were important enough that they, and their deaths, were mentioned in numerous winter counts, such as the No Ears and the Great Missouri winter counts for 1799, the year "when many pregnant women died."[6]

The White Buffalo Woman brings, along with the pipe, the philosophy upon which the Dakota peoples based their entire mode of living. She enjoins them to pray, every minute of every day, and to view each day as sacred. Said Eastman: "In the life of the Indian there was only one inevitable duty — the duty of prayer — the daily recognition of the Unseen and Eternal. His daily devotions were more necessary to him than daily food."[7] As described by the Oglala holy man, Black Elk, every dawn was a holy event and every day was a holy day. In *Soul of an Indian,* Eastman (Ohiyesa) expressed it another way. "Every act of his life is in a very real sense, a religious act."[8]

Secular pursuits and spiritual activities were not compartmentalized as they often are in the Christian church. The red man viewed the white man as lackadaisical in the observance of his faith. Ohiyesa's grandmother was scandalized when she heard of the Christian-style worship where attendance on and prayer to one's maker was limited to Sunday. She conveyed this disapproval to her grandson, for decades later Charles Eastman observed: "He (the Indian) sees no need for setting apart one day in seven as a holy day, since to him all days are God's."[9]

This was one of many differences between the white man's and the native's faith — even though they professed many of the same philosophies—charity/generosity, brotherly love versus "all our relations." Many years after his "Americanization," Eastman was scathing in his condemnation of white man's faith as it had evolved in modern times: "....the religion that is preached in our churches and practiced by our congregations, with its element of display and self-aggrandizement, its active proselytism, and its open contempt of all other religions but its own, was ... extremely repellent.... the professionalism of the pulpit, the paid exhorter, the moneyed church, was an unspiritual and unedifying thing."[10]

In this story about the origins of their most sacred rituals, *Wohpe* (the White Buffalo Calf Woman) reminds the people of their interrelationship with all that lives upon this earth. For what is humanity without the plants and the animals who provide food, clothes and shelter? The White Buffalo Women enjoined the Dakota to remember that all the peoples of the earth, the four-legged, the two-legged and the winged ones, are sacred and should be treated with respect. In this context, the earth is also mother, for it is the earth who provides life to all plants and creatures, and at all times, so the Dakota people must show respect and honor to their sacred mother, the earth.

Another message from *Wohpe* was that women should be honored. The man who defiles her should be castigated severely, with punishments including death. That the Dakota honored this tradition is documented in the Big Missouri winter count entry for 1828 where a man was killed after beating his wife.[11]

It is Grandmother and Mother Earth who are invoked by *Wohpe*, and not the sacred Father, and the earth (the female principle) is placed under the protection of the Dakota. Also in the tale, it is the women and children, and not the men, who are served first by *Wohpe*. This tradition has found its reflection in the oaths of the many warrior societies where no warrior could eat as long as any women or children remained hungry.

This extended to the very old. Each age of life was precious, and each made its contribution to society, which should help dispel the myth that the elderly were casually abandoned once they became burdensome to the tribe. The fact that the Dakota have not one but several cautionary tales about desertion indicates that abandonment of the old was viewed with condemnation.

In one such Dakota legend, relayed by Pond, a young man came upon an old woman in a deserted camp. Even though he had no horse, he picked her up and carried her on his back. When he caught up with the band, the brave's friends teased him and told him that he looked ridiculous, like a horse carrying an old woman on his back. The brave commented that there was more shame in those who had forgotten and left an old woman behind than in him for carrying such a burden. He would, he said, care for her even if they were attacked. Not long after he made this vow, they came upon the enemy. Undaunted, the warrior put the old woman on the ground and continued to defend her even when the others retreated. Impressed with his generosity and bravery, the people asked him to be their chief, but he replied with disdain: "Give your gifts to this woman whom you have wronged." They made her chief, and from that point on she sat on all the chiefs' councils.[12]

Abandonment was rare. In the woodland era, when they operated from an established summer base camp it would have been unnecessary and would have happened only under the most extreme circumstances. In times of great need for mobility, the old may have been left in the village with suitable guards. If evacuation required speed or the movement of the entire tribe, those who could not travel would remain in the summer camp, and the event was marked with solemnity and ceremony for the sacrifice they made. Yet there were recorded instances when the tribe found the individual alive, well and tending to the business of the camp when they returned to their summer base.

In the Lakota creation story, it is a woman elder, as bringer of wisdom, who suspects Inktomi when he tries to entice humanity to the earth's surface. A woman also guarded the path to the afterlife and judged men's souls. Although some stories credited *Waziya* (the spirit of the north) to this sacred post, others say a woman, perhaps as his representative, sat in judgment.

The spirits of the dead followed a prescribed path to a river. The water was spanned by a single log, or slippery tree. Along the river's edge lived an old woman, called *May owichapaha* ("She who pushes them over the bank").[13] The old woman would listen as the warrior recounted his personal history. Those whose spirits she believed unworthy were swept from the bridge, or over the bank, into the rushing torrent below where they must deal with the water spirits, among the most evil of all beings. Those she found worthy were allowed to continue unhampered across the tree. On the opposite bank, the road forked. The worthy were directed to take the right-hand fork to attain union with *Wakan Tanka* in the spirit world. Swept along by the current, the unworthy were doomed to follow the second, left-hand path when they climbed from the river and wander the earth forever as ghosts.

A woman also figured in the myth about the end of days. The Dakota refer to the end times as the two red and blue days[14] when it was believed the moon would turn red and the sun blue. Similar in concept to the rapture, it was the time when all the living beings would be turned into spirit. However, it was not evidently an event to be hurried because somewhere at the end of the world lives a grandmother, who is as old as time itself. Each day she toils, sewing beads onto a buffalo robe. As she shuffles back and forth between her beadwork and her kettle, her faithful hound unravels her work, for if she ever completed the robe, the world would come to an end, and so a woman protects humanity from ultimate destruction through her eternal labors.

In the faith of the Dakota, the woman's role is pivotal during certain ceremonies and women held the pipe during their enactment. Thus, women performed a vital function in some of their most important rituals. No sun dance could be begun without her. As they prepared for the sun dance, men and women would gather to sing the sacred songs as a woman chopped down the sacred pole around which the men would dance. As the pole is erected, women are called upon again to sing. The woman who felled the tree sits in a sacred space during the ceremony. Maidens also officiated at the dance. These chaste women had to prove their virtue by the ordeal of "biting a snake,"[15] a variation on the biting the knife. During the sun dance women danced next to their husbands or brothers, and they could contribute their flesh as a sacrifice to the good of the community, although they were never pierced as the male dancers were.

Women also took part in the *wanigi*

The fast formed the basis of many ceremonies, including the *inipi* and the sun dance. Charles Eastman believed their ability to go without food for long periods of time revealed the strength of the tribe. Often a warrior was called upon by his vows to give up his dinner in order to feed those who had nothing. Pictured here, a Lakota man "cries for a vision" through fasting and chanting to the Great Mystery. Photo by Edward S. Curtis, c. 1907, and published in *The North American Indian*, by Edward S. Curtis (Seattle, Wash.): Edward S. Curtis, 1907–30, v. 3, opp. p. 68. From the Edward S. Curtis Collection (Library of Congress).

wicagluhapi, or the "keeping of the soul" ceremony. The purpose of the rite was to ensure that the spirit rested in peace after death. All told, it took a year and required great sacrifice during which the participants had to forego normal life. While a man was often nominated as the keeper, it was a woman who took formal care of the sacred bundle.

Many warrior societies had women members. The *Tokala* (Fox) Society and *Cante Tinza* (Brave Hearts) each had women singers.[16] So it seems that a woman's voice was pleasing to the divine. According to Ohiyesa (Eastman), the Medicine Lodge, exclusive to the woodland Dakota, had women as full-fledged members.

Women whose brothers belonged to the No-flight Society were allowed to join in their dances, just as they joined in the sun dance. The women also celebrated their husbands' and their brothers' victories in the *Iwakicipi*, or scalp dance. Women were active participants in the horse dance. They walked in the procession, carrying the staffs and the flags which were essential to the ritual. They marked the four cardinal points around the circle, representing the sacred aspects of the four winds and the four directions.[17] Women also joined the *ipsica waci,* the jumping dance, and the *naslohan wacipi,* dragging one's feet dance.

They officiated at the sacred ball game, and four virgins took a ritual part in the final releasing of the soul. Grandmothers, women of repute who were wise in years, were selected to carry the superheated stones so essential to the *inipi* or sweat lodge. Each stone represented the gifts of Grandmother Earth; therefore only a grandmother was entitled to such a sacred trust. Like the pipe, the purification ceremony was integral to every other rite the Dakotas performed, including both the sun dance and vision quest. Without this ritual of purification, where the participant was cleaned from the inside out, no candidate was able to participate in any other sacred rite.

The Dakota had both holy men and holy women. Women had a medicine that was uniquely their own. Known as a *Wakan winyan,* they were divided into three main groups: *wapiyapi* or curers, *wakan kaga* or performers, and *wihmunga,* witches. The *wapiyapi* included both *wapiye wakan* and *pejuta winyela,* herbalists. The *wapiye wakan* often were married to holy men and assisted their husbands in healing ceremonies. Both had a knowledge of herbs. Also it was the older women, those past menopause, who were keepers of sacred objects.

Both men and women could have spider medicine, a gift from Inktomi, and both men and women could become *Heyoka,* if they had had dreamt of Wakinyan or his representatives. The *Heyoka* were *wakan kaga,* or performers who taught by example. According to Powers, the tradition is an ancient one. In his book *The Medicine Man,* Thomas Lewis describes the initiation of a female *Heyoka.* The ceremony relayed to Lewis by Holy Dance took place two decades ago, meaning the practice probably continues to this day.[18]

The last category of woman with magical powers was the witches. The *wihmunga* were feared, for it was believed that they could inflict disease rather than cure it. They were blamed for any unexpected and unexplained occurrence. In an interview with Walker, Thomas Tyon ascribed magic to Double Women, those who had seen *Anog Ite* either in a waking vision or sleeping dream. This gave them special powers, including skill in quillwork. Tyon referred to them as doctors and said: "Whoever walks about at night is very afraid of these Double Woman dreamers. They do not wish to hear their voices."[19] Since a *wihmunga*'s power was in her voice, it would appear that Double Woman dreamers were considered witches.

A woman, even who did not have a special medicine of her own, would often accompany a medicine man to leave offerings. As such, she represented her family and her clan. She would place the tobacco pouches around a sacred site, and the holy man would pray, asking the divine to bless a certain endeavor, help a loved one or heal the sick.

Dakota women also had their own sodalities and societies beyond the warrior societies. The *Katela,* or "Strike Dead" society was formed to celebrate the victories of their husbands, brothers and sons. They danced carrying their husbands' weapons, and one man, selected to represent the enemy, would be rushed and struck by the women dancers. Similarly they had medicine societies such as the *Wakan okolakicye* for those who had dreamt of elk, buffalo or horses. The women of these societies supplied war medicine and received a share of the spoils of war.[20]

Little is known of women's societies since few white researchers of the 1800s were interested in them. However, it is unlikely that they would have learned much even if they had asked, for the secrets of these societies would never have been shared outside the group and most certainly would not have been revealed to any man, much less a white one. Ohiyesa was one of the few privileged with such information since his grandmother was a singer, a medicine woman, a midwife, an herbalist and a member of the Turtle Lodge, who hoped to see him follow in her footsteps and be initiated as a medicine man.[21]

Many parallels about the elevated status of women in religion can be found among the other tribes. Discussing the plains tribes as a whole, Dr. Colin Taylor found women's influence in Native American faith profound: "...women's societies performed the various ceremonials, particularly those associated with food and production, bountiful harvests and buffalo calling. There were symbolic links between women and buffalo, chastity and ritual, fertility and intertribal warfare."[22]

The highest honor accorded a Dakota woman was to become a buffalo woman, and Black Elk considered the rite, the *Taktanka Lowanpi*, among the most important. It was brought to the *Oyate* to combat the influence of *Anog Ite* (Two-faced Woman) among the young and impress upon them the sacred duties they possessed as the mothers of the tribe.

When a young girl had her first menstrual flow (*tonwon*) she would be put in a special tipi to protect her from *Anog Ite* and Inktomi the trickster. After her *tonwon* was completed, her parents would prepare for the ceremony. The parents made a new lodge that would then become her residence.

As with all rites, days were spent in the preparation, consecration of the area and the lodge. The pipe dedicated to the four directions was then smoked. Each step was precise. The prescription of sacred numbers (see Chapter 15) followed, although certain intricacies of the proceedings varied according to the vision of the holy man who conducted it.

The day of the ceremony began with the invocation to the dawn, and an entreaty to the winds to give mild weather. An altar was made upon a mound of earth where a buffalo skull was placed. Arranged around the skull were a ceremonial staff, pipe and fire stick. As the sky turned red, the holy man asked the dawn's blessings upon the proceedings.

The woman would then be brought to the lodge and seated at the north side of the tipi. The holy man would cense the area with burning sage and adjure evil spirits (*Iya, Inktomi* and *Anog ite*) to stay away. The woman was instructed in the proper way of sitting and she assumed the correct posture. Then the holy man told her of his vision from which she could learn about her adult responsibilities.

In the ceremony relayed by Walker in *Lakota Belief and Ritual*, the medicine man cited three animals, the spider, the turtle, the lark, and said: "The spider is industrious and makes a tipi for its children. It provides them with plenty of food. The turtle is wise and hears many things and does not tell anything. Its skin is like a shield so that arrows cannot wound it. The lark is cheerful and brings warm weather. It does not scold its people. It is always happy."[23] Then he cautioned her against laziness and sloth, elaborating on the potential disaster for herself, her family, her hearth and her home should she succumb to them.

He then danced the buffalo dance, pawing the earth and charging the woman to brush against her side, and then advanced head-on. After each pass her mother placed a garland of sage over right and left breast and in her lap as form of protection. The woman drank the juice of the chokecherry. Red, it was considered *wakan* water, a symbol of the sacred water of life. The holy man then drank, followed by the attendants and observers of the ritual the tipi. The woman shed her old dress, as she shed her old life as a child, and it was given away to the needy. Her hair was redressed, the part painted red as a symbol of her new status. Later that day during the feast, the woman was then presented to the community as a new buffalo woman. She had eagle feathers tied in her hair as symbols of her virtue and fidelity,[24] and a man if he wished to marry her could make an offer at this time.

Compared to the European women of the time, Dakota women held considerable status among their people. This was recognized by their deep involvement in tribal ceremonies, such as the sun dance and the sacred ball game, in tribal societies, including the both the *akitcita* and warrior societies.

Elsewhere women's role, particularly in religion, was being negated. Mary Magdalene's position among the apostles was relegated to that of a reformed prostitute, while in the Protestant church not even the Blessed Virgin was held as divine and her participation in the sacred birth reduced to that of a "vessel." While white women of the period were cloistered and hidden from view, the Dakota woman not only performed special duties within their faith, but she dominated many of their most sacred rites.

She and her mothers before her were recognized as the founder of the clan, and it was through a woman that the Dakota became linked to the divine and their prayers heard. A woman judged men in death and a woman held back the end of days. Thus, Dakota women were acknowledged in their tradition and religion as the lifeblood of their community. They formed its backbone, its spine, without which the Dakota people and the world as we know it would have ceased to exist.

15. Matters of Faith

One day Wohpe came to Tate. "It is time," she said, "for me to give you my father's message. The world is without direction until your sons establish them. The directions are located at the world's edge. The time it takes your sons to accomplish their goal will become a year, which you will rule, and the amount of time you choose to give to each is up to you. Once their directions are found, your sons will live there. The land will become theirs, so dividing the earth into four parts, and your sons will be as spirits. Yum will stay a child — the spirit of love, fun and games."

Tate bowed his head, For he did not wish to see his children leave. Yet he could not disobey his brother Skan. He called his son to him and said: "It is time for you to leave this lodge and take your place in the world." He relayed Wohpe's instructions, adding: "You have four days to prepare."

Each had questions, except Okaga who gazed silently at Wohpe and wondered why she had sent them from her side. The youths set to work, each after his fashion. Angry, sullen, Yata refused to hunt. Why should he be sent from his father's tipi? The irresponsible Eya dawdled, for surely there was always tomorrow to prepare. Lazy Yanpa idled away the hours when he was supposed to hunt, and he returned empty-handed. Only Okaga killed a deer and brought it back for Wohpe to dress. The next two days passed as the first had, with the three bringing nothing while Okaga returned with an antelope and then a moose for Wohpe.

On the fourth day, Okaga did not want to hunt. Instead he went to sit by a spring beyond the pines. An old woman hobbled into view and fell at his feet. Okaga got up to help her. She thanked him and asked him what grieved him so. Okaga told her about Wohpe, and she laughed. He grew angry. She shook her head. "You need no help from me there. Still," she swung her arm around her camp site, "you have been kind to me. You may take whatever pleases you to give to your beloved."

He scowled, for nothing pleased him that day. As he stood up, Okaga crushed some sweetgrass underfoot. Okaga bent, plucked a few blades, sniffed it and smiled. He would not go home empty-handed. Outside the lodge he handed the garland to Wohpe. She accepted it and placed it next to her heart and so it became sacred to her and to the Dakota people.

The day of their departure, Wohpe gave the antelope robe and meat to Yata, the deer to Eya and the moose to Yanpa. For Okaga, she had nothing. Tate called upon his fellow spirits. He asked Skan to help his children, Inyan to defend them, Wakinyan to smooth their path and Maka to guide them.

As the four turned their backs on the tipi, Wohpe pulled Yum aside, gave him a bag and a circle of fur. "Give this to Okaga and return." He hastened to do her bidding.

Far away, the old man wizard Wazi listened to Skan. "When Anpetu colors the sky red, go and find your grandsons. Help them on their way, but do not follow. If you obey, you will be free to wander this earth as you please."

The first day the sons traveled without direction, for there was none. That night, they sat. The older brothers spread out their robes and ate their wasna. They laughed at Okaga

Religion was extremely personal and solitary. The individual prayed alone with the prairie sky as his chapel. Prayer accompanied all activities. Prayers could also be formal as part of a ritual or rite. The photograph pictures a Oglala man named Picket Pin, wearing a breechcloth and holding a pipe with its mouthpiece pointing skyward. A buffalo skull lies at his feet. Photograph taken by Edward Curtis, c. December 26, 1907. Part of Edward S. Curtis Collection (Library of Congress). Published in *The North American Indian,* Edward S. Curtis (Seattle, Wash.) 1907–30, Suppl., v. 3, pl. 91.

since he had neither meat nor robes. He took out the bag that Yum had brought to him from Wohpe and opened it. Inside, he found food. He ate until his appetite was sated.

The next morning Wazi approached the fire. Yata, Eya and Yata eyed him suspiciously. They talked among themselves. They would share no food with the stranger. The youngest, Okaga, offered Wazi the bag. Wazi took it and sniffed it. "This is the food the Spirits give to those they love. Cherish it, eat of it and your life will prosper. Did your receive anything else?" Wazi asked. Okaga revealed the circle of fur. "The cloth of the Spirits. Guard it, and treat it well. If you do not, she who gave it to you will turn her face from you." Then Wazi placed the circle on the ground and it spread until he had a fine blanket.

Jealous of his brother's largesse, the irritable Yata snapped at Wazi: "I am hot. If you are a wizard, then prove it. Make shade for us." The old man waved his hands at the sky and clouds rolled in to cover the sun. Then Wazi instructed them to make smoke and rub it on their feet. Wazi bound eagle plumes to their ankles. "With these, you will stride from hilltop to hilltop." And he guided them to the place that was the edge of the world. They traveled as swift as an eagle to the foot of a mountain beyond which lay their path. Wazi warned them that once they found the trail, they must walk as mortal men and not use the sacred eagle feathers to speed them on their way, and then he left them.

The following day, clouds still covered the sky. The brothers stared up at the dark mountain that towered above their camp with foreboding.

"How do we know if he was Wazi?" argued Yata, "It could have been Inktomi sent to trick us. "Eya and Yanpa agreed. They did not want to climb the mountain. It looked too tall.

"We must do as bidden," Okaga said, and he took the lead. The brothers trailed far behind. On the summit, Okago found a lodge. The booming voice that issued from the open door gave no welcome. "Leave, Okaga," it said. "You have no business here."

Far below Yata hung back, but his brother, the ever reckless Eya, knew no fear. He began to climb and when he reached the top he saw a nest of bones. Curious, he walked to the lodge.

Inside the voice boomed: "Who are you?"

"I am," he said, "Eya, son of Tate, who would learn more of you and your strange nest."

"You wish to learn. Then you are welcome to stay, Eya son of Tate. I will teach you." Seeing that their brother had not been harmed, Yata and Yanpa advanced into the clearing, but voice gave them no welcome. "Pass," it said.

As the brothers disappeared over the peak, a column of smoke rose from the tipi and began to take shape. It was a thing frightening to behold. It had neither body nor head, yet it contained within its many parts a sharp beak, many beating wings and huge talons.

Eya held his ground and mocked. "Your voice so tiny and small scares no one. Your beak and teeth scare no one."

The spirit of storm chuckled. "I am Wakinyan; I am Heyoka which you have now become. From this day forth you will do everything backwards. If it is night you, will say day. If it is good, you will say bad. Together we will teach the people and we will purify the world." Wakinyan changed into a giant. "The directions that you choose will be the only things on this earth that are fixed; everything else will change. Go, little Heyoka, but tell your brothers nothing of what I have said." And so Wakinyan kept his word to his brother, helping the son along the way.

Eya joined his brothers on the other side of the mountain. They found Wazi waiting on the path. The wizard nodded to Eya. "Take a rock and put it next to the trail. This is the first of the four directions. When each have found their place, Eya, you will return to build your tipi here." Yata started to protest, and Wazi turned to face him. "By holding back, you have proven yourself unworthy and have given up your rights as firstborn. To Eya is given this place of honor. From now on each of you will be subordinate to him." So said, he vanished.

With Eya in the lead the brothers continued along the world's edge, but Yata brooded that he had been usurped by his brother, and the two argued until Wakinyan had to intervene. He sent a swallow to act as Eya's messenger, thereby confirming his choice.

The clouds that Wazi had

While prayer could be individual — so Slow Bull kneels before his maker and Pin Pocket, pictured previously, stands — the sacred pipe was the centerpiece upon which ritual and prayer were built. Some elements remained the same. The pipe itself was offered to the four directions and *Wakan Tanka* as shown in both photographs. Here medicine man Slow Bull squats down, holding the pipe in ritual manner as he prays to the Great Mystery. Photograph by Edward Curtis, c. December 26, 1907. Edward S. Curtis Collection (Library of Congress).

called forth still covered the sun, and each day grew colder than the one before. Then one evening as they set up the night's camp an old man approached, his face covered by his robe. They thought he was Wazi and proposed a game of stones to idle the hours away. Four days passed as they played, with Yata winning. He cheated. Then his fortunes began to change, and he exploded, accusing their guest of cheating.

"You should know. You have been cheating," the old man chided, "and if you cheat, you will be cheated." He lifted the blanket to reveal the features not of Wazi, but of Inktomi the trickster.

He faded, and the clearing echoed with his laughter. As Yata bemoaned the loss, Wakinyan appeared. "Four days have come and gone, and you have lost time because you neglected your quest and frittered away your time to gamble. When your quest is done you will become spirits whom no man can see. No one will know where are, where you come from nor where you have gone." So it was decreed that the brothers would become as the wind, impermanent and transparent, but further punishments awaited. "Okaga, who let his brother gamble away his flint, has lost the ability to make fire. Yata who cheated shall never sit in the banquet hall of spirit, and Eya who let this happen shall lead no one."

Ashamed, the brothers continued, and the weather grew colder still. When three moons had passed, Wazi again materialized before them. He told Yata to place a block of ice upon the ground. In this cold, harsh place, he had found his home and he would build his tipi next to Wazi's loge, and the magpie became Yata's messenger — a bird of ill omen befitting an angry master.

The brothers traveled on until they arrived at a lake which they could not cross. The trail that led between the world's and water's edge was narrow. Unktehi, the water demon, pursued them until they were exhausted. They prayed to Inyan for protection, and he answered. Boulders appeared on their path. They scrambled onto the rocks where Unktehi could not follow. The brothers clambered along the rough edge of the lake for another moon until they reached a place of dry parched earth. They traveled for days without water until they thought they saw a second lake. They turned from their path, but as they advanced, it retreated, and when the day drew to a close, they were no nearer than they had been. Inktomi rose before them to mock them. "Sons of Tate, I have fooled you again. You strayed from your path to chase an illusion."

Far, far away, the maiden Wohpe felt their thirst. She hurried down to the stream, picked up a shell from the water and drank. Her thirst was satisfied. She gave the shell to Wakanka[1] and asked her to take it to her beloved. The old woman flew to the brothers. Okaga offered her food from his bag. She tasted it and nodded her approval. "This is the food of Spirit given by one who loves you, and she has something else for you now." Wakanka passed the shell to Okaga. "Drink from this and your thirst will be appeased."

So armed, they continued across the desert until they reached a place where the grass grew long. They heard a cry, and the brothers ran until they found Anpetu weeping in the grass. He told them that he too had been fooled by Inktomi who had stolen his colors away. Wazi appeared before them. "Cry no more, Anpetu; Skan places this judgment upon you. For your folly, you have lost your place as the lord of the day. From this time forth, you shall rule only in the margins of day and night." He turned then to Yanpa and said: "Fix a wand upon the trail." An owl settled upon the wand. "This is your home and the owl is your messenger, for it is lazy like you, sleeping when others work." He nodded to the brothers. "I will visit you no more. Okaga. When you reach the place where the sun casts no shadows you will have reached your goal."

The moon grew dark and then round again when the four arrived at a grove of trees laden with fruit. A beast in the form of a man came to them and offered to trade fruit for their wasna. Three of the brothers agreed, but when the man asked for the bag, Okaga refused. Yanpa ate and ate of the fruit, and the man told him, "There is another tree with fruit sweeter than this one." And he led Yanpa into the forest.

Yanpa plucked the fruit from a branch, tasted it and fell as if dead. When he woke, his mouth tasted bitter. The beast-man was gone. In his place stood Inktomi. "Because you have neglected your duty to satisfy your hunger, no food will satisfy you until you return to your father's tipi and so too your brothers will know hunger who gave up the fine wasna of Wohpe for tainted fruit."

He vanished and Yanpa was left lost in the woods. Yanpa called to his messenger. Owl flew from tree to tree, and Yanpa, weak with hunger, followed him from the forest. Disheartened, the brothers continued on the trail. At night they lay down and hunger gnawed at their bellies. Only Okaga was not affected and he sat up to play his flute. One night a voice whispered. "A woman's bones," it said. The tune faltered on his lips.

He glanced around the camp and his gaze fell upon a small bird. "Whose bones are these?"

"Wohpe," it whispered. "Go to her now."

He eyed the whippoorwill, and then rose to pack his things. The

Each day began with prayer and invocation to the sun. Many ceremonies, likewise, began with invocation as shown here: a Dakota man holds a pipe, with right hand raised skyward reaching toward *Skan* and *Wakan Tanka*. Photograph by Edward Curtis, c. December 26, 1907. Edward S. Curtis Collection (Library of Congress) from *The North American Indian*, Edward S. Curtis (Seattle, Wash.), Edward S. Curtis, 1907–30, Suppl., v. 3, pl. 109.

next morning, Okaga informed his brothers that he must leave. Yanpa argued. Surely, Skan would punish him as the others had been punished. But Okaga dismissed his brother's words. What he did, he did for love.

He ran and he ran until he came to a river. Then, placing his precious circle and bag on his head, he crossed, but water splashed on them, wetting them, and when he stopped to eat, he found no food in his bag. When he spread the circle on the ground, it did not spread. Unable to sleep, he continued on. The next day he came to a swamp. Unktehi came to harass him, but he played his flute and drove the demon away. Then he arrived an a sandy plain. He took his shell from his pocket, but found no water there. He pressed on until he could walk no more. He stumbled and fell. Wazi woke him in the morning, but Okaga was so parched and weak, he could not move. Wazi carried him into the wood, made a fire and fed him. Then he scolded him. "What are doing so far from your appointed path?"

"Wohpe is in trouble. A whippoorwill told me and the whippoorwill does not lie. Only I can help her. I will go to find her at my father's tipi, unless she tells me herself that I should not come."

Far away Wohpe heard him as he spoke to Wazi. She felt his thirst. She pulled her half of the shell from her pouch and drank, but the water was bitter. She passed her hand over the shell to sweeten the water. Then she turned to Wakanka. "The other half saved the brothers in the past, this half will save them again. Take the shell to Okaga. He will recognize it as the sister to the shell he now possesses and tell him what was asked."

Wakanka hurried to Okaga, and relayed Wohpe's message: "This shell is a sign that all is well with Wohpe. Now hurry. For twelve days you must journey alone. When you meet your brothers, you will fix your direction, by putting this shell on the ground. When your quest is done, return home. She will be waiting for you." As Wakanka faded from the fireside, she said: "Since Inktomi tricked you by speaking over the song of the whippoorwill and what you have done you have done for love, the whippoorwill will always sing the song of love."

Following her instructions, Okaga came upon his brothers. He put the shell on the ground and it grew into a shining tipi that contained all the colors that Anpetu had lost. A meadowlark lighted on it and so became Okaga's messenger.

Thus, the four directions and their season were set, creating the four times of the year. The brothers returned to their father's tipi through many adventures, for Gnaski and Inktomi were not finished with them yet. But the brothers were wiser now, not so easily distracted, and they had their messengers to guide them. When at long last they arrived home, Okaga and Wohpe were wed and the youngest, Yum, came to live with them in the south where the summer sun always shines. Eya, the Heyoka, made his home in the west, in the land of the autumn winds. The belligerent Yata lived in the north, the home of snow and ice, while idle Yanpa stayed in the east, in the land of perpetual spring.[2]

The pipe also had its place in meditation. Crying for a vision took many forms, including simple meditation. By smoking the pipe, the supplicant's prayers are sent to the heavens as promised by **Wohpe** or the White Buffalo Calf Woman, who brought the pipe to the people. This shows an unnamed man seated on a flat rock (Cheyenne River Medicine Rock). This position was particularly advantageous, for the individual was then connected to *Inyan*, mystery of stone, and grandmother/mother earth (*Maka*). Photo taken by Edward S. Curtis in 1907.

The story introduces the reader to one of the most important concepts of Dakota faith, the principles of fours. The four sons establish the four directions and become the spirits of the four winds, Wani. They come to personify the seasons they represent, and their personalities explain each season's vagaries. Each is assigned his position accordingly as like is placed with like. The warmth and bounty of summer mirror the generous spirit of Okaga (south). The irascibility and fury of Yata are reflected by winter's harshness. The blaze and glory of autumn are best illustrated by the spirit of rash and reckless Eya, and Yanpa finds his home in lazy spring which is, like him, sluggish and reluctant to emerge from its warm winter bed.

By going to the four corners of the world, Tate's sons give earth its directions, and in giving it direction, they gave it stability. According to Lakota tradition only the directions remained constant; all else changed. Their journey created not only the four seasons, but the four times (day, night, month, year). Thus, the tale presents the quadripartite divisions the Dakota had for nearly everything. There are four sacred colors, four superior mysteries or divines, and four cardinal virtues—*woksape* or wisdom; *woohitika* or bravery; *wowacintanka* (fortitude); and *wacantognaka* (generosity). Even the heavens consisted of four "elements," the sun, moon, sky, and stars. The number four was also used in building sacred structures, such as the sweat lodge and the sun-dance lodge.

Four meant balance and as such, the number was pleasing to the divine. It was found in the Dakota cross or four-cornered circle, the cross within the circle. The latter, the circle, represented the sacred hoop which encompassed all the Dakota people. The north-south axis of the Lakota cross embodied the "red road" of spirit, roughly equivalent to the Christian straight and narrow path. The northern path led to the land of the forefathers where the Buffalo People reside. Meanwhile the east-west axis was known as the blue or black road which represented materialism and greed, or the wrong way. The west in the physical world was the place from which most storms originated, where the sun set; thus, it represented darkness and the thunderbirds.

Tob, meaning four, also described sets of four allied mysteries, which could be compared to the triunes of gods, or tripartite system, of ancient Egypt. The four directions were known as *Tob kin*. *Tobtob kin,* or four times four, includes the major mysteries: *Wi (wikan),* the sun; *Hanwi (hanwikan),* the moon; *Skan (taku skan skan),* motion, or that which moves the sky; and *Tate,* the wind. *Tobtob kin* as noted by Walker are outlined below.

TOBTOB KIN WALKER (1917)[3]

Wi	Skan	Maka	Inyan
(sun)	(energy)	(earth)	(stone)
Hanwi	Tate	Wohpe	Wakinyan
(moon)	(wind)	(falling star)	(thunder beings)
Tatanka	Hunonpa	Tate tob	Yumni
(bull buffalo)	(two-leggeds)	(four winds)	(whirlwind)
Nagi	Niya	Nagila	Sicum
(spirit)	(ghost-life)	(spirit-like)	(potency)

In *Sacred Language,* William Powers divides *tobtob kin* into *wakan kin* (the *wakan* or divine) and *taku wakin* (something sacred). These two categories he further delineates as *wakan ankatu* (the superior *wakan*), that which came first, and *wakan kolaya* (kindred *wakin*), those beings who were created second. Tate's sons would be included on the latter list. This was followed by *Wakan Kuya* (subordinate *wakan*). This group included both buffalo and man, and *Wakalapi* (*wakan*-like), the spirits or souls, ghosts and "power" that fuels sacred things.[4]

WAKAN TANKA

	Wakan Kin		*Taku Wakan*
Wakan ankatu	*Wakan kolaya*	*Wakan Kuya*	*Wakalapi*
Wi	Hanwi	Tatanka	Nagi
Skan	Tate	Hununpa	Niya
Maka	Wohpe	Tate tob	Nagila
Inyan	Wakinyan	Yumni	Sicun

Powers's designations of superior and subordinate suggest that some of the mysteries were more important than others, and from one perspective this was correct since each was consid-

Dance formed a sort of visual prayer, a celebration of the divine similar to the processions of the Catholic Church. This photographic print was taken by Remington in 1903. The dancer wears long headdress of the Lakota and holds the a peace pipe.

ered secondary to *Wakan Tanka*, although some historians contend that the idea of Great Mystery or Great Spirit was unknown to the Sioux before the introduction of Christianity. The Oglala Good Seat said in an interview recorded for James R. Walker: "In old times, the Indians did not know of a Great Spirit...."[5]

Good Seat seems to hold a minority view. Certainly, the creation myth of the Lakota speaks of *Inyan* whose spirit is *Wakan Tanka* who endows everything with life, and *Inyan* as stone becomes the foundation upon which everything else is built. Similarly in another document recorded by Thomas Tyon also for Walker, Tyon discusses the belief in a pervading spirit that contained all the others as an established concept. "*Wakan Tanka* was the Great Spirit. He was above all spirits."[6]

Writing much later, Colin Taylor agreed, saying that: "Such concepts are the essence of Plains Indian religion, an acute awareness of some all pervading force — the power or moving force behind the universe — that emanates from unknown sources and to which a special name was given."[7]

In his book *Indian Boyhood*, the Dakota Charles A. Eastman (Ohiyesa) discusses the Great Mystery, and again the term is used as if the idea were a long-established one. Thus, Eastman preferred the term "mystery" to spirit as the more accurate description of something unknowable and unknown. Good Seat's description emphasizes this concept of mystery. "*Wakan* is anything that is hard to understand."[8]

The injunction given to the young was "be attentive," which implied that the Great Spirit, or the Great Mystery, was present in every act, every thing, every instant.[9] Prayers were given as food was being prepared, before eating and during the meal. Prayers accompanied the harvest of wild rice and as they gathered their food. There were special prayers to be said at the moment of plucking a flower or an herb. Some called upon a particular mystery, and in some cases, the prayer was specific to the plant being gathered. Prayers preceded and followed the hunt. So all acts became religious observances and all prayers, whether addressed directly or indirectly, went to *Wakan Tanka*.

The first recorded use of the term *Wakan Tanka* to a white man can be dated to the 1700s. However, its absence does not mean that the term had not been part of the vernacular for a period of time before the whites heard it. Recall that the language is divided into two separate units, the sacred and everyday speech, and historically speaking, some words once used solely by holy men have made their way into common usage. Thus, the rather late introduction to the white man of the words *Wakan Tanka* does not mean that the concept did not exist prior to that time. Walker himself suspected that once *Takuskanskan,* in common speech, came to be known by the abbreviated name *Skan* (in sacred language), *Wakan Tanka* replaced *Skan* as the supreme being and creator. Thus, *Skan* or *Takuskanskan* of earlier years was in fact the Great Spirit by another name.[10]

The belief in multiple gods is not unique to the native. It has been shared by all cultures if one reaches far back enough in time and is still practiced today by Hindus. The original meaning of pagan is "country-dweller," which described a person who not only lived close to his environment, but whose life and livelihood depended upon it. Still, most polytheistic faiths acknowledge that one god was pre-eminent. The Greeks had Zeus, same as the Romans' Jupiter. Only European arrogance rampant in that era would suggest that the native mind could not conceive of a supreme being, that the Dakota had no belief in an overall force that ordered the universe, and it would be presumptuous to think that the Great Spirit was a Christian innovation.

The Dakota world was peopled with spirits great and small. The latter powers, called *Wakalapi*, were not unlike the English fairy, brownie or sprite, whose aid could be solicited in time of need. In *Soul of the Indian* Ohiyesa defended the polytheism of his ancestors: "Naturally magnanimous and open-minded, the red man prefers to believe that the Spirit of God is not breathed into man alone, but that the whole created universe is a sharer in the immortal perfection of its Maker. His imaginative and poetic mind, like that of the Greek, assigns to every mountain, tree, and spring its spirit, nymph, or divinity either beneficent or mischievous. The heroes and demi-gods of Indian tradition reflect the characteristic trend of his thought and his attribution of personality and will to the elements, the sun, the stars, and all animate or inanimate nature."[11]

Many of these beings were evil. Besides *Anog Ite, Iyo* and *Gnaska,* who once had sat at the great banquet, there was *Unktehi,* the mother of all demons and water monster, and *mini watu* (water spirits) who were her offspring. *Can oti* (tree dwellers) haunted the forests. *Ungla* were roughly equivalent to goblins and *Gica* might be compared to dwarves. While the Dakota considered these creatures supernatural, they did not necessarily believe they were divine. Many spirits were neutral, and there were those whose mischievous acts benefited mankind and those whose bad deeds produced good results. Among the divine, *Inktomi* is probably the best example of the latter, for he teaches with his tricks and often brings warnings to mankind.

Which divinity took precedence remained a matter of debate for early white observers, and each seemed to have reached a different conclusion. Pond listed *Unkteri*; Henderson Eastman, *Unktahe,* and Walker *Skan* or *Takuskanskan.* Writing in the 1830s from an outsider's perspective, Pond claimed Minnesota Dakota worshiped bones (*Unkteri*) which he identified as mammoth bones and the Santee identified as a giant buffalo.[12] In the latter belief, the Santee were not incorrect. Whether or not the bones were buffalo or mammoth, a giant buffalo did once exist and would have become part of their collective memory. Mary Henderson Eastman

The Ghost Dance that so frightened white settlers was a manifestation of the Christian church. It was imported from the west, where a Paiute man saw Christ in a vision. The dance was supposed to cause the earth to rise up against the white man and subsequently bring back the buffalo and spirit of the ancestors. The illustration shows the Oglala at Pine Ridge Agency. It was drawn by Frederic Remington from sketches taken on the spot and used in *Harper's Weekly*, Dec. 6, 1890, pp. 960–961.

agreed that the woodland Dakota revered sacred bones, but according to her, the name was *Unktahe*.[13]

One wonders if they were referring to *Unktehi* (the mother of all evil beings), whose bones, according to legend, form the Badlands. Particularly when one considers the phonetic spellings used during the period, compare *Unktahe*, *Unkteri* and *Unktehi*. Were they one and the same? The Siouan tribes of the far southeast, in the Carolinas, Georgia and Florida, also had a water monster known as *Unktena*.

Some might contend that this means the Dakota worshipped evil; however, since they were "canoe Indians," water formed an important part of their culture. The area around the Great Lakes is dotted with thousands of lakes, ponds, rivers and waterfalls, places of great mystery and beauty. Waterways provided freedom. Meanwhile floods spelled disaster and drowning would have taken their toll. It seems logical then that they would have learned to fear *Unktehi*, the water demon and her offspring, and want to appease them.

Further west, in Lakota cosmology water had no power — not even the ability to hold it. Hence its power flowed back up to the heavens, making *Skan* predominant. This disparity does not show a conflict between the tribes of woods and plains; rather it reveals an evolution in point of view.

When the Lakota and Nakota moved onto the American prairies, they would have been confronted with an uninterrupted sky. Anyone who has ever stood on the plains is awed by its immensity and can understand the precedence that *Skan* (the heavens) took in the Lakota faith. Meanwhile floods, the provenance of *Unktehi*, did occur and were recorded in the Yanktonai winter counts for the year 1825. Still floods were rare while the onslaught of the winds was a constant. The storms that rode the heavens could be seen for miles. Therefore, one might surmise the change in emphasis resulted from a change in environment, with all its new challenges and the demands it placed upon the people.

As noted in the story of the White Buffalo Woman, the land (*Maka*) too was sacred. So was stone (*Inyan*). White reporters—both Pond and Henderson Eastman—spoke disparagingly of the Dakota's reverence for "sacred rocks," a reverence they shared with the Lakota. As a holy man Sitting Bull kept *wakan* stones. In the 20th century the Lakota holy man Fools Crow also claimed his power from stone. Wahpeton Ohiyesa explained the concept with a more sympathetic view: "...water-worn boulders, are regarded as sacred, or at the least adapted to spiritual use." Rocks formed the altars for such ceremonies as the Maiden's Feast. However, Ohiyesa used another name for stone than the more familiar *Inyan*. "For the rock we have special reverent name—'Tunkan' a contraction of the Sioux word for Grandfather"[14]—that is, *Tunkasila* in Lakota or *tunkasidan*, Dakota.

The sun was also held in high esteem, as Eastman explained: "The Sun and the Earth, by an obvious parable, holding scarcely more of poetic metaphor than of scientific truth, were in his [the Indian's] view the parents of all organic life. From the Sun, as the universal father, proceeds the quickening principle in nature, and in the patient and fruitful womb of our mother, the Earth, are hidden embryos of plants and men." He elaborated on their reverence for their environment: "The elements and majestic forces in nature, Lightning, Wind, Water, Fire, and Frost, were regarded with awe as spiritual powers, but always secondary and intermediate in character [to *Wakan Tanka*]."[15]

The Lakota openly acknowledged the influence of the stars, so *Wohpe* (Falling Star) as White Buffalo Woman brings the sacred rituals to man. The Morning Star represented the light of knowledge over darkness, and the east, and the eastern part of the tipi, symbolized this light. The "red road" of spirit had its immortal reflection in the sky, the Milky Way (*Wanaghi Tachanku*), where the heroes returned to the stars.

The Black Hills (*Pte Ska*) mirrored the heavens, and the plains tribes followed spring constellations from site to site within the Black Hills. Thus, in their migration, the Lakota mirrored the movements of the sun, as they traveled sun-wise across the face of the map. The constellations associated with the Black Hills included:

- Dried Willow or *Canshasha Ipusye*, watched from winter camp on the spring equinox;
- the Seven Little Girls (Pleiades) or *Wincinchala Sakowin*, greeted from Harney Peak during thunder's welcoming;
- *Tayamni* or Buffalo, part of life's welcoming in peace;
- *Ki Inyanka Ocanku* (the center of the "Race Track"), which was mirrored in *Pe Sla* (a bare hill)
- The Bear's Lodge (or Bear's Hearth), Mato Tipila, which includes Castor and Pollux and was viewed from Devil's Tower, during the summer solstice, just prior to the sun dance.

The celestial Race Track from the origin myth of the Black Hills was divided into *Cangleshka Wakan* (sacred hoop) and *Tayamni Cankahu* (the Animal's Backbone). The sacred sites enclosed by the terrestrial Race Track included Bear Lodge Butte, Ghost Butte, Thunder Butte and Old Baldy. Devil's Tower, beyond the Black Hills, forms the Buffalo's Head, with the face, Bear Butte as the Buffalo's Nose, and *Inyan Kaga* as the Black Buffalo Horn.

Besides the "Race Track," the Lakota observed another important group of stars around the winter solstice, including *Wichapi Owanjila* (Polaris); *Wakinyan* or Thunderbird (Gamma Draconis and 2 stars from "Ursa's bowl"); *Wichakihuyapa* (the Big Dipper); *Tayamni* or Buffalo

White settlers overreacted to the Ghost Dance and the frenzy with which it was celebrated. Their reaction led to one of the worst atrocities committed by the U.S. government against the Dakota peoples at Wounded Knee. The picture from a wood engraving for *The Illustrated London News*, Jan. 3, 1891.

(Sirius, Rigel, and Aldaberan); Capella, the "Fireplace," which contains parts of Leo and Gemini; *Canshasha Inpusye* or Dried Willow which consists of Triangulum and Aries; *Hehaka* (the Elk, which was part of Pisces); *Keya* (the Turtle); *Zuzuecha* or Snake (Canis Major and Columba); and *Wanagi Ta Chanku* (the Spirit's Road) or Milky Way.

The seven stars of the Big Dipper are said to correspond to the seven Lakota council fires. *Towin*, the Blue Woman Spirit who assists midwives with births, resides in the center of the dipper where Fallen Star's mother fell. The Dipper is said to carry the water for the celestial sweat lodge ceremonies, and to ferry the spiritual essence of deceased people to the Milky Way.

The stars that followed a predicted path across the heavens represented stability. The stars' position in the sky foretold the progression of the seasons and ruled the migration of the tribe. Therefore, meteors were viewed with suspicion. On November 12, 1833, a spectacular meteor shower was seen all across the northern United States. As stars mirrored the earth below, their sudden movement portended disaster, an end to stability. The "year the stars fell" (*Wicahpi hinhflpaya*) was a momentous event that was recorded in 34 versions of the Dakota, Nakota and Lakota winter counts.

The solar eclipse in 1867 would have been viewed with equal terror, as *Wi* turned his face from the heavens. Perhaps with cause, for at the end of the Civil War, the white man turned his gaze upon the west, and nine years later, the Battle of Little Bighorn precipitated the U.S. government's campaign of systematic persecution and extermination of the free Lakota peoples.

European recorders viewed the faith of the aboriginal inhabitants as primitive, with its multiplicity of gods. The Dakota faith reflects the complexity and the subtlety of their minds. Their religion is flexible, making allowances for individual needs. The emphasis changed not only between tribes but between people within a particular band.

As with the Biblical Genesis, there are variations in their creation myths. Such variants do not invalidate the legends any more than Genesis, with its two different accounts of creation, invalidates the Bible. Instead they reveal much about the character and growth of a people over time. The stories shifted and changed as the attitudes of people changed. Thus, in a tradition that is purely oral, the emphasis changed with the storyteller and the message or moral that he or she wished to stress at the time.

Similarly which spirit took precedence presented no confusion for the Dakota as it did for their white observers. Their beliefs were distinctly personal. Said Ohiyesa (Charles Eastman): "The American Indian was an individualist in religion as in war. He had neither a national army nor an organized church. There was no priest to assume responsibility for another's soul. That is, we believed, the supreme duty of the parent."[16]

Worship was a private affair. Each person greeted the day in prayer alone. Said Eastman: "It [worship] was solitary, because they believed that He is nearer to us in solitude and there

Dancing was also used to correct imbalances. Many types of dances and celebrations were restricted to night hours. Curtis, who photographed the Dakota extensively, also visited many other tribes. This print shows a night dance meant to restore an eclipsed moon. By dancing in a circle around a smoking fire they hoped to cause the sky to sneeze, thus restoring the moon to its proper place in the sky. Photomechanical print/photogravure (c. November 13, 1914), Edward S. Curtis Collection (Library of Congress). Published in *The North American Indian* by Edward S. Curtis (Seattle, Wash.) 1907–30, Suppl. v. 10, pl. 355.

were no priests authorized to come between a man and his Maker.... It was silent, because all speech is of necessity feeble and imperfect."[17]

Thus, whether one of the *wakan kin* (spirit beings) became elevated over the others became purely personal, their precedence often revealed to the individual in a vision. This being then became a patron, known as *sicun* or guardian. Priority could also be dictated by the situation. If the supplicant wanted to bring rain he would call upon the spirit of the storm, if he wished to bless the buffalo hunt, he would call upon the spirit of the buffalo or the spirit of the predator wolf.

Not only did the Dakota show more respect for individual freedom in their faith, they revealed more humanity and greater charity in their dealings with the European invaders. Certainly they felt no great compunction to convert others to their religion and did not condemn those who did not believe as they did, and never in their history did the Dakota display the wanton cruelty the Christians did in their rush to convert the native peoples to an alien religion.

Mystery	*Element*	*Sire*	*Provenance*
Inyan (whose spirit is Wakan Tanka)	Stone	None	Foundations
Skan	Air, heavens, or sky	Inyan	Motion
Maka	Earth	Inyan	Support, sustenance
Wi	Sun	Skan	Light, warmth
Hanwi	Moon	Skan (?) Wi	Night, dreams
Tate	Wind	Skan	change
Wani Wiopeyata Waziyata Wioyanpa Itokaga	Collective noun — 4 directions West wind North wind East wind South wind	Tate + Ite	Autumn, rest Winter, snow and ice, hibernation Spring, rebirth Summer, bounty
Yumni	Whirlwind	Tate + Ite	Love and games
Unk	Water	Maka	Contention, mother of evil beings
Wakinyan	Thunder	Inyan	Storms, active principle, or
Ksa		Inyan hatched by Wakinyan	Wisdom who became Inktomi
Inktomi	Spider	Transformed by Skan from Ksa	trickster
Iya		Iyan + Unk	Evil
Gnaski		Iya & Unk	demon
Wohpe	Falling Star	Skan (?) Hanwi+Wi	White Buffalo Calf Woman
Wa / Wazi	First man	Skan	Wizard, old man of the north
Ka/Kanka/Wakanka	Fist woman	Skan	Sorceress
Ite (Anog Ite)	Wife of Tate	Wa + Ka	Duplicity

16. Medicine and Power

In days long gone, a young man played his flute, and all who heard it fell in love with him, for he had elk medicine, the medicine of love. Any woman who heard it would leave family, lover or husband and children behind to follow the warm notes to their source, and there she met the handsome warrior. He would open his blanket to her, wrap it around her and whisper sweet words in her ear. Although his music inflamed the passions and his medicine spoke of love, his heart was cold and unyielding. He would have his way with her until he had used her up and then he would throw her away like an old moccasin.

He did this with not one, but many women, leaving them brokenhearted until no one trusted him. But when he played his flute, they forgot common sense; they forgot their duty and went to him, until there was not one heart he had not wounded with his elk arrows.

One day he left to go on a hunt and he did not return. His worried mother would look out over the prairie and his father rode along the plain to no avail. The moon grew fat in the sky, and they waited. When Hanwi decided to cover her face, they went to a medicine man who had a way with lost things. He had stones powerful enough to find anything, treasured possessions or cherished son.

The father loaded the pipe; the mother presented the gifts she had gathered to the medicine man. The father lit the pipe and passed to him as the mother told him about her son's disappearance. The old man nodded, for he had heard. He accepted their gifts and said he must consult the spirit of the stones. The couple withdrew to await the decision of the stones. Later the medicine man went to their lodge and stood outside their tipi. The woman gasped and rushed to give him entrance.

"I am sorry," the holy man said, "your son is dead." Then he told them where they would find his body.

The mother wailed, tore at her braids and collapsed into her husband's arms weeping. "Oh, what are we to do? Our only son is gone."

The grieving father held her close. "I must go," he said, "and bring him back so we can place him among his ancestors."

The father scooped ashes from the fireplace and sprinkled them into his wife's hands. She spread them on his face and rubbed them into his skin, and then she built the travois that would carry her son's body with her own two hands. She would not stay behind, but rode with her husband and the medicine man to carry her son home to his final resting place.

The body lay exactly where the stones had said, a knife sticking from his chest. He had been murdered. Some said naught while others murmured behind their hands that he had deserved it, but all were uneasy. Whether discarded lover or angry husband no one knew for sure, but a murderer was living in their midst.

While others whispered, the family erected the scaffold. The mother prepared the body. They would neither wash nor eat until their duties to their son were complete. The mother made him the finest buffalo robe and soft buckskins. She beaded his moccasins. He was a handsome man in life, so she would have him look his best in the afterlife.

On the appointed day they took their son to his final resting place. The mother slashed

Captain Seth Eastman, Charles Eastman's grandfather and Mary Henderson Eastman's husband, painted many native scenes. This picture of his, entitled *Medicine man curing patient*, shows a healer at work. The lithograph was created by C. Schuessele for P.S. Duval and published in *Indian Tribes of the United States* by Henry R. Schoolcraft L.L.D. Philadelphia: Lippincott, Grambo & Co., 1851, pl. 46

her arms and beat her breast, and her blood fed the grass beneath her feet. The father moaned and moaned as if he would raise the dead with his voice.

The village looked on in wonder and shook their heads. For days, neither moved, but the band could not wait for them to work through their grief. The herd had wandered north and they must pursue it. Reluctantly, the parents left their boy to join their tribe.

One evening many days' ride away from their original camp, as the village settled down to sleep, they heard a ghost flute playing a haunting melody, an elk song that warmed the heart, but froze the soul. And they knew that the son had followed. Then they heard him speak:

> "Long I thought I understood the magic of love,
> "And I used it to do my bidding.
> "Now I am alone and I am doomed to wander this way,
> "Throughout eternity."

―⁂―

Like many other societies, the Dakota held a belief in ghosts. Ghosts were restless spirits who clung to their mortal remains or, as in the story above, those with unfinished business who were tied by their sins to those they had wronged in life. Ghosts also included those who had been deemed unworthy and pushed into the raging river by (She Who Judged Men's Souls), or they had taken the wrong path to the afterlife.

Meanwhile in sickness and in death, Dakota holy men and women and medicine men and women ministered to the needs of the people. They were integral to the spiritual and secular life of their band. They found lost objects, as in the story above. They treated the sick. They conducted the ceremonies and provided blessings upon the people. They sent their prayers to the almighty and interpreted the visions and dreams of the tribe.

Like priests, but unlike their Christian counterparts, they did not separate themselves from the people — retreating to monasteries or hiding behind a cassock and collar. They had had their gifts bestowed by the divine. As people of power, they held great power within their community. They were part of the governing counsel. They were consulted in cases of war and they sanctified the war party. No battle was enjoined without their blessing.

White recorders often use the terms holy men and medicine men interchangeably. The Dakota, however, made a distinction. Both were blessed by spirit, yet each performed a different function within the village environment. As George Sword explained to Walker: "*Wicasa wakan* is the term of the Lakota priest of the old religion; a Lakota medicine man is *pejuta wacasa*. The white people call our *wicasa wakan*, medicine men, which is mistake. Again, they say *wicasa wakan* is making medicine when he's performing ceremonies. This also is a mistake. The Lakota call a thing medicine only when it is used to cure the sick or wounded..."[1]

Medicine, *pejuta*, was wrongly interpreted as "magic" or power by white reporters who observed the ceremonies associated with healing with skepticism and suspicion and viewed them as pure chicanery. Thus they ignored the most obvious usage: medicine as in treating the sick or effecting a cure. In *Black Elk Speaks*, Joseph Epes Brown delineated three different types of medicine men: the *Wapiye*, who used herbs; the *Yuwipi*, who used "magic"; and ghost doctors.[2]

Holy men meanwhile ministered to the spirit. The *wicasa wakan* or holy men and the *winyan wakan* (woman) officiated at the rites. They acted as the counselors during the *inipi* and guides for those seeking the vision quest. They interpreted dreams and were consulted in matters large and small. The path of a *wasica* or *winyan wakan* was revealed to him or her in a vision. Robert Utley made another distinction. "*Wichasa* [*wicasa*] *wakan* were dreamers— men who had experienced dreams with sacred content or who had attained visions of powerful spiritual meaning. Not all dreamers were holy men, but all holy men were dreamers."[3]

The power of the shaman and healer could run along familial lines, but a vision was still necessary to confirm it. In *Indian Boyhood*, Eastman relayed a tale of a mother who believed she had bear medicine. She wanted to have her son initiated as a bear medicine man. The boy claimed to have had the vision, but Ohiyesa wondered if the boy did not say this to please his mother.[4]

The individual may also have shown a natural aptitude, or in the case of the *pejuta wacasa*, he or she might have been chosen as apprentice to another. Thus, Ohiyesa's grandmother taught him about herbs so that he might someday take over her position as healer within their community.

> **Medicinal Herbs**[5]
>
> Among the medicinal arsenal of the herbalist *wasica/winyan pejuta* were:
>
> - *Taopi Pejuta*, used for wounds, powder, stirred in a cup of water.
> - *Keya Ta Cante* turtle heart dried and powdered, used for wounds.
> - *Canli Wakan* holy tobacco, used for wounds, smoke in pipe and pipe pointed at the wound.
> - *Hante Pejuta* cedar medicine, used to disinfect, burned in a fire and in sweat house, chewed and put on the scalp lock.
> - *Icahpahu Pejuta* the pith of the soap weed, used for swelling, mixed with water and used as a poultice.
> - *Pejuta To* (blue medicine) used for anemia, powdered infusion which is drunk.
> - *Sinkepte tawote Pejuta* (calamus root) for delirium and mental illness. The patient chews it or the doctor chews it and spits it in the face or over the head of the patient.
> - *Pejuta Skuya* (sweet medicine) used for menstrual troubles. Powdered, made into a tea and then taken.
> - *Wahpezizila pejuta* also known as "yellow leaves medicine." It was used with swellings, mixed with water or grease and rubbed in the affected part.
> - *Tazi-yazan pejuta* (yucca) powdered and drunk for upset stomach.

The distinction between holy men and medicine men often became blurred. For example, holy men treated the sick; but they did not usually use herbs as the *pejuta wacasa* did. Said Sword, holy men carried bags or bundles, but they did not carry medicine (*pejuta*) or herbs in their bags, they carried something else sacred or *wakan*.[6] Yet some did maintain knowledge of herbs. Sitting Bull, who was a holy man rather than a medicine man, understood the medicinal properties of roots and herbs, carried them with him and used them to treat the sick.

Another form of holy man was the "magician." He had both the ability to curse or to cure and was viewed with suspicion by the rest of the tribe. Said Sword: "He was *wapiye wicasa* when he makes someone well. *Wakan skan wicasa* when he makes someone ill."[7] The magician made charms that allowed their bearer to be victorious at games orè to win the love of men and women. Their charms could also kill. These wizards were known as *Hmugma wicasa* or *Wicahmunga*. According to William Powers, the *Wicahmunga* were practitioners of black magic. Their power came from *Gnaskinyan* or *Gnaska*, sire of all evil demons, and it was carried in their voices. They would hum and the vibrations would carry their intent for good or for ill to their target.

Powers gives a different set of divisions for holy men from Sword. Powers considered medicine men a subset of the former. His classification of the *Wicasa Wakan* included the *Wapiyapi* (literally, one who makes over and renews) or curer; and the *Wakan Kaga*, "kaga" meaning performance. The *Wakan Kaga* officiated at sacred ceremonies, and the *Wicahmunga*, the magician or wizard, and the *wikte* (transvestite).[8]

Healers could either belong to a society or work as sole practitioners. Included among the latter were:

- The *Yuwipi wicasa*, who held séances;
- *Hohu iyapa*, which means "to hold the bone," who sucked disease from the body;
- And the *pejuta wicasa*, who used herbs.

The *Mato wapiye*, meanwhile, belonged to a society, the Bear Society, which gave him his medicine. Like the *pejuta wicasa*, bear medicine people used herbs, and a knowledge of herbs was bear's gift to man in ancient times. Bear, representing both strength and wisdom, endowed its worker with the ability to treat wounds received while on the warpath or in hunting accidents. This included broken bones, inflammations, and wounds that became infected. Many medicines were represented by a society, but not all society members became healers. Some became performers, such as the *Mato* (bear) *kago*. Still others were warriors.

Other animals too had curative powers, that were specific to the animal. The buffalo, associated with women, gave its members knowledge of female complaints. Another name used for buffalo medicine men was "They who sung over the menses," and it was the medicine men of this society who officiated at the initiation rites of the buffalo woman.

Ohiyesa's grandmother was endowed with turtle medicine. Like buffalo, turtle medicine imparted upon its bearer power over women's diseases, conception and birth, so she became a midwife and an a herbalist.

Eagle acted as the messenger between *Wakan Tanka* and man. Crazy Horse and Sitting Bull were examples of holy men, rather than medicine men, blessed with eagle medicine. Eagle bestowed its initiate with the ability to cure gallbladder disease and tuberculosis.

Members of wolf medicine society officiated at ceremonies of war and held dances prior to war parties. Warrior wolf endowed its medicine men and women with the ability to treat wounds of war. They were renowned for their skill at removing arrows.

Additionally, there were mole, badger, weasel and mink medicine. Mole endowed one with knowledge of roots and their curative powers. Their healers also used dirt from moles' tunnels, untrodden upon by men, which was sprinkled on the affected part to effect a cure. Those who had the power of badger specialized in the treatment of children. The use of mink and weasel medicine has been lost to antiquity. Medicine bags of both kinds exist and conveyed both spiritual power and spiritual protection to their owners, although it was better not be in too close contact with the skins, for to sleep with a weasel skin was to invite disease into your bed.

Spider medicine, endowed by the trickster god Inktomi, was one of the most complex. The power could be dangerous to its bearer. Powers spoke of one woman who had been killed by its medicine.

Not all mentors were animal. Ghost doctors (*wanagi pejuta*), referred to by Brown, treated heart attacks and strokes through the power of the pipe and herbs.[9]

The *Yuwipi* healer did not have a specific lodge. Although each could claim an animal mentor, the animal varied. Some *Yuwipi wacisa* got their power from spider. An allied medicine was woodpecker medicine which was associated with thunder and storms, or *Wakinyan*. Fools Crow was an example of *Yuwipi* man who based his power on woodpecker.

In addition, the *Yuwipi* practitioner worked directly with spirits. They could foretell the future, find lost objects, communicate with the dead, and give demonstrations of magic. It is most likely that the "jugglers" referred to in early accounts were *Yuwipi* men. As Pond described them: "They knew how to release themselves when bound fast, hand and foot with cords."[10] This practice is still used in the *Yuwipi* healing ceremony today.

The *Yuwipi* healing began when the sufferer approached the medicine man with a pipe and asked for help. The pipe would be smoked and instructions given for preparations. This was followed by a sweat lodge and the singing of sacred songs. The final ceremony would take place in a totally darkened structure. *Yuwipi* man would be bound and blindfolded. As the *yuwipi* practitioner communed with the spirits who told him the cure, the participants would often hear mysterious noises, animal sounds and alien howls. When the spirits left, blue lights would flash and then, when illumination was provided, the *Yuwipi wicasa* would be found unfettered and sitting next to the altar he had created before the rite. When he destroyed the altar the cure was complete. The ceremony would end with sacred songs and the smoking of the pipe.[11]

Powers' second category of holy men, the *Wakan Kaga* or performers, were those who had dreamt of a man twice and an animal twice, although traditions varied and some said three times. A person would become were *Heyoka kaga,* if he or she had dreamed of coyote. There were also *hehaka* (elk) *kaga, mato* (bear) *kaga, sunkmanitu* (wolf) *kaga, tatanka* (buffalo) *kaga, zuzeca* (snake) *kaga,* and horse dancers. *Wakan Kaga* also had curative powers. For example: Elk and deer dancers were able to treat ailments of the heart and create aphrodisiacs. Horse dancers healed maladies of the head, such as mental illness and nightmares.

The position of the *Kaga,* or performers, was taken seriously. An entry in the 1774 No Ears

The last scene of the last act of the Sioux war is a print that shows a native warrior laid to rest on a scaffold. Another warrior, medicine man or family member is seated next to it, with a horse lying on the ground beneath. In the background, one can see wolves and coyotes have gathered. The purpose of the scaffold in Lakota tradition was to present the body to the heavens (*Skan*). It remained on the scaffold unless disturbed. Meanwhile the woodland Santee used scaffolds to prevent scavenging until the body could be buried. The wood engraving, created by H.F. Farny, was published in *Harper's Weekly*, v. 35, no. 1782 (February 14, 1891), p. 120.

winter count illustrates how seriously when it recorded that year's main event: "They killed *Heyoka* impersonator,"[12] and again in 1788 when two *Heyoka* impersonators were killed for performing the ceremony without having earned the right to do so.[13]

Dakota women could become endowed with medicine or power, becoming healers or holy women. These were divided by Powers into three basic categories, the *winyan wakan* (sacred woman) which included the *wapiyapi*, or *wapiyape winyan*, and the *pejuta winyan*. Women also could be *Wakan Kaga or* performers such as the *Heyoka kaga*, and women were not immune to the dark arts, for they had *Wihmunga* practitioners, or witches.[14]

Another category of *wakan* men were the *Wikte*, men who dressed as women. Early settlers believed them to be homosexuals or simply cowards who hid not behind, but inside the skirts of women. However, most were married and the fathers of children, and they were often recorded as participating in war parties. One of their assigned and sacred tasks included the care of the sick and the feeble. The *Wikte* acted as go-betweens for a woman and her male intended, so it was considered propitious to have a child named by a *Wikte*,[15] although the names were often crude.[16]

Like the sacred pipe, the sacred transvestite found expression in many tribes. The Illini had their *Ikoneta*, or what the Frenchman La Salle called *berdache*. By the time of the Joliet and Marquette expedition in 1673, the institution had existed for more than a generation.[17] Father

Jacques Marquette observed: "They pass for Manitous. That is to say for Spirits."[18] Unlike the Lakota *Wikte,* the *berdache* sacrificed much to accept this calling to a woman's role, for they were prohibited from battle.

Wakan men and women spoke the sacred language which was understandable only to them, although the terms used were similar to those used in common tongue. A person could be bestowed through vision with more than one medicine or power, such as Fools Crow who was one who "bore the bone" and held the powers of woodpecker. Similarly, the medicine man could be endowed with the medicine of more than one animal. Holy men could be medicine men and medicine men could be holy men. However, many like Sitting Bull were one or the other and not both.

Their expertise in treating the typical ills of the tribe was recognized and emulated by settlers. In the 1700s, John Lawson spoke admiringly of the Carolina Santees' use of sassafras. Further west, the woodland Dakota used the available spikenard to treat many of the same ills. Yet the medicines so successful against the normal afflictions of the tribe proved totally ineffective against the relentless march of European diseases, such as measles, cholera and smallpox, that followed the path and preceded the white trader wherever he went. Still their response to these foreign diseases revealed an elemental logic. They attempted quarantine, but usually by the time they recognized the problem, it was too late. The carrier had been let into their midst.

When death came, mourners would cut their hair and men blackened their faces. The Siouan tribes of the Carolinas would also "smoake" their faces. Said Eastman: "The outward signs of mourning for the dead are far more spontaneous and convincing than is the correct and well-ordered black of civilization. Both men and women among us loosen their hair and cut it, according to the degree of relationship or devotion. Consistent with the idea of sacrificing all personal beauty and adornment, they trim off likewise from the dress its fringes and ornaments, perhaps cut it short, or cut the robe or blanket in two. The men blacken their faces, and widows or bereaved parents sometimes gash their arms and legs till they are covered with blood. Giving themselves up wholly to their grief, they are no longer concerned about any earthly possession, and often give away all that they have to the first comers, even to their beds and their home. Finally, the wailing for the dead is continued night and day to the point of utter voicelessness; a musical, weird, and heart-piercing sound, which has been compared to the 'keening' of the Celtic mourner."[19]

Mourners dressed in rags for the duration of their mourning period and would not wash until a ritual feast was given. Women in particular were expected to give everything away at the death of the husband, and if she did not do so, then her neighbors helped her by divesting her of her possessions.[20] During this period they were to think no bad thoughts, neither were they to scratch themselves unless they used the branch of a chokecherry.[21] They were to fast, and if they ate, they were supposed to stop eating while still hungry.

Mourners were considered *Wakan* and stayed in mourning for a period of at least one month, often longer. During this time they would participate in the *inipi* ceremony and receive instructions about their duties from a holy man or a holy woman. They were told to isolate themselves and to grieve, but remember those of their relations who were living, and when they were ready to come back to the camp, they should shoot a deer and prepare a feast where they would be welcomed back to the world of the living.[22]

Dakota funerary rituals reveal that they treated the dead with both dignity and respect. When a person died, the family would retrieve the body if it happened outside the home and carry it on a travois back to camp. The travois was not attached to a horse or a dog, as would happen when transporting goods; rather an individual, usually a family member, would pull it. The distance to be traversed did not matter, with bodies carried hundreds of miles if the tribe happened to be in a camp that was far from the tribal burial grounds. In the 1840s, Mary Henderson Eastman described the death of Deer Killer, who instructed his wife to place food so his soul might be replenished on his journey. He clung to life since he wanted to buried near the land of his birth, but once he extracted her promise to return him to his native village, he died, and his wife carried his body on her back to his homeland, a trip that took several days to complete.[23]

The body was then dressed in clothes and moccasins that were the best that the family had to offer. The dead were wrapped in as many blankets and buffalo robes as the family possessed. The body was placed upon a scaffold or up in the branches of a tree for a period of time which varied, depending on the time of year or the personal request of the individual.

White writers found the custom of scaffolding barbaric, but Samuel Pond defended it, viewing it as necessary during the winter months when the earth was frozen hard. By elevating the body, they protected it from scavenging animals until the burial could be accomplished.[24] The custom had historical precedent elsewhere. The Siouan tribes of the Carolinas created a platform for their dead, even though their winters were not nearly as brutal as those of Minnesota, Canada and Dakota Country. Exposure allowed the flesh to fall from the bones. The skeleton could then be interred in a burial mound or a grave. If the family was forced to move, the bones were taken along with them. One can also find European antecedents with similar customs among the Celts.[25]

Like the Siouan of the east, the woodland Dakota eventually buried their dead. Visiting the Mdewakanton in 1823, William Keating described their coffins. "Sometimes a trunk (purchased from a trader), at other times a blanket, or a roll of bark conceals the body of the deceased."[26] Burial, however, seems to be a later innovation. In 1679, Father Louis Hennepin said that the Santee chief Aquipaguetin carried the bones of important relatives with him,[27] as the Carolina Santee did during Lawson's time.

Meanwhile the prairie Lakota left the body exposed so that the physical remains could feed the animals who had so often in life fed the Indian. In *The Sacred Pipe*, Joseph Epes Brown explained the spiritual significance of scaffolding for the prairie tribes. "It is in this manner that the gross body is given back to the elements from which it came; it is left exposed to the agents of heaven; the four winds, the rain, the winged ones of the air, each of which — and with the earth — absorbs a part."[28]

Food was left by the grave or the scaffold, along with any possessions prized by the deceased. Some viewed the gift of food as foolish, indicative of their superstitious nature and primitive culture, but Pond described the custom as no more strange than the European tradition of leaving flowers—neither, he indicated, could be enjoyed by the deceased—and the Dakota knew that the dead did not partake of the food that was left for them. It was done as a mark of respect.[29]

In cases where the person was of high rank or particularly beloved, the family might leave the individual in death as he had lived, inside a lodge. Said Eastman: "As a special mark of respect, the body of a young woman or a warrior was sometimes laid out in state in a new teepee, with the usual household articles and even with a dish of food left beside it, not that they supposed the spirit could use the implements or eat the food, but merely as a last tribute. Then the whole people would break camp and depart to a distance, leaving the dead alone in an honorable solitude."[30]

If grief was particularly acute, or if it was believed that the spirit did not rest easy, the mourner might initiate the Keeping of the Soul ceremony, one of the seven sacred rites brought by *Wohpe*. Lasting a full year for the participants, it required absolute commitment on the part of the person who undertook it. During this time, the individual lived only half a life. Activities were restricted by any number of prohibitions. The keeper was not allowed to work, to handle weapons or, in later periods, to touch metal. This meant very real sacrifice for himself and his family. The male could not hunt. The woman could not cook or gather food. Meals had to be supplied, through the generosity of family and friends. Since knives as weapons could not be touched, this prohibited the scraping of hides or the cutting of meat. In addition, no dissension was allowed within the lodge where the soul was kept, and people of bad reputation were not permitted to enter.

The purpose of the rite was to cleanse the soul of the dead in preparation for the afterlife. In *The Sacred Pipe*, Black Elk explained the reasoning behind the tradition. The rite "...so purifies it that it and Spirit become one, and it is able to return to the 'place' where it was born and need not wander the earth as in the souls of bad people."[31] Furthermore, the Dakota believed the ceremony helped the people to remember that death was a part of living and above all to remind them of *Wakan Tanka* who is above all dying. According to Black Elk, at first the Keeping of the Soul rites was only held for great leaders, but later it became standard for all good people.[32] Others said that its use was restricted to those who would not rest easy. However, any family could perform it as an act of devotion to the loved one and the passing of children was often honored by the Keeping of the Soul ceremony.

The rite began with the cutting of a lock of the deceased's hair. A holy man would be solicited to officiate. The hair would be wrapped in buckskin and put in a place of honor. The pipe would be smoked and instructions given. During the year as others hunted, the keeper would go to an adjacent hillside, smoke his pipe and send his voice to the heavens, praying for a bountiful hunt. Any buffalo cow killed near him became his, but he could not skin it. Shoulder meat was considered especially *wakan*. This and the hide would be taken to the woman who kept the bundle; she would dry it and turn the hide into a robe. She would use the meat to make *wasna* and save it until the day the soul would be released.

Once dedicated, the buffalo robe was used to cover the bundle whenever it was taken outside. A war bonnet was placed on top of the robe to honor the soul in death. On sunny days, the soul bundle would be hung on a tripod, facing south, and displayed out of doors so members of the band or family could bring gifts and pray to it. The gifts were retained and given away to the poor and the needy at time of release. Helpers assisted the keeper, but only the keeper could carry the bundle, which was held against the breast. When it was taken inside, it was offered to the four directions.

When a year had passed, the day for release was selected. Tobacco was sprinkled to each of the directions and entreaties were given to the Great Mystery to ease the spirit along the way. When all was made ready, the Keeper walked "sun-wise" around the lodge and sat in the place of honor. The wife went to her tipi and brought back the bundle. She would stand in front of the keeper of the pipe and hand him the bundle. The bundle was then placed on an altar, consisting of a depression in the ground to represent a buffalo wallow, upon which two pipes lay crossed. The ritual dedications of the pipe were observed as the holy man explained the reasons and history behind the ritual.

The food that had been set aside was offered to the bundle and then given to four virgins. They were then covered with the robe. Thus sustained, the women in turn sustained the spirit of the departed and the tribe. A post was erected to contain the soul. It was addressed throughout the ceremony. As soon as the bundle was taken outside, the soul was considered released. The ceremony was followed by a feast where the gifts and possessions of the deceased and those acquired during the year were given away to the poor.

The Keeping of the Soul seems to be have a shared custom, between the tribes of the woodland and plains. Pond tells of a Santee family keeping a lock of the hair for a period of time until it was released, in this case, by carrying it to battle against an enemy.[33] Wahpeton Ohiyesa gave more details about the woodland Dakota version of the ceremony. "A lock of hair of the beloved dead was wrapped in pretty clothing, such as it was supposed that he or she would like to wear if living. This 'spirit bundle,' as it was called, was suspended from a tripod, and occu-

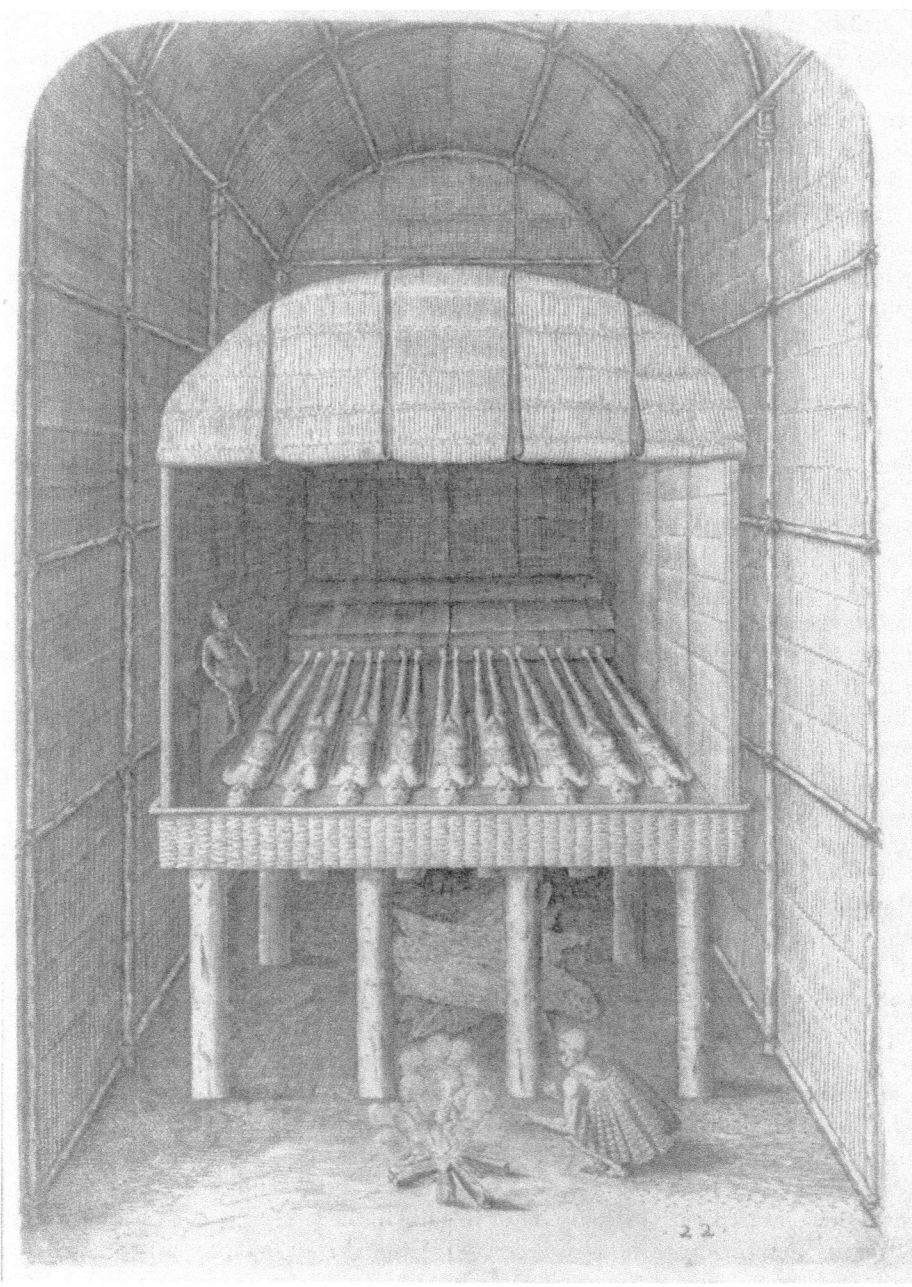

This watercolor by John White portrays the burial customs of the eastern Santee, although the illustration depicts an Algonquian burial house. The Siouan tribes of the Carolina also placed bodies on a raised platform. A priest squats by a fire beneath the platform which sped the drying process, after which the bones would be interred in a tomb mound. In some instances, the body was left undisturbed and the burial house itself was covered in mud, becoming the mound. Library of Congress Rare Books Collection: Engraving by Theodor de Bry after a watercolor by John White in *Wunderbarliche, doch warhafftige Erklärung, von der Gelegenheit vnd Sitten der Wilden in Virginia ... / Erstlich in engelländischer Sprach beschrieben durch Thomam Hariot, vnd newlich durch Christ. P. in Teutsch gebracht.* Franckfort am Mayn: Gedruckt bey J. Wechel, in Verlegung D. Bry, 1590, plate 22.

pied a certain place in the lodge, which was the place of honor. At every meal time, a dish of food was placed under it, and some person of the same sex and age as the one who was gone must afterward be invited to partake of the food. At the end of a year from the time of death, the relatives made a public feast and gave way the clothing and other gifts, while the lock of hair was interred with appropriate ceremonies."[34]

The Dakota view of life and afterlife was complex. A man's life force was centered around his breath or *ni*. When alive, the person contains *waniya* (breath of life), and he has *nagi* (spirit) that warns him of danger. In the afterlife, breath (*ni*) became *niya* (ghost) and his spirit, *nagi*, became *wanagi* (sacred spirit).[35] A person also possessed called *nagila* (like spirit). These "spirits" in plural were referred to as *nagipila*.[36] Like the Egyptions with their *ba* and their *ka*, the Lakota had a spirit and they had other "spirit-like" selves. After death, a man's *wanagi* would linger near the body. After a time, the spirit would travel to the land beyond the pines, guided by the man's *nagi*.[37]

With a multiplicity of spirits contained within an individual, it is not surprising that the Dakota expressed a belief in reincarnation. Mary Henderson Eastman knew chiefs who claimed to have lived a previous life. Ohiyesa (Charles Eastman) concurred: "Many Indians believed that one may be born more than once, and there were some who claimed to have full knowledge of a former incarnation."[38] Meanwhile in their document on the "Foundations" of the Lakota faith written for James Walker, Thunderbear, John Blount Horn, Thomas Tyon, and George Sword disagreed, saying: "Men have one spirit. It left the body when it was dead. It went to the spirit world. Some said this was in the west. Some said this was in the south."[39]

The road traveled in death began in life. Called the red road of spirit, it has been compared to the Christian's straight and narrow path. Thus the Dakota recognized that the journey a soul followed to attain the spirit world after death began in this one.

Once the mortal soul was released, it traveled this spirit path to the river to be greeted by *May owichapaha* ("She who pushes them over the bank")[40] who then sat in judgment over Dakota souls. In Lakota cosmology the Milky Way, called *Wanaghi Tachanku,* was the trail of spirits. The association with the Milky Way and spirit world was shared with other cultures in Central and South America. Where the Milky Way splits, it was believed the divine Arbiter stood. The *nape* or Hand, which consists of Orion's belt and sword, and Rigel and Eridanus Beta, was also linked to Lakota afterlife beliefs. In this context, people who lived an immoral life were forced to the nebula, leaving them tumbling through space forever. Those who lived a proper life took the other road to *Wanaghiyata*, the promised home of departed souls.

In the spirit realm the worthy continued to live much as they did on earth, hunting and feasting, but without many of its drawbacks. The Santee of Carolina shared this belief. Analogies can be drawn between the spirit land of the Dakota and Valhalla of the Norse. However, Eastman argued that: "The idea of a 'happy hunting-ground' is modern and probably borrowed, or invented by the white man. The primitive Indian was content to believe that the spirit which the 'Great Mystery' breathed into man returns to Him who gave it, and that after it is freed from the body, it is everywhere and pervades all nature, yet often lingers near the grave or 'spirit bundle' for the consolation of the friends, and is able to hear prayers."[41]

Meanwhile those who were afraid to cross the bridge, or who got pushed over the bank, were doomed to wander the earth as ghosts. Their land of the restless dead was found in the north, where Wazi the Wizard lived, in the realm of Yata. The Dakota hold many beliefs about ghosts. For instance "If a man sees a ghost no harm will come of it. If he hears a ghost, bad luck will follow, and if they hear a ghost mourning then someone in the family will die soon."[42] Hearing a ghost was believed to cause strokes which only a ghost medicine man could cure.

Similarly if a war party saw a ghost who gave a victory shout, triumph would follow. If the ghost grieved, then the battle would be lost. Ghosts could also portend the outcome of a battle for the people who remained within the village. If they heard ghosts singing a victory song, then the war party had won the day; if the ghosts sung a mourning song, then their warriors had died.

Ghosts were best avoided or appeased. People sought protection against these displaced spirits. A part of every meal would be given to them, with food spilled next to the hearth, as the supplicant prayed: "Ghosts say for me I will live long."[43] Thus, the Dakota urged their ancestors to intervene for them with the divine.

Ghosts could cause mischief. As a war party went to battle an animal would be killed and left behind to distract any ghosts and prevent them from following the warriors into battle. If a person heard an owl at night it was a warning and they would prepare a ghost feast, which should not be confused with the ghost dance—the latter, which so frightened white settlers of the time, was actually an offshoot of the Christian faith. A ghost lodge was called when a man killed a white buffalo, as was recorded in the 1848 Big Missouri winter count when a man known as Yellow Spider "obtained a white buffalo hide."[44] This means the ghost lodge as a rite existed before the ghost dance.

The victorious warrior too had to appease the spirits of those men he had vanquished, for it was believed that the *nagi* which inhabited the scalp lock or scalp would seek revenge on the victor. Some followed a full thirty-day mourning period. Another abbreviated rite consisted of thrusting the pole, from which the scalp hung, out of the smoke hole to release the souls of the warriors contained therein. This rite showed a great deal of respect for a fallen enemy whose remains were treated with reverence.

Dakota customs find their reflections across the globe. For example, the Norse buried a man with his possessions, his weapons and his boat, either on dry land or at sea. Even today Christian mourners place some prized possession or a small memento in a loved one's coffin to be taken with them into the grave. Dakota dressed their relations in their finest, as people do today. Such shared traditions show that reactions to grief cross all races, religions and boundaries.

The Dakota had, and continue to have, a firm belief in an afterlife. The principle of *ni/niya* and *nagi/wanagi* is not unlike the distinction we make between spirit and soul. Likewise little difference can be found between Valhalla, the Egyptian "Field of Reeds," or the Moslem and the Christian concept of heaven and what Eastman refers to as "the Happy Hunting Ground." The Dakota spirit path has both reward and retribution for the good or the ill done in life—a concept found in most faiths—while the association of this path with the Milky Way is another that is shared with many cultures, in the Old and New Worlds.

Some of what the early recorders viewed as the Native American's more barbaric rituals, such as scaffolding, have their European equivalents. Archeological digs in Hambeldon Hill, England, revealed pieces of human bones in a causeway outside an enclosure. After studying the bones, scientists concluded that they had been left exposed deliberately to allow birds to pick them clean.[45] Other excavations, like the one at Wayland Smithy in Oxfordshire, seem to confirm this point. Bones found within the tomb had been gnawed by rats. Elsewhere (Skendelby, Lincolnshire) bones contained snail's eggs, an above-ground creature. Each site indicates that the body had been exposed to the elements for a time before internment.[46] So the Dakota tradition of exposing a loved one was not unique and could be considered comparable to the Egyptian process of drying the human remains in preparation for the final funeral.

The Dakota belief in ghosts is also shared between cultures. Hauntings remain a topic of discussion to the present day. Hours of scientific analysis and equipment are devoted to their study, to either prove or disprove their validity. A large segment of the population have no doubt about their authenticity and even many skeptical profess uncertainty. Ghosts, or at least a belief in them, seem to be another universal.

The priests of the Dakota did not withdraw from their people as did Catholic monks. The holy men and women and the medicine men and women lived among the people they treated, providing comfort and suffering many of their same losses. In Pond's time, they were paid for their services, but Ohiyesa remained convinced that this was a later manifestation which occurred after the arrival of the white man when the hunting economy had been destroyed and the tribe had been influenced by the concept of the "paid exhorter." Prior to that time, they received sufficient payment through the accepted custom of generosity.

The rituals associated with healing so roundly condemned by the missionary often proved instrumental to its success. Belatedly white doctors on the reservation have come to recognize that their patients respond better to modern medicines if a *Yuwipi* man is an active participant in the individual's treatment. Doctors have acknowledged that faith is an important component in the healing process, and none deny the "placebo effect."

While their cures contained a measure of magic, their use of herbs was based on scientific evidence, provided much the same way new medicines are tested today, through trial and error. Their medicines and cures were more than adequate to their needs until white men brought new diseases against which they had no immunity and no defense. The catalogue of *pejuta* on page is incomplete. Many more herbs were harvested and utilized, and their use often picked up by the white man to treat his own ills. Their skill in treating broken bones and other wounds is evidenced by the number of people who survived such injuries with few ill effects, visible scars or crippling disabilities.

17. Send a Voice

A young man desired to go on a vision quest, for he was sure that he was destined to do great deeds and become a medicine man. As a hunter and a warrior, he had proven himself to be courageous, and his parents were good honest people. He consulted a holy man and made the arrangements. When the appointed day quest arrived, two holy men prepared the inipi. He breathed the breath of the Grandfathers, in the steam. Then, they took him to a hilltop where they had dug a vision pit. They instructed him to cry for a vision, to ask in humility for the spirits to send a voice.

The first night he kept himself awake, crying aloud, ready to wrestle with the vision the spirits sent. As day dawned, a voice spoke to him from the mists. "There are other places you could have gone. Why have you come here and why don't you leave us in peace? You have kept us awake all night. Animals and birds, even the trees could not sleep."

The youth ignored the rebuke, spending the another day and a night in the pit, begging for enlightenment, but it did not come. The next morning the youth discovered a boulder standing on the edge of the pit. The young man stared and the boulder began to rock, falling backward. It rolled back up to the mountain top. Then with a rush and roar, it tumbled back down again. The young man scrambled from the pit. The boulder crashed down upon the place where he had sat. Then it leapt back to the summit, only to roll back down again. Again and again it rolled to the hilltop and back, landing atop the pit four times.

The young man returned to the village to consult the holy men, but they sent him back to the pit. The next dawn, the voice came again and told him to leave, but the youth did not listen. He cried all day and night until he was hoarse.

When sun rose, the voice boomed over his head in anger. "Why are you still here?" it asked.

With the foolishness of youth, the boy answered defiantly. "I can not help it. I am doing as instructed by the most holy men of our village, and who are you to tell me what to do? I am going to stay until they come to fetch me."

The mountain shook and roared. The wind began to blow. The boulder appeared again, poised on the peak. Lightning struck the mountaintop. The rock swayed and then toppled over. Moving slowly at first, it rolled until it came crashing down upon the pit.

The holy men arrived on the fourth day to find the youth crouched next to a tree, and he told them that no vision had come. Then he relayed the tale of the stone; the old men muttered among themselves and then turned to face him.

"You angered the spirits. You went after a vision like a hunter after buffalo or a warrior after scalps. You did not listen, instead you fought with the spirits when they came to you. You may have seen nothing, but we hope you have learned your lesson. Suffering alone does not bring a vision, nor does courage, nor willpower. The spirits come to you in many ways, and you must listen. You must obey. If you had remained silent as asked, perhaps, they would have given you a vision, for spirits come only to those who seek them with true humility born of wisdom and patience."[1]

A group of eastern tribesmen gathered around a campfire; some appear to be holding rattles. Rattles, like flute and drums, carried the community's prayers to the Great Spirit. Another creation of John White, this watercolor depicts the worship of the Virginia tribes in the 1500s. Dugout canoes appear on the river in the background. Library of Congress Rare Book Collection: Engraving by Theodor de Bry after a watercolor by John White in *Wunderbarliche, doch warhafftige Erklärung, von der Gelegenheit vnd Sitten der Wilden in Virginia ... / Erstlich in engelländischer Sprach beschrieben durch Thomam Hariot, vnd newlich durch Christ. P. in Teutsch gebracht.* Franckfort am Mayn: Gedruckt bey J. Wechel, in Verlegung D. Bry, 1590, plate 17.

Prayers found expression in public ceremony, and few life events were not recognized by ceremony; for example, the blessing of a newborn's umbilical cord, which was thought by the Dakota to contain a person's soul. The rite was similar to the old custom of taking of one's measure in medieval Europe. It was believed that the human soul resided in an individual's shadow. The shadow, or soul, was measured by a piece of string, and them the string, like the Dakota umbilical cord, was blessed, kept in a pouch and worn as an amulet to protect its bearer from evil. Ritual marked a youth's transition into adulthood. Other rites existed, such as those that adopted individuals into different sodalities.

Religious dances were common. Held to ensure a good hunt, initiate a war party or celebrate its return, they comprised a sort of visible prayer and could be compared to the pageants and processions found in Christian churches both past and present. Dances as religious events included the thunder dance, the sun dance, the horse dance, the buffalo dance, the deer dance and the elk dance, to name only a few. According to Utley, the horse dance was a later manifestation and found its origins in Sitting Bull's time after he rescued his grandchild from a river on horseback. He asked the child to be brave and promised a dance would be held in his honor, if he did not stir from his seat astride the horse.[2]

Dances were held often in conjunction with other rituals and rites, such as the maiden feast, and could be considered inseparable from them. Some ceremonies and dances were unique to a person or a tribe. The woodland Dakota performed the medicine dance, which all holy men/women and medicine men/women attended. Neither the Nakota nor the Lakota had its like. Pond suggested that the medicine dance was an import. Other tribes celebrated the medicine dance, including the Ojibwa, the Winnebago, and Sauk and Fox, and the Arikara. Unsure of its origins, Pond admitted that medicine dance may have originated with the Dakota and been adopted by

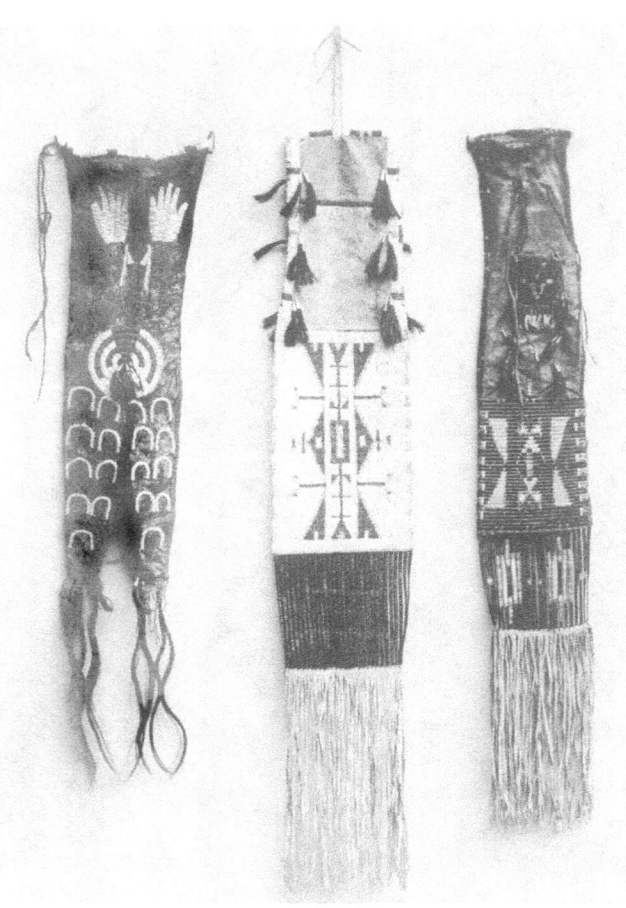

The Dakota made bags and pouches for many purposes. The most important were those connected to ritual uses, the medicine pouch of the medicine or holy men and women and the pouch that contained an individual's umbilical cord, to name only two examples. Pictured here are pipe bags and tobacco pouches photographed by Edward S. Curtis and published in *The North American Indian,* Edward S. Curtis (Seattle, Wash.) Edward S. Curtis, 1907–30, v. 3, p. 26. From the Curtis Collection (Library of Congress).

the adjacent tribes, only to be dropped by the western Nakota and Lakota as they moved onto the plains.[3]

Ohiyesa agreed that the medicine dance was a recent innovation among the Dakota, an import from the Algonquin tribes of the east. He believed that it was created as a buffer against Christian missionaries. The medicine dance barred the common man from entry, which he said reflected the exclusivity practiced by the Christian church.[4]

If extreme circumstances forced the abandonment of a wounded, infirm or elderly male, the woodland Dakota performed another ceremony called the "making of the enemy." The man would be armed and attacked by the other braves of the tribe, giving him death with honor and dignity as befitting a warrior rather than a slow, ignoble death which would result from starvation and exposure.

Feasts, such as *Wakan* feasts, were another part of the religious life. The maiden feast and the other associated fidelity feasts, such as *isnala kic'un*, the "being alone" ceremony, celebrated the virtue of the Dakota people. The Minnesota Santee, who normally disdain eating raw meat, held the feast of raw fish. Its celebration usually resulted from a vision and was convened to avert disaster.[5] Mary Henderson Eastman referred to a dog feast, which may have been the *Heyoka* feast, although in *Lakota Belief and Ritual,* Walker mentions a dog feast associated with the *Hunka* ceremony[6] and later states: "the principal viand, at this, as it is nearly at all formal feasts of the Lakotas, was boiled dog meat."[7]

Rituals were often instigated by an individual, and their target could be an individual, as in the *Yuwipi* healing ceremony where the medicine man engaged the support of spirits to cure a patient. Rituals could also be used for the good of the group. The most important rites of the Dakota peoples were multi-layered, with each ritual representing a step that led to another, and together they created a whole. The rites that formed the backbone of their faith were found in the seven sacred rites brought to the Dakota by the White Buffalo Calf Woman, *Wohpe*. Listed by the Oglala holy man Black Elk[8] in 1953, these include:

- *Canupa Wakan*—the pipe ceremony.
- *Inipi kaga*—the sweat lodge ceremony or purification rite.
- *Nagi yuhapelo*—the keeping of the soul.
- *Hanblecheyapi* (Dakota *Hambeday*)—crying or lamenting for a vision.
- *Wawakyag Wachipi*—the sun dance.
- *Hunkapa* (*Hunka Lowanpi*)—making of relations, or adoption ceremony.
- *Tapa Wanka Yap*—the throwing of the ball, or sacred ball game.

The Dakota tribes shared the pipe ceremony (*canupa wakan*). Indeed, the pipe or calumet was common to all the tribes of the eastern United States, the Great Plains and the American southwest. The Dakota reasoned that air, represented by smoke, was the one element that bound everything together. They recognized that every creature needed air, and each breath inhaled took in air previously circulated elsewhere, air that had touched another being, another essence, or had been exhaled by someone else. So it was that air linked all things together. Years later, quantum physics has confirmed their belief, for the solidity of matter is an illusion. In truth, objects are little more than a mass of gyrating particles of protons, neutrons and electrons. Air passes through apparently solid objects and unites us all.

The smoke itself represented *Wohpe*, who took Dakota prayers to the Great Mystery. The *canupa wakan* (pipe ceremony) provided the foundation for every other rite or ceremony in Dakota tradition. No decision, no trade, no alliance or act of import, no dance, no negotiation or religious observance was completed without the *canupa wakan*. The *inipi* (sweat), the *yuwipi* (healing) ceremony, the *hanblecheya* (crying for a vision), the bull buffalo dance, the sun dance, the sacred ball game, every initiation and every council began with the pipe. The pipe ceremony and prayers preceded the hunt and the war party. If a man went to a medicine man for healing, he brought tobacco and his pipe. No deal was struck nor oath taken without the pipe.

The concept of the sacred fours, or *tob,* found physical expression in the pipe ceremony and in other Dakota rituals. Dedication to the four directions took place during the sun dance and initiations. In the *Hanblecheya* the petitioner walked the four-cornered circle, where directions were marked with wands or sticks. During the horse dance women stood in these honored places. The center was marked by a large staff, or spirit pole, for all knowledge came from *Wakan Tanka,* who was represented by the center.

To smoke the pipe in a *wakan* manner required dedications to the four directions, above (*Skan*) and below (*Maka*) during each phase of the rite. Before filling it, the empty pipe was dedicated. As the pipe was filled the holder stopped at each direction and put a pinch of tobacco in the bowl for the four. Once the pipe was lit, the smoke was offered by inverting the bowl and pointing the mouthpiece to the appropriate direction.

With each step of the dedication, ritual words were spoken. Certain prayers were pre-

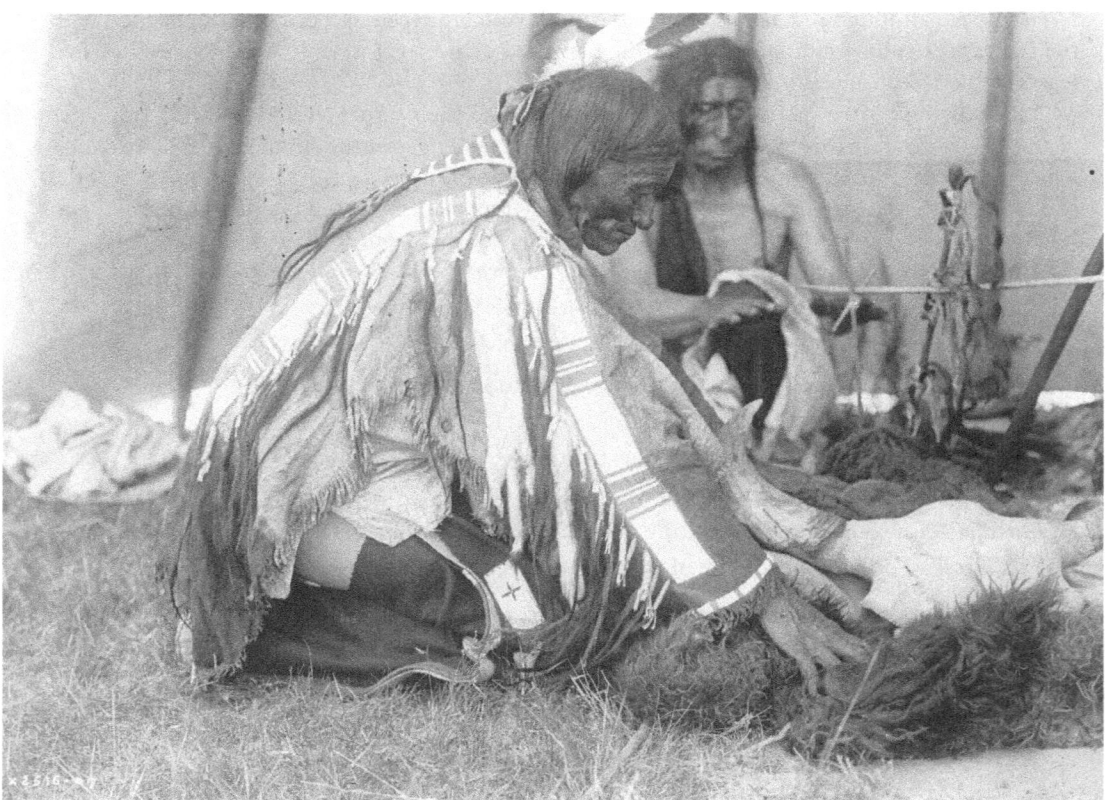

The *Hunka* ceremony was the most photographed of all Lakota ceremonies, probably because it was a public celebration of honor for the individuals and the tribes involved. Although Curtis's spelling omits the nasalized "n" and divides the words in unusual locations, the term *Hu Kalowa Pi* is still recognizable as *Hunka Lowipi* (the latter word meaning sacred songs). Another name for the making of relatives ceremony was "They sang over each other with horse tails." In this interior shot of a tepee, a man kneels on ground and removes the buffalo hide from the skull on the ground. Behind the altar, another male warms his hands by fire. Edward S. Curtis Collection. Published in *The North American Indian,* Edward S. Curtis (Seattle, Wash.): Edward S. Curtis, 1907–30, v. 3, p. 76.

scribed by tradition. Others were revealed by spirit to the speaker. Often the prayer was appropriate to the occasion or action. The petitioner may ask for wisdom, for spirit to send a voice during a weighty decision, or the supplicant may ask to be led down the correct path, in sending a vision. Each prayer required appropriate dedication, for these were not a hurried people who would rush matters of spirit, and it did not matter how many times an act or words needed to be repeated.

The oaths, the steps, the various dedications must be followed faithfully and consistently. Said Pond, divine "displeasure was incurred rather by transgressions of the arbitrary rules; for example, smoking the wrong pipe at the wrong time, might provoke them.... It was dangerous for the Dakotas to omit any of the prescribed ceremony in the *wakan* feast as it is for some Christians to eat meat on Friday."[9]

The next layer in Dakota observance was the purification ceremony, or the *inipi*. Ohiyesa pointed out in *Soul of the Indian*: "There are two ceremonial usages which, so far as I have been able to ascertain were universal among American Indians, and apparently fundamental. These have already been referred to the as the 'eneépee' or vapor-bath and the 'chan-dú-hu-pah-yú-za-pee,' or ceremonial of the pipe. In our Siouan legends and traditions the two are preeminent, as handed down from the most ancient time and persisting to the last."[10]

The purification rites of the Dakota and other Native American people can be compared to the Christian baptism which is supposed to cleanse the person from the taint of original sin. Unlike baptism, the Dakota did not believe that a single rite of purification was sufficient. It needed to be performed again and again throughout a person's life as human foibles resurrected themselves.

The lodge was called *ini ti*. It was constructed with four-by-four pieces of wood. One end would be anchored and bent, and the opposite end would be thrust into the ground. The second stick would be treated likewise, creating an arched cross (+). The next two would form a similar cross at a 45-degree angle which was superimposed over the first (×). Altogether they created a circle or a dome upon which hides were hung.

The structure was round rather than conical or square since it represented the womb of the sacred mother, *Maka*. The circle carried into the earth, it created a sphere which signified the grandmother or the totality of earth.[11] A hall made of woven branches or hung with hides led to the entrance to the lodge. The door into the *ini ti* was small, requiring the participant to bow or crawl to get inside, for as the story illustrates only in humility can man meet his Creator. Christians follow a similar practice when they get on their knees or they bow their heads to pray.

The sweat was unisexual; although both genders practiced ritual purification, they did it separately — men with men, women with women. The fire was set up outside the door. The firekeeper's walk, or grandmother's path, was a specified length, seven paces. Each step represented a stage in the rite of purification. The first, purification by fire; the second, understanding one's limitations; the third, leaving what is not needful behind; the fourth, accepting one's strengths; the fifth, correct action; the sixth, spiritual support; and the seventh, rebirth.[12]

The participants would enter and turn left, moving sunwise around the circle, to take their respective places. By no means would they move straight across the structure or turn right. The holy man sat in the place of honor opposite the door. A grandmother selected for her virtues brought the stones which were then passed to the holy man who ran the ceremony.

Water would be sprinkled on the superheated stones to create the steam, which was also known as Grandfather's breath, *tunkashila oniwan*. Steam, like smoke, represented the breath of spirit. It was the breath of life, the *ni*. The steam cleansed. Songs were sung; prayers were offered each time water was poured over the rocks, and the steam carried the prayers to the heavens. If the ceremony was held for a specific purpose, the prayers addressed the pertinent issues — such as healing or in preparation for another religious event.

Like the pipe ceremony, the *inipi* could be performed as a single entity or, more often than not, to prepare the participant for other ceremonies. Dancers attended a sweat as a precursor to the dance. A sweat was part of the vision quest (*hanblecheya/hambeday*): when the petitioner received his instructions, and when the *hanblecheya* ended, he returned to the sweat lodge where the vision would be interpreted.

The *Hanblecheya* was held during significant events in the life of the individual. It was part of coming of age for the young Dakota male. According to Robert Utley: "Somewhere between the ages of ten and fourteen, the boy solicited the counsel and instruction from a holy man, purified himself in a sweat lodge, and went to a remote hillside to fast and struggle until the vision came. Afterward, the holy man interpreted the vision and helped devise a special fetish or design to summon the power when needed."[13] The petitioner could also compose a song as a result of the vision, and the holy man might place him under a taboo. Sometimes the youth would receive his adult name or his spirit name during the *Hanblecheya*.

The rite could also be undertaken in times of trouble to seek answers, advice or inspiration about issues that were important to the individual or to the tribe as whole. Crazy Horse lamented for a vision several times a year.[14] The holy man or the medicine man would cry for a vision in preparation for other rites, as noted in Walker's description of the bull buffalo ceremony.[15]

Said Black Elk: "But perhaps the most important reason for lamenting is that it helps us

This photograph shows the completed altar. The skull was a symbol of virtue; the nostrils were stuffed with sage to consecrate it. The holy men sit behind the newly constructed altar. Popular subjects for Curtis, the men, Slow Bull, Saliva, and Picket Pin, have been pictured elsewhere conducting various rites such as the invocation. Edward S. Curtis, c. 1907. Published in *The North American Indian* by Edward S. Curtis (Seattle, Wash.) 1907–30, v. 3, p. 80.

realize our oneness with all things, to know that all things are our relatives; and then in behalf of all things we pray to *Wakan Tanka* that he may give us knowledge of Him who is the source of all things, yet greater than all things."[16]

Both men and women could seek a vision. Women had female assistants rather than male, but both subjected themselves to fasts. The *inipi* preceded the *hanblecheya* and was part of it, as was fasting. The most common, but by no means only, form of *hanblecheya* was walking the four-cornered circle. Before the rite, the holy man or woman would prepare a circle far from camp atop the region's tallest hill. Grass would be stripped away, and wands placed to mark the four directions with a large staff at the center.

After the sweat lodge, the petitioner would be sent to the circle. The man went alone along the path indicated, wearing only a loin cloth and moccasins and carrying a blanket. He may, if he chose, divest himself of these objects and enter the circle as he was born, naked. With their sense of modesty, it seems unlikely that a woman would do the same.

Once the petitioner entered the circle from the east, he/she would walk it, not by following its circumference. Instead the supplicant would move to the center, turn and walk to the first directional wand and then go back to the central staff. He would continue to do this, moving sunwise, until he had walked to each of the four wands, thereby honoring the four directions, always returning to the center from which all things came. This was known as walking the four-cornered circle. Certain songs were sung and prayers said. The petitioner would continue to walk the circle until he or she received a vision, the four days had passed, or the individual dropped from exhaustion. If the latter happened, then the lamenter would resume the march as soon as he/she was physically capable, and continue until the vision came or the four days completed. Although Black Elk also said that the petitioner could choose to work in silence or sit in quiet meditation, for silence allowed the voice of spirit to be better heard.

The *hanblecheya* almost always came as a form of ordeal that tested the limits of the supplicant's endurance. Records indicate there were other forms *hanblecheya* could take. The person could fast and dance while staring at the sun, a form of self-sacrifice which also found its expression in the sun dance.[17] Before the battle of Greasy Grass (Little Bighorn), Sitting Bull slashed his arms over 100 times to receive a vision.[18] In the tale related at the beginning of the chapter, as elsewhere in the American southwest, an individual might be buried alive or placed in a pit, a facsimile of his grave in which he would spend for four days and four nights, facing his fears and his own mortality. It is said that a Crow warrior once floated in a canoe on a lake for four days and nights, waiting for a vision. The ordeal then became the fast, forced confinement and inactivity.

Not all vision quests were successful. If an individual did not get a vision, the *hanblecheya* could be repeated up to four times. If after the fourth time the person still had not received a vision, he was not allowed to try again. He was considered suspect. Continued silence on the part of the spirits was seen as an indictment, and the person was not to be trusted.

The vision quest was shared not only between the Dakota tribes of woodland and plains, a form of it was practiced from the Inuit of the north to the Maya of the south, although some experts refer to the latter as true "shamanism" where only the priestly caste could address the spirits. Evidence exists that Clovis man also performed some form of vision quest, making the rite not only nearly universal in its practice in the Americas but one that reached far back into antiquity. Europe had its equivalents. The Greek priestesses of Apollo were visionaries. The soon-to-be-installed knight performed a vigil the night before the ceremony where he knelt with his arms and prayed. The Laplanders of Finland and many of the aboriginal peoples of Africa, Polynesia, Australia and Asia continue to practice a form of vision quest to the present day.

While the *hanblecheya* was strictly individual, the sun dance involved all the members of the tribe and its many bands. Said Utley in *The Lance and the Shield: The Life and Times of Sit-*

ting Bull: "The sun dance was to the tribe what the vision quest was to the individual — a great outpouring of religious devotion and supplication aimed at securing tribal power and well-being."[19] More than one tribe would take part. The Mdewakanton would come from Minnesota, and Wahpeton from Canada and the Yankton from Nebraska or Iowa. After 1845, the Cheyenne also attended.

The sun dance took place in midsummer — in the moon of chokecherries (July)[20] or in the moon of fattening (June) when the moon itself was full[21] and the "hearth of the *mato* (bear)," or the dog star, was highest in the sky. It was usually held somewhere near *Paha Sapa*, the Black Hills. The rite lasted for twelve days. The first four featured the ceremonies for women and men, along with the initiations into various sodalities. The second four were committed to instruction of the participants. The final four were dedicated to the performance of the dance itself.[22]

Ohiyesa (Eastman) relayed the history of the dance as it was practiced by the Santee. "In the old days, when a Sioux warrior found himself in the very jaws of destruction, he might offer a prayer to his father, the Sun, to prolong his life. If rescued from imminent danger, he must acknowledge the divine favor by making a Sun Dance, according to the vow embraced in his prayer, in which he declared that he did not fear torture or death, but asked life only for the sake of those who loved him. Thus, the physical ordeal was the fulfillment of a vow and a sort of atonement for what might otherwise appear to be reprehensible weakness in the face of death. It was the nature of confession and thank-offering to the 'Great Mystery,' through the physical parent, the Sun, and did not embrace a prayer of future favors." Eastman believed the piercing of the flesh was a perversion of the original. "It is noteworthy that the first effect of contact with the whites was an increase of cruelty and barbarity...."[23]

Because of the custom of piercing, which early traders and pioneers found horrifying, more has been written about the sun dance than any other ceremony. The purpose of the sun dance as it later became practiced was to ensure the prosperity of the entire Dakota nation for the upcoming year, and in keeping with their beliefs about sacrifice, they believed they must shed blood, as *Inyan* did in creating the heavens and the earth, for who among a grateful humanity could do any less? Men were pierced as they danced around the pole "so their people might live," while women could also con-

The first step of any sacred rite was the smoking of the pipe, and the *Hunka* ceremony was no exception. It began with the sacred pipe, or *chanupa*. This photograph shows the Dakota holy man Saliva as he kneels by the altar with the pipe in his hands. The Dakota did not like to have photographs taken during the rite, so the photography of the *Hunka* ceremony ends with the ritual's beginning. The picture was taken by Edward S. Curtis at the same time as the others, c. 1907, although not used in his book.

tribute a piece of skin, approximately one-inch square, to adorn the post from which the men were suspended.

Due to its intricacies and the number of participants, the sun dance was the most elaborate of all their rituals. The preparations took weeks, even months, and the participants had to plan a year in advance. The dancers were expected to volunteer early. The participation of a dancer in the ritual put not only himself, but his entire band in harmony with the cosmos. The male dancer had to purify himself and must remain abstemious for a period of up to a year. Tribe members were expected to contribute food to the feasts that would follow and the preparations of *wasna* and jerked beef began long before the actual event.

During the first phase of the ceremony, the sun dance lodge would be built of 28 poles, one each for the days of the "moon" or month. Later the holy man and dance leader would select the sacred tree. The tree was always cottonwood, which, it was believed, had special properties. A chosen, or chaste, woman would fell it, and the tree would be brought back to the camp, raised and dedicated. The post would then be adorned with the flesh of the contributors.

The dance began with a procession. Selected candidates would be attached to the tree, their skin pierced with awls and then tied to the tree by leather thongs. One of the dancers would have four buffalo skulls attached to his back, which he would drag back and forth until the thongs tore through his skin.

The rest of the dancers would run from the periphery of the circle to the center and back three times, building up speed each time. After the third flight, the dancer moved with such force that the pegs were torn from his chest. Some of the dancers would literally be hauled up the pole where they would dance suspended in mid-air. The thongs ripping free of flesh acted as a reminder that the people were torn away from their connection to the Great Mystery during the process of birth. Likewise it reinforced the idea that everything — from the grass that grows, the grazing buffalo and man that fed upon it — is ultimately dependent on the Sun.

The sun dance was one of the most important rites; it was for the community what the vision quest was for the individual. Pictures of the sun dance as practiced by the Lakota are virtually nonexistent. However, the building specially constructed was photographed in 1911: a log building with a sod roof. The people stand outside looking in. Credit: J.A. Anderson.

Others could join the dance; women danced with their husbands and their brothers, children with fathers. Women and children were not pierced, but many of the former contributed flesh to the poles. Any of the dancers could rest if they chose. However, it was a point of honor to continue to dance without a break.

To sacrifice oneself for the good of one's people was a great honor, and those who did so were rewarded. They were then allowed to paint their legs red during ceremonial occasions as a symbol of their participation in the sun dance. Often the dancers would receive a vision as a result of the ordeal that the dance entailed, and from those visions would come predictions that affected the entire tribe. One notable example is Sitting Bull's vision of soldiers raining down from the sky. Jumping Bull did the honors, piecing his mentor's flesh with an awl 50 times on each arm and placing the skin on the dance pole. Then Sitting Bull danced, at which time he received the image which he later described to Black Moon.[24]

The Dakota were not alone in this custom. Some form of self-immolation rite was common throughout the Americas. The Mayan chief would pierce either his tongue or his testes to gain a vision of the future. Once forewarned he could plan accordingly to ensure the health and well-being of his people. A form of sun dance was practiced by every tribe across the plains. The Mandan had their *Okeepa* ceremony where braves were pierced and then hung from rafters of a lodge to honor the buffalo, who gave them life.

Another of the seven sacred rites was the *Hunka* or adoption ceremony. The buffalo symbolism of the *Hunka* ceremony found its reflection in other Native American tribes, including the Omahas' and Poncas' *wawan* and the Pawnees' *Hako* ceremonies.[25] Called "making relations," it was one means of making peace with a neighboring tribe. It formally declared that the two tribes were as one family.

The origins of the ceremony are shrouded in myth. Some authorities believe it to be an import from another tribe. Some cite the Arikara as the originator; others, the Cheyenne; and still others, the Mandan. Some Dakota claim that it was performed before the White Buffalo Calf Woman visited the tribe, at a time when all the bands lived in the land of the pines. Most legends, however, credit it to *Wohpe*. The Lakota Black Elk also attributed it to *Wohpe,* as one of the sacred seven promised to the people, but said the oath was fulfilled later when the Lakota Matohoshila (Bear Boy) received the ceremony from *Wakan Tanka* during a vision quest.[26]

One story told by John Blount Horn provides a date of origin. According to him, before the year "many pregnant women died" (1799), adoption was celebrated by a simple feast. Following the deaths, the people decided that they had angered the spirits because their children were given away without proper ceremony, and no adoptions took place for five years until someone expressed a desire to adopt an old couple who needed the protection of a family. The people discussed this in council and some went to seek a vision, which provided the rite used today, suggesting the *Hunka* ceremony dates to 1805.[27]

As the story indicates, the adoption ceremony was not only used as a way to make peace, it was used within the tribal setting between individuals. The adopted child would become as one's own sons or daughters. An old man or old woman became one's adopted parents. People of similar age became siblings. It solidified a friendship ever since. Said Eastman: "Friendship is held to be the severest test of character. It is easy, we think, to be loyal to family and clan, whose blood is in our own veins. Love between men and women is founded on the mating instinct and is not free from desire and self-seeking. But to have a friend, and to be true under any and all trials, is the mark of a man!"[28]

The importance of the *Hunka* ceremony among the Lakota people was reflected by the fact that it found its way into the No Ears winter count of 1805,[29] and later it was mentioned in the 1843 and the 1845 Yanktonai winter counts, first when "Iron White Man was honored" and second when "His Horse Runs was adopted." Sitting Bull's uncle adopted the son of Red Fish in

1856, an event recorded in Minneconjou, Hunkpapa and Brule winter counts. This tradition was followed by Sitting Bull himself when he adopted the *Hohe* (Assiniboin) youth and named him Jumping Bull.

John Blount Horn described the obligations of the *Hunka*. "If any other Indian was a *Hunka*, the Oglala would treat him like a brother."[30] The individuals were then like any other family member despite tribal affiliations. The *Hunka* would not take another *Hunka's* horses, his women and children, or make him captive. If some other Indian took him as prisoner, the *Hunka* was honor bound to help — to mount a war party to effect a rescue and to retrieve any property that was lost. If a *Hunka* was hungry, their adoptive relatives would feed them. If they were in need, the other would provide for them. The ceremony emphasized importance not only of friendship but of kinship and reinforced the concept that all are related.

Once adopted, the *Hunka* would paint his face with the *Hunka* stripe of red on forehead and cheek.[31] The ceremony was often referred to as waving of horsetails since a part of the rite included waving wands with strands of hair from a horse's tail over the heads of the participants. Wands with corn then followed. The horsehair and corn were symbols of prosperity. The act reminded the participants that their prosperity and livelihood had become inextricably linked or bound as *Hunka*.

The sacred ball game was another rite shared by many tribes throughout the Americas. The Maya had a form of it, as did the Siouan tribes of the east. As with other ceremonies, the ball game was an metaphor. The ball represented the world or the universe, and the skill with which the game was played revealed the players' skill in handling life. When the Mayan king played the game, his prowess and skill in playing it indicated his ability to maintain control over the world symbolized by the ball. In this way, the ball game was not unlike the races the Egyptians held for their pharaohs. In the early kingdom period, the pharaoh physically participated. When he was too old to run, he was too old to rule. Eventually, though, it became a symbolic gesture with an athlete hired to run in the king's stead.

The sacred ball game of the Dakota, however, consisted of four teams. Four goals were set up at each of the four corners. The four teams represented the denizens of this world, in other words, the four-legged (mammals), the two-legged (man), the winged ones (birds) and those that swim or creep (reptiles/fish). The ball represented *Wakan tanka,* and the goal was not to get control over the ball and keep it, but to share the responsibility between the different teams and to make sure that the ball never touched the ground.

A woman officiated, standing in the center of the playing field and holding the ball or universe in her hands. She represented the buffalo. A child was also brought in to sit beside her to symbolize the four stages of life. The woman would throw the ball in each one of the directions to be caught by one of the teams. The fifth time the woman would throw it straight up, at which time there would be a scramble as many tried to capture it. Gifts and blessings were bestowed upon those who had caught the ball.

Whether the Dakota game of lacrosse achieved the same status as the sacred ball game is difficult to say since it was often played for its entertainment value alone. Lacrosse was shared among all the tribes of the Great Lakes, and contained many of the same elements as the sacred ball game. A holy man was required to make and bless the balls used in the game. Elsewhere Pond described lacrosse matches performed in conjunction with funeral proceedings, which suggests a sacred function.[32]

Religion formed both the warp and the woof in the tapestry of everyday life. Dakota rituals and faith were interwoven into every aspect of their existence. It was inextricably intertwined with their concept of themselves as a people. Religion was inseparable from family and no discussion of their history would be complete without it. Their religion supplied not only the cause, but often the ways and means of celebration. It provided emotional support and psychological unity within the framework of community.

The only representation of the inside of the sun dance lodge in the Library of Congress collection is an engraving which shows one of the more controversial aspects to the ceremony: that of pierce, titled: *Young bucks proving their endurance by self-torture*, Jules Tavernier & Frenzeny. The wood engraving was created by A. Measom and published in *Harper's Weekly*, January 2, 1875, pp. 8–9.

Dakota ceremonies reflect their modesty and their humility as a people. The Dakota were diffident in their dealings with the divine. They entered the *ini ti* on their knees, approaching their maker as humble supplicants. Such a properly prayerful attitude is also found desirous in the Christian faith, but rarely achieved. Meanwhile the Dakota celebrant made himself worthy of the divine through personal sacrifice, fasts, and rites of cleanings.

Many of their rites were shared, not only between tribes on this continent, but also across continents. The sweat was universal among American tribes and shared with the Scandinavians. The Greeks, the Romans and the medieval Christians each had their visionaries, their oracles, their prophets. The present-day Laplanders of Norway have their practicing shamans. The Dakota were not unique in their vision quests, but they made them democratic, with visions, and the seeking thereof, accessible to every man and woman, to young and old alike, and they gave credence to the insight of each participant as a message of the divine.

Many tribes had some form of self-immolation ritual. The Dakota who chose to make such a sacrifice were always volunteers, whereas in other tribes the individual may be an unwilling victim. The Skidi Pawnee and the Natchez were the only two North American tribes to practice human sacrifice, the victim inevitably a member of an enemy tribe. In European, the old faith also practiced human sacrifice, requiring the death of the helpless or weak, often in the form of infanticide. The Celts were known to sacrifice children. Elsewhere some of our highest civilizations—including the Greeks and the Romans—also performed human sacrifice or a form of infanticide to please or appease some god. The sacrifice of an innocent, and in the end an unwilling victim, in person of Jesus Christ is the basis of the Christian faith.

Meanwhile, the Dakota never asked any of their people, or even their adversaries, to do anything against their will and yet they found many volunteers within the tribe willing to make a sacrifice for the good of the people.

18. The Pursuit of Happiness

The year had been a good one. The hunt was successful and the flow of maple sap unusually abundant. Even the corn harvest had come early. When midsummer arrived it was time for the great feast. Bundles of tobacco and invitation wands were sent far and wide, and the village hummed with activity as the people prepared for the upcoming festival. Each contributed his share, wild rice, fresh meat, berries, and turnips.

Soon the other bands began to arrive and tipis sprouted like mushrooms around the camp. The elders of the various tribes were called together to discuss who would make the balls for the game that would be held as part of the feast. The herald rode from camp to camp, shouting the name of the man selected: "Cankpi-yuha (Keeps the Club)."

That evening Keeps the Club arrived at the circle leading a small child of a scant four winters by the hand. The boy clutched his bow and arrow in his other hand. The medicine man pulled himself upright and threw the boasts of the warriors back at them, saying: "If Wahpetonwan wins then he," the medicine man indicated the boy beside him, "shall lose his child's name, 'Hakadah' and become known as 'winner.' If the Light Lodges win, the name shall be given to any child they choose."

The field was selected on a narrow strip of land between stream and lake. The day of the game arrived, and the akitcita rode among the people to ensure no one strayed onto the playing ground.

The players advanced to the field. Some had painted themselves with the likeness of the rainbow or with the graceful colors of Anpetu, the sunset sky. Others had adorned themselves with the glowing white stripe of the milky way or jagged zig-zag of the lightning bolt. Many depicted animals on their persons, those fleet of foot or swift of wing whose powers they hoped to invoke.

The four most powerful men were stationed in the center of the field. Another approached the group, threw his head back and trilled at the sky. The first ball was thrown up and the men tried to catch it in their nets. War whoops filled the air as the other players rushed to the middle of the field, sticks flailing. Dust rose and bodies blocked all view of the ball.

Suddenly it shot through the air toward the Mdewakanton goal. The Kaposias cheered. Others ran to grab it, but the Kaposia failed to catch it in his net. It struck the ground and one of the Wahpeton leapt upon it. The band shouted encouragement. Leaping and bolting, the warrior evaded the many Kaposia who sought to seize him. He ran but fifty paces before his progress was arrested.

Again and again the ball was volleyed back and forth, yet neither one tribe nor the other could gain the advantage. The herald announced it was time to change balls. The game began anew. The red ball was tossed and grabbed by the one man and then another, moving inexorably toward the north side of the field

The other team blocked and the ball disappeared from view under the roiling mass of players. Suddenly one of the Wahpeton emerged from the crowd, the sphere clutched in his hand, and raced across the field. So fast was he that he was known by the name "Antelope."

The game of lacrosse was shared by many tribes. Both the Ojibwa and the Dakota played it. A version of the game was played by the Siouan tribes of the east where a clay cup replaced the Dakota net. Pond and Eastman described the playing field and the rules of the game. This representation of lacrosse came from a music cover showing Native Americans and white men playing on opposite teams. The lithograph was created by W.C. Chewett 7 Co. in Toronto, and published between 1830 and 1910.

> *The people shouted his name. Two Kaposia warriors bore down on him from either side. Antelope neither veered nor slackened his pace. The Kaposia warriors collided. Antelope achieved the goal unimpeded and the Wahpeton won the day.*
>
> *That night after the feast, the medicine men led the one they called "pitiful last" into the circle, and conferred upon him a new name, and that's how Ohiyesa got his name.*[1]

Despite its hardships and responsibilities, life presented many opportunities for play, and games were pleasing to *Yumni*, lord of love and games. Many children's games were educational, preparing them for their adult roles. Boys had miniature bows and arrows to hunt small game. Target practice served a dual purpose, entertaining as well as honing an important skill. Often such contests took place when contestants were running or riding on horseback, where it was the chance shot that won the day.

The young participated in hunts both mock and real. In fact, like children of all ages, they found that anything observed, anything the imagination conceived, could be turned into a game, from running like wild horses upon the wind to an imitation buffalo hunt. Ohiyesa, in *Indian Boyhood*, described just such a game where one group of boys set off on to the prairie,

The picture, *The exercises of Youth*, depicted by Jacques Le Moyne in an engraving by Theodor de Bry is just as accurate in 1800s as it was in the 1500s. Shown here, young men shot arrows, wrestled, raced and pitted their strength against another, testing those skills they would need to survive as adults. After a watercolor by Jacques Le Moyne, the Bry engraving appeared in *Brevis narratio eorvm qvæ in Florida Americæ provicia Gallis acciderunt: secunda in illam nauigatione, duce Renato de Laudoniere ... anno MDLXIIII. Qvae est secvnda pars Americae ... / Auctore Iacobo Le Moyne, cui cognomen de Morgues ... Nunc primùm Gallico sermone à Theodoro de Bry Leodiense in lucem edita: Latio verò donata a C.C.A. Francoforti ad Moenvm:* Typis I. Wecheli, sumtibus vero T. de Bry, venales reperiutur in officina S. Feirabedii, 1591.

bearing meat. They represented the quarry. After a respectable interval, the second group, the hunters, followed with the goal to capture the meat from the "buffalo."

Boys practiced strategy in their game "war on bees" described in Chapter 11, and as boys of most cultures have done throughout the centuries, Dakota children held other kinds of mock battles. One form was described by Eastman as a cruel sport. Mud balls were placed atop a willow branch. It was pulled back and released, flinging the mud balls at the opposing side. The projectiles smarted, and another element of the "work" of play became apparent. The participants were expected to suffer their injuries in silence, and any who exhibited weakness would be teased or shunned. After the battle, the boys often imitated the rites and ceremonies of their parents, which, if they had been observed, would have gotten them in trouble, for religion was not to be taken lightly or recreated in jest. Yet for the child who wanted to emulate his parents, nothing was exempt. Ohiyesa took part in an imitation medicine dance as a child, complete with lodge, medicine bags and initiation.[2]

There was also a game of exchange, called "White Man." Two of the children would be selected to act the part of the white trader. They would be painted with white clay and given "birch hats." Fur attached to their chins with string became beards, and white bark tied over the chest represented white shirts worn by the traders. These "white men" came to barter, with sand for sugar, dried leaves for tea and ground earth as gunpowder.[3]

Agility and speed were prized by young and old alike, and numerous running games and contests helped children develop these skills. Footraces were common among all ages. Men competed against men; boys against boys; women against women and girls against girls. Endurance was as important as speed. Thus, the track was designed to test stamina, and the prize went to the one who finished the race and not the fastest.

Inflated bladders were used as balls in the sacred ball game of the Lakota. Meanwhile the woodland Dakota children played lacrosse like their parents. Balls were fashioned from many different materials, such as wood or the rough hair of buffalo.

Walker listed numerous games played by young Oglala. "Children romped and played with whip tops, horn tipped javelins, bows and arrows and a kind of miniature bowling, with two stone balls about the size of walnuts and cylindrical blocks about two inches in diameter and two inches in length.[4]

Boys participated in wrestling matches, which were not the one-on-one affairs familiar

Celebrations and feasts were often synonymous. Few celebrations occurred without a feast. At such public events deeds of valor were sung to edify the tribe, or a man may wish to compose and sing about his deeds of valor after a victory. A person's deeds or accomplishments were also sung as part of his funeral. Such songs were probably sung inside the tipi at night to teach the young the Dakota traditions. The photograph shows two Dakota men playing hand drums outside of a tipi. Photographic print taken by Edward S. Curtis, c. 1908. Edward S. Curtis Collection (Library of Congress). Published in *The North American Indian*, Edward S. Curtis (Seattle, Wash.): Edward S. Curtis, 1907–30, v. 3, p. 82.

now, but consisted of massive numbers of contestants similar to the medieval melee. If a participant sat, he was free from the threat of being tackled, and the winner was literally the "last man standing."

In the summer months, swimming rounded out play. Often the daily chores, such as watering the horses, would turn into games, as a child grabbed an animal's tail and was towed across the river in yet another form of a race, or he rode a log on the river's current.

Until the age of eight, girls were welcome to join in the rough-and-tumble activities that the boys pursued. Girls participated in many of the same games, for their lives were also bound by the same necessities and presented with many of the same dangers. They would learn to shoot an arrow. When it came to warfare, speed profited them as much as it did the boys, so they ran in footraces. Girls swam and rode when time permitted and opportunity presented itself. Girls also had games of their own, more tailored to the role they would eventually fulfill. They played with dolls, made of hulled corn cobs dressed in beaded finery lovingly wrought by their mothers. Girls also had miniature tipis to use with their dolls.

Winter held its own amusements. Dakota children, like most others, enjoyed sledding. The woodland Santee used bark to make a sled. A hole was bored in one end where a string was tied. The boy rode, standing one foot in front of the other, down to the end of the hill. The plains Nakota and Lakota fashioned sleds from the ribs of a buffalo. After all the meat was cleaned off the bones, "six or seven long ribs fastened together at the larger end served the purpose [of a toboggan]. Sometimes a strip of bass-wood bark, four feet long and about six inches wide, was used with considerable skill."[5]

Sleds almost certainly presented the children another chance to pit their skills one against another in the form of a race. Boys would skip sticks across a frozen pond much like children today skip stones across water. Both men and boys participated in this activity. Another game mentioned by Ohiyesa but not described was called wands and snow arrows. Children also had tops made of heart-shaped wood, horn or bone. These were whipped with long thongs of leather tied to a stick. Between two and fifty boys would play tops at one time, steering them along an obstacle course, over hills of snow and tossed into the air onto the ice.[6]

Many adult pursuits were an extension of childhood play, such as target practice and footraces. After the arrival of the horse, horse races figured largely in Dakota entertainment. Wrestling seems to be an activity of the young. Young and old enjoyed throwing knives, and played a game similar to mumbet-peg.

Many games were more sophisticated. Men had a form of dice made of astragalus bones of the antelope or deer,[7] although the game of dice seemed to be preferred by women. Dakota women used plum stones which had marks burnt into them. John Lawson described a similar game played by the Siouan women of the east with dice made of "Kernels or Stones of Persimmons, which are in effect the same as our Dice, because Winning or Losing depend on which side appear uppermost and how they managed to fall together."[8] Dakota women used a wooden bowl filled with plum stones. The bowl would be shaken and then set down hard enough to cause some of them to jump from the bowl. Women's games of dice were not as raucous as men's, but they were more numerous and women would often spend hours playing plum stones.

Men played a game known as moccasins. Said Walker: "The more enticing and popular game of moccasins was a contest of skill and wits."[9] This game was played by both the woodland Santee and the tribes of the plains.

The Dakota game described by Pond had gone through a transformation by 1834. Originally it had been played with a nut, stone or pebble, and four moccasins. In the late period, a bullet replaced the stone and mittens replaced the moccasins. In many ways it is similar to the present-day game of ball and cups. Four mittens—one with a bullet hidden inside—would be placed in a row. The contestants had to guess which contained the bullet. When a participant

In this posed photograph, Mato Wanarsaka teaches his son to shoot. In fact, a Dakota boy began such lessons long before the age portrayed in the photograph. He received his first bow and arrows as soon as he was old enough to walk, and he began to hunt squirrels and small birds as soon as he was capable. Contests honed the skill so important to survival. Photo by Herman Heyn, c. June 20, 1900.

succeeded, then it was his turn to hide the ball.[10] The game often involved the rest of the village who would come and sing a specific set of songs and beat a drum as an accompaniment. The fact that songs evolved around the game suggests a religious significance was once ascribed to the event. Wagers were often placed, and in some instances, a player would be bankrupted.

The Lakota variation, relayed by Walker, was more complex. Both relied on a person's ability to read people. However, the Lakota retained the use of moccasins, and required four stones, one differing significantly from the other three, often with three painted white and one black. Four people played, two against two. A rod was given to one team and a drum to the other. Sixteen counting sticks were divided evenly at the beginning of the game. The moccasins were laid side by side between the opponents. One of the players hid the pebbles one under each of the moccasins while his partner sang and beat on the drum. The opposing players used the rod to lift the moccasin which they believed covered the odd pebble. If correct, they would win a counting stick, take the drum and hide the pebbles. If they picked the wrong stone, they lost a counting stick and must guess again.[11]

The Santee of Carolina also played a game based on counting sticks. Lawson described it in his journals. "Their chiefest Game is a sort of Arithmatick, which is managed by a Parcel of small split Reeds, the Thickness of a small Bent; these are made very nicely, so they part and are tractable in their Hands. They are fifty one in Number, their Length about seven Inches; when they play, they throw part of them to their Antagonist; the Art is, to discover, upon sight how many you have, and what you throw to him that plays with you. Some are so expert at their Numbers, that they will tell you ten times together, what they throw out of their Hands. Although the whole Play is carried on with the quickest Motion ... some are so expert at this Game as to win great Indian Estates by this Play. A good Sett of these Reeds, fit to play withal, are valued and sold for a dress'd Does-Skin."[12]

Adults also had less sedentary pursuits. Lacrosse, so popular in the east, was no longer played in the west. Eastman explained that lacrosse continued to be played by the Sisseton and the Santee Sioux in the late period while Shinny was played by the Lakota and Nakota of the plains.[13]

Pond witnessed a lacrosse match and gave a description. The playing field was leveled and boundaries set about a half-mile apart. The goal of the game was to throw the ball over the boundary. The ball was made of wood and smaller than a baseball. The sticks were hickory,

Dakota girls often had miniature tipis, similar to dollhouses. Here three girls, of the Northern Cheyenne Indian Reservation, pose at play with their tipis and their dolls The photograph was taken in 1909 by Julia E. Tuell at Lame Deer, Montana.

bent at one end into a small hoop, about three inches in diameter, across which several strings were tied in a cross-hatch design. The nets were of no great depth, meaning that the ball could be easily jostled from the cup. Whole tribes would play, with hundreds of players on the field. After the ball was thrown all the players would try to capture it. As with the modern game, the ball would be tossed from one player to another, flung toward the goal or, if a clear path presented itself, the player could run with it. If the ball fell to the ground, there was often a battle over it. So it would criss-cross the field until the goal was achieved and the winners able to bring the ball safely across their boundary.[14]

A form of lacrosse was shared with the Siouan tribes of the Carolinas. In the eastern version, called *Chenco,* a clay cup cradled in a forked stick replaced the net of the woodland Sioux.[15]

Women also played ball games. The woodland Dakota women would play lacrosse in the summer months. During the winter, they played a game that resembled present-day hockey. Playing on ice, such as a frozen river or pond, the women would knock a ball about the field with sticks between one and another. The Siouan tribes of the east also played a land-bound version of the same game. In his *Voyages,* Lawson mentions: "Another Game managed by a Batoon and a Ball...."[16]

People bet on games, both men and women. Bets were placed during the major lacrosse tournaments.[17] Almost every competition was an occasion to bet upon the victor, for gambling too pleased *Yumni (Yum),* the lord of games.[18] Pond viewed Dakota gambling with true ministerial asperity. "They wasted their time, and sometimes lost what they could not well spare; but they had no large fortunes to lose.... The loss of property which they incurred was not irreparable and caused only a temporary inconvenience."[19]

Stakes were quite literally staked, hung on sticks in sight of any onlookers, which allowed the one accepting the challenge to refuse to play and stake his property against anything of lesser value.[20]

Games often had religious significance or presaged certain events. The gambling losses were viewed with equanimity, but a game's outcomes were taken seriously. Games that passed quickly foretold a good hunt. Continual defeat or games that went slowly with no clear victor were cause for alarm. Repeated loss was often attributed to witchcraft, and a holy man would be called in to get rid of any evil spirits.[21]

Games and gambling were noteworthy enough events to be included in the winter counts of both No Ears and Battiste Good for 1780 where Slukela[22] lost everything in a game of *haka* (similar to lacrosse) and was left naked and alone.[23]

Entertainment was not confined to games. Social feasts could be held at any time, by anyone for any reason, such as for marriage or the blessing of the umbilical cord. A feast would be announced to celebrate an event — like a victory in war or at the games or because the hunt had been successful, which gave rise to feasts of thanksgiving. Often social gatherings turned into impromptu meetings during which the men discussed the business of the tribe. Societies held feasts in which the tribe not only contributed but often participated. Many feasts were religious events: the making of a buffalo woman, *Wakan* feasts, the *Heyoka* feast, and feast of raw fish.[24] A feast also marked the release of the soul. Numerous dances were held, such as the thunder dance, sun dance, scalp dance, and war dance. Each had its feast. While having serious intent, they also entertained, and often warriors were called upon to tell stories of their exploits, so children learned the history of the tribe.

A specific society may choose to celebrate in isolation, as happened with the medicine dance, and so it become a social event for certain select individuals. With societies for men and women, and most people belonging to more than one, this created many opportunities to enjoy life.

As a people, they both worked and played hard, and in the quiet of the night, the grandparents or parents would regale their children with tales of great heroes or stories of religious

Foot races sharpened another vital skill, endurance. All ages and both genders participated. The racers ran to prove not only speed but endurance. The arrival of the horse changed the emphasis, with horse races replacing the footrace. A scrub-race on the plains shows men engaged in a horse race, from a Lagarde engraving for *Harper's Weekly* of a picture by J.D. Smillie in the watercolor exhibition, published in the March 4, 1876, issue on page 184.

import, passing on their history from one generation to another. The child would be asked to repeat it the following day[25] and explain the lesson hidden therein. Children would be asked to share with their parents the activities of the day, what they had done, what they observed, and often lessons could be drawn with from these experiences. Sometimes, a child's chance observation of buffalo or deer might provide the direction of the next hunt.

Each band had its storytellers who were also holy men and among the most valued members of the village, keeping as they did the oral tradition of the people. The storyteller would also be called upon to entertain during a feast or religious event. Among the storytellers' most prized possessions were bundles of small sticks painted to represent the important events of history. The sticks were notched with the number of years since that particular event occurred. In the west, the winter count drawn on a buffalo hide was used along with the counting stick as a means of recording tribal history.

The Dakota, like all the native people, were not dour as we have been led to expect. Said Ohiyesa: "There is scarcely anything more exasperating to me as the idea that the natives of this country have no sense of humor and no faculty for mirth.... I don't believe I ever heard a real hearty laugh away from the Indians' fireside."[26] The Dakota were known for their pranks, which were for some reason more often played between brothers- and sisters-in-law.[27]

The natives soon learned to become tight-lipped after years of repeated discourtesy and downright abuse from the white settlers. It was deemed better to keep silent than draw attention to oneself or to have what was said be ridiculed and misconstrued.

The picture that emerges is of a people who knew how to have fun. It was incorporated into feasts and celebrations, and in the games they played. Toil could just as easily become an occasion for recreation. When the chores were finished, then sport and diversion took over. Games could be educational, honing important survival skills; stories not only entertained, they taught the traditions and the history of the people, and games were adapted into religious rituals. Thus, after fasting and sacrifice came feasting and celebration. Just as the Dakota did not preclude prayer from work, neither did they exclude joy from religion.

19. Wasicu

Many winters ago, Inktomi was selected for a sacred quest. Because he had named all things, he knew all the languages of man and Wakan Tanka appointed him as messenger. Inktomi went from tribe to tribe.

He ran into the first camp, shouting: "Beware. Beware! There is a new man coming, and he is like me, Inktomi, a trickster and a liar. His skin is white; his legs are long, and he brings many new things, most of them bad."

The chiefs listened and then they called council to discuss this new man and what should be done. Inktomi did not tarry, for he must tell everyone of this new man, and he hurried away. When he reached the edge of the camp, he shot a web up into the sky and climbed to the heavens, so they knew he spoke true.

Next Inktomi visited the Lakota in his human shape. He pointed to the west, saying: "I am Inktomi and I have come from Wakan Tanka to warn you. A strange sound is coming. A new voice. A new man. He is coming across the great waters to steal all the four directions from you. This man is clever, but he has no woksape. He has knowledge, but he is not wise. He brings greed, and he weaves pretty lies wherever he goes."

Then Inktomi rolled up into a ball. He spun and he spun until he took the familiar form of spider. As spider, he crawled into his web, and away he sped to see the Arapaho and tell them of the arrival of the new man.

"He speaks fair words," Inktomi said, "but do not trust him, for he lies. He brings death and destruction. He will steal the land, the air, the buffalo, the grass and the trees, and he will give you a new life, but not a good one."

The people muttered among themselves — "how can he bring life and death?" they asked — but Inktomi had left to spread the word.

After the Arapaho, he went to the Crow, the Pawnee, the Shoshone, and everywhere he told same tale. "A new man approaches who is not one of us. He has no grandmothers or grandfathers on this land. He brings many things. He brings disease and he brings death. He brings hate and prejudice. He speaks no language that you can understand. Do not listen to his words, for they are false."

And after Inktomi had visited all the tribes, he returned to his own people, the Lakota, and again he said: "Remember, his word is not to be trusted. He lies and his lies never end. You shall know him as 'wasi-manu,' the stealer of all things, and 'wasicu,' fat-taker, for he will take the fat of the land, leaving you nothing."

The worried chiefs asked if there was aught they could do. "Is there no hope?"

"Maybe," Inktomi replied, "you will be able to break this dark hoop of falsehood and deceit."

And with this cryptic message, Inktomi returned to the heavens on his magic web. Many winters came and went, the Oyate hunted the great buffalo unhindered. The women worked as they had always done, giving birth to generations, and the people forgot about the new man whose coming was foretold.

After the Santee uprising in 1862, all the Dakota tribes in Minnesota were rounded up and their warriors put on trial. Three hundred were convicted to death by hanging, although Lincoln gave a last-minute reprieve to most of them. This lithograph depicts the execution of thirty-eight Santee Braves in Mankato, Minnesota, on December, 26, 1862. Later it was discovered that two of the men hanged had been among the men reprieved. The print comes from Milwaukee Litho & Engraving Co. Lithograph, c. 1883 by John C. Wise.

> Then one day a man approached the village. His skin was white and his legs were long. He carried a cross in one hand and a thunder stick in the other. This man spoke sweet words of peace. He talked of a Great Spirit who loved all his children. He spoke of brotherhood, just like Wakan Tanka who told the Lakota that "all are related." He brought bright, shiny toys and sticks that spat fire, and for a while the people were duped.
>
> Then one day the white man happened upon an old woman as she dug up the prairie. When she returned to her tipi, she was covered in spots. She sickened and died, and the Lakota realized that this man who spoke so fair carried disease that jumped from the white man to the red, and as the people started to die, the Lakota understood too late that the "wasicu" man was already among them.[1]

Heretofore, little reference has been made about the impact of white culture on the Dakota except to record their growing influence on trade, dress and tribal migration. The records and the observations of early white explorers offer a glimpse into the life of the tribe, but every attempt has been made to view this as an internal history—the Dakota as a nation-state as it grew and developed. Little mention has been made of the devastation wrought by the white man, yet no history of the tribe would be complete without it.

Wasicu or *wasicun* is the name the Dakota gave to the white man. With its root *"sicun"* meaning guardian, it appears flattering. However it translates as devil or demon. One of the lesser demons, to be sure, but a devil just the same. Nothing — neither climate nor migration — had a more profound influence on the original inhabitants of this continent than the arrival of European diseases.

The Spanish carried smallpox on their ships to the Americas in 1558 or 1560. It first appeared at Rio de la Plata, or Silver River, on the southeastern coast of South America. Having no natural immunity, "more than a hundred thousand Indians" of the region's native population died as result of smallpox within two years. Further north, the Pilgrims brought plague, or possibly typhus, to New England when they landed at Plymouth Rock in 1620.[2]

The English also brought with them measles and cholera. Meanwhile smallpox had made its way to the upper east coast of North America and worked its way inland in little more than three-quarters of a century, or seventy-seven years to be precise. The Huron suffered an outbreak of either smallpox or measles in 1637 and again in 1639 through 1640. As traders the Dakota would have met and interacted with the Huron at trade fairs. Whether the Huron epidemic made it into Dakota communities during this period is not recorded.

However, the Kansa to their west suffered a fifty percent decrease in population before first contact with the Europeans. The date defined as contact is a bit fuzzy. The first European to meet the Kansa was Spanish explorer Juan de Onate in 1601, which many define as "contact." By 1673 Marquette's map correctly noted the location of the Kansa, but long-term contact (the second accepted meaning of the word contact) with the French did not occur until 1750. If one accepts the meeting with Juan de Onate as "contact," then smallpox reached the Kansa with phenomenal speed, traveling up the waterways of the Mississippi to arrive in forty years and some forty years before its appearance among the Huron. More likely contact refers to the latter, which indicates they suffered through the pandemic of the 1700s.

With outbreaks at the Huron camps to their east and the Kansa to their west, it seems unlikely that smallpox would have skipped the Dakota completely, especially when one considers the pandemic. The ravages of smallpox would go a long way to explain why the four hearths of the Santee, more than half of the accepted seven tribes, comprised only 20 percent of the total population of the Dakota peoples. Their position in the east made them more accessible and susceptible to the disease. As a trading people the Santee would have had direct contact with the whites. They would have been the first hit and the hardest hit of all the Dakota nation.

Further south and east, disease cut great swathes through the native population. James Mooney estimated the Carolina Santee had a population of 1000 in 1600.[3] By the time John Lawson explored the Carolina interior in 1700, the eastern Santee numbered less than 90 — a loss of 90 percent in a few scant generations. Likewise the Congaree population went from 800 to forty[4] and the Sewee from 800 to 57.[5] Said Lawson, "Small-Pox has destroy'd many thousand of these Natives.... There is not one sixth Savages living within two hundred Miles of all our Settlements as there were fifty Year ago." Smallpox "destroyed whole Towns without leaving one Indian in the Village." Speaking specifically of Siouan Congaree, he wrote: "They were a small People, having lost most of their Numbers by ... Small-pox which hath visited them often."[6]

The Siouan Catawba were still a great nation in Lawson's time. However, they did not remain untouched. They suffered from successive incursions of smallpox in 1697, 1738, and 1759. Each epidemic was suspected of killing between one-half to two-thirds of the tribe.[7] In 1760, smallpox struck the Cherokee. The South Carolina militia burned all fifteen of their villages, along with their crops.

From a reenactment of the Indian encampment at Wounded Knee, with U.S. troops surrounding the camp. The film producers chose to ignore, or chose not to replicate, the conditions at the time. The Minneconjou from the Cheyenne River began moving to Pine Ridge after Big Foot was placed on a list of people to be arrested for participating in the Ghost Dance. During the march of 150 miles the temperature dropped severely to well below zero. On December 28 the small band was intercepted by the Seventh Cavalry led by Major Samuel Whitside. That night Whitside mounted two Hotchkiss guns, capable of shooting shells for two miles, on top of a rise strategically aimed so they could rake the entire village. The staged photograph is part of a six-picture set which relate to the filming of the movie, *The Indian Wars*, on Pine Ridge Reservation in 1913. Buffalo Bill was the main consultant for the film, with Major Brennan. For Miller Studio, Gordon, Neb. November 10, 1913.

The Delaware received blankets from a smallpox hospital in 1763, which some believe was a deliberate act, an early form of germ warfare during the closing years of the French and Indian War. As a result, Delaware villages were ravaged, and smallpox had become pandemic across the Americas.

Using Mooney's figures as a baseline, this means that nine out of ten people died from diseases like smallpox. Compare the 90 percent against the 50 percent death-rate suffered by parts of Europe during the period of the Black Death. Only when one views these figures does one grasp the real impact of European diseases on the native population. This was a process that would be repeated over and over again as the white man moved west. Everywhere the Europeans arrived the native population was devastated by disease. Often disease preceded the white explorer, brought into the village by another member of the tribe who had had the unhappy luck of meeting a carrier.

The Dakota were no exception. It's doubtful the Minnesota Santee were omitted from the pandemic, although the first recorded mention of smallpox comes from the winter counts of Iron Crow and No Ears. The former, "Iron Crow's account," described the year 1792 as the winter when many pregnant women died; that same year No Ears "saw two white women."[8] Both the Big Missouri winter count[9] and that of No Ears[10] mention 1799 as the winter when many pregnant women died — possibly indicative of rubella (German measles), alternatively credited to smallpox, although credited in the Big Missouri winter count to an extremely cold winters.

Winters counts of many Dakota tribes refer to the period from 1779 through 1780 as the year when smallpox "used them up." The Sicangu (Brule) had experienced five separate outbreaks before they met Lewis and Clark in 1805, the Oglala five, the Yanktonais four and the Minneconjou three.[13] The No Ears winter count recorded outbreaks among the Oglala of some "rash" (either measles or smallpox) in 1782, 1818, and 1845.

The first recorded outbreak of smallpox among the Dakota struck the Minnesota Santee in the middle 1830s. It swept through Yanktonai camps in 1837, 1838 and 1839. Cholera hit the river villages of the woodland Dakota in 1846 and 1847.[14] The Oglala also suffered from an epidemic of cholera, brought to them by white settlers traveling along the Oregon Trail in 1849. The Big Missouri winter count lists epidemics in 1819 and 1851. Two Yanktonai band names may date from this time of death and destruction: "the band that wishes life" and "the few that lived."

The Arikara, Mandan and the Assiniboin were among the hardest hit of the plains tribes. The Mandan consisted of nine villages in 1750. Fifty years later there were only two. The Mandan suffered two additional smallpox epidemics in 1780 and 1837. The last incursion of smallpox reduced the population from approximately 1600 to 57.[13] The Crow caught it from the Hidatsa and before 1800. The outbreak lasted three years, reducing a tribe of 2000 lodges to 300.[14] The Algonquin Blackfoot lost three-quarters of their population to smallpox in 1837, and it struck again in 1845 and 1851 with a death toll of 30 percent each time.[15] Smallpox reached the Assiniboin in 1840. Their losses were estimated at seventy-five percent.[16] The Arikara lost between seventy-five and eighty percent of their population.[17]

The prairie Lakota were attacked on several fronts, receiving smallpox from the Ojibwa through trade on the Missouri River and further west from the Shoshone. William Walker of Hudson Bay Company recorded his impressions of the 1781–1782 epidemic: "The smallpox is rageing all around Us with great violence, sparing very few, the Indians lying Dead around the Barren Ground like rotten sheep, their Tents left standing and Wild beasts Devouring them."[18]

Many of the differences between the woodland Dakota and their prairie brethren — in dress and deportment — found their origins with the arrival of white men. The Yankton and the Lakota moved onto the plains to trap the beaver desired by the European traders. Meanwhile the Dakota, the middlemen, adopted the European broadcloth as a part of their regular attire, a process that was expedited by the loss of precious game, hence hides, in their territory as they competed with white settlers for food and territory.

Unless one reaches back to the first explorers like Radisson, the Dakota do not fare well in the eye of the later white recorders, Samuel Pond and Mary Henderson Eastman. Each reports episodes of violence usually coupled with drunken debauchery. Yet they came to observe the woodland Santee when the culture was already in disarray after the tribe became dependent upon European goods. With the loss of hunting grounds, men lost their traditional place within the family as provider. Add alcohol to that volatile mix and the natural result is violence, neither of which had been mentioned about either the woodland Santee or the plains Nakota/Lakota by the earliest observers. Later testimony states such behavior was commonplace among the tribes in the post-reservation era.

European traders brought alcohol and relied on it for income since it, unlike durable goods bought by the Indians, needed to be replenished constantly. The Hudson Bay Company soon saw the advantage of making brandy a staple of the fur trade. In the year 1700, they sold seventy gallons. By 1750, volume had increased to 2000 gallons. In 1764, over fifty thousand gallons of rum were sold to the Indians by the traders of Forts Detroit and Pitt. George Morgan imported some 8000 gallons of liquor to his trading post at Kaskaskia in Illinois for sale to the natives. That same year (1767) Fort Pitt brought in 6500 barrels of rum, and it was believed that their competitors traded twice that amount. The Detroit Commissary of Indian Affairs, Jehu Hay, estimated that merchants exchanged 24,000 gallons of rum a year for furs.[19]

The speed of the transition among the woodland Dakota astounds. The Santee whose military prowess had so impressed Lieutenant Governor Patrick Sinclair in 1776[20] were viewed as "the most notorious beggars" by Major Steven Long in 1815.[21] In 1823, the great chief Red Wing was described by Count Beltrami as "an old man of hideous aspect ... a beggar withal." Later William Keating saw them as a "noble ruin."[22]

By 1836, Gideon Pond, Samuel Pond's brother and fellow missionary, said: "They must be drunk — they could hardly live if they were not drunk. — Many often seemed as uneasy when sober, as a fish does when on land. At some villages they were drunk months together. There was no end to it. They would give guns, blankets, pork, lard, flour, corn, coffee, sugar, horses, furs, traps, anything for whiskey. It was made to drink. It was good — it was wakan. They drank it, — they bit off each other's noses, — broke each other's ribs and heads, they knifed each other. They killed one another with guns, knives, hatchets, clubs, fire-brands; they fell into the fire and water and were burned to death, and drowned...."[23]

Thus within sixty years, or three scant generations, the transformation was complete, and the Santee went from Sinclair's "undebauched" to Gideon Pond's "drunk for months" at a time. Lawson described a similar transformation that took place among the Siouan tribes of Carolina, who went from free peoples to having the British as absolute masters in less 10 years, which he attributed in large part to alcohol.

European missionaries bemoaned the trade in alcohol which they thought interfered with Christian conversion, and many natives were willing to listen to the missionaries since they espoused philosophies similar to their own. The Christian concept of brotherly love resembles the Dakota belief of *Mitakuye Oyasin* "all our relations." Yet practice and implementation of Christian brotherly love seemed lacking, particularly where the red man was concerned. Ohiyesa condemned the Christian missionaries. "They spoke much of spiritual things, while seeking only the material. They bought and sold everything: time, labor, personal independence, the love of a woman, and even the ministrations of their holy faith."[24] Additionally he defended the faith of his ancestors when he said: "It is my personal belief, after thirty-five years' experience of it, that there is no such thing as 'Christian civilization.' I believe that Christianity and modern civilization are opposed and irreconcilable, and that the spirit of Christianity and of our ancient religion is essentially the same."[25]

Christian charity and the Dakota *wacantognaka*, generosity or gifting, also appear similar at first glance, but upon closer examination, the European model was flawed. Their generosity or lack of it was universally condemned by Native Americans. In 1610, Samuel de Champlain brought a young Huron with him to France, who was horrified by the poverty he saw.[26] In 1636, Gabriel Sagard agreed when he said: "they blamed us greatly [for the great number of needy and beggars]."[27]

John Lawson's quote best sums up the disparity between the cultural ideas of charity that rings throughout the centuries as condemnation of the European model. "They [the natives] naturally possess the Righteous Man's Gift; they are patient under all Affliction and have a great many natural Virtues.... They are really better to us, than we are to them; they always give us Victuals at their Quarters, and take care that we are arm'd against Hunger and Thirst: We do not so by them, but let them walk by our Doors Hungry."[28]

Contrast the European model of Christian charity against Dakota custom of gifting where a person gave to the point of "utter impoverishment"[29] and the greatest leaders were inevitably the poorest. Said Eastman: "The true Indian sets no price on either his property or his labor. His generosity is only limited by his strength and his ability."[30] Food was divided equally, and no man of worth ate as long as any other member of the tribe went hungry. Warrior oaths

Nothing more poignantly illustrates the final destruction of tribal tradition than the pictures that come from Indian School, Carlisle, Pa. One of the students has been identified as the son of the Lakota chief American Horse. This photograph shows six boys working in the school's laundry, which was one of the many classes that white Americans felt were important to teach. The photograph print, cyanotype, was taken between 1901 and 1903 by Frances Benjamin Johnston, photographer. Part of the Frances Benjamin Johnston Collection, Library of Congress.

required a man to give his share to the elderly or any women and children who had no provision. Meanwhile white man's charity was inevitably conditional, usually being dependent upon the Indians becoming "civilized" Christians, in essence, "white."

Throughout our interaction with them, the European and the American historians have continually underrated native culture. It has long been pictured as small pockets of primitives, individual tribes that dotted — and under-utilized — the landscape; a simple people who gathered their food, hunted and rarely interacted with other tribes except through occasional raids and sorties; who fought nonsensical battles against "habitual" enemies, using the most primitive, and savage, means necessary. History proves otherwise. Brutality, particularly in the form of scalping, appears to be a European import.

People point to the lack of domesticated animals and the absence of the wheel as proof of their primitive nature. Yet animals were not domesticated in the Old World until 12,000 BCE. The horse was first tamed between 4000 and 6500 years ago around the Urals along the steppes of the Ukraine, among other places. Meanwhile radiocarbon dates of human artifacts found on the east coast of America indicate a human presence here 50,000 years ago, long before the concept of domestication occurred to man anywhere.

Further radiocarbon dates locate human habitations in the southern tip of the New World, revealing a culture advanced enough to have established a permanent a village 13,000 years ago. The llama of South America was tamed by the Incas around 4000 BCE, around the same time horse in the Eurasian steppes.

Meanwhile horses here were the size of dogs, not good candidates for use as mounts, and dogs were already in use as beasts of burden. Many of the animals available were not the best product for domestication. To the present day, the American bison and the pronghorn antelope have proven resistant to training, even though we have had five hundred years to tame them. The pronghorn tends to die and the bison simply does not submit to the will of a human master.

The animals present at the time of human appearance on this continent included the megafauna, weighing between 1100 and 2200 pounds. North America then was the home of the mammoth, the ice-age camel and the giant beaver. The short-faced bear stood twelve feet tall and would have been a formidable adversary. The vegetarian North American ground sloth had twelve-inch claws while the people who traveled down to South America (the B-haplography) would have found a predatory ground sloth equal in size to its northern counterpart. The mastodon roamed freely while the saber-tooth tiger, which stood three feet at the shoulder, saw man as another prey species.

The large herbivores were innocent of human contact. In a very real sense, the prey of the first hunters was naïve of the threat presented by man. For the new arrivals the Americas would have been a land of plenty. With game readily available, there would have been little need to domesticate animals for consumption. It has long been said that necessity is the mother of invention, and the limited populations would not have felt any lack for many generations.

The Native Americans have been credited with the extinction of the megafauna; however, it has now been proven that the first inhabitants lived alongside these giants for thousands of years without making a significant dent in their population. They may even have arrived with them when sea levels were 250 feet below what they are now. The megafauna did not die out in the Americas until 11,000 years ago, as the result of global warming trend. Survival in cold climates requires mass, which slows metabolism and prevents heat loss. Even today the southern raccoon and the Florida panther (the same species as the mountain lion, puma or cougar) are smaller than their northern counterparts. The ice age was perfectly to suited to the megafauna. When the planet warmed, these creatures would not have been able to adapt to the new temperatures. Significantly the pygmy mammoth was the last to succumb to the climate change.

The original inhabitants of North America domesticated corn from a grass which our sciences have yet to identify. Even genetics has been unable to shed light on the origin of corn. The natives not only cultivated it, but they developed more varieties of corn than botanists have been able to generate in the five hundred years since European habitation of the Americas.

A land locked by the ice was not particularly amenable to the wheel, but the concept of the wheel was not unknown to the Indians. Even after the glaciers melted, it remained impractical, considering the terrain. American civilizations flourished in some of the harsher environments— the Peruvian Andes, the Mayan jungle and the swamps of the Mexican highlands, where the wheel would have been an encumbrance. Even in Egypt, the wheel had limited usefulness during the construction of the pyramids. The wheeled wagon would have met impediment in the Incan Andes, the soft sands of the Yucatan, and the marshland surrounding the Aztec city of Tenochtitlán. In Mexico, transport by boat was preferred, while in the mountainous Andes, the llama served the purpose as pack animal. The wheel would have had no appeal where it gave no advantage, just as domestication required biddable animals capable of being domesticated. The fact that some of the most advanced civilizations thrived in the most unforgiving environments does not suggest a people who were in any way backwards, rather it reveals native engineering skill and genius.

The historians of the Victorian era rejected the natives of this continent as too primitive to be the mound builders, but again science proved otherwise, from the first rough studies of skulls to present-day genetics where the genetic material from remains found in grave mounds have been compared against today's tribes and revealed a direct line of descent that link the latter to the former. While the Minnesota Santee do not claim to be among the builders, the Carolina Santee were, and the Dakota were certainly among their inheritors.

The historians have dismissed Dakota oral traditions as myth even after science and other disciplines have provided evidence that validates their tales. Many of their legends, such as *Wasicu* at the beginning of this chapter, record actual events. Linguistics provides the proof that the Dakota and their offshoots have traveled from coast to coast — north, south, east and west — as their stories claim. It can be found in the presence of their language. If one accepts that the Dakota peoples entered this continent across the Bering Strait, then one must accept the fact that they would have been to the furthest reaches of the north and west coasts. If one recognizes the spread of Siouan tongue, including Santee, to the east coast and the south coast, with the Biloxi, then one also must acknowledge that their verbal tradition is true. Not myth or legend, but fact. The controversial presence of the X (European) haplogroup in Dakota samples could provide further proof that the Dakota themselves resided in the southeast. If the presence of a European-style spear point is evidence of European presence on this continent 15,000 years ago, and this group then intermarried with the native population and bequeathed their genes to them in the form of the X-haplogroup, this suggests that not only were the Dakota living in the southeast, but the tribe existed as a separate genetic entity at that time, meaning their culture dates back further than anyone previously thought. If the X-haplogroup came from the Vikings, it also suggests that the Dakota had traveled as far east as the settlement of Vinland.

The Dakota may have planted their corn, gathered their food and hunted to provide meat

One of the goals of the Indian School was to turn Indian children into farmers. This photograph comes as an indictment. Pictured here, once proud native sons, whose ancestors not only roamed free but managed to conquer a continent, dig in the dirt for potatoes. Their efforts are overseen by an instructor in the background. Carlisle Indian School, c. 1900, Frances Benjamin Johnston Collection, Library of Congress.

for their families, as the Europeans imagined; but their world, their political map, was anything but simple. They, as did all American tribes, developed alliances with any number of different groups throughout their history. When circumstances and needs changed, old alliances and old enmities dissolved. At one time, the Lakota would have fought by the side of their Santee relations against the Ojibwa, but as they moved farther west, new hostilities occurred as new territorial disputes accrued, and in the end, they concentrated their efforts against the Shoshone, the Pawnee and the Crow.

The Europeans saw the aboriginal American as technologically impoverished, without either metal or gunpowder. However, a form of metallurgy was known and used by the mound builders, who could work copper into fine jewelry and breastplates. Meanwhile, not all of the technologies brought by the early settlers, such as gunpowder, were of European origin. Rather they were an import from another land where the Europeans themselves were viewed as the primitives.

The conquistadors and those that followed thought they were creating order, bringing advancement and development to the savages. However, the tribes had had regular dealings with each other through exchange for generations. Trade routes that traversed the continent, allowing the movement of goods from coast to coast, were of long standing. The Dakota ranged far as traders, traveling east to the St. Lawrence River, up to the region around the Hudson Bay and down to the tip of Lake Michigan to attend the fairs which were held at centers that had existed for hundreds, possibly thousands of years. In the west, they traveled to the Tetons, participating in a large trade network.

The tribes were not, as many believe, isolated. The extent of interaction is reflected not only in the movement of goods, but the movement of ideas as shown in modes of dress or fashion and in religion. It represents free exchange across tribal boundaries. The Dakota and Lakota women borrowed styles of dress from both east and west, as the other tribes borrowed from them. The Dakota adopted new materials into their designs as they became available to them. They accepted dentalium shells with as much enthusiasm as ribbon. The universality of the sweat lodge and the pipe ceremony across the continent also suggests the free interchange of ideas and a commonality in native philosophy. The sun dance too was shared among many tribes.

The native American people devised a universal language, sign language, which allowed people of diverse language groups to communicate with each other, which had no European equivalent at the time of contact. It was centuries before white men adapted this concept to their needs and longer before any attempt was made to create a language that could potentially be understood by all. In many ways, the civilized countries of the world lag behind, for the sign language of Spain cannot be not understood by the deaf in England, and people remain resistant to giving up their own language and national identity to adopt Esperanto, a process thrust upon the native who was forced to learn English and leave his old language behind.

The Europeans took much and gave little in exchange. The loss of Dakota territory in the late period before the Plains Wars is reflected in the history of McPherson County, Kansas, along the Smoky Hill River which at one time represented the southernmost boundary of the Oglala *Kayaksi*. In 1850, cattle drivers battled the Cheyenne.[31] In 1867 and again in May of 1869, both the Sioux and the Cheyenne are mentioned doing battle against the other resident tribes including the Osage and the Pawnee at Sharps and Spellmen Creek respectively.[32] Fear of the tribes was so great that the Home Protection Company was formed and a "civilian" fort built in 1869. In 1871, the Oglala and the Pawnee went on the war path. The raids lasted for a full thirty days.[33] After that time, the Sioux disappear from county histories, while the Cheyenne remained, which reflects the fact that Lakota territorial claims were starting to shrink and the plains tribes grew compact as they withdrew further north.

After stealing their lands, the Americans then went about the systematic destruction of the native peoples and their cultures. Present-day historians debate Dakota status as a nation, since they had no central rule, but the United States government recognized the Dakota as a nation state until March 3, 1871, when a rider attached to an appropriations bill denied national status to the tribes. Ironically the same year that Congress stripped them of tribal citizenship, the Supreme Court took away native rights to become citizens of this country since they were "distinct and independent political communities, retaining the right to self-government."[34]

The siege on the native peoples continued in other forms. In the years between 1880 and 1890, between 2.5 and 3 million buffalo were killed in the state of Kansas alone as part of a government campaign not only to exterminate the animal but eradicate the people who depended on it. By attacking their livelihood, the government forced the tribes to farm the meager plots that were allotted them in place of the territories that they once possessed.

The Dawes Act of 1887, authored by Congressman Henry Dawes, provided allotment of lands to Indians on the reservations, and allegedly "extended the protection of the laws of the United States and the Territories over the Indians." If an allotment was sold, "purchase money for any portion of any such reservation shall be held in the Treasury of the United States for the sole use of the tribe" and "shall be at all times subject to appropriation by Congress for the *education and civilization* of such tribe or tribes...." It further stipulated that "nothing in this act contained shall be so construed as to affect the right and power of Congress to grant the right of way through any lands granted to an Indian, or a tribe of Indians, for railroads or other highways, or telegraph lines, for the public use, or to condemn such lands to public uses...." It also offered citizenship to any native who had separated from the tribe and had "adopted the habits of civilized life."[35]

To get on the Dawes rolls, Native Americans had to "anglicize" their names. At the same time, the act prohibited religious ceremonies associated with naming, in direct violation of the First Amendment. Either directly or indirectly, the Dawes Act made the practice of their traditional religion, and any manifestations thereof, illegal. This included their dances, their stories and their art, anything that might have religious connotation or symbolism. Their rites, such as gifting, were outlawed. *Hunka* or adoption as it was practiced by the Dakota became illegal. Thus, a nation which claims to be founded upon the principle of religious freedom denied the first citizens of this continent their faith.

To this end, children were removed from their homes and taken to Indian Schools in order to educated, civilized and repatriated as Americans. They were taught "practical" things like baking, potato digging, woodworking, cabinetry, how to do laundry and farming. These were skills which they already used in digging *mdo* and cooking their daily meals, or skills the youngest would have acquired if they had been left to learn them in their home environment. The attack on their culture was as total as it was absolute. The students were bereft of the protection and support of family and tribe. The schools negated their culture, treated it and any reminders of it harshly. Their hair was shorn; they ate in large communal dining rooms; they were forbidden to speak their native tongue, and punishments for violation of these rules were severe.

The apparent return to old mores, represented by the Ghost Dance, terrified white settlers in 1890. The Pine Ridge Indian Agent wired the government for protection against the tribes who, he said, were acting "wild and crazy." However, the Ghost Dance religion founded by a Paiute, Wavoka, was an offshoot of the Christian faith. Its rites included baptism and its precepts were those professed by Christianity. Wavoka preached to his followers: "You must not hurt anyone or do harm to another person. You must not fight. You must always do right."[36]

People who knew the Lakota well recommended moderation in U.S. response to their celebration of the Ghost Dance. One-time Indian agent Valentine McGillycuddy was sent in to survey the situation. He told the government: "I would let the dance continue.... If the Seventh-Day Adventists prepare their ascension robes for the second coming of the Savior, the United

The Indian School set out systematically to remove the Indian from the Indian. Their hair was shorn; the students dressed in the fashions of the period, and they were forbidden to speak their native tongue. Gone were the intimate family scenes of tribal life with meals around the fire, to be replaced by the mass dining hall, pictured here. Cyanotype print taken in 1903 by Frances Benjamin Johnston, photographer. Frances Benjamin Johnston Collection, Library of Congress.

States Army is not put in motion to prevent them. Why should not the Indians have the same privilege?"[37] The U.S. government did not heed his words.

One direct result of the government's reaction to the Ghost Dance was the assassination of Sitting Bull on December 15, 1890.[38] It found its most horrific expression eleven days later at Wounded Knee where hundreds of Brule were slaughtered as they attempted to return to Red Cloud reservation (see photograph) for refuge after a warrant had been issued for their arrest because they practiced the Ghost Dance.

Charles A. Eastman (Ohiyesa) was among those children trained in an Indian school. He later went on to be trained in Boston as an M.D. and was assigned as a doctor to Pine Ridge Agency in 1890. He was present at the time of Wounded Knee and an eyewitness to the atrocities. When he went to retrieve the wounded, Eastman reported that they found the body of a woman three miles from the camp: "...they had been relentlessly hunted down and slaughtered while fleeing for their lives."[39] His report tells of horror after horror. "When we reached the spot where the Indian camp had stood, among the fragments of burnt tents and other belongings, we saw frozen bodies lying close together or piled one upon another. I counted eighty bodies of men who had been in council."[40] The survivors had been left untended for two days by the time Eastman arrived. "Under a wagon, I discovered an old woman totally blind and entirely helpless. A few had managed to crawl away to some place of shelter, and we found in a log store near by several who were badly hurt and others who had died reaching there."[41]

His experience explains the observations he made in *The Soul of an Indian* when he said bitterly: "But it was not so easy to overlook or to excuse national bad faith. When distinguished emissaries from the Father at Washington, some of them ministers of the gospel and even bishops, came to the Indian nations, and pledged to them in solemn treaty the national honor, with prayer and mention of the God; and when such treaties, so made, were promptly and shamelessly broken, is it strange that the action should arouse not only anger, but contempt? The historians of this white race admit that the Indian was never the first to repudiate his oath."[42]

The Dawes Act that allowed for citizenship of any non-reservation "civilized Indian" did not include those who lived on reservations. It wasn't until 1924 that the U.S. Congress generously extended citizenship to the first citizens of this continent, the Native Americans, including those on the reservation. It took another act of Congress, "The American Indian Religious Freedom Act of 1978," to allow the natives the right to worship in the old ways. Up until that time, a few brave souls like Black Elk had protected the old traditions to hand down to the next generation.

Even after they were permitted to practice their religion, controversies continue to arise as the result of clashes between the native faith and the U.S. government. In *Lyng v. Northwest Indian Cemetery Protective Association* (1988), the Supreme Court narrowly defined the federal government's responsibility to protect religious freedom. The court allowed for the U.S. Forest Service to construct a road through a cemetery which would "destroy the ... Indians' ability to practice their religion." Thus, religious customs continue to be regulated by the federal government.

The Native American Graves Protection and Repatriation Act became public law on November 16, 1990, although further clarification must have been necessary, for in 1993 the federal law known as the Religious Freedom Restoration Act was passed. Three years later in 1996, an executive order instructed federal agencies to accommodate Native Americans' use of ceremonial sites. Cases still continue to accrue. On, November 1, 2005, the U.S. Supreme Court reiterated the freedoms provided by the 1993 act, saying that members of the Native American Church could ignore laws that interfered with the practice of their faith.

Curiously, in denying self-knowledge to others, white Americans have lost precious knowledge about themselves. Most chronicles of the Dakota begin with their "discovery"; for example, the first meeting between the Sioux and Jean Nicolet in 1640. Even now, their history continues to be treated as if it did not exist until the European came along to document it. The Lakota/Dakotas' own records, the winter counts, the myths and legends have been largely ignored until recently, yet they reflect important milestones in the history of the tribe and need to be further studied.

Until people acknowledge that the history of America must include the history of the aboriginal Americans and not just that of European descendants, it will remain incomplete. With much of Europe's past quite literally buried under its present and therefore unobtainable, learning about the native civilization may be essential to the understanding of development of human culture as a whole. Thus, the reconstruction of Native American history becomes imperative to our comprehension of man's overall social development.

Chapter Notes

Chapter 1

1. *Wakan* means sacred or mysterious, while *tanka* is big. Now commonly translated as Great Spirit.
2. Father Sky, or the heavens.
3. A quote from the documentary film *Atomic Physics,* filmed by J. Arthur Rank Organization, Ltd., 1948.
4. Colin G. Calloway, *One Vast Winter Count* (Lincoln, NE: University of Nebraska Press, 2003), 25–26.
5. Calloway, 26.
6. Douglas Summer Brown, *The Catawba: The People of the River* (Columbia, SC: University of South Carolina Press, 1966), 11.
7. Frank C. Hibbens, *Digging Up America* (New York: Hill and Wang, 1961), 15.
8. Dr. J.D. Figgins originally named the species after Dr. E. Taylor, head of Colorado Museum; also known as *Bison antiquus* and *Bison occidentalis*, which were far larger than the present day *Bison bison.*
9. Hibbens, 15.
10. Hibbens, 13.
11. Calloway, 31.
12. Clark Wissler, *Indians of the United States* (New York: Anchor Books, 1989), 66–67.
13. Hibbens, 18.
14. The term haplogroup comes from "haplo," the Greek word for "single." It represents a collection of closely related and linked genes which are inherited as a unit.
15. Wissler, 200.
16. Calloway, 30.

Chapter 2

1. Adaptation of story told by Ohiyesa in Charles A. Eastman, *The Soul of an Indian* (Lincoln, NE: Bison Books, 1991), 123–130.
2. John Lawson, *A New Voyage to Carolina* (Chapel Hill, NC: University of North Carolina Press, 1968), 219.
3. Lawson, 62.
4. Charles A. Eastman, *Indian Boyhood* (Lincoln, NE: Bison Books, 1991), 33–45.
5. Eastman, *Boyhood,* 117–118.
6. Calloway, 3.
7. Lawson, 213.
8. Sweat lodge.
9. Lawson, 48.
10. Lawson, 23.
11. Lawson, 27–28.
12. Douglas Summer Brown, 16.
13. Douglas Summer Brown, 15.
14. Douglas Summer Brown, 15.
15. Douglas Summer Brown, 16.
16. James Mooney, *The Siouan Tribes of the East* (Washington DC: Smithsonian Collection, 1994), 71–73.
17. Lawson, 28.
18. Hibbens, 97.
19. Hibbens, 99.
20. Henry Clyde Shetrone, *The Mound Builders* (New York, NY: D. Appleton and Company, 1930), 6.
21. Eastman, *Boyhood,* 191.
22. Eastman, *Boyhood,* 192.
23. Roy W. Meyers, *History of the Santee: United States Indian Policy on Trial* (Lincoln NE: Bison Books, 1967), 7.
24. Douglas Summer Brown, 14.
25. Douglas Summer Brown, 17.
26. Douglas Summer Brown, 29.
27. Samuel W. Pond, *The Dakota or Sioux in Minnesota as They Were in 1834* (St. Paul, MN: Minnesota Historical Society Press, 1986), 44.
28. Pond, 174.

Chapter 3

1. Translated as the "heart of the mysterious land," Devil's Lake, North Dakota.
2. Adapted from a story told by Smoky Day to the young Ohiyesa. Eastman, *Boyhood,* 192–194.
3. Eugene Buechel, *A Grammar of the Lakota: The Language of the Teton Sioux Indians* (Rosebud, SD: Saint Francis Mission, Rosebud Educational Society, 1939), 7.
4. Pond, 77.
5. Buechel, 200.
6. Buechel, 202.
7. Buechel, 30.
8. Buechel, 31.
9. Ceasre Marino and Leonard Vigorelli, *The Sioux Vocabulary 1823: In the Archivio Beltrami of Count G. Luchetti, Filottrano, Italy* (Kendal Park, NJ: Lakota Books, 1995), 43–44.
10. Marino and Vigorelli, 44–45.
11. Buechel, 32–34.
12. Marla N. Powers, *Oglala Women: Myth, Ritual and Reality* (Chicago, IL: University of Chicago Press, 1986), 80.
13. Buechel, 6.
14. Roberta Carkeek Cheney, *Sioux Winter Count: A 131-Year Calendar of Events* (Happy Camp, CA: Naturegraph, 1998), 58.
15. George Fronval and Daniel DuBois, *Indian Signals and Sign Language* (New York: Wings Books, 1994), 73.
16. Fronval and DuBois, 72.
17. Marla N. Powers, 62–64, 80; James R. Walker, *Lakota Society* (Lincoln, NE: Bison Books, 1982), 46–49.

Chapter 4

1. Adapted from Sicangu (Brule) tale told by Lame Deer as relayed to him by his Santee grandmother. Richard Erdoes and Alfonso Ortiz, eds., *American Indian Myths and Legends* (New York: Pantheon Books, 1984), 93–95.
2. Walker, *Society*, 14.
3. Colin F. Taylor, *The Plains Indians* (London: Salamander Books, Ltd., 1997), 40.
4. Robert M. Utley, *The Lance and the Shield: The Life and Times of Sitting Bull* (New York: Ballantine Books, 1993), 211.

5. Walker, *Society*, 13.
6. Walker, *Society*, 14.
7. Meyers, 21.
8. Meyers, 27.
9. Meyers, 45.
10. Pond, 5.
11. Meyers, 45.
12. Taylor, 38.
13. Walker, *Society*, 12.
14. Walker, *Society*, 133.
15. Cheney, 27.

Chapter 5

1. Adaptation of "The Story of the Pet Crow." Mary L. McLaughlin, *Myths and Legends of the Sioux* (Lincoln, NE: Bison Books, 1990), 136–141.
2. Jack Weatherford, *Indian Givers: How the Indians of the Americas Transformed the World* (New York: Fawcett-Columbine Books, 1988), 138.
3. Weatherford, *Indian Givers*, 135–136.
4. Weatherford, *Indian Givers*, 142.
5. Weatherford, *Indian Givers*, 124.
6. Lawson, 204–205.
7. Pond, 66.
8. Lawson, 204.
9. Lawson, 43.
10. Walker, *Society*, 30.
11. Walker, *Society*, 38.
12. Utley, 162.
13. Utley, 183.
14. Taylor, *Plains Indians*, 40.
15. Pond, 179.
16. Cheney, 58.
17. Lawson, 43.
18. Walker, 29.
19. Walker, 30.
20. Walker, 38.
21. Walker, 30.
22. Walker, 33.
23. Walker, 38.
24. Walker, 29.
25. Utley, 125.
26. Utley, 211–212.
27. Walker, 21.
28. Walker, 22–23.
29. Walker, 35.
30. Utley, 21.
31. Taylor, 40.
32. Utley, 18.
33. Utley, 101.
34. Pond, 66–69.
35. Elijah Blackthunder, *Ehanna Woyakapi: A History and Cultural Record Commissioned by the Sisseton Wahpeton Sioux Tribe*, Sisseton, SD, 1972.
36. Eastman, *Boyhood*, 217.
37. Eastman, *Boyhood*, 226.
38. Utley, 135.

Chapter 6

1. Lawson, 200.
2. Josephine Paterek, *Encyclopedia of American Indian Costume* (London: Norton, 1994), 112.
3. Paterek, 112.
4. Taylor, *Plains Indians*, 126–127.
5. Pond, 32.
6. Meyers, 2.
7. Meyers, 8.
8. Eastman, *Boyhood*, 47.
9. Eastman, *Boyhood*, 40.
10. Paterek, 113.
11. Pond, 33.
12. Taylor, 125.
13. Paterek, 113.
14. Taylor, 133.
15. Taylor, 140.
16. James R. Walker, *Lakota Belief and Ritual* (Lincoln, NE: Bison Books, 1991), 165–166.
17. Lawson, 180.
18. Pond, 37.
19. Walker, *Society*, 133.
20. Pond, 42.
21. Meyers, 20.
22. Meyers, 16.
23. Meyers, 18.
24. Pond, 41.
25. Pond, 41.
26. Pond, 42.
27. Walker, *Society*, 81.

Chapter 7

1. Adapted from a story told by Dakota storyteller Smoky Day to Ohiyesa, c. 1858. Eastman, *Boyhood*, 126–137.
2. Cheney, 29.
3. Cheney, 30.
4. Walker, *Society*, 124.
5. Walker, *Society*, 136.
6. Eastman, *Soul*, 10–11.
7. Meyers, 18.
8. Pond, 26.
9. Weatherford, *Indian Givers*, 84.
10. Weatherford, *Indian Givers*, 85.
11. Pond, 27.
12. Eastman, *Boyhood*, 32.
13. Eastman, *Boyhood*, 235–236.
14. Lawson, 51.
15. Eastman, *Boyhood*, 87.
16. Eastman, *Boyhood*, 88–89.
17. Eastman, *Boyhood*, 55.
18. Calloway, 37.
19. Pond, 54–55.
20. Pond, 29.
21. Eastman, *Boyhood*, 87.
22. Peter C. Mancall and James H. Merrell, *American Encounters: Natives and Newcomers from European Contact to Indian Removal, 1500–1850* (New York: Routledge, 2000), 544.
23. Jack Weatherford, *Native Roots: How the Indians Enriched America* (New York: Fawcett-Columbine, 1991), 68.
24. Weatherford, *Native Roots*, 70.
25. Eastman, *Boyhood*, 91.
26. Weatherford, *Native Roots*, 79.
27. Weatherford, *Native Roots*, 69.
28. Walker, *Society*, 83.
29. Eastman, *Boyhood*, 25.
30. Walker, *Society*, 92.
31. Walker, *Society*, 81.
32. Walker, *Society*, 92.
33. Walker, *Society*, 80.
34. Pond, 49–50.
35. Cheney, 22.
36. Cheney, 23.
37. Cheney, 28.
38. Eastman, *Boyhood*, 95.
39. Walker, *Society*, 93.

Chapter 8

1. Eastman, *Soul*, 14–15.
2. Calloway, 36–37.
3. Calloway, 37.
4. Eastman, *Soul*, 76–78.
5. Eastman, *Soul*, 142.
6. Eastman, *Boyhood*, 171–174.
7. Eastman, *Soul*, 15.
8. Eastman, *Soul*, 47.
9. Joseph Epes Brown, *Animals of the Soul: Sacred Animals of the Oglala Sioux* (London: Element Books, 1997), 52–54.
10. Walker, *Belief*, 218.
11. Eastman, *Boyhood*, 54.
12. Walker, *Belief*, 168.
13. Utley, 30.
14. Joseph Epes Brown, 25–26.
15. Utley, 30.
16. Utley, 30.
17. Walker, *Belief*, 127.
18. Joseph Epes Brown, 24.
19. Walker, *Belief*, 223.
20. Joseph Epes Brown, 32.
21. Walker, *Belief*, 266.
22. Walker, *Belief*, 121–122.
23. Eastman, *Soul*, 43–45.
24. Utley, 5–6.
25. Eastman, *Boyhood*, 3.

Chapter 9

1. Adapted from McLaughlin, 78–80.
2. Mancall and Merrell, 221.
3. Hibbens, 112–113.
4. Cheney, 17–18.
5. Walker, *Society*, 135.
6. Cheney, 20.

7. Walker, *Society*, 136.
8. Cheney, 22.
9. Cheney, 29.
10. Meyers, 16.
11. Mancall and Merrell, 36.
12. Calloway, 160.
13. Mancall and Merrell, 225.
14. Wissler, 206.
15. Calloway, 302.
16. Calloway, 309.
17. Calloway, 240.
18. Calloway, 241.
19. Calloway, 241.
20. Pierre Esprit Radisson, *The Voyages of Peter Esprit Radisson: An Account of His Travels and Experiences Among the North American Indians, from 1652 to 1684,* transcribed from the original manuscript in the British Museum (London: Peter Smith, 1943), 282.
21. Meyers, 12.
22. Mancall and Merrell, 544.
23. Meyers, 17–18.
24. Pond, 85.
25. Pond, 169.
26. Pond, 170.
27. Mancall and Merrell, 544.
28. Mancall and Merrell, 544.
29. Mancall and Merrell, 545.
30. Wissler, 183.
31. Walker, *Society*, 128.
32. Walker, *Society*, 130.
33. Cheney, 18.
34. Utley, 102.
35. Cheney, 14.
36. Walker, *Society*, 130–131.
37. Cheney, 15.
38. Walker, *Society*, 131.
39. Taylor, *Plains Indians*, 43–45.
40. Meyers, 27.
41. Cheney, 16.
42. Cheney, 17.
43. Pond, 172.
44. Cheney, 15.
45. Walker, *Society*, 132.
46. Cheney, 17–18.
47. Mancall and Merrell, 546.
48. Mancall and Merrell, 545.
49. Pond, 170.
50. Pond, 173.
51. Taylor, 43.
52. Taylor, 44.
53. Taylor, 44.
54. Walker, *Society*, 134.
55. Meyers, 35.
56. Meyers, 36.
57. Cheney, 20.
58. Cheney, 23.
59. Cheney, 24.
60. Cheney, 25.
61. Cheney, 25.
62. Cheney, 29.
63. Cheney, 30.
64. The Wahpeton name for half-breed traders of Canada.
65. Eastman, *Boyhood*, 257.
66. Radisson, 210–211.
67. Radisson, 213.

Chapter 10

1. From the White River Sioux, Erdoes and Ortiz, 258–260.
2. Pond, 60.
3. Eastman, *Boyhood,* 14–15.
4. Eastman, *Boyhood*, 18.
5. Radisson, 214.
6. Meyers, 9.
7. Calloway, 230.
8. Calloway, 230.
9. Meyers, 13.
10. Meyers, 13.
11. Meyers, 6.
12. Wissler, 183.
13. Meyers, 13.
14. Meyers, 29.
15. Walker, *Society*, 125.
16. Douglass Houghton, in a letter written September 21, 1832. Henry Rowe Schoolcraft, *Narrative of an Expedition Through the Upper Mississippi to Itasca Lake* (New York: Harper & Brothers, 1834), 254–255.
17. Meyers, 14.
18. Walker, *Society*, 125–126.
19. Calloway, 369.
20. Meyers, 19.
21. Calloway, 370.
22. Walker, *Society*, 127–128.
23. Mancall and Merrell, 546.
24. Walker, *Society*, 129.
25. Douglas Summer Brown, 29.
26. Mancall and Merrell, 543–544.
27. Mancall and Merrell, 546.
28. Mancall and Merrell, 547.
29. Walker, *Society*, 130.
30. Walker, *Society*, 131.
31. Cheney, 14.
32. Mancall and Merrell, 546.
33. Walker, *Society*, 131.
34. Mancall and Merrell, 550.
35. Cheney, 15.
36. Meyers, 25.
37. Cheney, 15.
38. Meyers, 31.
39. Walker, *Society*, 132.
40. Cheney, 16.
41. Reuben Golden Thwaites, *Original Journals of the Lewis and Clark Expedition, 1804–1806,* Vol. 6 (New York: Arno Press, 1969), 98.
42. Mancall and Merrell, 547.
43. Meyers, 28.
44. Walker, *Society*, 132–133.
45. Mancall and Merrell, 547.
46. Meyers, 30–31.
47. Walker, *Society*, 133.
48. Walker, *Society*, 133–134.
49. Meyers, 38–39.
50. Walker, *Society*, 135.
51. Mancall and Merrell, 550.
52. Mancall and Merrell, 544.
53. Mancall and Merrell, 551.
54. Meyers,
55. Cheney, 21.
56. Meyers, 40–41.
57. Walker, *Society*, 136–137.
58. Meyers, 51.
59. Meyers, 51.
60. Cheney, 25.
61. Walker, *Society*, 138.
62. Walker, *Society*, 139.
63. Mancall and Merrell, 550.
64. Meyers, 61.
65. Cheney, 25.
66. Meyers, 58.
67. Cheney, 26.
68. Mancall and Merrell, 552–553.
69. Walker, *Society*, 140.
70. Cheney, 27.
71. Walker, *Society*, 140.
72. Walker, *Society*, 141.
73. Meyers, 105.
74. Meyers, 79–80.
75. Meyers, 98.
76. Walker, *Society*, 142.
77. Walker, *Society*, 143.
78. Utley, 23–24.
79. Walker, *Society*, 143.
80. Meyers, 104.
81. Meyers, 104.
82. Walker, *Society*, 143–144.
83. Cheney, 31.
84. Walker, *Society*, 144.
85. Mancall and Merrell, 552.
86. Mancall and Merrell, 556.

Chapter 11

1. Based on the story "Tonwayah-pe-kin: The Spies," by Mary Henderson Eastman and published in *Dahcotah: The Life and Legends of the Sioux Around Fort Snelling* (Afton, MN: Afton Historical Society Press, 1995), 113–117.
2. Eastman, *Soul*, 108.
3. Radisson, 207.
4. Meyers, 6.
5. Meyers, 8.
6. Meyers, 19.
7. Eastman, *Soul*, 108.
8. *Michigan—A Guide to the Wolverine State* (New York: Oxford University Press, 1941), 235.
9. Francis Whiting Halsey, *The Old New York Frontier* (New York: Charles Scribner's Sons, 1900), 312–314.
10. Walker, *Society*, 138.
11. Eastman, *Boyhood*, 56.
12. Eastman, *Boyhood*, 67.
13. Walker, *Society*, 72.
14. Pond, 120–121.
15. Walker, *Society*, 86.
16. Meyers, 6.
17. Meyers, 8.
18. Lawson, 207.
19. Francis Parkman, *The Conspiracy of Pontiac* (New York: Literary Classics of America, 1991), 544–545.
20. Eastman, *Boyhood*, 28.

21. Eastman, *Boyhood*, 28.
22. Utley, 23.
23. Sara F. Wakefield, *Six Weeks in Native Tepees* (Norman, OK: Oklahoma University Press, 1997), 69.
24. Walker, *Belief*, 260.
25. Walker, *Belief*, 264.
26. Walker, *Belief*, 268–269.
27. Walker, *Belief*, 267.
28. Utley, 18.
29. Walker, *Belief*, 264.
30. Utley, 101.
31. Utley, 101.
32. Walker, *Belief*, 270–276.
33. Eastman, *Boyhood*, 144.
34. Eastman, *Boyhood*, 143.
35. Eastman, *Boyhood*, 144.
36. Fronval and Dubois, 73.
37. Eastman, *Soul*, 131.
38. Pond, 121–122.
39. Pond, 171.

Chapter 12

1. Herald, or town crier.
2. An adaptation of two stories found in Eastman, *Boyhood*, 181–187, and Mary Henderson Eastman, 43–51.
3. Eastman, *Boyhood*, 183.
4. Eastman, *Soul*, 99.
5. Marla N. Powers, 88.
6. Pond, 150.
7. Pond, 150.
8. Pond, 71–72.
9. Eastman, *Soul*, 41.
10. Eastman, *Boyhood*, 105–106.
11. Pond, 109.
12. Pond, 108.
13. Pond, 106.
14. Eastman, *Soul*, 108–110.
15. Eastman, *Soul*, 94.
16. Pond, 76.
17. Lawson, 184.
18. Eastman, *Soul*, 104–105.
19. Eastman, *Soul*, 114.
20. Fronval and Dubois, 25.
21. Pond, 109.
22. Pond, 76.
23. Eastman, *Boyhood*, 22.
24. Eastman, *Boyhood*, 20.
25. Eastman, *Boyhood*, 17.
26. Eastman, *Boyhood*, 20.
27. Eastman, *Soul*, 9–10.
28. Lawson, 184.
29. Eastman, *Soul*, 100–101.
30. Eastman, *Soul*, 103.
31. Pond, 170–171.
32. Radisson, 207.
33. Gabriel Sagard-Thèodat, *Histoire du Canada et Voyages que Les Frères Mineurs Recollects y ont faicts pour la Conuersion des Infidelles* (Paris, 1636), 241–242.
34. William F. Ganong, *New Relation of Gaspesia with the Customs and Religions of the Gaspesian Indians by Father Chrestien LeClercq* (Toronto, 1910), 241–242.
35. Wakefield, 76.
36. Douglas Summer Brown, 78.
37. Eastman, *Boyhood*, 50.
38. Eastman, *Soul*, 34.
39. Eastman, *Soul*, 37.
40. Lawson, 43.

Chapter 13

1. Eastman, *Soul*, 42.
2. Eastman, *Soul*, 65–66.
3. Radisson, 213.
4. Eastman, *Soul*, 41.
5. Taylor, *Plains Indians*, 95.
6. Eastman, *Soul*, 99–100.
7. Walker, *Society*, 51.
8. Pond, 137.
9. Eastman, *Soul*, 41.
10. Marla N. Powers, 81.
11. Walker, *Society*, 51.
12. Those who dressed as women.
13. Pond, 140–141.
14. Walker, *Society*, 42.
15. Eastman, *Soul*, 40–41.
16. Pond, 139.
17. Pond, 74.
18. Wakefield, 76.
19. Cheney, 22.
20. Marla N. Powers, 88.
21. Taylor, 91–92.
22. Utley, 7.
23. Pond, 47–48.
24. Walker, *Society*, 43.
25. Eastman, *Soul*, 30.
26. Mary Henderson Eastman, xv.
27. Cheney, 58.

Chapter 14

1. Adapted from the story as told by Black Elk. Joseph Epes Brown, *The Sacred Pipe: Black Elk's Account of the Seven Rites of the Oglala Sioux* (Norman OK: University of Oklahoma Press, 1953), 3–9.
2. Walker, *Society*, 130.
3. Eastman, *Soul*, 33–34.
4. Eastman, *Soul*, 41.
5. Utley, 7.
6. Walker, *Society*, 130; Cheney, 22.
7. Eastman, *Soul*, 45.
8. Eastman, *Soul*, 47.
9. Eastman, *Soul*, 46.
10. Eastman, *Soul*, 19–20.
11. Cheney, 22.
12. Pond, 179.
13. Joseph Epes Brown, *Pipe*, 29.
14. Joseph Epes Brown, *Pipe*, 19.
15. Walker, *Belief*, 190.
16. Marla N. Powers, 86.
17. Thomas H. Lewis, *The Medicine Men: Oglala Ceremony and Healing* (Lincoln, NE: Bison Books, 1990), 109.
18. Lewis, 145.
19. Walker, *Belief*, 166.
20. Marla N. Powers, 88.
21. Eastman, *Boyhood*, 22.
22. Taylor, *Plains Indians*, 95.
23. Walker, *Belief*, 249.
24. Walker, *Belief*, 252.

Chapter 15

1. Also known as *Kanka*, the witch, the mother of *Ite* and *Wazi's* wife.
2. Adapted from the story, "The Four Directions and the Fourth Time." D.M. Dooling, *The Sons of the Wind: The Sacred Stories of the Lakota* (Norman, OK: University of Oklahoma Press, 1985), 45–114.
3. Taylor, *Plains Indians*, 62.
4. William K. Powers, *Sacred Language: The Nature of Supernatural Discourse in Lakota* (Norman, OK: University of Oklahoma Press, 1986), 122.
5. Walker, *Belief*, 70.
6. Walker, *Belief*, 102.
7. Taylor, *Plains*, 61.
8. Walker, *Belief*, 70.
9. Joseph, Epes Brown, *Pipe*, 62.
10. Walker, *Belief*, 31–32.
11. Eastman, *Soul*, 121–122.
12. Pond, 87.
13. Mary Henderson Eastman, 157.
14. Eastman, *Soul*, 81.
15. Eastman, *Soul*, 13–14.
16. Eastman, *Soul*, 27.
17. Eastman, *Soul*, 4.

Chapter 16

1. James R. Walker, "The Sundance of the Teton Dakota," Part 2 (*Anthropological Papers of the American Museum of Natural History* 16), 152.
2. Joseph Epes Brown, *Animals*, 62.
3. Utley, 28.
4. Eastman, *Boyhood*, 169–171.
5. Walker, *Belief*, 93.
6. Walker, *Belief*, 92.
7. Walker, *Belief*, 92.
8. William K. Powers, 181.
9. Joseph Epes Brown, *Animals*, 63.
10. Pond, 105.
11. William K. Powers, 71.
12. Walker, *Society*, 126.
13. Walker, *Society*, 128.
14. William K. Powers, 194.
15. William K. Powers, 188.

16. Walker, *Society*, 127.
17. Mancall and Merrell, 121.
18. Mancall and Merrell, 122.
19. Eastman, *Soul,* 150–152.
20. Pond, 166–167.
21. Walker, *Belief*, 164.
22. Walker, *Belief*, 163
23. Mary Henderson Eastman, 175–176.
24. Pond, 162–163.
25. Michael Parker Pearson, *Bronze Age Britain* (London: The English Heritage Library, 1993), 28.
26. Meyers, 45.
27. Meyers, 8.
28. Joseph Epes Brown, *Pipe*, 14.
29. Pond, 165.
30. Eastman, *Soul*, 153.
31. Joseph Epes Brown, *Pipe*, 11.
32. Joseph Epes Brown, *Pipe*, 11.
33. Pond, 169.
34. Eastman, *Soul*, 154–155.
35. Walker, *Belief*, 70–71.
36. Walker, *Belief*, 73.
37. Walker, *Belief*, 72.
38. Eastman, *Soul*, 167.
39. Walker, *Belief*, 102.
40. Joseph Epes Brown, *Pipe*, 29.
41. Eastman, *Soul*, 156.
42. Walker, *Belief*, 104.
43. Walker, *Belief*, 164.
44. Cheney, 28.
45. Pearson, 28.
46. Pearson, 46–47.

Chapter 17

1. Adapted from a Brule tale relayed by Lame Deer at Rosebud Reservation in 1967, recorded by Richard Erdoes and published in Erdoes and Ortiz, 69–72.
2. Utley, 34.
3. Pond, 93–94.
4. Eastman, *Soul*, 64–69.
5. Pond, 99–101.
6. Walker, *Belief*, 239.
7. Walker, *Belief*, 253.
8. Joseph Epes Brown, *Pipe*, vii.
9. Pond, 108.
10. Eastman, *Soul*, 78.
11. Thomas E. Mails, *Fools Crow: Wisdom and Power* (Tulsa, OK: Council Oaks Books, 1991), 104.
12. Archie Fire, Lame Deer, and Helene Sarkis, *The Lakota Sweat Lodge: Spiritual Teachings of the Sioux* (Rochester, VT: Destiny Books, 1994), 35–37.

13. Utley, 28.
14. Joseph Epes Brown, *Pipe*, 45.
15. Walker, *Belief*, 249.
16. Joseph Epes Brown, *Pipe*, 46.
17. Utley, 32.
18. Utley, 138.
19. Utley, 31.
20. Utley, 31.
21. Joseph Epes Brown, *Pipe*, 67.
22. Utley, 31–32.
23. Eastman, *Soul*, 55–56.
24. Utley, 138.
25. Taylor, *Plains Indians*, 85.
26. Joseph Epes Brown, *Pipe*, 101.
27. Walker, *Belief*, 203–204.
28. Eastman, *Soul*, 49.
29. Walker, *Society*, 131.
30. Walker, *Belief*, 204.
31. Walker, *Belief*, 197.
32. Pond, 166.

Chapter 18

1. Adapted from a story told by Ohiyesa. Eastman, *Boyhood*, 36–45.
2. Eastman, *Boyhood*, 70–72.
3. Eastman, *Boyhood*, 72–73.
4. Walker, *Society*, 64.
5. Eastman, *Boyhood*, 69.
6. Eastman, *Boyhood*, 69–70.
7. Walker, *Society*, 64.
8. Lawson, 180.
9. Walker, *Society*, 64.
10. Pond, 117.
11. Walker, *Society*, 67.
12. Lawson, 180.
13. Eastman, *Boyhood,* 66.
14. Pond, 114–117.
15. Lawson, 62.
16. Lawson, 180.
17. Pond, 117.
18. Walker, *Society*, 66.
19. Pond, 118.
20. Pond, 117.
21. Walker, *Society*, 89–90.
22. Masturbator.
23. Walker, *Society*, 126–127.
24. Pond, 96–101.
25. Eastman, *Boyhood*, 51.
26. Eastman, *Boyhood*, 267.
27. Eastman, *Boyhood*, 268.

Chapter 19

1. Adapted from the Brule tale "The Coming of the Wasichu," published in Erdoes and Ortiz, 491–496.

2. Mancall and Merrell, 61.
3. Lawson, 24.
4. Lawson, 23.
5. Lawson, 17.
6. James H. Merrell, *The Indians' New World: Catawbas and Their Neighbors from European Contact to the Era of Removal* (Chapel Hill, NC: University of North Carolina Press, 1989), 19.
7. Douglas Summer Brown, 181.
8. Walker, *Society*, 129.
9. Cheney, 13.
10. Walker, *Society*, 130.
11. Calloway, 421.
12. Meyers, 68.
13. Wissler, 198.
14. Calloway, 241.
15. Wissler, 106.
16. Wissler, 178.
17. Calloway, 419.
18. Calloway, 423.
19. Mancall and Merrell, 197–198.
20. Meyers, 19.
21. Meyers, 32.
22. Meyers, 44.
23. Meyers, 68.
24. Eastman, *Soul*, 22.
25. Eastman, *Soul*, 24.
26. Calloway, 220.
27. Sagard-Thèobald, 241–242.
28. Lawson, 243.
29. Eastman, *Soul*, 101.
30. Eastman, *Soul*, 103.
31. Edna Nyquist, *Pioneer Life and Lore of McPherson County* (Shawnee Mission, KS: McPherson County Historical and Archeological Society, 1932), 161.
32. *The History of the Canton Community, 1864–1988* (Canton, KS: History Book Committee, 1988), 13.
33. *The History of the Canton*, 14.
34. Cheney, 35.
35. *U.S. Statutes at Large*, Vol. 24, 388 ff.
36. Dee Brown, *Bury My Heart at Wounded Knee* (New York: Arena Books, 1987), 435.
37. Dee Brown, 437.
38. Dee Brown, 437–438.
39. Charles A. Eastman, *From the Deep Woods to Civilization* (Lincoln, NE: Bison Books, 1977), 111.
40. Eastman, *Woods to Civilization*, 111–112.
41. Eastman, *Woods to Civilization*, 113.
42. Eastman, *Soul*, 23.

Bibliography

Ball, Eve. *Indeh: An Apache Odyssey.* Norman, OK: University of Oklahoma Press, 1980.

Blackthunder, Elijah. *Ehanna Woyakapi: A History and Cultural Record Commissioned by the Sisseton Wahpeton Sioux Tribe.* Sisseton, SD, 1972.

Brown, Dee. *Bury My Heart at Wounded Knee.* New York: Arena Books, 1987.

Brown, Douglas Summer. *The Catawba: The People of the River.* Columbia, SC: University of South Carolina Press, 1966.

Brown, Joseph Epes. *Animals of the Soul: Sacred Animals of the Oglala Sioux.* London: Element Books, 1997.

_____. *The Sacred Pipe: Black Elk's Account of the Seven Rites of the Oglala Sioux.* Norman, OK: University of Oklahoma Press, 1986.

Buechel, Eugene. *A Grammar of the Lakota: The Language of the Teton Sioux Indians.* Rosebud, SD: Saint Francis Mission, Rosebud Educational Society, 1939.

Calloway, Colin G. *One Vast Winter Count.* Lincoln, NE: University of Nebraska Press, 2003.

Cheney, Roberta Carkeek. *Sioux Winter Count: A 131-Year Calendar of Events.* Happy Camp, CA: Naturegraph, 1998.

Clark, William Philo. *The Indian Sign Language.* Lincoln, NE: Bison Books, 1982.

Dooling, D.M. *The Sons of the Wind: The Sacred Stories of the Lakota.* Norman, OK: University of Oklahoma Press, 2000.

Eastman, Charles A. *From the Deep Woods to Civilization.* Lincoln, NE: Bison Books, 1977.

_____. *Indian Boyhood.* Lincoln, NE: Bison Books, 1991.

_____. *The Soul of an Indian.* Lincoln, NE: Bison Books, 1991.

_____. *Soul of the Sioux.* Boston: Houghton Mifflin, 1910.

Eastman, Mary Henderson. *Dahcotah: The Life and Legends of the Sioux Around Fort Snelling.* Afton, MN: Afton Historical Society Press, 1995.

Erdoes, Richard, and Alfonso Ortiz, eds. *American Indian Myths and Legends.* New York: Pantheon Books, 1984.

Farnell, Brenda. *Do You See What I Mean?: Plains Indian Sign Talk and the Embodiment of Action.* Austin, TX: University of Texas, 1995.

Fronval, George, and Daniel DuBois. *Indian Signals and Sign Language.* New York: Wings Books, 1994.

Ganong, William F. *New Relation of Gaspesia with the Customs and Religions of the Gaspesian Indians by Father Chrestien LeClercq.* Toronto, Canada, 1910.

Grinnell, George Bird. *The Cheyenne Indians: History and Society.* Lincoln, NE: University of Nebraska Press, 1972.

Halsey, Francis Whiting. *The Old New York Frontier.* New York: Charles Scribner's Sons, 1900.

Hibbens, Frank C. *Digging Up America.* New York: Hill and Wang, 1961.

History of the Canton Community, 1864–1988. Canton, KS: History Book Committee, 1988.

Lame Deer, Archie Fire, and Helene Sarkis. *The Lakota Sweat Lodge: Spiritual Teachings of the Sioux.* Rochester, VT: Destiny Books, 1994.

Lawson, John. *A New Voyage to Carolina.* Chapel Hill, NC: University of North Carolina Press, 1968.

Lewis, Thomas H. *The Medicine Men: Oglala Ceremony and Healing.* Lincoln, NE: Bison Books, 1990.

Mails, Thomas E. *Fools Crow: Wisdom and Power.* Tulsa, OK: Council Oaks Books, 1991.

Mancall, Peter C., and James H. Merrell, eds. *American Encounters: Natives and Newcomers from European Contact to Indian Removal, 1500–1850.* New York: Routledge, 2000.

Marino, Ceasre, and Leonard Vigorelli. *The Sioux Vocabulary 1823: In the Archivio Beltrami of Count G. Luchetti, Filottrano, Italy.* Kendal Park, NJ: Lakota Books, 1995.

McLaughlin, Mary L. *Myths and Legends of the Sioux.* Lincoln, NE: Bison Books, 1990.

Merrell, James H. *The Indians' New World: Catawbas and Their Neighbors from European Contact to the Era of Removal.* Chapel Hill, NC: University of North Carolina Press, 1989.

Meyers, Roy W. *History of the Santee: United States Indian Policy on Trial.* Lincoln, NE: Bison Books, 1967.

Michigan — A Guide to the Wolverine State. New York: Oxford University Press, 1941.

Michno, Gregory F. *Lakota Noon: The Indian Narra-

tive of Custer's Defeat. Missoula, MT: Mountain Press Publishing, 1997.

Mooney, James. *The Siouan Tribes of the East*. Washington, DC: Smithsonian Collection, 1894.

Nyquist, Edna. *Pioneer Life and Lore of McPherson County*. Shawnee Mission, KS: McPherson County Historical and Archeological Society, 1932.

Parkman, Francis. *The Conspiracy of Pontiac*. New York: Literary Classics of America, 1991.

Paterek, Josephine. *Encyclopedia of American Indian Costume*. London: Norton, 1994.

Pearson, Michael Parker. *Bronze Age Britain*. London: The English Heritage Library, 1993.

Pond, Samuel W. *The Dakota or Sioux in Minnesota as They Were in 1834*. St. Paul, MN: Minnesota Historical Society Press, 1986.

Powers, Marla N. *Oglala Women: Myth, Ritual and Reality*. Chicago, IL: University of Chicago Press, 1986.

Powers, William K. *Sacred Language: The Nature of Supernatural Discourse in Lakota*. Norman, OK: University of Oklahoma Press, 1986.

Radisson, Pierre. *Voyages of Peter Esprit Radisson: An Account of his Travels and Experiences Among the North American Indians, from 1652 to 1684*. New York: Peter Smith, 1943.

Sagard-Theodat, Gabriel. *Histoire du Canada et Voyages que Les Fr(res Mineurs Recollects y ont faicts pour la Conuersion des Infidelles*. Paris, 1636.

Schoolcraft, Henry Rowe. *Narrative of an Expedition Through the Upper Mississippi to Itasca Lake*. New York: Harper & Brothers, 1834.

Shetrone, Henry Clyde. *The Mound Builders*. New York: D. Appleton and Company, 1930.

Taylor, Colin F. *The Native Americans: The Indigenous People of North America*. London: Smithmark Books; 1991.

_____. *The Plains Indians*. London: Salamander Books, Ltd, 1997.

Thwaites, Reuben Gold. *Original Journals of the Lewis and Clark Expedition, 1804–1806*. Vol. 6. New York: Arno Press, 1969.

U.S. Statutes at Large, Vol. 24. Congressional Library.

Utley, Robert. *The Lance and the Shield: The Life and Times of Sitting Bull*. New York: Ballantine Books, 1993.

Versluis, Arthur. *Native American Traditions*. Shaftsbury, Dorset, UK: Element Books, 1993.

Wakefield, Sarah F. *Six Weeks in Sioux Teepees: A Narrative of Indian Captivity*. Norman, OK: University of Oklahoma Press, 1997.

Walker, James R. *Lakota Belief and Ritual*. Lincoln, NE: Bison Books, 1991.

_____. *Lakota Society*. Lincoln, NE: Bison Books, 1982.

_____. "The Sundance of the Teton Dakota," Part 2. *Anthropological Papers of the American Museum of Natural History* 16.

Weatherford, Jack. *Indian Givers: How the Indians of the Americas Transformed the World*. New York: Fawcett-Columbine Books, 1988.

_____. *Native Roots: How The Indians Enriched America*. New York: Fawcett Columbine, 1991.

Williamson, John P. *An English-Dakota Dictionary*. St. Paul, MN: Minnesota Historical Society Press, 1992.

Wissler, Clark. *Indians of the United States*. New York: Anchor Books, 1989.

Young Bear, Steve, and R.D. Theiz. *Standing in the Light: A Lakota Way of Seeing*. Lincoln, NE: Bison Books, 1994.

Index

Abbott, C.C. 7
Abnaki 134
Acorn 91
Acosta, Jos(de 6
Adovasio, James (Dr.) 8
Agriculture 31, 48, 49, 84–89, 115, 116, 117, 125, 138
Akitcita (marshals or police) 55, 56, 57, 58, 59–60, 62, 63, 93, 96, 108, 110, 129 152, 155, 162, 181; town crier (Yamaha) 59–60, 162; women as 176
Algonkin-Wakashan 7
Algonquin 29, 30, 44, 56, 118, 120, 122, 144, 153; battles with 131, 133, 135; beadwork 75, 76
Alibamu 11
Allouez, Claude Jean 133
American Horse 141, 143, 151
American Indian Religious Freedom Act of 1978 255
Amerindan 8
Anasazi 116
Antiquities Act 7
Apache 119
Aquipaguetin (chief) 214
Arapahoe 138, 141, 144, 243
Arikara (Ree) 11, 49, 75, 77, 120, 122, 123, 125, 138, 140, 141, 222, 230, 247; Lakota blockade of 139, 143, 145
Assiniboin (*Hohe*) 25, 41, 42, 94, 118, 120, 122, 125, 136, 138, 145, 146, 168, 247
Athapaskin 116, 119
Atwater, Caleb 22
Aztec 116, 250
Aztec-Tanoan 7

Baker, William C. 184
Bandelier, Adolf 7
Bear Boy 230
Bear Ears 137
Beltrami, Giovanni (Count) 31, 248
Bering, Vitus 6
Betrothal 178
Big Bellies *see* Chief's Society
Big Crow 146
Big Foot 49
Big Missouri winter count 49, 87, 98, 116–117, 123, 124, 127, 138, 143, 145, 175, 181, 187, 218, 246

Big Road 140
Biloxi 12, 20, 26–27, 251
Bite the Knife Ceremony 164
Biting the Snake 189
Black Buffalo 141
Black Elk 187, 191, 209, 212, 223, 226, 230
Black Hawk 142
Black Hawk's War 142
Black Hills (*Paha Sapa*) 100–101, 138; *Wamaka Og'naka Icante* (the heart of everything that is) 101, 203–204 228
Black Moon 230
Black Road (the way of materialism) 199
Black Rock (warrior) 139
Blackfoot (Algonquin) 49, 120, 124, 136, 182, 247
Blackfoot (Sioux) *see* Sihasapa
Blue-and-Red Days 189
Blue Thunder 143
Blunt Horn (warrior) 145
Blunt Horn, John 42–43, 46, 59, 156, 217, 230, 231
Bradford, W.R. 16
Brides' price 177–178
British 27, 30, 31, 120, 123, 134, 135, 137, 139, 140, 150, 169
Broken Leg Bird 137
Brown, Joseph Epes 104, 108, 209, 211
Brown Robe (warrior) 145
Brule *see* Sicangu
Buechel, Eugene 29, 30, 32, 44
Buffalo 86, 91, 92, 93, 94, 122, 138, 139, 140, 143, 185, 242; buffalo hunt 97–98, 123; economic value of 124, 125, 187; white buffalo 98, 104, 186, 210
Buffalo Woman 191; rite *Tatanka Lowanpi* 191–192
Bull Bear (chief) 144

Caddoan/Caddo 11, 116
Cahokia 23, 24
Caitlin, George 49
Calloway, Colin G. 92, 100, 101, 102, 137
Cancu, Clifford 41
Cangleska Oyate (Hoop Nation) 39, 60
Cangleska Wakan (Sacred Hoop) 39, 199

Cannibalism 87
Caral 8, 115
Carver, Jonathon 45, 79, 118
Catawba 6, 12, 20, 23, 24, 25, 27, 119, 137, 172, 245
Cayuga 11
Cayuse 124
Champlain, Samuel de 248
Chardon, F.A. 126
Charles, Thomas 56
Chavin 115, 116
Chepoussa 132
Cherokee 11, 20, 137, 245
Cheyenne 118, 123, 124, 138, 139, 141, 143, 144, 151, 152, 154, 228, 230, 252
Chickasaw 11
Chief's Society 41, 57, 58, 59, 60, 61–62, 152, 154, 155, 156
Children 171–172, 183, 187; education 241–242; gender training 172; play and games 235–239; training for war 152
Chinook 120, 176
Chippewa *see* Ojibwa
Choctaw 11
Cholera 213, 245, 247
Chotanka 23
Chumash 11
Clark, William 48, 123, 124, 125, 127, 139, 141, 175, 247
Cleveland, W.J. (the Rev.) 48
Cloud Man (chief) 144
Clovis 8, 115, 227
Comanche 120, 134
Congaree 12; river 119, 245
Conquering Bear 145
Constellations 203–204
Corn (maize) 84, 86, 88–89, 91, 93, 181, 234, 250, 251
Coronado, Francisco Vasquez de 119
Cotterill, R.S. 20, 24, 26, 27
Council 41, 55, 57, 58 254; Council House (*iyokihe*) 56, 58; council of all tribes (1825) 141
Coup 161; count coup146, 157, 158; coup stick 130
Courtship 178–178; flute (*cotanka*) 178
Crazy Horse 19, 52, 64, 157, 211, 226
Cree 69, 118, 120, 122, 127, 134, 138
Creek 1, 112
Crow 12, 41, 43, 118, 120, 124, 125,

265

129, 130, 138, 139, 141, 142, 144, 145, 146, 147, 227, 243, 247, 252
Culbertson 47, 51

Dakota (woodland Sioux) 1, 2, 11, 12, 18, 19, 23, 24, 29, 30, 32, 39, 41, 43–46, 56, 77, 79, 87, 88, 89, 96, 98, 201–202, 213, 217, 236, 237, 238, 245, 246, 248; civil war 136; dress 66, 70, 118 121, 123, 131; government 62–63; wars 132, 133, 134, 142, 143, 144
Davis, Edwin Hamilton 22
Dawes, Henry (congressman) 243
Dawes Act of 1887 253–255
Death beliefs 209; afterlife 188–189, 217; judgment 188–189, 217; *May owichapaha* (she who pushes them over the bank) 188–189, 217; mourning 169, 213–214; *Nagi* 217, 218; *Nagila* (*Nagipila* pl.) 217; *Ni* (breath) 217, 225; *Niya* 217; *Wanaghi Tachanku* (pat of spirits) 217; *Wanagi* 217, 218; *Waniyi* 217
Deer Killer 213
Delaware 246
Deloria, Vine, Jr. 15, 49, 78
Denig, Edwin 176
De Smet, Pierre 48, 182
Desoto, Hernando 20, 22
Detroit, Battles of 153; (in 1747) 134; (in 1763) 135, 151
Dezhnyov, Semyan Ivanov 7
D'Iberville, Pierre Le Moyne (Governor) 122, 134
Dickson, Robert 139
Disease 1, 22–23, 46–47, 49, 125, 126, 140, 213, 210, 211, 219, 244
Dishonesty 167, 168; punishment of 167–168
Divinities and spiritual beings 199–200; *Anp/Anpetu* 3, 193, 196, 198, 234; *Can oti* (tree dwellers) 201; *Eya* 174–175, 193–198, 199; *Gica* (dwarves) 201; *Gnaski* (*Gnaskinyan*) 198, 201, 210; *Han* 3; *Hanwi* (*Hanwikan*), the moon 3–4, 199, 207; *Inktomi* (*Unktomi*) 3–5, 15, 18, 28, 107, 113, 159, 188, 190, 191, 194, 196, 197, 198, 201, 243; *Inyan* 3, 5, 76, 100, 102, 199, 200 203, 228; *Ite* (*Anog Ite*) 2, 4, 28, 76, 165, 178, 190, 191, 201; *Iya/Iyo* 3, 201; *Ka* (*Kanka/Wakanka*) 4, 5, 165, 196, 197; *Ksa* 3–4, 107, 108, 164, 165; *Maka* (earth) 3–4, 15, 203, 224, 225; *Mini watu* (water spirits) 201; *Nagi* 217, 218; *Nagila* 217; *Niya* 217; *Okaga* or *Itokaga* 106, 108, 174–175, 178, 186, 193–198; *Sicun* (guardians) 206; *Skan* (*taku skan skan*) 3–4, 165, 193, 196, 198, 201, 202, 224; *Taku wakan* 98, 166, 199; *Tate* (wind) 3–4, 165, 174, 193, 196, 199; *Tob* (four) 199, 244; *Tob kin* (four directions) 199; *Tobtob kin* (collectively, the mysteries) 199;

Tunkan (Eastman) 203; *Ungla* (goblins) 201; *Unk* (*Unktehi*) 3–4, 15, 18, 39, 165, 196, 197, 201–203; *Unkahe* (Henderson-Eastman) 201–202; *Unkteri* (Pond) 201–202; *Wa* (*Wazi*) 4–5, 165, 193, 194, 195, 196, 197, 217; *Wakan Tanka* 3, 4, 12, 28, 39, 44, 66, 100, 102, 185–186, 187, 188, 189, 210, 227, 231, 243, 244, 200–201, 203, 215, 224, 230; *Wakinyan* 3, 100, 165, 190, 195, 210; *Wani* 198; *Waziya* (*Waziyata*) 188; *Wi* (*Wikan*) 3–4, 16, 41, 165, 203; *Wohpe* (White Buffalo Calf Woman) 174–175, 186–187, 188, 193, 194, 196, 197, 198, 203, 214, 223, 230; *Yanpa* (*Wioyanpa*) 174–175, 193–198, 199; *Yata* (*Wioyata*) 174–175, 193–198, 217; *Yum* (*Yumni*) 4, 174–175, 193, 194, 198, 235, 241
Divorce 165, 176–177, 181
Dog Feast 223
Dorsey, James Owens 6, 47
Double Woman Dreamers 190
Douglass, A. E. 7
Dowry 178
Dragging one's feet dance (*Naslohan wacipi*) 190
Duluth, Sieur 134, 153

Eastman, Charles (Ohiyesa) 18, 19, 63, 70, 77, 87, 89, 92, 93, 96, 101, 102, 103, 104, 106, 108, 110, 111, 127, 131, 150, 152, 153, 154, 158, 163, 164, 165, 167, 169, 170, 176, 179, 183, 184, 187, 188, 200, 201, 203, 204, 209, 213, 214, 215, 217, 218, 219, 225, 228, 230, 235, 236, 238, 248, 254
Eastman, Seth 19, 184
Elderly: as teachers 241–242; treatment of 172, 188–189
Erie 11
Eskaleut 8
Eskimo 24
Eskimo-Aleut 7
Etowah 116, 119

Faribault, Oliver 93
Fasting 169–170
Feast of Raw Fish 223, 241
Fidelity 163, 165
Figgins, J.D. 7
First Amendment 253
Flame winter count 123
Flinders-Petrie, William 7
Folsom 7
Fools Crow 203, 210, 213
Forsythe, Thomas (Major) 126
Franklin, Benjamin 56, 151
French 30, 31, 120, 132, 134, 135, 136, 169; introduction to 43; trade 120–122, 127, 133, 137; wars with 123, 133, 134, 135
French and Indian War/Seven Years' War (1754–1763) 135, 136, 246
Funerary rites 2, 19, 213–214; at

the death of an enemy 149–150, 215; funerary dress 73, 213; *Nagi yuhapelo* (*wanigi wicgluhapi*/ keeping the soul) 19, 169, 189–190, 214–217; scaffolding 214

Gallineaux, Joseph 126
Games and entertainment: archery 152, 235, 237, 238; "arithmetick" 240; ball games 237; bowls 237; "buffalo hunt" 235–236; chenco 18, 241; counting sticks 238, 239; dances 236, 241; dice 238; feasts 241; foot races 235, 237, 238; gambling 238–239, 241; *Haka* 241; horseback racing 152, 235 238; humor 242; lacrosse 18, 231, 237, 240–241; moccasins 239–240; mud whips 236; plum stones (pips) 238; shinny 240; skip sticks 238; sledding 238; storytellers 242; swimming 238; tops 237; wands and snow arrows 238; war on bees 152, 235; "white man" 236–237; wrestling 237–238
Gatschet, A.S. 6, 11
Generosity 169–170; views on European 171, 248–249
Germ warfare 136, 246
Ghosts 189, 209, 217–218; ghost dance 253–254; ghost lodge 218
Gifting 170
Good, Battiste 20, 27, 138, 143, 151, 241
Good Seat 200
Goodyear, Albert 9
Government: *Akitcita* (enforcers of the law) 55, 56, 57, 58, 59–6; *Itancan* (chief/s) 41, 56, 57, 59; *Naca Ominicia* (chiefs' society) 41, 57, 59, 60; *Tiospaye* (band) 41; *Wakiconza* (tribal council) 56, 57, 58; *Wakicun* (clan's council representative) 63; *Zuya wikasa* 152
Grattan, G.L. (Lieutenant) 145
Grattan Massacre 145
Greasy Grass, battle of (Little Bighorn) 58, 64, 137, 227
Great Man 141
Greenburg, Joseph 8, 10
Gros Ventre 140, 142
Guardians spirits 104, 105

Hale, Horatio 6, 11
Hamilton, Henry 150
Hammond, James Henry 20
Harney, William S. (White Beard) 145
Hay, Jehu 248
He Crow (warrior) 144
Headdress 76–77, 155, 156, 157, 158
Headmen 54, 56, 57, 58, 59, 63, 129, 157
Henderson-Eastman, Mary 70, 179, 181, 183, 184, 201, 202, 203, 213–214, 223, 247

Hennepin, Louis 45, 70, 87, 150, 153, 214
Herbs (*pejuta*) 209, 210, 219; chart 210
Hewett, Edgar L. 7
Heyoka 62, 104, 105, 106–107, 157, 195, 198, 211, 212, 222, 241
Hidsata 12, 41, 75, 118, 120, 122, 124, 125, 131, 137, 138, 139, 143, 144, 247
His Horse Runs 230
Hokan 11, 13
Hokan-Siouan 7, 11–13
Holmes, William Henry 7
Holy Dance 190
Holy/Medicine men/woman 209–213, 219, 222, 226; *Hmugma wicasa* or *Wicahmunga* (wizards) 210; *Hohu iyapa* (to hold the bone) 210; *Pejuta wicasa* (herbalist) 190, 209, 210; *Pejuta winyela* (women herbalist) 190, 212; *Wakan Kaga* (performers) 190, 210, 211–212; *Wanagi pejuta* (ghost doctors) 211; *Wapiyape winyan* 212; *Wapiyapi* (herbalist) 190, 209, 210; *Wapiye wakan* (herbalist) 190, 210; *Wasicun wakan* (holymen) 96; *Wicasa wakan* (holyman) 209, 210; *Wihmunga* (witches) 190, 212; *Wikte* (transvestite) 178, 210, 212–213; *Winyan wakan* or *Wakan Winyan* (holy woman) 190, 209, 212; *Yuwipi* (magician) 210, 211, 219, 223
Honesty 164; views of 167
Hopewell 116
Horse 96, 98, 106, 125, 170; first recorded trade 94, 122; introduction to 123; raids 138
Hough, Walter 7
Housing 19, 44, 46, 49, 50, 77–78, 126
Hrdlicka, Ales 7
Hunkpapa (End of the horn) 47, 48, 49, 51, 52, 61, 62, 123, 125, 127, 129, 142, 143, 145, 146, 155, 231
Hunting techniques 92–98
Huron (Wyandot) 11, 56, 118, 120, 132, 133, 134, 135, 137, 161, 245

Illini 26, 43, 121, 132, 133, 134, 212
Inca 115, 249, 250
Indian Removal Act 126, 142, 144
Indian Trade and Intercourse Act 126
Infidelity 165; punishment 165
Inkpaduta 41, 44, 145
Insignia 155–157, 160; badges 62; eagle feathers 157–158; paint 156–157; religious 231
Iowa 12, 20, 23, 26, 44, 87, 118, 123, 132, 134, 139, 141, 142, 144, 166
Iron Crow winter count 87, 123, 124, 137, 139, 140, 141, 143, 144, 145, 175, 245
Iron Tail 59

Iron White Man 230
Iroquois 11, 26, 29, 56, 132, 133, 134, 136, 153
Itazipco (Sans Arc/without bows) 43, 77, 140

Jackson, Andrew 142
Jefferson, Thomas 6, 22, 56
Joliet, Louis 212
Jumping Bull 145, 155, 230, 231
Jumping Dance (*ipsica waci*) 190

Kansa (Kaw) 12, 24, 26, 118, 132, 134, 245
Karok-Shasta 11
Kathio, Battle of 134–135
Kaw *see* Kansa
Kayaksi 144
Keating, William 44, 46–47, 214, 248
Kickapoo 118, 120, 132, 134
Kindle winter count 126
King George's War, War of Austrian Succession (1740–1748) 134, 135
King William's War (1687–1697) 134
Kiowa 139, 140, 141, 144
Kirk, Brian 8
Kiuska (violators) 44
Kiyuksas (split offs) 144
Koch, Albert 6
Kroeber, Alfred L. 7

Lakota 1, 2, 5, 12, 18, 19, 24, 29, 30, 32, 43, 46, 47, 48–52, 63, 89, 92, 94, 96, 98, 120, 122, 123, 125, 136, 138, 139, 140, 141, 142, 143, 144, 145, 202, 222, 223, 237, 238, 240, 243, 247; dress 69, 70, 72, 73, 243
Lasalle, Sieur de 132, 212
Lawson Johann (John) 12, 18–19, 21, 22, 23–24, 29, 33, 56, 58, 66, 68, 77, 91, 153–155, 167, 170, 172, 213, 214, 238, 240, 240, 245, 248
Leavenworth, Henry (Colonel) 141
LeClercq, Christien 171
Lederer, John 171
Lejeune, Paul 41
Le Seuer, Pierre-Charles 48
Lewis, Meriwether 48, 123, 124, 127, 139, 175, 247
Lewis, Thomis 190
Liosel, Regis (Little Beaver) 123, 124
Little Bighorn, battle *see* Greasy Grass, battle of
Little Crow 146
Lone Dog winter count 49, 78, 126, 143
Long, Steven (Major) 248
"Loups" 134
Lyell, Charles 6
Lyng v. Northwest Indian Cemetery Protective Association (1988) 255

Mackinac 136, 140
Making an Enemy (ceremony) 223
Mandan 24, 75, 78, 118, 120, 122, 124, 125, 131, 136, 137, 138, 139, 142, 144, 230, 247

Mankato 155
Maple sugar production 89, 183
Marest, Joseph 153
Marquette, Jacque 150, 212–213
Marriage 177–180; buried man 178; *ikiciyuze* "to join together" 178; wedding feast 180
Mascouten 118, 120, 132, 134
Mass hanging (Mankato, MN) 161
Master Guardians 104–105
Maya 84, 115, 116, 227, 230, 231, 250
Mazpegnaka (wear metal in the hair) 43
McColloh, James 22
McGillycuddy, Valentine 253–254
McJunkin, George 7
McLaughlin, Marie L. 108
Mdewakaton 2, 19, 23, 43–44, 45, 60, 75, 77, 98, 137, 146, 155, 166, 214, 228, 234; estimated value in trade 124
Measles 213, 245; German measles 246
Medicine Lodge (Santee) 222; dance 222, 223, 241; women in 176, 190
Menominees 118, 120, 134, 136, 140, 141, 142
Merriweather, Andrew 10
Metal Ornament (warrior) 137
Meyers, Roy 1, 44
Miami 118, 132, 133, 134
Michigamea 132
Minneconjou; Mnikowoju (planters beside the stream) 48, 49, 126, 142, 143, 231
Mipissing 133
Missisauga 134
Mississippi culture 116
Missouri 12, 26, 134, 138, 141
Mitakuye Oyasin (all are related) 102, 103
Mobilian 119
Moche 115
Modesty 164
Mohawk 11
Mooney, James (Dr.) 20–21, 22, 24, 245, 246
Morality 187–188
Morgan, George 247
Morgan, Lewis 6, 10, 11
Morton, Samuel George 6, 22
Murder 167
Muskegon/Muskhogean 11, 119

Na-Dene/Nadene 7, 8
Nakota 1, 2, 12, 23, 43, 46–48, 89, 96, 120, 122, 123, 132, 134, 136, 138, 140, 141, 142, 143, 144, 145, 202, 222, 223, 238, 240
Natchez 11
Native American Graves Protection and Repatriation Act 255
Navajo 119
Nazca 116
Nelson, Nels C. 7
Nez Perce 124
Nicolet, Jean 255
No Ears winter count 77, 87, 116,

118, 123, 136, 137, 138, 139, 140, 141, 142, 143, 144, 145, 151, 175, 187, 210, 230, 241, 246, 247

Oath (vows) 168, 169, 170, 181, 188, 225, 230
Occaneechees 119
Oceti Sawakin 2, 4, 41, 44, 52, 134
Ofo 20
Oglala (Scatter their own) 2, 43, 48, 49, 57, 58, 62, 125, 137, 138, 139, 142, 143, 144, 145, 237, 247, 252; civil unrest 144
Ohiyesa *see* Eastman, Charles
Ojibwa (Chippewa) 75, 76, 94, 118, 120, 123, 127, 132, 133, 134, 135, 136, 137, 140, 141, 142, 144, 154, 155, 222, 247, 252
Okeepa (Mandan) 230
Olmec 116
Omaha 12, 24, 26, 118, 132, 138, 139, 141, 230
Onate, Juan de 245
Oneida 11
Oneota 118, 131
Onondaga 11
Oohenunpa (Two Kettle) 49, 140
Osage 6, 20, 24, 26, 118, 132, 134, 139, 144, 252
Oto 12, 20, 26, 132, 134, 138, 141, 142, 144
Ottawa 118, 120, 132, 133, 134, 135, 137, 141, 142, 153
Oxaca 11

Paine, Thomas 56
Parkman, Francis 153
Paterek, Josephine 66
Pawnee 11, 134, 138, 142, 143, 144, 145, 146, 147, 230, 243, 252; Skidi 141
Pearson, Philip Edward 20
Penutian 7
Perrot, Nicolas 133
Piaute 253
Pike, Zebulon 44, 124, 139
Pipe bearers 62
Pipestone 39
Polygamy 171, 179–180
Pomo 11
Ponca 12, 26, 118, 132, 139, 142, 144, 230
Pond, Gideon 248
Pond, Peter 79, 87
Pond, Samuel 24, 29–30, 31, 35, 56, 62–63, 73, 75, 77, 79, 87, 122, 124, 131, 158, 159, 160, 164, 166, 167, 170, 178, 179, 180, 181, 182, 188, 201, 203, 214, 215, 219, 222, 225, 238, 247, 248
Pontiac 135, 153
Pontiac's War 135
Posnansky, Arthur 8
Potawatomi 118, 120, 132, 134, 135, 141, 142
Powatan 20
Powell, J.W. 7, 22
Power animals 104, 105
Powers, Marla 36
Powers, William K. 210, 211

Prayers 187–188, 200–201, 222, 224–225
Pueblo 116, 119
Punishment 59–60, 62–63, 165, 166, 167, 170, 188; of children 183; and women 180

Quapaw 12, 20, 132
Queen Anne's War (War of Spanish Succession) 134, 135
Quivera 119

Radisson, Pierre (Peter) 69–70, 106, 120, 127, 133, 150, 160, 170, 176, 247
Red Cloud 52; 1880 census 184; reservation 254
Red Feather 57, 146
Red Fish 230
Red Rabbit 108
Red Road (of spirit) 199, 217
Red Weasel 146
Red Wing 133, 135, 248
Ree *see* Arikara
Relationship names 32, 36–38; roles 172
Religious Freedom Restoration Act 255
Religious precepts 172, 199; views on European faith 187–188; *Wacantognaka* (generosity) 102, 170, 199, 248; *Woksape* (wisdom) 114, 199; *Woohitika* or bravery 131, 152, 199; *Wowacintanka* (fortitude) 131, 152, 199
Revolutionary War 20, 21, 136–137, 150
Ribas, Andrés Pérez de 6
Riggs, Stephen 31
Rites and Rituals 187; *Canupa* (pipe ceremony) 114, 124, 160, 168, 173, 185–187, 189, 223–225; *Hanblecheya*–Dakota *Hambeday* (vision quest) 111–112, 169, 190, 220, 223, 224, 226–227; *Hunka* (making relatives) 160, 223, 230–231; *Inipi* (sweat lodge) 96, (women in) 176, 190, 220, 223, 225–226, 227; *Nagi yuhapelo* (keeping the soul) 169, 189–190, 214–217; *Tapa Wanka Yap* (sacred ball game) 189, 190, 192, 223, 224, 23; *Wawakyag Wachipi* (the sun dance) 169, 222, 223, 224, 227–230, 241, 252; women in 176, 189, 192, 228–229

Sacred Arrow 144–145
Sagard, Gabriel 171, 248
Salinan-Seri 11
Salish 118
Saone 48, 140
Sans Arc *see* Itazipcho
Santee 2, 12, 18, 19, 21, 23, 24, 25, 26, 27, 28, 29, 42, 43–46, 48, 66, 70, 73, 75, 77, 87, 93, 94, 98, 103, 120, 122, 123, 124, 126, 127, 167, 170, 213, 213, 215, 217, 228, 240, 245, 246, 251, 252; alliance with Iowa 134; Santee Uprising (1862)

131; war with Ojibwa 133, 135, 136, 142; warfare 133, 134, 137, 140
Sapir, Edward J. 7, 8
"Sarastau" 134
Sarpy, Thomas Lestang (Yellow Eyes) 126
Sauk and Fox 118, 120, 123, 126, 132, 133, 134, 137, 138, 141, 142, 144, 222; united tribes 134
Scalp Dance (*Iwakicipi*) 159, 241
Scalping 149–151
Scalplock 73, 149–150
Schoolcraft, Henry Rowe 22, 47
Seielstad, Mark 10
Seminole 11
Seneca 11, 153
Sewee 12, 27, 245
Sexual roles 32, 92, 152, 179, 181–183; training 164, 172
Shakopee 155
Shawnee 118, 132, 134
Shetrone, Henry Clyde 21
Shirt wearers 62
Short Ears 144
Short Hair *Pahin ptechala see* Chief's Society
Short Man 142, 143, 145
Shoshone 124, 144, 147, 243, 247, 252; Bad Arrows 142
Sibley, Henry Hasting 59, 131
Sibley, John 24
Sicangu (Burned thighs/Brule) 48–49, 58, 126, 138, 143, 145, 231, 247, 254
Sihasapa (Sioux Black Foot) 48, 49, 140, 143
Silent Eaters *see* Chief's Society
Sinclair, Patrick 150, 248
Sisseton 42, 43, 45, 46, 62, 70, 76, 78, 87, 88, 145, 158, 240; estimated value in trade 124
Sitting Bull 52, 58, 60, 62, 104, 107, 108, 137, 145, 155, 156, 203, 210, 211, 213, 222, 226, 230, 254
Sluke Raka 137, 241
Smallpox 1, 48, 49, 125, 136, 138, 143, 144, 163, 184, 213, 245, 246, 247; pandemic 245, 246; vaccination 140
Societies: Badgers *Ihoka* 59, 75, 104, 110, 155, 181; Bear *Mata* 75, 103, 104, 157, 211; Braves or Strong Hearts *Cante Tinza* 59, 62, 152, 155, 156, 190; Buffalo dance(r)s 75, 104, 156–157, 210, 211, 222, 223; Crow owners *Kangi yuha* 59, 75, 110, 155; Deer dancers 211, 222; Elk *Hehaka* 104, 207, 211, 222; Elk/Buffalo and Horse Dreamers *Wakan okolakicye* 191; Heyoka 62, 157, 190, 194, 198, 210, 223; Horse dancers 190, 210, 211; Kit Fox *Tokala* 59, 62, 75, 104, 108, 155–156, 167, 181, 190; Mandan or no flight *Miwatani* 62, 109, 155, 181, 190; Omaha 75, 76, 110, 155, 156, 181; Otter *Ptan* 104, 155, 157; Owl 155, 157; Sacred Bow

110; Strike Dead *Katela* 190–191; Tall ones 75; Turtle 191, 210; Wand Carriers *Sotka yaha* 59, 155; White Horse Owners *Ska yula* 62, 157; White marked *Wikin ska* (Chief's Society) 57, 58, 59, 61–62, 152, 155, 156; Wolf (*Sunkmanitu/Hanskaska*) 106, 157, 211; women in 190, 192
Spanish 21, 24, 30, 31, 119, 120, 122, 123, 124, 245
Speck, Frank G. 20
Spider-like (warrior) 146
Spirit Lake massacre (1857) 43, 145
Squire, Ephraim 22
Standing Bull 138
Striped Face 142
Sugaree 12
Supreme Court 253, 255
Susquehana (Conestoga) 11
Swadish, Morris 8
Sweet grass 193
Swift Cloud 145
Sword, George 209, 210, 217

Taboos (*tehila*) 106, 110, 169; of warfare 152; and women 165
Taliaffero, Lawrence (Major) 126, 141
Tasagi (chief) 42
Tatankachesli (dung of the buffalo) 43
Taylor, Colin (Dr.) 191, 200
Tequistlatecan 11
Theft 168; views on 167; *Wamanon'* (thief) 167
Thomas, Cyrus 22
Thunder dance 222, 241
Thunderbear 217
Ti-tanka 78
Tipi 77–78
Tipi tonka 18, 77, 87, 181–182
Titowan 19, 24, 29, 30, 42, 48–52, 61, 62, 70, 75, 122, 123, 137, 139
Tiyopa (gate or entrance) 60
Tiyotipi (Soldiers' Lodge) 59
Tobacco 87, 96, 170, 182, 186, 190, 214, 234
Tokahe 4, 19
Toltec 116
Totem 102, 104
Trade: alcohol 126, 136, 139, 142, 145, 176, 247–248; beaver 121, 122, 123, 127, 139, 247; buffalo 122, 123, 124, 139, 176; centers 118–120, 122; corn 124; embargo 124, 141, 143, 147, 152; guns 121, 122, 123, 124, 127, 134; horses 94, 122, 123, 124, 125–126; pipestone 122; rights 138; rituals in 124, 127; rivalry 139; routes 115, 118, 120, 140, 252,
Trapping 92–93, 94–96, 122, 123, 138, 139, 247
Treaties 141–142, 160, 168–169; with the Cheyenne/Arapaho144–145; with Crow at Pine Bluffs 141; first Fort Laramie treaty (1857) 127; of 1825 141–142; peace referendum between Santee, Sauk and Fox (1723) 134; peace with Kiowa 140; *Portage de Sioux* (July 1815) 125, 141; Santee with U.S. (September 23, 1805) 124, 139; Santee with Sauk and Fox (July 15, 1830) 126, 141–142; Santee with Sauk and Fox (1844) 144; Santee final cessation of lands (September 29, 1837) 127, 144; Santee Treaty (June 19, 1858) 145; Traverse des Sioux (1851) 145, 146; truces with Assiniboines 136
Treatment of prisoners 153–155
Trousseau 178, 179
Truteau, Jean Baptiste 122
Tuma 11
Turner, George 184
Tuscarora 11
Tutelo 6, 27
Tyon, Thomas 59, 76, 155, 156, 190, 200, 217

Unktena (water spirit of the Eastern Siouan Speakers) 202
United States 7, 8, 9, 11, 12, 18, 20, 29, 114, 119, 123, 124, 125, 126, 137, 139, 141, 142, 143, 144, 145, 146, 147, 161, 169; tributes paid to Lakota 139
Units of measure 122, 128
Usner, David H. 114
Ute 124, 147
Utley, Robert M. 41, 156, 182, 209, 222, 226, 227

Virginity 164, 229; maiden feast 162–163, 222, 223; male equivalent 162
Virtue 163; challenges to 163–164; *isnala kic'un*, the "being alone" ceremony 163, 223

Wabasha 137, 150, 155
Wahpeton 23, 42, 45–46, 60, 62, 70, 76, 77, 87, 93, 96, 103, 131, 158, 166, 179, 203, 215, 228, 234, 235; estimated value in trade 124
Wahpukte 42, 44, 60, 61, 119, 134, 140, 145; estimated value in trade 124
Wakan Feast 223, 241

Wakefield, Sarah 155, 161, 171, 180–181
Walker, James R. 48, 56, 62, 155, 157, 178, 179, 190, 200, 201, 209, 217, 223, 226, 237, 238, 239
Walker, William 247
Wamdesapa (chief) 42
Wanbli gleska 39, 186
War of 1812 139, 141
War, rules of 152; division of property 153; treatment of prisoners 153–155
Warren, William W. 133
Washington, George 56
Washo 11
Wasna (pemmican) 91, 181, 193
Wateree 27
Wavoka (Piaute) 253
Waxshaw 1, 56, 58
Weapons 96–97, 158–160
Weatherford, Jack 96
Weyuha 23
White, Richard 138, 147
White Bull 142
Wi Jun Jon 167
Wichita 11, 120
Wild rice 89–90, 181
Wilford, Lloyd A. 23
Winnebago (Ho-chunk) 12, 20, 26, 118, 120, 139, 141, 144, 222
Wissler, Clark 11, 141, 146, 151
Woccan 12, 27
Women 96; dress 66–70, 73; in government 56, 58, 176, 184, 188; introduction to white women 123; and language 32; and property 106, 176; and rape 185–187, 188; in religion 186, 187, 189, 192, 228–229, 231; rights 179; rights with children 171, 179, 182; social-sexual roles 92, 172, 179, 181–183; status 165, 186, 187, 188, 190, 191; suicide rates 180; in trade 106, 124, 127, 176; value 176, 177, 178; in war 152, 153, 154, 176; women's societies 190–191
Wounded Knee 254–255
Woyakapi, Ehanna 62
Wyandotte *see* Huron

Yamaha (town crier) 59, 162
Yankton (End Dwellers) 2, 29, 43, 46–47, 51, 61, 77, 94, 98, 118, 120, 122, 137, 140, 141, 144, 145, 146, 228, 247; dress 69
Yanktonai (Little End Dwellers) 43, 46–48, 61, 118, 122, 123, 127, 137, 140, 141, 142, 143, 145, 247
Yellow Spider 218
Yuma 11

www.ingramcontent.com/pod-product-compliance
Lightning Source LLC
Chambersburg PA
CBHW081546300426
44116CB00015B/2768